*Great Lakes Indian
Accommodation and Resistance
during the Early Reservation Years,
1850–1900*

EDMUND JEFFERSON DANZIGER, JR.

The University of Michigan Press / Ann Arbor

{ FOR MARGARET }

my life's partner

Copyright © by the University of Michigan 2009
All rights reserved
Published in the United States of America by
The University of Michigan Press
Manufactured in the United States of America
♾ Printed on acid-free paper

2012 2011 2010 2009   4 3 2 1

No part of this publication may be reproduced, stored
in a retrieval system, or transmitted in any form
or by any means, electronic, mechanical, or otherwise,
without the written permission of the publisher.

A CIP catalog record for this book is available from the British Library.

Library of Congress Cataloging-in-Publication Data

Danziger, Edmund Jefferson, 1938–
    Great Lakes Indian accommodation and resistance during the early
reservation years, 1850–1900 / Edmund Jefferson Danziger, Jr.
        p.   cm.
    Includes bibliographical references and index.
    ISBN-13: 978-0-472-09690-9 (cloth : alk. paper)
    ISBN-10: 0-472-09690-7 (cloth : alk. paper)
        1. Indians of North America—Great Lakes Region (North America)—
History—19th century.   2. Reservation Indians—Great Lakes Region
(North America)—History—19th century.   3. Indian reservations—
Great Lakes Region (North America)—History—19th century.   I. Title.
E78.G7D367   2009
977.004'97—dc22   2008047858

Contents

Map of Great Lakes Indian Reservations, 1850–1900 iv
Preface and Acknowledgments vii

Introduction: A Homeland and Its People 1

PART ONE. MAKING A LIVING

1. Agriculture on the Great Lakes Homelands 31
2. Old and New Alternatives to Reservation Agriculture 60
3. The Homeland Becomes a Checkerboard: Allotment and Location Tickets 95

PART TWO. BATTLING FOR THE MIND AND SOUL

4. The Education Crusade 123
5. Traditional Spirituality versus Christianity: Finding a Balance 156

PART THREE. WHO SHALL RULE AT HOME?

6. Reservation Politics: The Challenge of Shared Governance 187

Conclusion: Moccasins in the Mainstream 220

Notes 255
Bibliography of Works Cited 297
Index 313

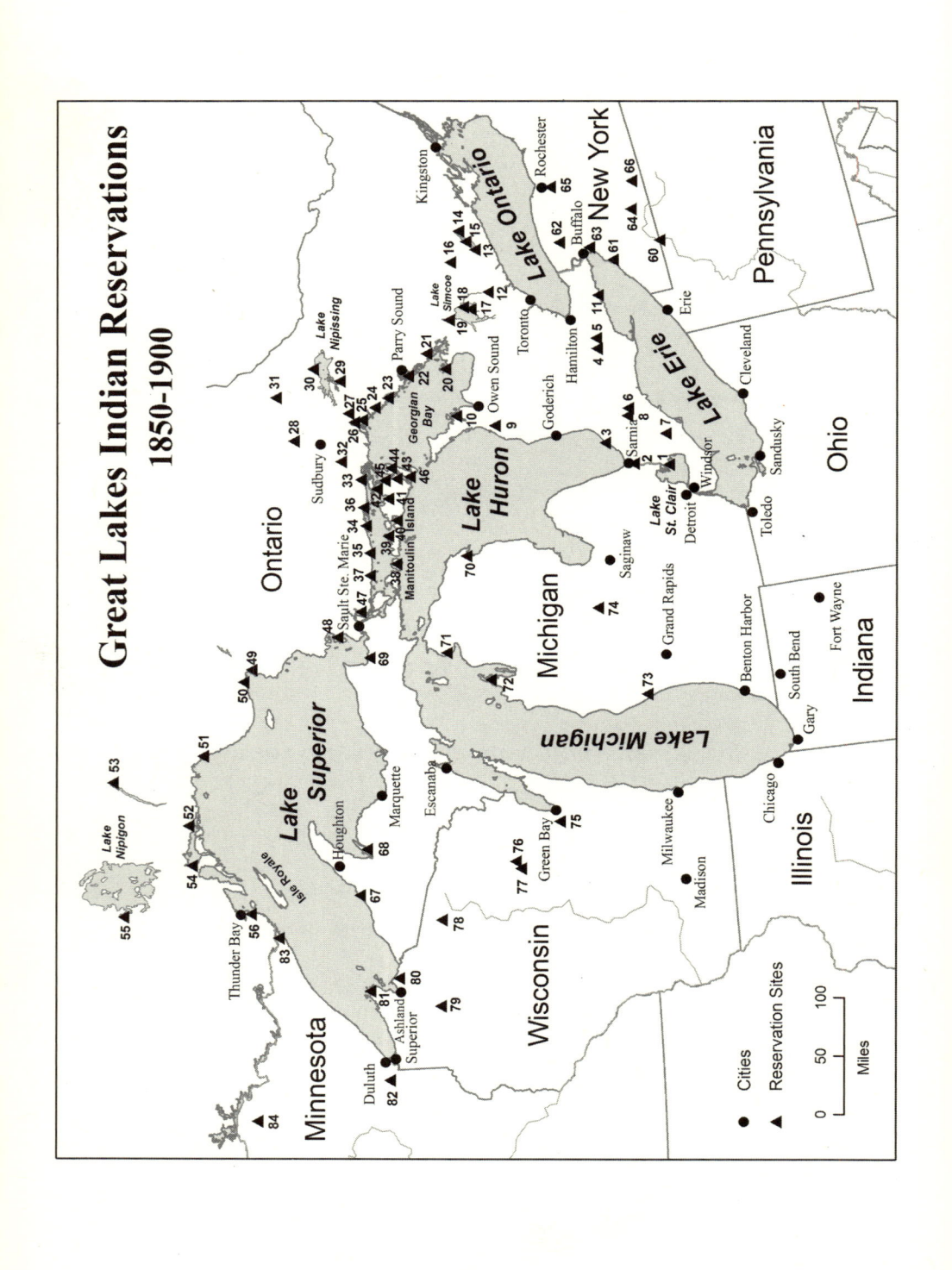

Great Lakes Indian Reservations 1850-1900

Canada

1 Walpole Island
2 Sarnia
3 Kettle and Stony Point
4 Six Nations
5 New Credit
6 Oneida (Onyot'a:ka)
7 Moravians of the Thames
8 Chippewa and Munsee-Delaware of Thames (Caradoc)
9 Saugeen
10 Cape Croker (Nawash)
11 Mohawk of Bay of Quinte (Tyendinaga)
12 Scugog
13 Rice Lake (Hiawatha)
14 Alnwick
15 Sugar Island (Alderville)
16 Mud Lake (Curve Lake)
17 Georgina Island
18 Snake Island
19 Rama
20 Christian Islands (Beausoleil)
21 Watha Mohawk (Gibson)
22 Perry Island
23 Shawanaga (Sandy Island)
24 Magnettawan
25 Henvey Inlet (Onewaiegoes band)
26 Point Grondin
27 French River
28 Lake Wanapitei (Tahgaiewenene band)
29 Dokis
30 Nipissing
31 Temogaming
32 Whitefish Lake
33 Whitefish River
34 Serpent River
35 Mississagi River
36 Spanish River
37 Thessalon
38 Cockburn Island
39 Sheshegwaning
40 Obidgewong
41 West Bay
42 Sucker Creek
43 Sheguiandah
44 Wikwemikong
45 Wikwemikongsing
46 South Bay
47 Garden River
48 Gloulais Bay (Batchewana Bay)
49 Michipicoten
50 Gros Cap
51 Pic River
52 Pays Plaat
53 Long Lake
54 Lake Helen (Red Rock)
55 Lake Nipigon (McIntyre Bay, Gull River, Island Point, and Jackfish Island)
56 Fort William

United States

60 Allegany
61 Cattaraugus (Seneca)
62 Tonawanda (Seneca)
63 Buffalo Creek (Seneca)
64 Oil Springs (Seneca)
65 Onondaga
66 Tuscarora
67 Ontonagon
68 L'Anse and Vieux Desert
69 Ottawa and Chippewa reserves on eastern end of Upper Peninsula
70 Iroquois Point
71 Little Traverse Bay
72 Grand Traverse Bay
73 Oceana and Mason Counties
74 Isabella
75 Oneida
76 Menominee
77 Stockbridge and Munsee
78 Lac du Flambeau
79 Lac Court Orielles
80 Bad River
81 Red Cliff
82 Fond du Lac
83 Grand Portage
84 Bois Forte at Nett Lake, Vermilion Lake, and on Grand Fork River

Preface and Acknowledgments

During the 1850s, Great Lakes aboriginal families began the difficult transition to reservation life within a region dominated by non-Indian newcomers. The natives' ability to move back and forth between the old ways and the newfangled ones brought by whites was a good omen and impressed forty-four-year-old British travel writer William H. G. Kingston. He visited an aboriginal village while his steamer was anchored off Christian and Beausoleil islands in Georgian Bay and marveled at the "living Red Indians" and their wigwams. "But a change has come over them," he noted. "Even now they are no longer the same people they once were; for . . . the good-natured, easy-going, laughing, idle, brown fellow of the present day contrasts greatly with the fierce Red warrior of a century ago." Kingston observed that most of the men did not wear "ill-made blanket coats"; indeed, "some even had on shooting-jackets and caps, and others black coats and trousers, and black round hats." But that evening, while back on his boat, the past paid a visit.

> Several canoes came off, some with squaws and their papooses, and others with men; but our friends had made an extraordinary change in their costumes, and had donned what they considered their ball-dresses. They were no longer the mute-like, respectable-looking citizens, in black coats and tweeds, we had seen in the morning; now huge plumes of many-coloured feathers decked their heads, and tails of foxes and other animals hung down their backs. Their faces were painted in stripes of red and black, while beads and feathers formed fringes round their waists, their knees and ankles. One carried a drum, and the rest bore in their hands war-clubs, tomahawks, and

calumets ornamented with feathers, while their feet were covered with embroidered moccasins. To be sure trousers and tweed coats could be seen from under the feathery and skin-coverings of bygone days; and one or two had put coloured shirts over their other garments to add grace and elegance to their costume. A funny jumble it was truly, the oddest mixture of the past and present I ever saw.

Once on board Kingston's steamer, aboriginal men performed a war dance while "uttering the most unearthly shrieks and cries."[1] Other tourists also must have thought it an odd mixture of past and present: birch-bark canoes tied to a Great Lakes steamboat while natives danced on the deck wearing both "savage" and "civilized" clothing.

Such sights were commonplace throughout the Great Lakes at this time. Thousands of moccasined Indians cautiously entered the Canadian and American mainstreams and, while preserving many traditions and their sense of Indian identity, developed ways to deal with an aggressively intrusive capitalistic world. The process lasted for many decades but was most challenging during the early reservation years between 1850 and 1900.

The scene of this accommodation and resistance could not be more important. Stretching 750 miles from east to west and covering ninety-four thousand square miles, the Great Lakes water system understandably became a barrier between the United States and Canada.[2] "We are separate countries today—separate and distinct" because of the Great Lakes, writes renowned Canadian author Pierre Berton.[3] The lakes were indeed a physical barrier, yet their historic role was more complex and grand. Vast resources—strategic water routes, furs, fish, timber, minerals, fertile farmlands—triggered a centuries-long struggle for dominance among Indian nations, the French, the British, and, later, the United States. The final confrontation was the War of 1812. It shattered Tecumseh's dream of holding back the American juggernaut. Over the next four decades, Great Lakes Indians surrendered most of their homeland north and south of the international border and began to refashion their lives on remnant portions called reservations. Here, chiefs and councils worked to revive Tecumseh's vision: to preserve what was left of their homeland, their sovereignty, their economic independence, and their distinctiveness as Indians.

They did so within the context of momentous changes that reached beyond the Great Lakes. Canada and the United States also stood at a crossroads. Industrialization, the rise of big business, urbanization, and a westward-expanding market system aided by railroads and steamboats were poised to transform the face and the heart of each country. Families between the Great Lakes and the Atlantic would no longer be as isolated, rural, and agricultural. All of this would occur at breakneck speed. What emerged by century's end were the origins of modern economies and societies.

Great Lakes Indians, besides facing an even more powerful and beckoning white mainstream, had to cope with insidious reservation intruders who worked and schemed to "civilize" and assimilate aboriginal men, women, and children and to control natural resources needed to support native families. The challenges faced by individual natives plus their chiefs and councils could not have been greater. No wonder Canadian and American policy makers, reformers, and reservation neighbors expected that within one generation—two at most—Indians would cease to exist as distinctive people and communities. The mainstream would surely claim them as it did the millions of European immigrants disembarking on North America's shores.

Fifty years after the reservation era began, these predictions proved false. Great Lakes Indian communities, though somewhat marginalized and assaulted from every direction by two separate nation-states, had survived. Moreover, they had preserved many of their core values, lands, and Indian identities. Forty thousand Indians also continued to shape the region's economic development. How could this be? How could hundreds of federal policy makers, altruistic reformers, missionaries, schoolteachers, Indian agents, and entrepreneurs be so wrong about the future of Great Lakes aboriginal communities and their homelands? How did native peoples negotiate the space between their traditional lives, which worked well for millennia, and the reservation life?

As important as this question is for understanding the heartland of two countries, historians have not addressed it in a comprehensive and comparative manner. Excellent studies abound about Indian policies in Canada or the United States, yet the only book-length examination of both nations' handling of aboriginal matters is Roger Nichols's *Indians in the United States and Canada: A Comparative History* (1998). Though that book is well written and insightful, its space did not permit a detailed discussion of Great Lakes reservations during the late 1800s. A handy, shorter overview of Canadian and U.S. Indian policies is provided in chapter 1 of Hana Samek's *The Blackfoot Confederacy, 1880–1920: A Comparative Study of Canadian and U. S. Indian Policy* (1987). Another important analysis of Indian experiences on borderlands west of the Great Lakes is David G. McCrady's *Living with Strangers: The Nineteenth-Century Sioux and the Canadian-American Borderlands* (2006). Most helpful have been monographs and scholarly articles that provide in-depth examinations of specific Great Lakes tribes before and during the reservation era or facets of reservation life, including religion, politics, and the development of resources, such as mineral and timber. These tightly focused studies are listed in this book's bibliography.

To understand how so many Great Lakes reservation communities—fifty-six in Ontario and twenty-five in the United States—persevered as Indians against enormous odds, one must go beyond existing general works and case studies. Fortunately, Great Lakes eyewitness accounts from the 1800s are voluminous and varied enough to answer fundamental questions about the early reservation years. The easier side of the story to tell is the role of government officials in Ottawa and Washington, D.C., and their field associates. Legislative acts and the annual reports of the Canadian Department of Indian Affairs and the U.S. Office of Indian Affairs leave little doubt about the motivations and actions of federal officials in their respective national capitals. Supplementing these materials are the field office records of Indian agents, including letters received and sent. Observers of federal reservation policies in action also included government farmers, schoolteachers, missionaries, travelers, newspaper reporters, and non-Indian neighbors.

Native responses to reservation life, especially the "civilization" and assimilation initiatives of Washington and Ottawa, were not documented in such detail. Nevertheless, the record is rather clear about the Indians' very active role in early reservation life. This included economic development, education, religion, and politics. Noticeable, too, in the documents was their awareness of events on other reservations, in recently ceded areas, and in national capitals. We know this because of comments made by reservation agents, schoolteachers, and missionaries. A more direct voice came from Indians who used the power of the pen and their facility with the English language to record observations and concerns in books and articles for public consumption or in petitions and letters intended for federal authorities. Field records of Indian agents, for example, are filled with letters from literate reservation residents requesting help with particular problems and from chiefs and councils demanding the righting of some wrong. The Indians' voice was also clear and assertive when they hired attorneys to defend reservation interests or asked local missionaries to articulate aboriginal points of view to the Canadian Indian Department or U.S. Indian Office. The aboriginal voice, though somewhat filtered, may be found as well in Indian agents' transcriptions or summaries of local council meetings or exchanges with groups of chiefs visiting the agency office. Finally, unrecorded Indian thoughts were acted out when some families refused to take up horse-and-plow farming, balked at giving up seasonal hunting-fishing-trapping-gathering of local food sources, and would not send their children to agency schools or listen to Christian evangelists. The viewpoints of chiefs and councils were equally clear when they fended off the efforts of Ottawa, Washington, and local Indian agents to dominate reservation decision making or to stop reservation delegates from carrying petitions to the national capitals and participating in regional Indian gatherings.

Resistance to the white man's civilization program was not the only set of actions that revealed Indians' perspectives. Accommodation also characterized their responses to Ottawa and Washington and to the many mainstream forces transforming the Great Lakes region. Indeed, Indian agency is the focus of this book. To underscore the independent responses of reservation people to the coercive plans of federal officials and to preserve a flavor of the times, I quoted rather extensively from nineteenth-century records.

These grassroots investigations revealed an answer to the central question about how Great Lakes Indians survived—as Indians. Having been consigned to reservations, they realized that their world was changing and that they, too, needed to change. Valiantly and creatively, they defended their cultural traditions as well as their economic and political independence. Reservation leaders, drawing on long-standing traditions of mutual respect and cooperation with non-Indians, sought a workable balance between the new and the old, between accommodation to altered circumstances and resistance in order to protect their peoples' resources and traditions. In short, they stepped cautiously into the shallows of the mainstream to try it out, but not far enough to be carried off and submerged. They chose which elements of each culture to keep or reject. This approach allowed chiefs and their followers to meet with varying degrees of success between 1850 and 1900 as they continued to shape their own history and that of the region.

Whether living on a reservation in Canada or America, natives responded in similar ways to their new circumstances. In part, this was because Algonquian and Iroquoian peoples lived on both sides of a porous international border, across which communication and travel were common. Ottawa and Washington also followed comparable Indian policies and organized field officials accordingly. Moreover, the winds of change that swept the Great Lakes during this period, especially the advancing line of white settlers and their market system, affected all aboriginal peoples of the region, north and south of the international border. Differences in Indian responses originated in part from the physical attributes of their reserves and the local climate, which, for example, might encourage or rule out farming as a way to make a living. Thus American and Canadian reservations, which shared much in common, became remnant homelands where Indian ways of life could still thrive and intermingle with selected features from the mainstream.

The nomenclature for this book supports this integration. The spelling of particular Indian groups varies a great deal among scholars and in the original sources. I have used the spellings suggested by the authoritative *Atlas of Great Lakes Indian History* edited by Helen Hornbeck Tanner and others (1987). Thus, for example, the term *Ojibwa* is used rather than other versions applied to these Indians: *Anishinabe, Chippewa, Chippeway, Mississauga, Ojibway, Ojibwe, Otchipwe,* and *Saulteaux.* A useful synonymy for all Great Lakes tribes may be found in the *Handbook of North American Indians,* volume 15, *Northeast,* edited by Bruce C. Trigger (1978). For the sake of variety, I use *American Indian, Native American, natives, aboriginal peoples, First Nations,* and *Indians* interchangeably for the indigenous inhabitants of the Great Lakes region. The term *reservation* is employed throughout and includes Canadian entities called "reserves."

The research on which this study rests could only have been completed with extensive support. Most important, Bowling Green State University (BGSU) and its Department of History provided released time and reimbursed expenses for trips to archives. A faculty research grant from the Canadian Embassy in Washington, D.C., also helped subsidize travel costs. Archivists at the National Archives and Records Administration (NARA) in Washington, D.C., its federal records center for the Great Lakes Region (GLR) in Chicago, the Archives of Ontario in Toronto, and the staff of Walpole Island Heritage Centre (WIHC) were especially helpful. Individuals who provided outstanding service included Mary Francis Morrow at NARA; Scott Forsythe at NARA's GLR center in Chicago; and Norma Altiman, Dean Jacobs, and David White of WIHC. Over the years, BGSU history graduate students provided invaluable assistance. They include Stephen W. Badenhop, Dwayne Beggs, Joseph Genetin-Pilawa, Phyllis Gernhardt, and Michael Kimaid. BGSU librarian Coleen Parmer helped me access our rich, printed government documents. Colleagues at BGSU and elsewhere offered guidance, camaraderie, and critical readings of my works in progress. Special thanks go to Tina Amos, Dean and Shirley George, Scott Martin, David T. and Paul McNab, James Miller, Donald Nieman, Diane Rohrer, Eileen Sawyer, DeeDee Wentland, and Leigh Ann Wheeler. Professor Yu Zhou, a warm and generous man, crafted with care the map of Great Lakes Indian reservations, 1850–1900. Finally, I am deeply indebted to family members for their long-standing support when Dad was working at home or away on research trips.

Although the pages of this book tell of another time, they are not just "old school" or ancient history. Their story is also about today, and its lessons carry across the ages. First is a warning. Lingering arrogance among nonnatives, born of ethnocentrism and the belief that they know what is best for others, not only produced the unfortunate Dawes Severalty Act and the Canadian residential school system but continued to threaten aboriginal self-sufficiency, sovereignty, and self-determination in the twentieth century. Second is an inspiration. The Great Lakes reservation story of the late 1800s is about culturally resilient native families and community leaders who battled against great odds to survive as Indians even though their moccasins entered, in varying degrees, the Canadian and American mainstreams. To present Indians otherwise—for example, as hapless and tragic victims who benefited little from reservation life—does them and history a great injustice. Equally misleading would be to picture all whites as dominating tyrants. The power of the Indian past was captured in part by President Richard M. Nixon in July 1970, when he remarked to Congress:

> But the story of the Indian in America is something more than the record of the white man's frequent aggression, broken agreements, intermittent remorse and prolonged failure. It is a record also of endurance, of survival, of adaptation and creativity in the face of overwhelming obstacles. It is a record of enormous contributions to this country—to its art and culture, to its strength and spirit, to its sense of history and sense of purpose.[4]

Reservation Indians of the Great Lakes, on both sides of the international border, earned their right to be included in this tribute.

Red Jacket, Seneca war chief. *(Courtesy Archives of Ontario, image RG 2-344-0-0-23.)*

Introduction

A Homeland and Its People

"*Brother: Listen to what we say,*" remarked Seneca Indian chief Red Jacket to white missionaries assembled at Buffalo Grove, New York, in 1805.

> There was a time when our forefathers owned this great island. Their seats extended from the rising to the setting of the sun. The Great Spirit had made it for the use of the Indians. He had created the buffalo, the deer, and other animals for food. He'd made the bear and the beaver, and their skins served us for clothing. He had scattered them over the country, and had taught us how to take them. He had caused the earth to produce corn for bread. All this He had done for his red children, because He loved them.[1]

The Great Lakes homeland of the Seneca and other native peoples was indeed a beautiful land of plenty, a place that shaped their cultures and their history.

Stretching 780 miles from east to west and covering 94,250 square miles, the Great Lakes form a magnificent yet mysterious treasure house. The lakes are muscular and dangerous, capricious and vulnerable. One approaches them with caution and humility, like a hiker in grizzly country or a kayaker atop the watery world of killer whales and sharks. Respect for these mighty freshwater seas appears in the rock pictographs of aboriginal peoples who have subsisted on their shores since time immemorial.[2] Newcomers from Europe also harvested the wealth of land and water—but with a vengeance: trapping fur-bearing animals nearly to extinction, clear-cutting seemingly endless forests, gouging out fortunes in iron and coal and copper, tapping lake fisheries, turning the sod, bridging the rivers, and harnessing mighty waterfalls. White entrepreneurs, with the aid of the Canadian and U.S. governments, also pushed aside native nations and planted scores of towns and cities while marketing the region's resources to customers throughout the world.

FIRST NATIONS

Prior to the Europeans' arrival, Indian villages dotted the region. Estimates of their population by the sixteenth century range from 60,000 to 117,000. Evolving aboriginal communities—diverse, autonomous, varied as the land itself—composed two language groups. Iroquoian speakers ranged south from Georgian Bay to the fertile lands encompassing Lakes Erie and Ontario. They included the League of the Iroquois and the Huron Confederation. On the eve of European contact, Iroquoians resided in year-round villages and benefited from an agricultural-based economy. Algonquians, who surrounded this Iroquoian island, extended westward through the Lake Superior–Canadian Shield country. The more southern bands farmed, while those living in cooler climates and on lands less suited to agriculture focused on hunting, gathering, and fishing. Besides providing food, Great Lakes woods and waters shaped the material cultures of Algonquians and Iroquoians. They fashioned dwellings, clothing, and canoes, for example, from the skins of local animals, tree bark, roots, and saplings. Spiritual beliefs, traditions, songs, art work, historical events, and sacred places, such as the graves of ancestors, also linked aboriginal peoples to their Great Lakes homeland.[3]

As I have explained elsewhere, native people looked at the land differently than later Euro-Canadian and Euro-American settlers.

> In part this reflected an intimate knowledge of woods and waters which came from extended residence in the Great Lakes region. But it was more than that. "When aboriginal people speak of the land," noted a Canadian Royal Commission, "they mean not only the ground that supports their feet; they also include waters, plants, animals, fish, birds, air and seasons—all the beings, elements and processes encompassed by the term 'biosphere.'" Furthermore, Ab-

original People "have a sense of kinship with other creatures and elements of the biosphere."[4]

Native inhabitants felt bound to one another as well as the land—in families, clans, and villages. Families included, besides the mother, father, and children, an extended network of uncles, aunts, cousins, and grandparents. Additional men and women might be added through marriage and adoption. Within this social unit, gender dictated one's work. Men hunted and fished; they fashioned tools and weapons; they politicked and made war. Equally important and respected was the work performed by girls and women: preparing food and other products from fish and game, farming, collecting wild plants, plus various household tasks. Females exerted great influence in all village matters, including politics and diplomacy. As the fundamental social institution, families educated and disciplined their members. They supported themselves economically with a network of mutual sharing and obligations that insured individuals would never be alone when in need. Village families also selected representatives to participate in local, clan, and tribal activities—from political councils to hunting and war parties.[5]

Village locations, appearances, and activities varied greatly depending on the community's economy. For example, there was a look of permanence about an Iroquoian town in the Mohawk Valley: such towns featured bark-covered, multifamily longhouses; perhaps a defensive palisade; and certainly vast fields of corn, beans, and squash. Conversely, an Ojibwa fishing settlement just north of Lake Superior would reflect the seminomadic lifestyle of its residents. Their numbers were less, and their oval, single-family wigwams were more portable, for the Ojibwa only remained as long as the fish were running. Canoes probably lined the beach, and nets were hung up to dry in the sun along with fish fillets. Seasonal shifts, which triggered changes in animal migrations or the ripening of plants, caused the Ojibwa to disperse once more. Despite such differences between a northern and southern aboriginal village, each remained an important home base for families and a fundamental unit of Indian culture.[6]

Similarities among Great Lakes aboriginal communities arose because of parallel responses to a shared environment as well as a diffusion of customs and technologies from village to village through a far-flung trading network. Intermarriage and military alliances enhanced communication links. At the same time, differences in historical traditions and languages between Algonquian and Iroquoian peoples profoundly affected their relations with one another and with Euro-Canadian and American newcomers before the reservation era of the late nineteenth century.

GREAT LAKES ALGONQUIANS

Algonquian-speaking nations (the native language term is *Anishinaabeg*), numerous and commanding vast resources north and west of present-day New York, played a prominent role in the Great Lakes heartland. Their hunting grounds fluctuated continually in response to Iroquois and European incursions, but by the late 1760s, they were located as follows. The southeastern Ojibwa or Mississauga ranged along the north shores of Lakes Ontario, Erie, and Huron as far as the eastern half of Michigan's Lower Peninsula. Beyond Sault Ste. Marie, the southwestern Ojibwa encircled Lake Superior. West of Lake Michigan and south of the Ojibwa's holdings lived the Menominee, Mesquakie (Fox), Sauk, Winnebago (Siouan speakers), and Potawatomi. The latter's country also embraced lands immediately below Lake Michigan and the extreme southern part of the Lower Peninsula. The western portion of the Lower Peninsula was dominated by the Ottawa, whose villages extended around the northern shores of Lake Michigan and east to Manitoulin Island. South of the Potawatomi, in the Wabash and Maumee valleys, lived the Kickapoo, Wea, Miami, and Ottawa. Other occupants of northern Ohio included the Wyandot (Iroquoian speakers), Delaware, and Mississauga.[7]

No matter which nation it belonged to, an Algonquian nuclear family lived under one roof and might contain from two to twelve members plus a few dependents, such as elders and orphans. As the core social unit, families were characterized by an egalitarian ethic and mutual reliance based on a clear division of labor between the sexes. This, in turn, was balanced with individual respect. The result was usually a dynamic and resourceful partnership. Men and women also felt bound to more distant kin in the village and beyond.[8]

A network of totemic clans furnished another avenue of friendship and aid for Algonquians. The Ojibwa of Lake Superior living within the United States, for example, inherited clan membership from their fathers. Each nuclear family therefore represented a segment of at least two clans. A totem— the name of a fish, bird, or animal—signified the clan's common ancestry. Totems were not worshiped or thought to yield special powers, like a personal guardian spirit, but Algonquians treated them with respect and worked totemic emblems into decorations on clothing, carved them on bows and war clubs, and etched them onto pendants. In the mid-nineteenth century, Lake Superior Ojibwa had about fifteen or twenty patrilineal clans, the principal ones being the crane, catfish, bear, marten, wolf, and loon. A clan's authority stemmed not from control of land or material goods but from dictating eligible marriage partners (custom forbid unions between members of the same clan) and from their chiefs' political power. When traveling to distant villages, an Ojibwa could also expect hospitality and help from fellow clansmen.[9]

Several clan segments and extended families composed an Algonquian band. Because they moved with the seasons, band size and makeup fluctuated. Single families scattered in search of game during the winter months, then regrouped in sizable settlements for spring fish runs and maple sugaring and at summer base camps. Northern bands roaming the Canadian Shield seldom exceeded one hundred people; those dwelling in milder, southern climates where farming was possible might reach four hundred members. Bands, which controlled their own hunting grounds and internal politics, were loosely bound together into nations, such as the Ojibwa, Potawatomi, and Ottawa, and in confederacies of nations, such as the Three Fires.[10]

Each Algonquian band and nation assured its survival by attentively nurturing the young. Fathers, mothers, and grandparents cared for and helped raise the children. In wigwams and villages where there was little privacy, adult behavior and public pressure for conformity guided the younger generation into their proper roles. Young Ojibwa south of Lake Superior, for instance, learned to convert the fisherman's catch and hunter's game into food and clothing. A female's tasks included constructing wigwams and their furnishings; chopping wood and gathering berries, rice, and medicinal herbs; and making birch-bark vessels and maple sugar. Young men, meanwhile, worked outside the home. They strived to become brave warriors and successful woodsmen by mastering the bow and arrow, war club, spear, traps and snares, and, particularly, the ways of the forest and its creatures. To establish good relations with the spirit world, parents urged both boys and girls to make prepuberty fasts. Hopefully they would receive a guardian spirit that henceforth could provide sound advice, knowledge, and perhaps the power to influence future events. In these and other ways, the Lake Superior Ojibwa taught their children the religious, economic, and political practices as well as the moral standards of the community.[11]

Though the Algonquin were marvelously adapted to their resource-rich environment, cooler climates prevented northern bands of Ojibwa and Ottawa from relying entirely on horticulture. Instead, small family groups followed a mobile subsistence strategy, moving whenever a nearby seasonal resource, such as blueberries and wild rice, became plentiful. Groups better able to raise vegetable crops included the Menominee, Potawatomi, Shawnee, Miami, and other tribes whose homelands ringed the milder,

Indian sugar makers. *(Courtesy Wisconsin Historical Society, image 5224.)*

southern shores of the Great Lakes. They, too, followed well-established migratory patterns that included a fall hunt and a move to the sugar bush in spring, but their lives were more sedentary, and their villages were larger.[12]

The Algonquian world contained a host of spirits that manipulated the weather, lured game to the hunter, controlled the corn harvest, and affected the family's health. Consequently, religious thought focused on placating these spirits, especially the lesser ones found nearby in animals, trees, rocks, and water. They all had life and the power to intervene for good or ill in family affairs.[13]

Like religious beliefs, methods for charming the spirits and harnessing their power for a particular purpose were highly individualistic among the Algonquian. The Lake Superior Ojibwa, for instance, used tobacco as an offering—a way to communicate between them and the spirit world. The plant, they believed, was especially pleasing to the spirits, so they used it in feasts and religious ceremonies. They threw pinches of it into the water before harvesting wild rice. Tobacco was placed at the base of a tree or shrub where medicine was to be gathered. When smoked in stone pipes, tobacco sealed treaties between tribes and agreements between individuals. Great respect might also be shown to forest creatures. Parry Islanders particularly venerated local bears, who seemed nearly human. To avoid offending the spirits of bears and other objects in their world, Algonquian families inherited from previous generations a multitude of taboos and ceremonial prac-

Ojibwa Indian deer hunt. *(Courtesy Wisconsin Historical Society, image 2103.)*

tices. Lest a powerful bear spirit be offended, Indians always explained to a killed bear why their families needed the meat for food. Hunters tried to honor the carcass; they carried it to their village rather than dragging it, then placed its skull on a tall pole, out of the reach of dogs.[14]

To transit such spiritual minefields, men and women sought wisdom and support from dreams, power visions, and medicine men. Villagers took very seriously knowledge obtained while dreaming, and projects often were initiated or abandoned based on visions of the future. Medicine men, who had particularly close relationships with the spirit world, specialized in curing diseases with herbs and ceremonies. Among the Ojibwa, some practitioners belonged to a highly organized priesthood, the Midéwiwin Society. Its members had a practical knowledge of plants; they knew how to compound medicines and release their power with ritual songs and elaborate healing ceremonies.[15]

Individualism and local autonomy characterized Algonquian organization as well as the group's spirituality and economic practices. Widely scattered and self-sufficient bands of no more than three to four hundred people constituted the basic unit of the rather informal political structure, in which individual families and villages maintained much independence. Personal liberty was particularly pronounced and operated within a shared Algonquian family of languages and many common beliefs. Neither family members nor chiefs could compel an individual to act in a certain way. A community's civil leaders, characterized by their generosity and humility, guided members with verbal persuasion and personal prestige rather than coercion. Even war chiefs could not force villagers to join an expedition. Civil chiefs presided at band councils and represented their people at national councils, which dealt with internal affairs plus land divisions and business transactions on the international level. All men and women past puberty participated in band councils' open discussions. In making decisions about the general welfare, the wisdom of experienced, wise elders, such as medicine men and war chiefs, guided thinking, and consensual democracy prevailed.[16]

Governed in part by their Great Lakes environment, the Algonquian people evolved cultures that gave them a satisfying life. Traditional activities, institutions, and beliefs were family-centered and tied to the rhythms of the seasons. Self-sufficient households, often isolated, lived in a loosely related political, economic, and social world of villages, clans, bands, and nations. Their spiritual universe included sorcery and medicine men. Somewhat fearsome were their Iroquoian neighbors, who lived around the eastern Great Lakes and demanded, with much authority, a lion's share of the resources.

THE LONGHOUSE PEOPLE

Several native nations comprised the Iroquois linguistic family. The Huron Confederacy and the Petun people hunted and farmed in the region north of Lake Ontario and along the shores of Georgian Bay south of Manitoulin Island and the French River. The Neutral and Wenro nations inhabited much of the north shore of Lake Erie, and across these waters, the Erie Confederacy commanded the southern coast. Directly eastward lived the Five Nation Iroquois (Seneca, Cayuga, Onondaga, Oneida, and Mohawk) along the Finger Lakes, the Mohawk Valley, and the upper Hudson River valley. To the south, on what is today the New York–Pennsylvania border, dwelt the Susquehannock. The Five Nations called themselves "Haudenosaunee"

(People of the Longhouse). They became the Six Nations in the early 1700s when they were joined by the Iroquois-speaking Tuscarora, who had been driven from their North Carolina villages.[17]

Multifamily longhouses epitomized the larger unity of the confederacy, which stretched, like families in an extended longhouse, across present-day New York State and beyond. The Seneca were designated the "keepers of the western door," the Mohawks the "guardians of the east." Construction of Huron and Iroquois homes was similar except their environment forced the Six Nations to depend more on elm-bark sheathing instead of the cedar favored by the Huron. Iroquois longhouses also varied in size. The largest one identified by archaeologists was in Onondaga County, New York, and reached 334 feet in length. Unlike Huron homes, the Iroquois houses were partitioned into individual family apartments with an open side facing a central aisle, where a fire was shared with the family opposite. The bark longhouse remained common well into the nineteenth century.[18]

Clustered together in palisaded villages, longhouses were usually arranged in rows around a square used for public meetings. The Iroquois chose these sites with at least three criteria in mind: proximity to drinking water and a navigable waterway; good farmland nearby, including an ample wood supply; and defensibility. Natural moats or heights of land were supplemented by fifteen- to twenty-foot-high fortifications complete with three rows of interlaced posts, galleries, and watchtowers stocked with water and stones. Settlements ranged in size from 30 to 150 longhouses. The larger villages, with perhaps three thousand residents, were called "castles." The exhaustion of the soil and wood supply near a town forced relocations about every twelve years.[19]

The basic unit of Iroquois society within the longhouse was the "fireside," a nuclear family comprised of a wife, her husband, and their children. Others residing within the building formed a maternal lineage of mothers, sisters, and daughters, plus their spouses and children. A matriarch, or the senior woman, guided longhouse affairs, which were central to the village's functions—from setting agricultural and ceremonial schedules to disciplining family members, controlling chiefs, and influencing decisions about war and peace.[20]

Within the longhouse, children learned a strong sense of family and community obligation. Toddlers helped their mothers carry river water and gather firewood. The older they got, the more services they supplied the household. Girls continued to help the women, while boys, in their games, cultivated courage as well as hunting and oratorical skills. As the youths matured, longhouse matrons took responsibility for arranging suitable marriages, especially for those who seemed to be overlooked in the courting process. When a match was made, senior women participated in the negotiations with a girl's family. Ultimately, both longhouses participated in much gift giving, feasting, and dancing to sanction and bind the couple.[21]

Like Algonquian societies, the Six Nations Confederacy was divided into clans, each with its own chiefs, elders, and warriors. Children belonged to their mother's clan and were supposed to welcome fellow clansmen as though they were brothers and sisters. Clans took their names from certain animals, which became the members' crests. Figures were often tattooed on their chests or displayed at the ends of longhouses. The Turtle, Wolf, and Bear clans existed throughout the confederacy, whereas the Deer, Beaver, Heron, Hawk, Eel, and Snipe were prominent in some nations but not in others.[22]

Iroquois women played preeminent roles in the clan system as well as the local economy. Their longhouses acted as independent food-production units. Husbands and wives, while working to support their families, stuck to a sexual division of tasks that was basic to Iroquois society. Men took on heavy building and land-clearing jobs that called for a large degree of physical strength or activities that took them away from the village for extended periods, such as trading and warfare. In their absence, females were charged with protecting family life and maintaining the household. Farming was women's work, too.[23]

For longhouse families, religion was inseparable from hunting, tending their crops, and other family activities. Iroquois everyday life was filled with so much uncertainty and danger that men and women regularly tried to placate the spirits. Using tobacco, villagers ceremoniously petitioned the gods to avert some bad spirit or expressed thanks for a good harvest and successful hunt.[24]

Respect for individual, longhouse, and clan autonomy—so clearly expressed in social gatherings, religious beliefs, and economic activity—was also central to Iroquois government. Chiefs and their counselors met publicly and set policy on the village level. Agenda items included issues of war and peace as well as local affairs, such as the regulation of farming, hunting, and fishing or deliberation on a criminal case.[25]

The effectiveness of village councils stemmed in part from the process for choosing civil leaders. Each clan was permitted a set number of chiefs, and upon the death of a titleholder, his successor was chosen by the clan matron. (The office could not pass to the chief's son, who would be a member of his mother's, not his father's, clan.)[26] As they presided over village councils and represented their clans at tribal and confederacy gatherings, chiefs were commanding persons but sported few trappings of power. Their authority came from possessing honorable qualities and respecting individual and clan autonomy. Headmen requested, rather than commanded, support from followers.[27]

Government beyond the village level consisted of national councils and the grand council at Onondaga, which was uniquely Iroquois. Its members came to visualize themselves as a united and powerful longhouse confederacy stretching across upstate New York. Their warriors and diplomats exuded self-confidence—even haughtiness—in dealing with other nations. Without this confederacy, the Iroquois could not have maximized their geographic advantage.[28]

Native neighbors courted and feared the New York Iroquois League. Later on, so did French, Dutch, and British officials. Diplomatic decisions of this mighty confederacy reverberated from Maine to the Carolinas and as far west as the Illinois country. For more than a century, they were the most powerful Indian group on the northern colonial frontier, including the lower Great Lakes. Europeans sometimes referred to the alliance as the Six Nations, but a more common name was the Algonquian epithet *Iroquois,* signifying "rattlesnake" or "terrifying man."[29]

FROM LORDS OF THE LAKES TO RESERVATION RESIDENTS

Chief Red Jacket, in his 1805 remarks to white missionaries, lamented that native peoples had at first taken European newcomers to be friends.

> They called us brothers. We believed them, and gave them a large seat [of land]. At length their numbers had greatly increased. They wanted more and more land; they wanted our country. Our eyes were opened, and our minds became uneasy. Wars took place. Indians were hired to fight against Indians, and many of our people were destroyed. They also brought strong liquors among us. It was strong and powerful and has slain thousands.
>
> Brother: Our seats were once large, and yours very small. You have now become a great people, and we have scarcely a place left to spread our blankets.[30]

Insightful and articulate though he was, Red Jacket had no way to foresee that the future would bring even more disruptive land loss and cultural change to the Great Lakes Indian people.

The four decades following the War of 1812 began the process. Enduring peace along the international border made native military allies less desirable. A declining fur trade further weakened their position. By the 1850s, government officials and entrepreneurial private citizens believed that exploitation of Great Lakes resources was essential to the future prosperity of Canada and the United States. "Let the merchants of Toronto consider," proclaimed George Brown in the *Globe,* "that if their city is ever to be made really great—if it is ever to rise above the rank of a fifth rate American town—it must be by the development of the great British territory lying to the north and west."[31] Develop they did—at a breathtaking and dizzying pace. Tidy farms and swelling cities blanketed the southern drainage basin of the Great Lakes by century's end. Meanwhile, farmers, lumbermen, miners, fishermen, town builders, tourists, and federal bureaucrats transformed many parts of the pristine northern hinterlands. Ontario's population was 2.1 million by 1891, double that of forty years earlier.[32] The growth of Great Lakes states south of the international border was equally dramatic. Between 1850 and 1900, for example, New York's population increased by 234.7 percent, Michigan's by 608.8 percent, Illinois's by 566.3 percent, and Wisconsin's by 677.5 percent.[33]

Several factors besides the commercial dreams of journalist-politician George Brown spurred Great Lakes developments. The scarcity of good farmland south of the Canadian Shield combined with exploding Canadian and U.S. populations to propel people into urban areas or north to more marginal lands. Industrialization and urbanization impulses within both nations created homes and work for those living around the southern lakes as well as markets for fish and raw materials, such as timber and minerals shipped from the northland "treasure trove."[34]

Two additional factors facilitated these events. First, a transportation revolution integrated Great Lakes industries, then linked them with distant western and eastern markets to help fuel the Industrial Revolution. Second, during the mid-1800s, the Canadian and U.S. governments continually opened Indian lands for resource exploitation and concentrated aboriginal families on remnant portions called "reservations." When officials permitted white settlement on western Manitoulin Island in 1866, for example, the aboriginal population was only 1,250. Within four years, noted historian James P. Barry, the island was "fairly well settled": "Between 1872 and 1880 its population grew by 15,000 people, largely drawn there by lumbering."[35]

The rush of white settlers and developers out to the Great Lakes, via the Erie Canal and other new transportation arteries, forced several Indian cession treaties north and south of the international border. American policy developed three variations in the Old Northwest. Removal was applied only to

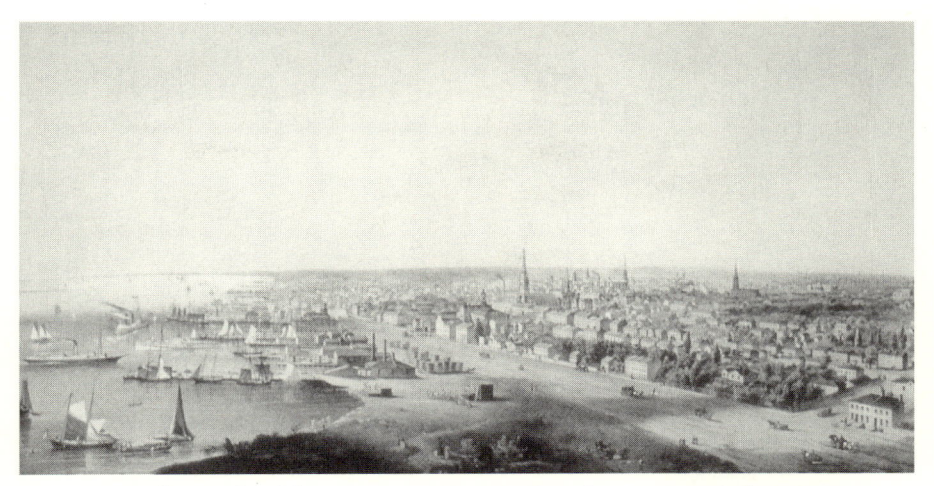

View of expanding Toronto, 1854. *(Courtesy Canadian Heritage Gallery, image 23234.)*

Booming harbor at Port Arthur, Ontario, 1885. *(Courtesy Canadian Heritage Gallery, image 21949.)*

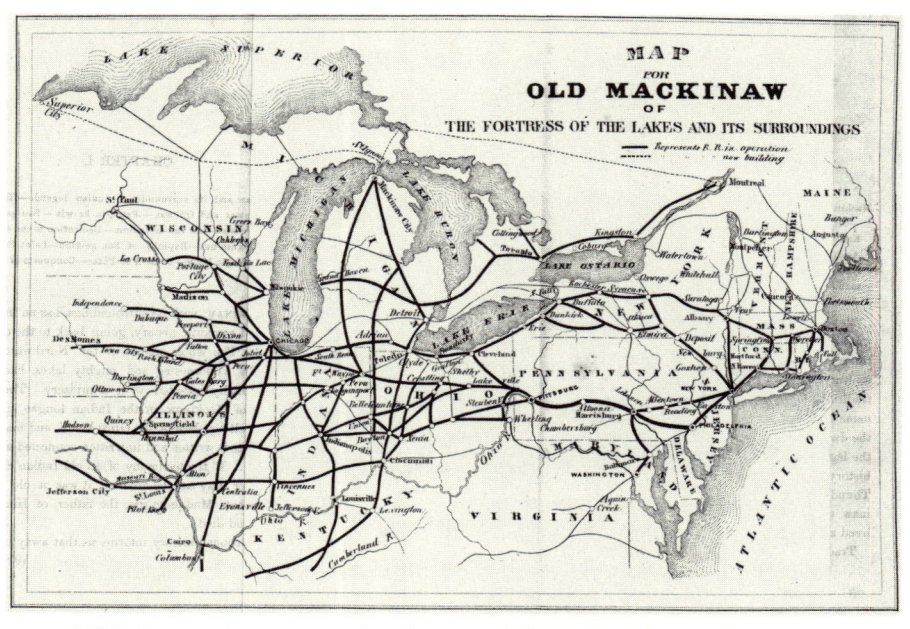

Mid-nineteenth-century railroad routes linking the Great Lakes to national and international markets. *(W. P. Strickland,* Old Mackinaw, or The Fortress of the Lakes and Its Surroundings *[Philadelphia: James Challen & Son, 1860], frontispiece.)*

native enclaves south of a line that ran from the eastern end of Lake Erie to Milwaukee, Wisconsin. This zone embraced fertile farmland and strategic real estate needed for booming midwestern settlements, such as Buffalo, Cleveland, Detroit, Chicago, and Milwaukee. Neither resource, it was argued, could be left in Indian hands. North of "the line" was an area of pine forests, marginally fertile soils, and long, tough winters. "This is the Midwestern Outback," writes environmental historian William Ashworth, "the area once referred to by Henry Clay in a famous Senate speech as 'a place beyond the remotest extent of the United States, if not in the Moon.'"[36] After Indians were elbowed aside to permit the development of prime timber and mineral resources, they retained only a few dozen restricted holdings. Last, Great Lakes Indian relocation or concentration differed from events elsewhere in the United States because of the nearby Canadian escape hatch. Ottawa, Ojibwa, and Potawatomi families, whose homes lay south of "the line" and who were targeted for removal to the west of the Mississippi, found refuge and then permanent homes east of Lake Huron and the St. Clair River.

This process, pretty much finished by the mid-1850s, removed some groups entirely from the Great Lakes. The Wyandot, Shawnee, Sauk and Fox, Kickapoo, and Illinois tribes settled west of the Mississippi. Iroquois, Miami, Ottawa, and Potawatomi villagers joined them but left many fellow tribespeople behind.[37]

Those living on American and Canadian Great Lakes reservations in the mid-nineteenth century faced an uncertain future. Their moccasins were at a crossroads. Indians had once enjoyed the freedom of adopting only those features of white culture that appealed to them. By the 1850s, the luxury of selectivity was no longer theirs. When chiefs touched their pens to cession and relocation treaties, aboriginal people began a new journey.

CREATION OF THE FIRST NATIONS' ARCH

Canadian reserves clustered along an arch that extended from the north coasts of Lakes Erie and Ontario to the remote western shores of Lake Superior. Aboriginal lands lay within the administrative unit of Canada West (formerly Upper Canada) until 1867; then they were incorporated into the new Dominion of Canada's Ontario Province. The arch's southeastern base, extending from the Amherstburg area to near Kingston, embraced diverse reserves created by pre-Confederation grants and treaties beginning in the late 1700s.[38] To make way for an exploding non-Indian population and to do what was best "for the red children of the forest . . . who wish to be civilized," Canadian federal policy makers in the 1830s hoped to concentrate the bulk of native nations on the Bruce Peninsula and the Manitoulin Island chain—similar to U.S. removal plans for Indian children south of the Great Lakes. But southern Ontario native communities resisted the move. Furthermore, land developers desired the timber, minerals, farmland, and other resources of the northern sites that were set aside for Indians. Additional native cessions followed. In the mid-1800s, government negotiators pressured the Saugeen Ojibwa into several land surrenders, which concentrated them on a fingernail reserve north of present-day Wiarton. Here, at Cape Croker, "where land was unfit for cultivation, they were not disturbed." The Canadian Department of Indian Affairs also decreased native control of Manitoulin. In 1862, just twenty-six years after promising that the island chain would be aboriginal territory protecting the Indians "from the encroachments of the whites," Canadian commissioners William McDougall and William Spragge signed an agreement at Manitowaning to open up the western portion of Manitoulin to non-Indian settlers. Treaty provisions assigned natives living on that part of the island to reserves. Proceeds from land sold to white settlers, "after deducting the expenses of survey and management," would be invested "for the benefit of the Indians." The large eastern portion of the island remained unceded.[39]

Algonquian nations on the north shores of Lakes Huron and Superior were not safe from covetous white miners and developers. In September 1850, at grand councils in Sault Ste. Marie, chiefs and principal men surrendered, in the Robinson-Huron and Robinson-Superior treaties, most of their territorial rights south of the height of land separating the Great Lakes basin from Hudson's Bay Company territory. In return, First Nations leaders accepted modest cash payments, perpetual annuities, and more than two dozen reserves extending in a broken line from Penetanguishene on the eastern shore of Georgian Bay to Fort William near Thunder Bay.[40] A First Nations arch of approximately nine to thirteen thousand Canadian Algonquian and Iroquoian people was in place, and the gates opened to an anticipated flood of nonnative settlers.[41]

By the mid-1800s, considerable diversity existed along the reservation arch. Its southern base included a seven-hundred-member Mohawk Bay of Quinté (Tyendinaga) Reservation. To the west, in the lake-spangled region around present-day Peterborough, about three hundred Mississauga lived on three reserves at Mud, Rice, and Scugog lakes.[42] The most populous and wealthy native community was Six Nations of the Grand River near Brantford. Its twenty-eight hundred residents had more than eight hundred thousand dollars in trust funds. Adjacent to Six Nations dwelt about two hundred Mississauga of New Credit. They had relocated here back in the 1840s because of pressure from white settlers along the western shore of Lake Ontario.[43]

Neighboring First Nations to the west also adjusted to the presence of an expanding white population. In 1857, four groups lived on reserves adjoining the Thames River: the Oneida (517 persons on 5,400 acres), Chippewa and Muncey (590 on 12,095 acres), and Moravians (259 on 3,189 acres).[44] Along the St. Clair River–Lake St. Clair–Detroit River waterway were three more reserves. A community of Wyandot, descendants of the Huron who had once held land on both sides of the Detroit River, lived on 7,770 acres in Anderdon Township at Amherstburg. The large Walpole Island settlement, nestled against the north shore of Lake St. Clair, was home for 824 Ojibwa, Ottawa, and Potawatomi in 1857. During the 1840s, the local Ojibwa population was engulfed by refugee Algonquians (Ottawa, Potawatomi, and Ojibwa) from the United States, fleeing Washington's removal program. Many were incorporated into the Walpole band, thereby forming a major settlement that grew to over fifty thousand acres. Much of the reserve, composed of six delta islands, was wetlands. Upriver, the Ojibwa of Sarnia retained an eight-thousand-acre reserve and numbered about 530. In addition to their main reserve, thirty-nine Sarnia Ojibwa inhabited five thousand acres on the Ausable River and at Kettle Point on Lake Huron.[45]

Along the First Nations arch to the northwest, approximately nine hundred scattered Mississauga still roamed the river and lake country and gathered in villages between Lake Ontario and Georgian Bay. The Saugeen, following the surrender of the Bruce Peninsula, divided into two bands. The Ojibwa of Nawash lived at Cape Croker and numbered over three hundred in the 1860s; the Saugeen community at the mouth of a river that bears its name was a little smaller.[46] Along Lake Simcoe's southern shore, Chief Snake's band of a little over one hundred members occupied Snake and Machego islands in the late 1850s. The Rama community, with a population of 201 in 1857, lived on sixteen hundred acres beside Lake Couchiching, which joined Lake Simcoe at Orillia.[47]

The Ojibwa of Lake Huron were estimated at over twenty-one hundred and assigned to reserves that dotted the eastern Georgian Bay coastline from Christian Island northward to the French River, then inland to Lake Nipissing. Here, they found good fishing, hunting, trapping, and gardening resources and probably were close to sacred sites. The names of aboriginal communities and their approximate populations at midcentury follow:

Beausoleil and Christian Islands, 233
Mohawk of Gibson, 140
Parry Island, 58
Shawanaga (or Sandy Island), 145
Magnetawan, 164
Henvey's Inlet, 176
French River, 81
Point Grondine, 59
Tahgaiewenene, 151
Dokis, 62
Lake Nipising, 90[48]

The Ojibwa and Ottawa who occupied Manitoulin Island reserves numbered about thirteen hundred in the mid-1800s. They, too, had accepted reserves and clustered in settlements from Wikwemikong on the unceded eastern end to Cockburn Island on the west.[49] The names of these settlements and their approximate populations follow:

Wikwemikong, 598

Wikwemikongsing, 130

South Bay, 61

Sucker Lake, 41

Manitowaning, 88

Sheguiandah, 113

Sucker Creek, 69

West Bay and Magnetawan, 118

Sheshegwaning, 117

Cockburn Island, 33[50]

Exploitation of natural resources along the mainland shore north of Manitoulin was obviously on the federal government's mind when negotiating the Robinson-Huron Treaty of 1850. Between five hundred and one thousand Indians thus accepted reserves at Whitefish Lake, Whitefish River, Spanish River, Serpent River, the Mississauga River, and Thessalon. Pending white settlement, most also continued their seasonal rounds of hunting, fishing, gathering, and gardening, like fellow Algonquians on Manitoulin and around Georgian Bay.[51]

The northern Ojibwa population of over two thousand that contended with Lake Superior's rugged, windswept coast thinned out greatly toward Fort William. Anchoring this arch of reserves on the southeast was Garden River, near Sault Ste. Marie. Its population in 1857 was 218.[52] Beyond the Sault, the Lake Superior reserves and their populations included Batchewana, 54; Michipicoton and Big Heads, 269; Pic River, 245; Long Lake, 311; Pays Plat, 54; Red Rock/Helen Island, 153; Lake Nipigon, 426, and Fort William, 416.[53]

U.S. RESERVATIONS AT MIDCENTURY

Three Lake Superior Ojibwa reservations lay in Minnesota by midcentury. Just west of Duluth and south of the St. Louis River was Fond du Lac, comprising five townships. The Grand Portage Reservation, in the extreme northeast corner of the state, 150 miles from Duluth, boasted one of the most beautiful shorelines on Lake Superior. But its rugged and stony fifty-one thousand acres offered little timber or farmland of value for the 363 members.[54] Article XII of the 1854 treaty encouraged the Bois Forte band to select a reservation, but by 1866 their chosen land at Vermilion Lake, some hundred miles west of Grand Portage, had not been defined, and the Indians ceded claim to it in a treaty that April. To compensate them, the United States laid out 107,509 forested and swampy acres at Nett Lake, forty miles northwest of Vermilion Lake and about the same distance from the Canadian border. Executive orders later established two other tracts for the Bois Forte: 1,080 acres at Vermilion Lake in December 1881 and one township on Grand Fork River at the mouth of Deer Creek in June 1883.[55]

Minnesota's neighbor to the east also retained a large aboriginal population. Journeying north from the more populous regions of Wisconsin, a traveler in the early 1860s would first come upon the Oneida Indians at the southern tip of Green Bay. About eleven hundred persons lived on a reservation of sixty-one thousand acres in Brown and Outagamie counties.[56] Before 1854, the peaceful Menominee, objecting to removal to the west of the Mississippi, continued to roam the northeastern part of the state near the river that bears their name on the Michigan-Wisconsin border. That year, the government set apart for them twelve townships on the upper Wolf River, forty-six miles northwest of Green Bay.[57] In 1856, the Menominee sold two townships to 407 members of the Stockbridge and Munsee nation, which earlier had occupied a tract on the eastern shore of Lake Winnebago.[58]

A fourth Indian group had no official reservations about which to complain. These included bands of Winnebago and Potawatomi who were remnants of tribes already removed from the state. An Indian agent counted 720 "strolling Potawatomi" in 1870. They followed a migratory, seasonal lifestyle in isolated and forested parts of central Wisconsin. About one thousand Winnebago also roamed that part of the state, although federal officials occasionally collected and transported them to some western location. But the "disaffected" Winnebago always returned to their homeland. Congress accepted this reality in 1881 and helped six hundred families to establish small, tax-exempt homesteads on lands of their choosing. Finally, over two hundred Rice Lake Ojibwa roamed Forest County, Wisconsin, and survived by hunting and fishing. They, too, had no reservation home, and Washington regularly provided relief for aged, sick, and destitute band members.[59]

Wisconsin's Lake Superior Ojibwa inhabited a series of northern reserves established for them in 1854. Directly east of Ashland, Wisconsin, lay the Bad River Reservation, roughly rectangular and containing slightly more than five townships. It was meant to support a large Indian population, which numbered 638 in 1888.[60] A presidential executive order in 1856 added sixteen sections to the one set aside for Buffalo's band of over three hundred persons, thereby creating the Red Cliff Reservation, whose red sandstone cliffs jutted into Lake Superior at the northern tip of Bayfield County.[61] The Lac Court Oreilles Ojibwa lived in Sawyer County, southwest of Ashland, on a tract of 69,136 acres. Their population in the 1880s was 1,170. In Vilas County to the east, a reserve of similar size, approximately four townships, was home to the Lac du Flambeau band.[62]

Eastward, across the border in Michigan, the Mackinac Agency contained 8,149 Indians in 1868. The federal government had allocated to several bands thirteen hundred square miles of reservation lands scattered mainly across the northern part of the state. An 1854 treaty set apart ninety square miles at the head of Keweenaw Bay for the L'Anse and Lac Vieux Desert bands. A township on Lake Superior was also reserved for the tiny Ontonagon band.[63]

Ottawa and Ojibwa communities accounted for more than half of the state's native population and were evenly split between Michigan's northern and southern peninsulas. Washington assigned those on the eastern end of the Upper Peninsula to four reservations, but families were still dispersed in coastline villages, from Grand Island to Waiskee Bay on Lake Superior, south along the St. Mary's River and on Sugar Island, and around the Lake Huron shore from De Tour west to St. Ignace. Across the Mackinac Straits, Ojibwa and Ottawa communities hugged the shoreline from Lake Huron's Thunder Bay, around past Mackinac City, and south along Lake Michigan as far as Grand Haven and Grand Rapids. The three largest reservations in the 1860s were at Little Traverse Bay (350 square miles for twelve hundred Indians), west of Grand Traverse Bay (150 square miles for seven hundred Indians), and in Oceana and Mason counties (144 square miles for twelve hundred Indians).[64]

In southeastern Michigan, an 1864 treaty tried to consolidate the sixteen hundred Saginaw, Black River, and Swan Creek Ojibwa on the Isabella Reservation in the interior part of the state. A decade later, only half had moved; the rest resided at seven or eight different places in their former homeland, the Michigan Thumb area, where they had bought property.[65]

Two other bands, vestiges of the once-mighty but now-dispersed Potawatomi, lived among whites in extreme southern Michigan. The three-hundred-member St. Joseph River group acquired land near Hartford in Van Buren County. Not far away, in Calhoun County, a smaller community of between fifty-five and eighty, known as the Potawatomi of Huron, owned 120 marginal acres.[66]

Other Indians "out of tribal relations" remained south of the Great Lakes—32 in Illinois, 240 in Indiana, and 100 in Ohio. They were mainly remnants of the previous generation of natives that had been pushed west of the Mississippi. Washington closed its Indian agencies in these three states and expected remnant families to blend into local populations and disappear. Not all of them did, as Stewart Rafert details in *The Miami Indians of Indiana: A Persistent People, 1654–1994*. "Free of federal supervision and the heavy handed control of a local Indian agent," he writes, the Indiana Miami "went about rebuilding their lives behind the frontier," increasing their landholdings to several thousand acres by the 1850s and fighting for tribal survival.[67]

South of Lake Ontario, five thousand reservation Iroquois also struggled for economic self-sufficiency. The Seneca remained the most numerous. Their 761-acre Cornplanter tract lay in Warren County, Pennsylvania. A gift from the Commonwealth in recognition of the chief's valuable service, this choice river bottomland was divided among his heirs. The Allegany Reservation to the north was considerably larger, comprised of 30,469 acres on both sides of that river in Cattaraugus County. Further north and halfway to Buffalo, the Cattaraugus Reservation, with 21,680 acres of fertile land, stretched along Cattaraugus Creek. Straddling Erie and Genesee counties was the 7,549-acre Tonawanda Reservation. Seneca from these tracts owned a fifth tract (640 acres at Oil Spring) on the eastern boundary of Cattaraugus County, which they leased to white farmers. The Cayuga, who numbered 184 in 1877, had no reservation and lived among the Seneca.[68]

Other Iroquois had New York homes. Farthest east were the Oneida. Their population was less than three hundred during the late nineteenth century. Like the Cayuga, they had no official reservation. Some Oneida lived on 350 acres (in Madison and Oneida counties) that were divided in severalty; the rest resided with the Seneca and Onondaga. The latter reservation was seven miles from Syracuse and embraced seventy-three hundred acres. Further west and a few miles from Niagara Falls was the 6,249-acre Tuscarora Reservation.[69]

FEDERAL GOVERNMENT POLICIES AND PROGRAMS

During the last half of the nineteenth century, Washington policy makers, renouncing the racism and removal policies of predecessors, set two goals for their Indian wards: continued reduction of native landholdings and the Americanization of "savage" reservation residents in preparation for integration into mainstream society. Several assumptions guided Uncle Sam's thinking. Frontiersmen would applaud the opening of Indian lands to white settlement as they had for over two centuries. Federal officials also hoped that "civilized" citizens would be a good influence on reservation neighbors. Certainly, the United States no longer had room for traditional Indian cultures whose inefficient use of the land included hunting, gathering, fishing, and, at times, bloody intertribal warfare.[70] "We are fifty millions of people, and they [Indians] are only one-fourth of one million," reported commissioner of Indian affairs Hiram Price in 1881. "The few," he argued, "must yield to the many." Advocates of civilizing the Indians believed, furthermore, that aboriginal peoples of the Great Lakes and elsewhere in America were capable of learning the English language and of adopting an alternative, superior mode of life. To "allow them to drag along year after year . . . in their old superstitions, laziness, and filth . . . would be a lasting disgrace to our government," claimed Price, who said that to transform the Indians into self-sufficient and productive citizens would be "a crown of glory to any."[71]

Besides Price's federal Office of Indian Affairs, which had legal responsibility for aboriginal peoples, a group known collectively as Friends of the Indian supported several Native American advocacy organizations established in the late 1800s, including the Indian Rights Association. The Friends of the Indian, writes historian Arrell M. Gibson, "mobilized public opinion on the 'Indian Problem' to the point that during the 1880s a greater number of citizens became interested in Indian affairs than ever before in American history." The movement they generated built on the reform traditions of Christianity and the antebellum era. Ethnocentrism, individualism, patriotism, and Darwinism also shaped their thinking, as did the conviction that past federal Indian programs had failed miserably.[72]

Meanwhile, north of the Great Lakes, the new Dominion of Canada assumed responsibility in 1860 for regulating Indian-white relations. Canada continued Britain's policy of native assimilation begun in the 1830s. It was also the government's duty, wrote secretary of state Sir George Murray in 1830, gradually to reclaim natives "from a state of barbarism" and introduce "amongst them the industrious and peaceful habits of civilized life." The rationale for aboriginal displacement and cultural transformation drew on prevalent Euro-Canadian views about laissez-faire economics, cultural—if not racial—superiority, their destiny to dominate the continent, and an evangelical Christian duty to protect and guide the "civilization" of backward aboriginal peoples. London decided that small, protected native reserves like those already occupied by the Iroquois and Walpole Islanders would be the best locale for Europeanization of its Great Lakes wards. It was hoped that these settled, agricultural communities would eventually be characterized by frame houses, barns, fenced fields, schools, and churches.[73]

To attain their common goals for the Indian, Canadian and U.S. governments used similar strategies. The keystone was a paternal reservation system: dozens of halfway houses that temporarily insulated Great Lakes native communities from society at large and simultaneously enabled federal government officials to control the civilization and assimilation process. Over the years, their methods became increasingly interfering and menacing. They included (1) promotion of Indian economic self-sufficiency through sedentary farming, allotment of reservation land in severalty, and conferring citizenship on natives who had jettisoned tribal ways; (2) formal education of Indian young; (3) replacement of "pagan" Indian beliefs and ceremonies with Christianity; and (4) an assault on aboriginal political leaders who resisted Ottawa's and Washington's acculturation program. For all persons concerned, the challenges of integrating aboriginal peoples into capitalistic, foreign cultures were momentous. Yet optimism prevailed in Ottawa and Washington.

To implement these plans, they turned to governmental agencies—the Department of Indian Affairs in Canada and the Office of Indian Affairs in the United States—and particularly to their field employees. Historians have severely criticized these paternalistic and often ineffective public officials. Historian Francis Paul Prucha concludes that "the [American] Indian service, upon which rested much of the responsibility for solving the 'Indian problem' of the post–Civil War decades, was itself a large part of the problem."[74] Opportunities for fraud corrupted many federal agents, who yearly handled large amounts of Indian money, annuity goods, and farm equipment. They also supervised the leasing of reservation lands and negotiated contracts for agency improvements. Ottawa's management of Indian affairs in the late nineteenth century has also been judged "unequal to the task."[75] As vulnerable, subject peoples, Great Lakes Indians ironically were harmed at times by the very persons charged with protecting them.

The Canadian Department of Indian Affairs derived its powers from the 1876 Indian Act. Like the department's counterpart in the United States, it was divided administratively into a central office and several field agencies. The modest headquarters staff in Ottawa (less than forty employees in the early 1880s) consisted mainly of clerks who handled the deputy superintendent general's voluminous correspondence and made copies in letterbooks. Initially, the Department of Indian Affairs was housed within the Crown Lands Department, and though it was transferred to the Department of the Interior in 1873, it continued to be the agent of expansion, focusing its energies on the sale of Indian lands and resources to white developers.[76]

Great Lakes Indian agents, whether directed from Washington or Ottawa, thus strived for similar goals and employed comparable administrative strategies and tools. History would demonstrate, however, that these elaborate Canadian and American plans did not always agree with aboriginal agendas.[77]

NATIVE RESPONSES

The reservation environment, as overseen by federal Indian agents, elicited mixed responses from natives and was often rent with factionalism. Canadian and American officials of the period quickly and conveniently categorized bands or intratribal blocs as "progressive" or "traditional," yet historian David Rich Lewis cautions that communities contained many interest groups that were sometimes in flux because of the variety of issues they faced. Furthermore, individuals, as Lewis discovered in his study of Northern Ute leader William Wash, "frequently transcend the bounds of static factional categories."[78]

Some Great Lakes aboriginal leaders and their followers abandoned hope of ever restoring traditional lifestyles and, pleased to remain in their traditional territories, pragmatically tried to make the best of reservation life. They took up farming, sent their children to school, attended church services, adopted "citizen's dress," and cooperated in many ways with the local Indian agent—all the while retaining their sense of identity as native peoples with distinct cultures and sovereign homelands. For others, the old ways beckoned more strongly, and they disregarded federal prohibitions in order to keep such customs alive. They scorned local Indian agents and the American and Canadian ways of life they represented—often with good reason.

These Indians fended off government programs in a variety of ways. Canadian native families passively but steadfastly refused to comply with various enfranchisement acts that called on them to drop their Indian status, allot their lands, and become citizens. ("Between 1857 and 1920," writes historian J. R. Miller, "only 250 individuals [in all of Canada] opted for full citizenship and loss of Indian status by means of enfranchisement.")[79] Some American Indians also steadfastly resisted government "civilization" programs. Agents regularly reported the presence of "pagan" groups and practices. These included religious ceremonies, speaking Indian languages, living in bark wigwams, and seasonal roaming around the woods and waters to hunt, trap, fish, pick berries, and gather wild rice and roots. Each summer, as they had for hundreds of years, the women raised corn, beans, and other vegetables. In 1890, the U.S. Census noted of the Indian population at Lac Court Oreilles in Wisconsin, for example:

> The pagan Indians adhere very tenaciously to their old customs. . . . The pagans have but very little education. A very small percentage of these can speak English. They take no interest in education, do not send their children to school regularly, and many do not send them at all.

Nearby Lac du Flambeau was not much better in Washington's eyes.

> This reserve can be called the stronghold of Chippewa paganism. . . . During the winter scarcely half of the Flambeau Indians can be found on the reserve. In summer they earn a livelihood by picking berries and also by hunting and fishing and by the charity of their white brethren.[80]

Great Lakes Indians were not "aggressive or hostile in dealing with the U.S. government," as historical archaeologist Charles Cleland points out; but they were persistent and, in many ways, successful in preserving their language and religious beliefs and, to some degree, their political, social, and economic systems.[81]

CONCLUSION

Past developments offered many clues about the coming reservation years. The winds of change that swept across the Great Lakes in the late 1800s transformed heartland and hinterland. Steamboats and railroads contributed to a transportation revolution that integrated Great Lakes industries, then linked them with distant western and eastern markets. This, in turn, stimulated the timber industry, farming, mining, commercial fishing, and tourism. The dreams that such merchants as George Brown held for the northwestern frontier seemed to be realized.

A key factor in this Great Lakes boom was the opening of aboriginal lands for exploitation. Ottawa and Washington responded primarily to developmental pressures from white constituents. Federal officials from both nations rationalized the process by claiming that the reservation system would better protect remaining Indian landholdings and provide a sanctuary where natives might be metamorphosed—with the help of "civilizing" agents, such as missionaries and teachers—into acculturated citizens. Minor policy and implementation differences existed north and south of the international border and will be discussed in later chapters. Most striking, however, were the common governmental objectives for Indian children. About these ambitious programs, U.S. and Canadian aboriginal peoples were rarely consulted. It was, as the Royal Commission later observed about the evolution of the Canadian Indian Act, a "dialogue of the deaf."[82]

Aboriginal community leaders understood what was happening on their reservations and across the Great Lakes, yet they did not capitulate to these events as submissive victims. Neither land loss nor assignment to reservations crushed them. Despite their relatively small numbers, lack of unity, and modest economic and political resources, they adjusted and resisted in a variety of ways as best they could. Usually, they altered traditions when it seemed necessary or desirable. Their choices were informed and not made solely because of government policy and the chiding of field officials about the advantages of "civilization." Likewise, Indians of the Great Lakes continued to defend their rights, to negotiate in good faith, and to play a prominent role in Great Lakes history.[83]

The dominant theme of this book is the historic struggle of the late 1800s between an expanding white frontier assisted by federal government employees, on the one hand, and far-flung aboriginal communities determined to preserve their autonomy and prosper in their Great Lakes homeland, on the other. Settlers, frontier developers, and federal bureaucrats possessed most of the economic and political power. Thus it was not surprising that nonnatives controlled the bulk of Great Lakes resources by century's end. Yet their campaign to transform aboriginal peoples and absorb them into the Canadian and American mainstreams took an unexpected turn. Embattled native leaders had their own agendas, which did not include a wholesale abandonment of their cultures and further surrenders of their homeland. Red Jacket reminded his white missionary audience earlier in the century:

> You have got our country, but you are not satisfied; you want to force your religion upon us. . . .
>
> Brother: the Great Spirit has made us all, but He has made a great difference between his white and red children. He has given us a different complexion and different customs. . . . Since He has made so great a difference between us in other things, why may we not conclude that He has given us a different religion according to our understanding? . . .
>
> Brother: we do not wish to destroy your religion, or to take it from you. We only want to enjoy our own.[84]

Their moccasins were about to enter the mainstream, but Indians would not be swept away by it.

Chief Red Jacket and his spiritual successors on Great Lakes reservations enjoyed some success in this high-stakes contest for the land and the soul of a people. The struggle began with the Ottawa and Washington campaign to turn their native "wards" into self-sufficient farmers and to create model agricultural settlements on each reservation. Once this was achieved, Indian agents, government farmers, teachers, and missionaries could reshape every aspect of native family life and prepare them for assimilation.

{ ONE }

Making a Living

{ 1 }

Agriculture on the Great Lakes Homelands

Peter Hill of Six Nations on the Grand River Reserve was part of a local agricultural community in the 1890s, and his ledger-diary revealed the seasonal cycle followed on a family farm as well as its links to the market economy. Each year in March, Hill, his wife, and their sons gathered and processed maple sap; they also cut firewood for their own use and to sell in Brantford, fifteen miles away, where they purchased processed food, medicine, machinery, and furniture. Splitting rails and repairing fences consumed most of the next month. For help with such major tasks and with cutting and drawing wood, building a home and barn, and haying and harvesting, farmers like Hill sponsored cooperative bees. In return, the Hills participated in their neighbors' bees. Each spring, the family plowed and disked their fields, then sowed oats, barley, clover, peas, potatoes, and corn. The women and children assisted with corn planting before they went berrying, both long-standing Iroquois traditions. The family periodically needed supplies of sugar, flour, tobacco, and matches, which they usually bought closer to home, at the local flour mill, rather than at Brantford. The focus of June and July was haying, harvesting wheat, and, with the help of neighbors, threshing. During the next two months, the Hills gathered in additional crops, manured the fields, and fitted them for winter wheat. Each fall, they took apples to the Brantford cider mill and, as a respite from the long stretch of hard work, attended the annual Six Nations agricultural fair. Before snow blanketed the ground, Peter Hill and his sons plowed under the field and garden stubble. Regular Saturday trips continued to Brantford, where Mrs. Hill sold butter, eggs, turkeys, and ducks. When winter gripped the countryside, Peter cut stove wood and transported logs to the mill to be fashioned into railroad ties.

The industrious Hill family produced an approximate gross cash income from farming of $280. Although this was modest, the family was fairly self-sufficient. With good credit, Hill obtained cash loans from non-Indians and hired day laborers when needed. Diversification of income from the sale of a variety of farm commodities (wheat, beans, hay, forest products, ducks, turkeys, eggs, and butter) strengthened this enterprising family's financial position. Fred Voget, who edited Peter Hill's ledger-diary, judged that he "could pass for any farmer of moderate circumstances in his day"; yet "his ethnicity meant a great deal to him," and he "had no apparent desire to lose himself in the wider society."[1]

In response to changes sweeping the Great Lakes in the late 1800s, reservation peoples like Peter Hill's family adjusted in ways necessary to feed themselves and preserve community autonomy. For hundreds of aboriginal families, especially in the south, this meant a major commitment to plow agriculture. The decision seemed reasonable; the land could support farming, and their communities had strong horticultural traditions. Furthermore, Canada and the United States offered technical assistance. Nearby markets also beckoned for Indian surplus crops. Even the more northern reserves, where farming was less feasible, took advantage of the economic opportunities offered by expanding regional industries: commercial fishing, railroad construction, shipping, and lumber.

Each Great Lakes Indian community during this time period faced enormous pressure from Washington and Ottawa to abandon traditional subsistence practices and wholeheartedly commit to farming as a full-time job. Both governments became obsessed with this policy, believing it was the key to Indian "civilization" and ultimate assimilation. The passing years would show whether or not aboriginal families could continue to support themselves and protect their homelands and core values while adapting to market forces, federal government farm programs, and Great Lakes weather cycles.

CANADIAN GOVERNMENT POLICY

The Canadian Department of Indian Affairs was absolutely certain that its wards must till the soil in order to survive and be accepted by their nonnative neighbors. In his December 1898 annual report, the deputy superintendent general of Indian affairs, James A. Smart, explained the program's underlying principles. "For the transformation of the nomadic denizens of the forest or prairie," he wrote, "the first essential is fixity of residence, and the formation of the idea of a home. Without that neither churches nor schools nor any other educational influence can be established and applied." Smart continued:

> Cultivation of the soil necessitates remaining in one spot, and then exerts an educational influence of a good character. It keeps prominently before the mind the relation of cause and effect, together with the dependence upon a higher power. It teaches moreover the necessity for systematic work at the proper season, for giving attention to detail, and patience in waiting for results.[2]

These plans for aboriginal peoples revealed much about the mind-set of policy makers who were to shape reservation history after the 1850s. To argue that natives must be taught about "home," "the necessity for systematic work at the proper season," "patience," and "attention to detail" showed the federal government's shocking ignorance about its Indian wards. Canadian historian J. M. Bumsted also notes that the goal of turning aboriginal families into settled farmers provided both a convenient rationale for taking their hunting grounds and a way to turn them into productive persons on minimal allotments. For a "primitive people" to accept agriculture was a first step up the "ladder of progress." After all, noted Hayter Reed, the deputy superintendent of Indian affairs, "Corn proceeds all civilization."[3]

Canada's Indian agricultural policy included persistent and paternalistic Indian Department supervision of local operations, through its control of aboriginal annuity funds (proceeds from land cessions that the Indian Department put out at interest) and reserve lands (including the harvesting of timber and leasing of portions to nonnatives). When individual reservation residents or a band council wished to purchase, with their own money, seeds and agricultural implements or to improve farms in other ways, they had to apply to their financial gatekeepers, the Indian Department. Christian missionaries supplemented the educational and agricultural work of the Indian Department. Evangelists realized that infant churches and schools could only succeed if aborigines remained on their reservations and abandoned seasonal cycles of hunting, gathering, and fishing throughout the region. Methodists, Moravians, and missionaries of the New England Company thus promoted cultivation of the soil from the pulpit. They also grew crops on model farms, worked side by side with natives in their fields, supplied them with seeds and implements, and established manual labor schools with model farms to instruct the young. Success, from the missionaries' perspective, was most obvious in southern Ontario, where the climate was conducive, native nations (especially the Iroquois) had horticultural traditions, and off-reservation wildlife habitats were fast disappearing. Moravians working among Delaware on the Thames, for example, reported in the 1880s that proceeds from their successful farm not only supported the missionaries but helped purchase seed drills, mowers, and reapers for reservation families. The Indian population of 268 relied on agriculture and farmed nearly nine hundred acres of potatoes, wheat, oats, and corn.[4]

The Indian Department presented annual statistics to document agricultural success. The 1878 Ontario native population of 15,711 reportedly cultivated 46,063 acres of corn, wheat, oats, peas, barley, rye, buckwheat, potatoes, and hay. To plant, harvest, and process these crops, the department enumerated an impressive number of aboriginal barns or stables, ploughs, harrows, wagons, fanning mills, threshing mills, other implements, and livestock.[5]

That Canadian Indians were not totally dedicated to farming was indicated by significant incomes from fishing ($25,431), fur sales ($25,890), and "other industries" ($29,203).[6] Such data, like that offered by the missionaries, suggested modest success in promoting Indian farming. Yet a close look at specific reservation events—beneath the level of summary, official reports—reveals a complex tale of economic continuity and change, with important regional differences.

ABORIGINAL RESPONSE TO CANADIAN FARM POLICY

Diversity characterized native reaction to Ottawa's farming program. On some reserves, many persons tried plow agriculture with encouraging results. In other communities, the record was mixed; some families energetically cultivated the soil, while neighbors maintained a seasonal hunting-gathering-fishing economy at times supplemented with off-reservation wage work. Still other native communities entirely balked at plow agriculture. Generally, these divisions were regional. In extreme southern Ontario, the moderate climate and fertile soil invited the planting of crops, which Indians had done for hundreds of years, although not on the scale desired by federal officials in the late 1800s. Six Nations and Walpole Island First Nation farmers were exemplary of this area. Further north, on the shores of Georgian Bay and Lake Huron, conditions were less inviting for fledgling farmers. Manitoulin Island reservations were typical. Even less a haven for agriculturalists was the frosty bush country north of Lake Superior, with its violent windstorms and hailstorms.

Also important to Indian farming were expanding Great Lakes nonnative populations and transportation networks. They offered natives new opportunities to sell agricultural surpluses; natural resources, such as timber; and their own labor. But the market system had its drawbacks; increased mechanization of agriculture in the late 1800s demanded greater capital investments from hard-pressed farm families, who were hurt, too, by falling prices for cash crops. To evaluate agricultural development within each of Canada's three main regions over time, several key questions must be answered:

1. How many reservation acres were cleared for farming?
2. How many residents tilled the soil full-time versus those who maintained a mixed economy?
3. What was the range of farm sizes and their supportive apparatus: farm buildings and improvements, equipment (plows, threshing machines), and livestock (cattle, draft horses, draft oxen, pigs, sheep)?
4. What support did federal agents, missionaries, and reservation cooperatives provide?
5. What were farm production statistics by crop?
6. Did farm families use the crops mainly for personal consumption or for market sales? If the latter, did this money merely supplement other income, or did families totally rely on farm revenue?

Southern Ontario

Judged by the preceding guidelines, southern Ontario aboriginal people worked vigorously to become self-sufficient family farmers. They brought numerous acres under cultivation and expanded operations during the closing decades of the century. As a sign of progress, agents regularly—and eagerly—reported new acres "broken." They also praised improved practices. For example, the Indian Department described in 1896 how the Moravians of the Thames were not cultivating more land but doing it better: "They keep the land clean, and plant their seed at the proper time; they find that a little extra work laid out on the land insures a better crop."[7]

More pessimistic field accounts focused on persistent farming problems. Indians still worked disappointing percentages of remarkably fertile reservations. Of Alnwick's 3,404.5 acres, approximately 2,460 were cleared in 1885, but white tenants farmed 1,325 of these acres. In 1886, the Moravians of the Thames, despite improving techniques, planted only about one-third of their reserve.[8]

Nevertheless, progress over time generally characterized developments in southern Ontario. Events on the Sarnia Reserve were illustrative. Initially, the Indian Department lamented the lack of agricultural advancement along this stretch of the St. Clair River. Not much land was farmed. Rather than clear new fields, natives worked the old plots until the soil was exhausted. "Indians," the department observed disparagingly, "generally do not like to expend labor on anything for which they cannot be immediately repaid." Anglican missionary E. F. Wilson reported in the late 1860s that the Sarnia band did "little beyond just ploughing an acre or two round their dwellings, and planting it with Indian corn and potatoes, or perchance with a small oat or wheat crop." By the 1890s, field reports were rosy; having obtained agricultural implements, strung miles of barbed wire fence, and planted more acres than ever before, the reserve anticipated a fine harvest.[9]

At midcentury, most reservation residents leased out their land instead of farming and maintained a traditional, mixed economy rather than focus entirely on agriculture. During the ensuing decades, full-time farming characterized several southern Ontario aboriginal communities. The evils of leasing prompted Ottawa to discourage the practice. About the Alnwick Reserve, the department observed in 1884:

> The greatest evil existing here is the anticipating of rents, in some cases from two to seven years. The Indian goes to the tenant and receives the money, or its equivalent, allowing a very large discount. The money is then injudiciously spent in a few weeks, and when winter comes, the families suffer from the want of food and other necessaries.

Furthermore, whites tended to exhaust the soils they rented. At Scugog, this harmful trend was reversed in the mid-1880s when the department seized crops grown by illegal tenants and refused to return them until the trespassers agreed to two stipulations: (1) that for each wagonload of produce removed from reservation land, "a full load of manure would be returned"; and (2) that they would no longer farm Indian land without the permission of the superintendent general of Indian affairs. The Scugog agent soon reported, "not a single acre has been worked by outsiders this season."[10]

Though reservation harvests increasingly supported local residents, they were still reluctant to rely totally on tilling the soil. Agency reports regularly noted how natives supplemented the yields of farm and garden by hunting, fishing, gathering rice, selling baskets, and working for lumber companies and neighboring white farmers. Still, the commitment to agriculture increased with time on southern Ontario reservations. By the 1890s, farming was central to the economies at Alnwick, the Moravians of the Thames, Sarnia, and some other reserves—particularly Six Nations and Walpole.[11]

Iroquois agricultural success on the sprawling Grand River Reserve was the result of physical toil amid financial adversity. By the mid-1850s, the Indians had only cleared about 10 percent of their lands. Cash was scarce to buy seeds whenever smut destroyed those in winter storage bins. Yet Six Nations persevered and ultimately enjoyed farming's fruits. Approximately one-third of the families had become commercial farmers by the early 1870s.[12] Two decades later, 3,425 residents cultivated 19,097 out of 43,696 reservation acres. Sixty acres was the normal farm size, although some reached three hundred acres, and their owners relied on hired workers.[13] General farming was by then fundamental to the Six Nations economy. Some family members nevertheless worked as laborers, carpenters, and masons; and "Several hundreds" still engaged in off-reservation, seasonal berry picking and flax pulling. Chiefs and councils discouraged such migratory activities by providing financial assistance only to Iroquois who worked their own farms.[14]

Remarkable improvements to the land and investments in livestock and machinery bore further witness to the importance of agriculture at Six Nations. By 1890, the reservation was dotted by 653 houses, while 307 barns and stables sheltered crops, livestock, and equipment. In that year, the implements included 398 plows, 305 harrows, 382 wagons and carts, 181 fanning mills, and 8 threshing machines. One visitor to the reserve in the 1880s "counted in his morning's drive five threshing-machines at work, all owned and managed by Indians."[15] Iroquois livestock holdings at this time were equally impressive: 689 cows, one hundred oxen, 1,147 young cattle, 759 horses, 203 sheep, and 1,686 pigs.[16] This enormous agricultural commitment yielded abundant, prizewinning crops that chiefly supported the large reservation population. In 1889, the Iroquois planted 14,333 bushels of seed, which yielded 121,839 bushels of corn, wheat, oats, barley, and potatoes.[17]

Given the challenges of clearing the land, equipping their farms, learning new skills, and enduring droughts and floods, fledgling farmers required—and got—considerable assistance. In the mid-1850s, help came from the Indian Department, which provided annuity monies and credit so that families hit by a bad harvest could get seeds for replanting. By century's close, the Six Nations council had established its own loan fund. Probably the most effective stimulus was support from fellow aboriginal farmers. In the 1860s, for example, the Iroquois established an agricultural society that sponsored a three-day fair each fall so farmers could display produce and handicrafts and compete for prizes. The Canadian governor-general provided a plow to the winner of the very competitive plowing match. The competitors' skills plus the quality of crops impressed large numbers of off-reservation visitors, including newspaper editors. In a backhanded attempt to be complimentary, one observed:

> No intelligent man could have attended this agricultural exhibition by the Six Nations Indians without being convinced of the great progress made during the past few years in the moral, intellectual, and physical condition of these tribes of the aboriginal inhabitants of Canada, whatever may be said to the contrary by superficial observers and commentators on Indian morality, progress and civilization.

Joseph Howe, secretary of state for the provinces, observed that these displays and Iroquois cultivation of the soil were generally "the best means of placing them [the Iroquois] as nearly as possible on a par with their white fellow subjects." In the 1890s, a branch of the Farmer's Institute offered workshops on the reservation about the latest farm technologies. That Iroquois farming had come of age greatly pleased the Indian Department, and in 1893, it noted that an agricultural exhibit that represented "the progress of the Indians of the Six Nations on the Grand River" was sent to the World's Columbian Exposition at Chicago.[18]

Besides the raising of abundant, prizewinning crops, tilling the soil influenced the Iroquois economy in other ways. Their diet came to include pork, hot biscuits, eggs, milk, butter, and canned homegrown fruits and vegetables. Families at first bartered surpluses for credit at nearby stores; then, having shown they could compete with whites at agricultural fairs, Six Nations farmers began marketing crops throughout the region including Brantford and Hamilton. Profits helped pay for farm improvements and for everyday needs, such as furniture and clothing. Participation in the market economy naturally had its drawbacks and required flexibility. During the agricultural depression of the 1880s, Six Nations farmers suffered along with others in Ontario; and when grain prices dropped in the early 1890s, the Iroquois shifted their focus to raising stock.[19]

Indian farmers also did well at Walpole Island First Nation. One indicator was the amount of land cleared on the ten-thousand-acre reservation. In 1843, this was only 600 acres, but by century's end, the figure expanded to 8,150. Equally impressive were the increasing acres cultivated: from 1,300 in 1875 to 3,218 in 1898.[20] The number of islanders who tilled the soil grew so steadily that the local agent reported in the mid-1890s that the Indians "are engaged for the most part in agriculture." The register of marriages at St. John the Baptist Anglican Church, for example, revealed that of the thirty-nine men married between 1898 and 1908, all were farmers except one listed as a stone and brick mason. (Women's occupations were not recorded.)[21]

The amount of livestock and farm implements owned and improvements made by household units likewise indicated the growing importance of agriculture on this reservation. By 1898, farmers living in ninety-six frame dwellings and 131 of log construction had fenced 3,218 acres and supported their operations with eighteen barns, 139 horse stables, seventy-five cattle stables, thirty storehouses, thirty-five milk houses, and thirty-two corncribs. Livestock figures—numbers of horses, cattle, sheep, pigs, and poultry—were equally impressive. Family subsistence strategies had thus noticeably changed in the late 1800s. Many Walpole households became distinct economic units as they moved away from collective band to family farming and from subsistence to commercial agricultural production. More and more, their farms resembled those of their non-Indian neighbors, complete with cultivators, reapers, hay rakes, and fanning mills.[22]

Somewhat counterbalancing these optimistic reports was another filed by an inspector of Indian agencies, J. Ansdell MacRae, in 1904. He lamented that only 48 of the island's 157 families farmed the land. The rest showed no signs of settling down. They earned a livelihood as laborers, by selling craft items, and in other pursuits. He estimated that about 20 percent made their living through off-reservation means.[23]

The Lake Huron Region

Farming, which significantly altered reservation life at Walpole, Six Nations, and elsewhere in southern Ontario, was less prominent among northern aboriginal peoples. On some reserves, not even the soil was suitable. One agent observed that the Henvey Inlet band was "very unfavorably circumstanced as far as agriculture." He explained, "Their reserve consists almost entirely of burnt, flat rock, with here and there a patch of dry, sharp sand, and occasional saucer shaped hollows in the rock, of from 1/4 to 1 acre in extent, in which has accumulated decayed vegetable matters." The Parry Sound superintendent observed, "The lateness of the spring, the short summer and frequent failure of the crops from dry weather and from early and late frosts discourage the Indians, who have never been much accustomed to go in for agriculture." Rather than rely on this newfangled and risky venture,

Parry Sound natives prudently diversified their labor—to the Indian Department's chagrin—by continuing to fish, hunt, and trap. They also sought seasonal work in nearby lumberyards.[24]

This preference for a time-honored, mixed economy with limited reliance on gardens (mainly corn and potatoes) typified reserves throughout the Lake Huron region, from Nawash and Beausoleil in the south to Shawanaga, Henvey's Inlet, Dokis, and Lake Nipissing in the east, as well as from White Fish River west to Batchewana. Men and women continued their seminomadic, seasonal rovings to harvest nature's bounty and provide services to neighboring whites as guides, sellers of crafts, and laborers. Ottawa's agents promoted farming by providing seeds, equipment, and livestock. Officials also cajoled and scolded. The 1858 Special Commission to Investigate Indian Affairs claimed that the Rama community, which avoided tilling the soil, was "dragging through a life disgraceful to humanity." Still, many Indians would not commit to farming full-time. A group at Lake Nipissing, in answer to the agent's "inquiry as to the amount of crop they had raised," replied, "The pine woods are my farm."[25]

Manitoulin Islanders had endured zealous promoters from the Indian Department since the 1830s. They thought that thousands of acres could be farmed by natives plus nonnative settlers. Not all agreed. One missionary described the area as "23,000 rocks of granite, dignified by the name of Manitoulin Islands." An Indian superintendent and his staff (a carpenter, a blacksmith, a mason, a cooper, a shoemaker, and some laborers) were headquartered at Manitowaning in the 1840s and 1850s and vigorously promoted a sedentary, farm-centered life for Ottawa, Ojibwa, and Potawatomi families drawn to live in the village. But the lack of good soil nearby and divisive factors, such as religion and political jealousy, weakened the Manitowaning agricultural experiment. By 1860, the village contained only ninety-six persons.[26] Seasonal job opportunities on the island also undermined native commitment to full-time farming.

Nevertheless, during the last half of the century, many islanders made noteworthy agricultural advancements. In 1875, their population was estimated at 1,465: 528 lived on the western, ceded portion of Manitoulin (Cockburn Island, Sheguiandah, Sheshigwaning, Sucker Creek, and West Bay), while 937 dwelt on eastern, unceded territory (South Bay, Wikwemikong, and Wikwemikongsing). By the 1890s, their numbers grew to 1,822.[27] Farms also expanded during these years—from 2,206 cultivated acres to 6,090 (including "made pasturage"). These were merely estimates, because of the Indians' difficulty in gauging family holdings, which reportedly averaged between two and ten acres. Another factor affecting the economic information supplied by natives was their reluctance to show Ottawa "how really well off they were," for fear "their payments might be reduced or withdrawn."[28] Still, native commitment to agriculture was firm. By the mid-1870s, ambitious farmers had built 257 houses and 173 barns. Island harvests that year included 7,108 bushels of corn, 14,294 of potatoes, 728 of wheat, and 291 of other crops.[29]

Indian Department support for Manitoulin agriculture played a part in this success. In the 1860s, shortly after the establishment of island reserves, federal agents distributed wheat seed to supplement corn and potato crops that early frosts more easily damaged. Issuance of draught animals, plows, and other livestock, together with instruction about their care, helped natives expand their farms. By 1875, they owned thirty-six horses, seventeen oxen, 184 cows, 288 hogs, and 253 sheep. Ottawa also supplied a safety net when nature turned against Manitoulin farmers. In 1868, for example, wildfires destroyed woods and crops on the eastern, unceded portion of the island. Responding to a call forwarded by a missionary stationed at Wikwimikong, the Indian Department supplied $340 worth of seed (fall wheat, rye, and timothy grass) and fifteen sacks of rice (two hundred pounds each) to feed destitute natives during the coming winter. Again in 1885, federal officials assisted islanders when extreme, penetrating cold threatened the loss of their cattle and destroyed seed potatoes in underground storage pits.[30]

Lake Superior

On Canadian reserves along Lake Superior's northern shore, including Lake Nipigon, terrain was even less hospitable to agriculture than near Lake Huron. Soil on the Michipicoton Reserve, for instance, was generally sandy and supported only a few "scrubby pine and tamarack." The lowlands could support farms but were subject to spring floods. The situation at Pays Plat was similar. The short growing season also hampered agricultural efforts along the North Shore.[31]

Consequently, the Lake Superior aboriginal nations, even more so than those to the south, continued to rely on a mixed economy of seasonal hunting, trapping, trading, fishing, and gathering. Natural resources still abounded on reservations and in the area ceded by the 1850 Robinson Treaty. Sparse white settlements did not restrict free-ranging native families. As discussed in chapter 2, Hudson's Bay posts dotted the region and provided a market for furs. The company also hired natives to transport goods and supplies. The Canadian Pacific Railway and local fishermen—commercial and tourist—also employed aboriginal workers.

Ojibwa farm family, Garden River Reservation, 1901. *(Courtesy Archives of Ontario, image S 16361, acc. 10748.)*

Natives nevertheless took advantage of the opportunities to cultivate the soil and enjoyed some success, especially at Fort William. The Indian Department promoted agriculture, as it did with the more southern reserves, by supplying communities with yokes of oxen, farming implements, and seeds.[32] The limited growing season and scarcity of good soil meant that neophyte farmers would concentrate their efforts on hay (to feed their livestock) and root crops, such as potatoes, beets, onions, carrots, and turnips. These harvests, together with cleared, fenced fields and the construction of permanent log and frame homes as well as outbuildings, illustrated an Indian commitment to farming for at least part of their subsistence. In 1894, natives from the Long Lake Reserve traveled by canoe, making over twenty-four portages, to meet their agent and obtain potato and turnip seeds. The Indian agent reported the next year that he had been so pleased with the root, wheat, and oat crops grown by a portion of the Red Rock band on Lake Nipigon for the past nine years that he exhibited their produce at the Port Arthur Agricultural Fair.[33] Once North Shore families planted their gardens and fields, they usually left the reserves to fish, hunt, and gather.

The Indian Department lavished its warmest praise on the Fort William native community, whose "progress" was exceptional. Before 1883, residents "farmed or gardened only the land cleared and used by their forefathers." No drainage ditches or bridges existed, and Indian efforts yielded perhaps one hundred bushels of root crops. Then the Indian Department began furnishing them with livestock and farm tools. Each family pledged to grow a share of the hay necessary to feed the animals. Families cared well for their oxen, cleared additional land, fenced it, and helped construct drainage ditches, bridges, and roads. By 1894, their farms, with the assistance of the Roman Catholic mission, produced five thousand bushels of potatoes, fifteen hundred of turnips, six hundred of carrots, three hundred of beets, two hundred of parsnips, and 186 tons of hay. They owned eleven horses, twenty cows, six oxen, three bulls, and twenty-three young stock. The agent happily remarked, "These Indians live no longer by the chase . . . and market their overplus farm produce to the whites."[34] Fort Williams' willingness to try agriculture with assistance from the Indian Department led to the draining of Whiskey Jack Lake to grow hay. The lake is "about one mile long and surrounded with tamarack swamp," the agent noted.

> This has been for many years a hindrance to their extending their farms further back and it limits their cattle range for feeding. During July [1892] they cut a ditch from this lake, twenty-five hundred feet long, leading into a ravine which carries the water into the Kaministiquia [sic] River. This involved an excavation of three thousand five hundred and sixty-five cubic yards mostly through soft, mirey muskeg and some clay, and the ditch looks like a small canal. It lowered the water of the lake about six feet and dried up the surrounding swamp referred to, which now grows tall waving hay where it was covered with water. They have already commenced extending their fences, and some are clearing land and enlarging their farms. This extensive work they could not have done without the assistance of the department. The levels were taken by an engineer and fifteen cents per cubic yard was paid for excavating.[35]

Fort Williams' focus on agriculture was impressive; still, the North Shore reservation population of 1,454 (west of Michipicoton) had cleared only 777 acres by 1898 and had cultivated just 536. Natives owned livestock valued at $3,150 and a considerable amount of farm implements, such as plows, harrows, wagons, carts, and sleighs. Families had built thirty barns, two horse stables, nineteen cattle stables, eight storehouses, and seven root houses.[36] Yet none of the bands put all of their economic eggs in the farming basket. The warm weather was capricious, the arable soil too limited, and other resources—traditional hunting, fishing, and gathering as well as new jobs working for the white man—safeguarded Indians against crop failure. As with Lake Huron native nations, the forests remained their farms. Here was security and predictability based on centuries of evolving knowledge about the natural world. Even in tough times, the woods offered sustenance to those who knew its ways.

In the early 1890s, the North Shore winter was especially harsh. By spring, many "Indians were all thin and poor in flesh." The chiefs of one band informed their agent of a starving woman and her young son who had traveled toward Nipigon House to get some food.

> She got so weak she could go no further; she had with her a fish hook bone found in every rabbit and used when they can get no other kind; she got a line of tough bark off the moose or leather tree, tied it to her bone hook and cut a hole in the ice of a small lake abounding with jack-fish. But she could get none without a bait. She then cut a piece of the calf of her leg for bait and succeeded in getting a fish. This fish made bait to catch more; and she and her boy lived and got to the Nipigon Hudson Bay Company's Post.[37]

AMERICAN FARM POLICY FOR INDIANS

As in Canada, the American government was firmly committed to changing Indians from hunter-gatherers and horticulturists into self-sustaining tillers of the soil whose specialized cash crop could be sold on the market. Federal agents fostered reservation agriculture in a variety of ways, including technical assistance in the form of agency farmers, agricultural equipment, livestock, seeds, and model farms, as well as restricting the use of Indian annuities and trust funds to farm improvements. Over time, cultivating fruit trees and forests even became part of Washington's master plan.

In 1890, for example, Indian commissioner Thomas J. Morgan instructed all agents and superintendents of native schools to observe Arbor Day so that parents and pupils would be awakened to the value and importance of tree culture. Local exercises were to include the planting by each child (or school class) of a fruit, ornamental, or forest tree. Boys and girls were also to be taught to care for young trees with proper supports, wrapping, mulching, and water. The U.S. Office of Indian Affairs would supply the trees but expected full reports about these celebrations from field officials.[38]

Farming on Great Lakes reservations in the United States was a story, like

Canada's, of continuity and change. Also as in Canada, there were important regional differences. An examination of native agriculture in New York, Michigan, Indiana, Wisconsin, and Minnesota clearly documents these characteristics.

ABORIGINAL RESPONSE TO AMERICAN FARM POLICY

New York

Historically, the New York Iroquois, like their Canadian relatives, were a corn-fed people. Upstate reservations included prime farmland, and industrious white neighbors offered useful examples of success with plow agriculture. Here, the Indian Office's ideal of self-sufficient farm families seemed achievable.

During most of the 1800s, New York natives advanced steadily toward this goal. An agent for the Cattaraugus and Tuscarora reservations noted in 1858, "There are farms which, in their management, appearance, and productiveness, compare favorably with the best farms occupied and managed by white men in the respective vicinities." By the mid-1860s, Indians on the Allegany, Cattaraugus, Tonawanda, Onondaga, and Tuscarora reservations farmed 13,345 acres and owned a total of 4,068 cattle, horses, and swine. Of the 1,738 Six Nations persons with jobs in 1890, 590 farmed the reserve, using 20,763.75 of its 43,399 tillable acres. Products of the land included corn, wheat, oats, barley, rye, buckwheat, sweet corn, hay, potatoes, turnips, peas, beans, beets, cabbage, apples, strawberries, blackberries, tomatoes, and other vegetables. Farmers also had obtained an impressive number of farm implements, including steam threshers and self-binding reapers.[39] In September 1877, the Iroquois Agricultural Society held its annual fair and cattle show on the Cattaraugus Reservation. Members exhibited over thirteen hundred articles. The society, formed in 1859, held its first fair in 1860. Soon each reservation built its own fairgrounds. Annual displays highlighted successful crops and well-bred livestock. Prizes awarded for these products and to the winners of horse races, footraces, and various games attracted large, appreciative audiences. The encouraging influence of agricultural fairs declined significantly by the 1890s. Their management, according to a federal report, "fell into speculative hands," and "being distrusted, the best farmers ceased to compete for premiums and withdrew their support." Except for at the Cattaraugus Reservation, all fairgrounds had been "converted to other uses."[40]

By century's close, farming in general had waned among the New York

Iroquois. Partly to blame was the national agricultural depression of the 1880s, which also hurt thousands of nonnative farmers. The reduction in livestock, together with neglected orchards, barns, fences, and other equipment, reflected hard times and changing economic interests. Iroquois farmers primarily fed their crops to their families rather than market them commercially, making capital for improvements scarce. Indian agents grumbled that some households still relied on a mixed economy of hunting, trapping, fishing, gathering, and gardening. Families either consumed these woodland products or sold them on and off the reservations. Surrounding forests also yielded timber, for which there were ready markets in Pennsylvania and New York. Wage work in nearby white communities was equally attractive. Females trained in household arts received good pay, while males sought jobs on large farms, as bark peelers at lumber mills or axmen for logging companies, and as track hands for the railroads. Agents further noted the Iroquois tendency to lease land to whites rather than till the soil themselves. At Onondaga, for example, whites farmed four-fifths of the cleared acreage.[41]

Michigan and Indiana

As in New York, Michigan native economic prospects looked good at first. Agents reported in the 1850s and 1860s that Indians, pleased with reservation assignments, had begun clearing the land and farming. Traditional trapping, hunting, and fishing also remained important parts of their mixed economy, as suggested by the following 1868 Indian Office figures:

acres of Indian land cultivated	10,651
Indian horses owned	1,117
cattle owned	659
swine owned	2,379
sheep owned	12
feet of lumber sawed	357,500
pounds of maple sugar made	382,778
barrels of fish sold	5,253
value of furs sold	$44,484[42]

Reservation families earnestly experimented with farming on the Lower Peninsula in Isabella, Oceana, and Mason counties as well as on less hospitable lands across the Mackinac Straits at Bay Mills (near Sault Ste. Marie) and at L'Anse to the west. Yet the northern reserves, as in Canada, were not conducive to farming. One visitor to the Sault had observed in the early 1840s:

> Fish is, & must continue to be their [the Indians'] principal article of food.... Game is becoming scarce, & will soon be gone. The land is cultivated with much labor, and expense, & would be but moderately productive, if the climate was sufficiently mild to bring vegetation to maturity.... During my stay there, there was on the night of the 10th of July a frost so severe as to completely kill the potatoe [*sic*] tops & beans that were then fairly up. Even the grass in some places was frozen. There is nothing that they can depend upon with certainty but fish & cold weather.[43]

Many Indians south of the Mackinac Straits cultivated family allotments, built homes and barns, and "may be considered very good farmers," commented H. J. Alvord, special Indian agent, in 1866. Even the L'Anse community supplemented their fishing, hunting, lumbering, and quarrying with farming and, in 1890, made one thousand pounds of butter, raised two hundred bushels of potatoes plus fifty tons of hay, and owned sixty cattle. Still, most Michigan Indian crops were consumed locally and not marketed. Of the Isabella Reservation's 11,097 acres, natives cultivated only 886 in 1886. "A few owned their own farms, employ a number of men, and have horses, cattle, and other stock," reported a census taker, who concluded disapprovingly, "The land of the reservation is generally of good quality, and if cleared and properly farmed would be quite productive, but they have not the capacity for prolonged labor of any description."[44]

Despite such worries, Washington vigorously promoted an agricultural ideal throughout Michigan. The July 1855 treaty with the state's Ottawa and Ojibwa provided seventy-five thousand dollars (in five equal, annual installments) for farm implements, livestock, building materials, carpenters' tools, and home furnishing. The Indian Office purchased these annuities in Chicago. Once goods arrived at the reservations, chiefs and headmen distributed them to farm families. Another stimulus to cultivate the soil was the government's Mount Pleasant Boarding School, established in 1893. Besides a conventional curriculum, the staff tried to teach "a practical and working knowledge" of agriculture, so that Indian students could "transact the business of a small farm" and develop "such habits and characters as will make them industrious, frugal, and reliable citizens." Girls, it was thought, needed a training that would "make them good and saving housekeepers, faithful and worthy wives." On the school's 360 acres, boys raised a variety of crops, tended orchards and vineyards, and cared for livestock—from chickens to draft horses. Teachers also sought to instill within each boy the ambition "to have a farm of his own when he leaves school and to work it himself and thus to be self supporting and to have a home garden and thus always to have plenty to eat."[45]

Washington's reservation allotment program, described in chapter 3, ultimately undermined this promising beginning, and by the turn of the century, Michigan Indians lived in a shocking state of poverty. Non-Indian neighbors absconded with much of their land base. A scarcity of capital and subsequent agricultural depressions hurt those who retained allotments and tried to farm. Other Ottawa and Chippewa, including graduates of Mount Pleasant Boarding School, continued to resist the government farming program. Yet the woods and waters no longer yielded sufficient sustenance, and unskilled native men and women had increasing difficulty finding good jobs outside their communities. White hostility and race prejudice, writes Charles Cleland, forced Indians "even farther to the margins of the American economy," where "about the only positions open were as domestics or unskilled laborers."[46]

Meanwhile, to the south, in Indiana, Miami Indians numbered over two hundred and held better agricultural land than northern Michigan natives. Yet not all aspired to become commercial farmers. Some leaders in the Peru area prospered. Gabriel Godfroy owned a 220-acre farm in the 1870s, which compared favorably to well-to-do white neighbors. His livestock included an impressive number of horses, pigs, beef cattle, cows, sheep, and chickens. Most Miami families in the Wabash and Mississinewa valleys still preferred a traditional, mixed economy of gardening, hunting, fishing, gathering, and intermittent work for whites.[47]

Wisconsin and Minnesota

Indians responded unevenly to agriculture in Wisconsin and Minnesota, as they did in Indiana, Michigan, New York, and Ontario. The old practices (seasonal hunting, trapping, fishing, gathering, gardening) remained important to roving bands of northern Ojibwa, Potawatomi, and Winnebago and even to the more settled Menominee farmers of central Wisconsin who had difficulty feeding their families. Meanwhile, lumber industry, railroad, and farm jobs in nearby white communities attracted disenchanted reservation Menominee and Oneida, plus the Stockbridge and Munsee. Hundreds of central Wisconsin natives nevertheless worked energetically, with assistance from federal field officials, to clear and farm reservation lands.

The Oneida had brought to the Green Bay area a strong agricultural tradition; thus their success during the late 1800s, though hard won, was not entirely surprising. In a November 1868 memorial to Congress and the president advocating changes in federal policy, Oneida chiefs observed, "We have become almost exclusively an agricultural people." After years of hard work, farm families had cleared portions of the reservation, planted crops and orchards, and improved their properties with fences and residences. A year later, the Green Bay agent judged that the Oneida were the most advanced and economically self-sufficient Indian group in the area. They farmed only about four thousand of the forty-five thousand acres classed as tillable, due in part to the dense forest cover, but families committed to agriculture produced impressive results. Their agricultural society held an annual fair. By the mid-1890s, federal officials lavishly praised the well-fed livestock, large barns filled with straw, and impressive variety of crops grown, including wheat, oats, rye, and potatoes, plus apple and cherry orchards. Many families lived in commodious, nicely painted frame houses. All this and their "neatness in dress and courtesy of manner" prompted a beleaguered Indian Office to remark that the Oneida "are civilized and in most respects on a level with the surrounding white population, in some traits their superiors, perhaps."[48]

The modest total acreage under cultivation nevertheless revealed that farming was not the Oneida's sole means of support. The average family, which cleared and grew crops on only about five acres, looked to thickly wooded sections of the reservation for other economic opportunities.[49] Many entrepreneurs logged tribal lands and grabbed the quick profits offered by off-reservation lumber mills in Green Bay, Howard, and DePere. Looting could not be stopped; the nation held its resources in common and seemed powerless to protect the public interest. By 1868, lumber mills surrounded Oneida lands like a wolf pack. Chiefs believed that four million feet of pine logs were illegally sold that year, many "below fair market value."

> Thus a few individuals have been able to appropriate to themselves much of the most valuable portion of it [reservation forest], to the great injury of others and other generations to come after them. They have also demoralized the tribe, incited quarrels, and produced constant conflict with each other and with the neighboring white men.

"One portion of the tribe are really robbing the other," bemoaned the agent in 1872. Oneida timber was exhausted six years later.[50]

Like the Oneida, the Stockbridge and Munsee of central Wisconsin resorted to a mixed economy of farming in garden patches (with 200 acres cultivated in 1886, out of 307 classified as tillable), lumbering, and off-reservation work for white settlers. By 1860, those who had not abandoned the reservation felt discouraged about farming prospects. The growing season was too short—good crops matured only once in four years—and their lands were thickly forested. Few men were hunters; besides, game had become scarce throughout the region. It gave the Green Bay agent "pain to say that their present state is most wretched." They had tried farming most industriously and might have succeeded at a better location. Thirty-five years later, the Stockbridge and Munsee were reading and writing English, and a federal government official argued, "There is no more reason why they should be treated as Indians than the people of Pennsylvania Avenue should be." But poverty had become entrenched. Nonfarm work was scarce, and Indians resisted the tough job of forest clearing and otherwise improving the land until they could own individual allotments. Any white person would feel the same, contended the Indian agent.[51]

For Menominee farmers, neighbors of the Stockbridge and Munsee, the heavily timbered, 231,680-acre reservation was a blessing and a curse. Initially, their forests, together with the expertise of agency employees, enabled ambitious Menominee to build mills, a model farm, schools, private homes, and various outbuildings and fences. They easily cleared pine trees from the sandy plains so that family farming could begin.[52]

Bear and Thunder clan members living west of the Wolf River opposed acculturation, but many families who settled to the east committed themselves to agriculture and mainstream American lifestyles. At an 1856 council meeting, one leader remarked to the local Indian agent, "I have seen [in Washington, D.C.] how mighty the white man is and this is because they till the earth." Three years later, the chiefs in council proposed traveling to the U.S. capital to get financial assistance; then each family could have the tools, cattle, and other necessities for farming and no longer rely on the chase. This Menominee faction ultimately built frame farmhouses, dressed in white man's clothes, and encouraged schools and Christian churches. By the mid-1890s, they raised corn, wheat, oats, hay, potatoes, and barley. They also owned cattle, hogs, and poultry that were sheltered in outbuildings.[53]

Menominee Civil War veterans, federal Indian agents, and missionaries championed these agricultural initiatives during the late 1800s. Indeed, Uncle Sam was so adamant about farming that as late as the 1850s, the northern superintendent of Indian affairs, Francis Huebschmann, threatened the Menominee with removal to Minnesota if they did not take up the plow. To help with the start-up costs of individual farms, Washington furnished seeds, livestock, and implements. If the crops of fledgling farms failed, Indian agents also issued them provisions.[54]

The Green Bay agency farmer assigned to the Menominee modeled good practices and offered individualized assistance. In the mid-1850s, he established an exemplary farm. It generated jobs for one hundred Menominee while training them in the fields, at the mill, and in the repair shops. By 1860, the staff cultivated four hundred acres and had ground 3,650 bushels of grain. Twenty-two years later, with Indian families working their own lands, the agency farmer's duties had changed. R. P. Benedict regularly visited Menominee settlements to encourage plowing and planting of their tracts and care for their rail fences. He helped with the harvesting and storing of the Indians' crops. When the fall hunting season beckoned up north, Benedict urged them not to leave until they finished farm chores, especially fitting the soil for the next growing season. During the winter months, he looked after agency cattle, mended fences, cut and delivered firewood to needy persons, and issued them rations.[55]

Even with the federal government's technical assistance and the determination of many Menominee, farmers faced lots of obstacles, including long winters and infertile soil. Ironically, these impediments included Washington's inflexibility and abuse of Indians by neighbors the Menominee were supposed to emulate. David R. M. Beck's thoughtful history of the Menominee emphasizes that paternalistic federal officials were bent on turning the Indians into "civilized," self-supporting agriculturalists and would not consider economic alternatives for decades, despite Menominee farmers' repeated failures to feed themselves. Natives forced to live on a modest-sized reservation and surrounded by a rising tide of whites survived because of their adaptability. When crops disappointed them year after year or when families were unable to clear sufficient land to support themselves, they looked to other pursuits. Fellow Wisconsinites also let down the Menominee. State officials claimed portions of the reserve, traders and lumbermen looted Indian resources, and the chiefs believed that at least one Indian agent embezzled their monies. Washington intended to alleviate Menominee suffering in the wake of poor harvests, but dishonest traders in cahoots with their agent—so the Indians charged—absconded with relief funds.[56]

Also underlying agricultural problems was reservation geography. Too much of it was "acres of wet and worthless marsh," complained one federal official. "It is difficult to conceive of locations more ill adapted to the support and wants of a people but little acquainted with the arts of civilization . . . [and encouraged] to abandon their former modes of life, and engage in the cultivation of the soil." The light soil quickly became exhausted, and native farmers faced the prospects of rebuilding their homes and clearing off more acres atop the fertile ridges covered with hardwoods. But these acres would only yield crops after much toil behind oxen and heavy plows. Late spring and early fall killing frosts and rust, a destructive plant disease, then reduced Indian harvests and added to discouragement. By 1870, the Menominee farmed only six hundred acres. Such conditions, lamented the Indian Office, forced the Indians back into the woods to rely again on hunting, fishing, and gathering.[57]

Despite these difficulties, the Menominee continued to cultivate more land, which totaled about thirty-five hundred acres in 1890. Most families owned teams of horses. They continued to improve their lands by digging wells and planting fruit trees. Profits from crop sales enabled the Menominee to buy additional equipment. Nevertheless, their farms were garden plots, averaging only four acres.[58]

Among central Wisconsin Indian nations, the Winnebago showed the least interest in agriculture. They lacked farming implements and raised no domesticated animals except for dogs and ponies. Families planted only small gardens of corn, beans, and pumpkins; then they journeyed to summer camps to pick blueberries and cranberries in the marshes. A special investigator echoed government bias against nonfarming Indians when he wrote in 1895 that Winnebago "life is nomadic" and that they had not "the energy, the thrift nor the management" to produce a crop on their homesteads.[59]

Farming was even more difficult for the Ojibwa who lived further north in Wisconsin. Besides an equally extensive tree cover, the Lake Superior growing season was so short and the climate so cold that only root crops and garden vegetables thrived, particularly potatoes, turnips, beets, parsnips, and cabbages. Federal officials promoted Ojibwa agriculture in several ways, as they did on other Great Lakes reservations. The 1854 treaty required it. In return for huge Indian land cessions, Washington created several reservations across northern Michigan, Wisconsin, and Minnesota; and annually for twenty years, the government was to supply native communities with household furniture, cooking utensils, farming implements, cattle, carpenters' tools, and building materials.[60]

On the Ojibwa reservations, which were so widely scattered that the Indian agent stationed at Ashland could not personally look after them all, the key provider of technical assistance was a government farmer. Under the agent's supervision, the farmer took responsibility for government property and issued annuity goods, such as seeds, to needy Indian families. Most important, he supervised and encouraged reservation agricultural operations.

"Show them you are interested in them," the Indian agent advised Bad River farmer Roger Patterson, "and I have no doubt you will in time see the results of your efforts." The farmer saw to it that planting was done properly and at the right time. If natives lacked teams, he used government teams to plow their fields. Each year, the Ashland agent and his superiors expected an increase in the number of acres cultivated. In April 1899, Agent S. W. Campbell ordered the government farmer at Lac du Flambeau to see that all tillable soil was planted. The agent pledged to visit the reservation to see if instructions were executed. Agency farmers also had to make sure that Indians used their seed potatoes wisely, retaining some for future use, and that families had stored food for the winter.[61]

Reservation Ojibwa working industriously and with guidance from agency farmers still needed help to plant and harvest their crops. Teams and plows remained in short supply well into the 1890s. Nor could fledgling farmers afford to hire teams at four dollars per day to work their fields. Moreover, those who obtained horses and cattle did not always care for them properly, in the judgment of federal officials. Each summer, the animals were turned out to look after themselves; but during the winter, the Indians provided neither shelter nor adequate hay for their stock. Too often, they died of neglect. Still, by 1899, Ojibwa families from Keweenaw Bay, Michigan, to Grand Portage, Minnesota, owned 669 horses, 553 head of cattle, 403 swine, and 5,603 domestic fowl. Clearly, the reservations were committed to farming. Obvious, too, was their ongoing need for federal aid. That year, the Ashland agent requested monies to repair eight Indian plows—just on the Lac Court Oreilles Reservation—because no government blacksmith was available to fashion new moldboards, plow points, plowshare bolts, wheels, handles, and braces.[62]

Such fitting of the soil was pointless unless Ojibwa farmers had seeds, and throughout the late 1800s, they relied on agency issues. Following a "disastrous" weather pattern during the spring of 1881, which first drowned the Lac Court Oreilles crops and then scorched a second planting with a drought, the agent met with local farmers in early June. He was pleased to find their fields ready to replant. Carrot, beet, pumpkin, rutabaga, and squash seeds were issued, which they "accepted as a blessing" and "with thankful hearts." In the spring of 1899, the government again rescued these farmers. The previous season, Agent S. W. Campbell had provided them four hundred bushels of seed potatoes, and the Indians had pledged to return the same amount to the government farmer. These would be kept for planting the following year. But the potato crop largely failed. Native farmers had only eight bushels to keep in reserve and no money to buy more. Unless the Indian Office once again provided the reservation with seed potatoes, Campbell warned, families would perish next winter.[63]

Together, the Indians' strong commitment to farming and the assistance from Washington yielded some agricultural success on the Wisconsin reservations. How much is difficult to measure because local agents became overly excited and hopeful about any land cleared for cultivation and any rise in reservation crop production. The 1879 report about Red Cliff and Bad River was especially upbeat. Residents seemed determined to increase their harvests. They had also improved their fences and cared better for livestock. According to the agent, all this indicated "that they are leaving their old indolent habits and assuming more of those we term civilized." The agent even proposed holding an agricultural fair to showcase native achievements. Three years later came a report from the Lac Court Oreilles farmer that "the days of the migrant Indians have passed; they are well off for provisions of all kinds."[64]

The amount of reservation land cleared for agriculture, together with increasing yields, warranted modest optimism. Community leaders, especially at Red Cliff and Bad River, pushed for improvements. In 1860, the chiefs authorized use of annuity funds from the 1854 treaty to clear enough land so that each family had a farm, cattle, and a comfortable home, as a way of encouraging people to remain on the reservation and become self-supporting. Clearing the heavily timbered reserves was a slow process, and the Indians always seemed short of teams and farm implements. Yet by 1890, Agent M. A. Leahy judged that the Ojibwa obtained much of their livelihood from farming. Granted, their fields were small and their techniques "necessarily crude and imperfect," but the harvests proved "encouraging." Once native men plowed and fitted the soil, the "industrious and energetic" women planted, cultivated, and harvested the crops.[65] The reported yields for 1899 follow:

oats	5,100 bushels
corn	2,450 bushels
onions	775 bushels
pumpkins	8,000 bushels
potatoes	18,723 bushels
turnips	5,882 bushels
beans	625 bushels
other vegetables	3,390 bushels
hay	1,550 tons cut

wood	5,160 cords cut
butter	3,490 pounds [66]

The Indian Office delightedly announced these figures as evidence of progress toward "civilization," and there was no question about the dedication of many Ojibwa to family farming. But cultivating the soil in Wisconsin's far north presented overwhelming problems. Besides the short growing season, the thick tree cover forced Indians to fight for every acre brought under the plow. In 1860, roving Ojibwa bands informed their agent that since they had no way to gain a living on the reservations, they would settle down and farm only if the government cleared their land. So they continued migrating with the seasons—hunting, fishing, picking berries, gathering wild rice, and making maple sugar. Yet this was a precarious existence. Half-starved Ojibwa families roamed about the northern Wisconsin settlements looking for work. Concerned white farmers and townspeople regularly sent petitions to the state legislature requesting Indian removal. Federal officials also disliked these off-reservation movements. "As long as he [the Indian] is compelled to seek a precarious subsistence by hunting and fishing," remarked their agent in 1890, "he will continue a savage."[67]

Also under the Ashland agent's supervision were reservations in northeastern Minnesota for the Fond du Lac, Grand Portage, and Bois Forte Ojibwa. Their northern locations meant that agriculture would be tough. Even so, the Indian Office held firm to its goal of self-sufficient native farmers and provided neophytes with limited quantities of seeds and equipment plus technical assistance from government farmers. The number of acres cleared and cultivated on each reservation remained modest throughout the last half of the nineteenth century, as were Indian harvests. These consisted of root crops, especially potatoes. At Fond du Lac in 1890, for example, the Ojibwa farmed only 400 acres out of 100,121. Up the coast that year, nearly every family at Grand Portage raised some potatoes. Still, these crops and others provided only one-third of the community's subsistence. Similar conditions prevailed on the Bois Forte reservations to the west.[68]

To survive, the northeastern Minnesota Ojibwa, like their counterparts in Wisconsin, relied on traditional hunting and gathering rather than trying to clear their thickly forested lands. A frustrated agent, W. R. Durfee, reported on the Fond du Lac Reservation in 1885, noting that it included one hundred thousand acres set aside by the treaty of 1854.

> During the last winter the parties named [four white men married to Indian women] [cleared a total of] 100 acres and this is more clearing

than has been done on the whole reservation in the preceeding [*sic*] 30 years, and at the same rate as during the past winter it would take just 1000 years to bring the whole territory into condition for cultivation.[69]

CONCLUSION

Farming was fundamental to many Great Lakes aboriginal families and to federal government agencies responsible for native welfare during the last half of the nineteenth century. This was not a story of utterly mistaken government expectations for its aboriginal wards or of outright betrayal. Nor was it a tale of great differences in policy and administration between the United States and Canada. As to Great Lakes natives, theirs was not an account of wholesale rejection of federal programs and a mulish persistence in time-honored ways. The history of Indian agriculture was far more complex and important than such one-dimensional renderings.

To a large extent, government policies and programs propelled events. Ottawa and Washington never wavered in their joint goal: transformation of nomadic hunter-gatherers and gardeners into settled and self-sustaining agriculturalists. Paternalistic policy administrators therefore stationed Indian agents and farmers on several reservations north and south of the international border, provided considerable technical assistance (usually subsidized by the Indians' own annuities and interest from trust funds), and micromanaged nearly every aspect of reservation economies, from timber sales to the size of family farms and use of livestock. When field agents reported impressive crop production figures, the smug "I told you so" of policy makers must have echoed throughout the halls of Indian departments in Washington and Ottawa.

Trouble arose because both federal governments held assumptions about Indian agriculture that, as time passed, proved questionable or downright false. The first was that Great Lakes aboriginal peoples could be persuaded to give up their seasonal hunting, fishing, gathering, and gardening economies in order to build permanent homes and rely entirely on sedentary farming. Otherwise, it was thought, Indians would perish. Alternative economic activities did not exist for them. Another faulty federal government premise was that reservations had enough good soil and frost-free days for crops to mature. Southern areas had a "high potential for Indian agriculture," noted Tanner's authoritative *Atlas,* because they had "more than 140 frost-free days." The upper portions of the Great Lakes (northern shores of

Lakes Huron and Superior, most of Superior's southern shore, plus northern sections of Minnesota, Wisconsin, and Michigan) turned out to have "fewer than 120 frost-free days" and could not support farming. The middle zone (in central Wisconsin, Michigan, and interior areas of southwest Ontario) offered only "limited potential" for Indian agriculture.[70] Inevitably, field agent reports from Henvey's Inlet, Manitoulin, Lake Superior, the Menominee Reservation, and elsewhere up north revealed that farming in these areas was a much tougher struggle than anticipated. Canadian and U.S. policy makers also made the questionable judgment that Indian resources must be micromanaged to the extent that not a penny of a native community's own monies or an acre of its timber could be spent or sold without federal approval. How Indian nations might have fared if given total freedom to develop their own resources will never be known, but federal paternalism probably was part of the economic development problem.

Finally, the economic situation in both Canada and the United States hurt Indian farmers. The value of crops dropped during the agricultural depression of the late 1800s. Simultaneously, the rapid mechanization of farming squeezed small operators, like Indians, who lacked the capital to retool and thus compete with wealthier neighbors.

Nevertheless, during the last half of the nineteenth century, many native communities committed to giving plow agriculture an honest try. Although part of their effort was ultimately undermined by a variety of factors over which they had little control, the accomplishments of energetic Iroquois and Algonquians were enormous: land cleared and cultivated, crops produced, permanent homes and outbuildings constructed, farm implements acquired and used, and livestock raised. Particularly notable were production statistics for Walpole Island and Six Nations and from upstate New York Iroquois reservations. Their residents harvested a variety of crops—grains, vegetables, fruits—and hosted agricultural fairs. At the 1877 New York Iroquois fair held on the Cattaraugus Reservation, for example, members displayed over thirteen hundred articles. The value of the farm products in 1898 was $15,668 for Walpole Island and $63,810 for Six Nations.[71] Many Indian households, like Peter Hill's at Six Nations, had become distinct economic units engaged in commercial agriculture.

Farm success was not based on a reservation's location in either the United States or Canada. Accomplishments germinated from suitable geography, gardening traditions, a solid commitment to plow agriculture, and a nutritive sprinkling of assistance from the Indian departments in both countries. The farther north native peoples lived within the Great Lakes basin, the less practical plow agriculture was. Zealous American and Canadian officials pushed aboriginal communities to farm, and some gave it an honest try, with government help, at such places as Manitoulin Island, Fort William, and Wisconsin's Menominee Reservation. They cultivated thousands of acres and planted seeds; they built houses and barns. Reported yields, like the Wisconsin Ojibwa's in 1899, were impressive. But short growing seasons, the high cost of clearing land, and the availability of off-reservation food sources and wages offered by white neighbors convinced North Country men and women over the years not to rely totally on farm crops. Pine woods and waters remained as their farms. A pattern of seasonal rovings to supplement their garden patches persisted on both sides of the international border, from Georgian Bay and Lake Huron west across Michigan and Wisconsin and as far north as Lake Nipigon and Grand Portage, Minnesota.

Because Indian nations, Ottawa, and Washington committed so much energy and so many resources to the farming initiative in the late 1800s, the consequences were illuminating. Whether planting corn on the Six Nations lands in New York and Ontario or potatoes along Lake Superior's northern shore, increased cultivation of the soil altered the lives of nearly all Great Lakes natives. Farming, especially in the south, influenced where they lived, how they furnished their homes, what they ate, the clothes they wore, and how men, women, and children spent their days. Farming created differences in wealth within reservation communities. Farming also affected relationships with nonnative neighbors. Some whites, for example, consumed Indian products of the soil, attended their agricultural fairs, and hired them as field hands.

As consumers and producers of goods and services, Great Lakes Indian peoples continued to shape the history of the region in cooperation with nonnative neighbors. At the same time, aboriginal communities resisted those who would seize their territories and forcibly replace traditional values. This was nothing new. For thousands of years, chiefs and their followers north and south of the Great Lakes had adjusted creatively to changing circumstances in order to survive as a people. In the late 1800s, their increased farming efforts were but another phase of the never-ending process of accommodation.

Adjustment meant continuity as well as change. Native people preserved some parts of their traditional economies. Perceptive Indian farmers, who had lived with nature's vicissitudes for centuries, grasped the inherent dangers of agriculture dependent on cash crops and at the whim of escalating costs of mechanization and market fluctuations. Shrewdly, they "hedged their bet." The further north that native communities were located, the more dependence on nonfarming resources, the subject of the next chapter, increased. It remained an important part of the Great Lakes Indian economy from Manitoulin Island to Menominee, Wisconsin, during the last half of the nineteenth century.

{ 2 }

Old and New Alternatives to Reservation Agriculture

Ashland, Wisconsin, was founded about the time the 1854 La Pointe Treaty created nearby Ojibwa reservations. The city has influenced reservation affairs ever since. I have elsewhere explained the early history of the area as follows:

> Flush times began in 1877 with the Wisconsin Central's first regular rail service between Ashland and key cities on Lake Michigan. As a port where rails and lake freighters met, it became an important shipping center. Forty miles southeast of Ashland lay the Gogebic Iron Range; the tapping of its fabulous ore deposits in the mid-1800s triggered a widespread mining boom, making Ashland a chief beneficiary. Trains hauled ore to its several loading docks, and ships then took the cargo to lower lake ports to feed the hungry furnaces of American steel mills. Brownstone quarried nearby and timber were also shipped from Ashland. By 1890, eight sawmills buzzed day and night. Four railroads served the town, whose population had climbed to 9,956.
>
> [While some members of the nearby Red Cliff and Bad River reservations farmed patches of land], several of the men found jobs [in town] more to their liking (at $1.25 to $2.50 per day) in Ashland mills, sash-and-door factories, and in cooper, blacksmith, and carpentry shops. After the survey and allotment of their reservation in the mid-

1870s, Bad River Indians realized additional monies from the lumber industry. Between 1886 and 1894, for example, forest products marketed among the lines of the two railroads that crossed the reservation amounted to $400,000. Indian men also worked in lumber camps driving logs down rivers and as choppers, sawyers, pilers, and loaders. Red Cliff and Michigan bands worked in sawmills and for mining companies as wood choppers and loaders. Some Red Cliff men signed on as deck hands aboard lake freighters; others operated a small fishing fleet which, with the use of gill and pound nets, brought back large enough catches to sell at nearby Bayfield. The Northern Pacific and the Duluth and Winnipeg railroads passed through Fond du Lac and furnished a market for Indian timber. Another outlet was the flourishing town of Cloquet, Minnesota, just east of the reservation. Young men worked in logging camps, at sawmills, and with the railroads while their families gathered berries, fished, and hunted. Some of the Grand Portage Chippewas were packers and guides into the remote mining districts of the United States and Canada.[1]

Events in northern Wisconsin and Minnesota during the late 1800s mirrored developments throughout the region, as the rapid growth of new industries and towns supplied off-reservation markets and employment opportunities for Great Lakes Indians. Also important were such long-established activities as fishing, trapping, and gathering. Natives chose this work rather than full-time farming for a variety of reasons. Perhaps their reservation would not support plow agriculture, or perhaps they feared depending on it entirely to feed their families. Others simply preferred alternatives to farm labor. Whether in Canada or the United States, natives relied on non-farming activities for sustenance. The further north they lived within the Great Lakes basin, the more pronounced their mixed economies were. That so many Indians earned a livelihood in this way underscored their ability to adapt to changing economic circumstances within the Great Lakes region and to exercise personal freedom about using resources both near and far. On a broader scale, reservation communities worked through chiefs and councils to develop and control their homeland's natural wealth.

Alternatives to agriculture were significant on at least two additional levels. First, Indian workers and their reservation property played vital roles in overall Great Lakes economic development during the late nineteenth century.[2] A second theme that surfaced was growing federal government control of reservation resources and the failure of these stewards to promote economic self-sufficiency and community self-determination.

View of a bustling Ashland, Wisconsin, and the Apostle Islands, 1867.
(Courtesy Wisconsin Historical Society, image 22972.)

LONG-ESTABLISHED ACTIVITIES

Fishing provided essential nourishment and was a valuable alternative to full-time farming, even on southern reserves, such as Walpole Island, where white neighbors pressed from all directions. As late as the 1880s and 1890s, the Scugog and Alnwick communities relied on fish as a "never failing source of food supply" as well as a commodity for sale.[3] This was even more common on northern reserves. Wandering artist Paul Kane commented in the late 1850s that the Saugeen Indians subsisted mainly on abundant fish catches at the mouth of the Saugeen River. Forty years later, seasonal fishing remained an important supplement to their farming. Fishing was also a chief occupation at the Nawash (Cape Croker) Reserve. It owned lands specifically set aside as fishing stations.[4] On the eastern Georgian Bay shore, many of the Gibson Mohawk still caught large quantities of fish, which they preserved for winter use by salting or smoking.[5] Further north, on Manitoulin Island and neighboring reserves, where fish was the main food for hundreds of Indian families, natives reported owning 180 sailboats, seventy-six rowboats, thirteen canoes, and 569 fishing nets in 1898. Natives fished for their own consumption and, at times, for commercial purposes.[6]

Along the St. Mary's River and Lake Superior's north shore, where farming alone could not sustain reservation communities, fish nourished native families. Some also worked the waters commercially. Entrepreneurs living at the Sault, Goulais Bay, Batchewana, and Michipicotin in the 1890s, for example, sold their catch to the Ainsworth and Ganley Company for between two and two-and-a-half cents per pound. Other Indians supplied wood for the company's steam-powered tugs. Further west, at the mouth of the Pays Plat River, reservation residents likewise profited from new markets. Natives with sailboats and good nets shipped tons of fish on ice each week between spring and the Christmas season and earned fifty to one hundred dollars per month.[7]

Similarly, south of Lake Superior and the international boundary, fishing for family consumption and, at times, market sales was essential to reservation economies. Michigan Indians sold 5,253 barrels of fish in 1868. For years, natives of the La Pointe Agency, headquartered in Ashland, Wisconsin, avoided settling on their reserves and continued roaming about the region, relying on the plentiful supply of fish.[8]

In response to reservation needs and Great Lakes markets, aboriginal fishing skills came to the fore. Sightseer William Fraser Rae, who journeyed from Newfoundland to Manitoba in 1881, portrayed the exciting scene at Sault Ste. Marie as follows:

> As a spectacle, the Rapids are very striking. For the distance of a mile the waters of Lake Superior rush down over shelving rocks; at intervals in the descent, islets, covered with trees, form obstacles to the hurrying waters which eddy and foam around them. In the eddies white fish lie and feed till they fall prey to the Indian fisherman.... For centuries the Chippewa Indians had made this a place of abode, living on the white fish that swarm in the Rapids. The mode of fishing is unlike any which I ever saw practiced. Two Indians stand upright at either end of a canoe and force it up the swift running stream. One attends to keep the canoe's head upstream while the other watches for a fish; on seeing one he scoops it out with a small net attached to a pole six feet long. The pole, with the net attached, is not easily handled on land; when a fish weighing ten to fifteen pounds is in it, the physical exertion required to raise the net must be great. There is a knack in this as in all other feats; but it is one which none but Indians are known to acquire. The Indians get 2 cents a pound for the fish they catch, which are packed in ice and sent to Detroit.[9]

Indians in store-bought clothes fishing for whitefish in the rapids of the St. Mary's River, Sault Ste. Marie, Michigan, ca. 1890. *(Courtesy State of Michigan Archives, from the Library of Congress's Detroit Publishing Company Collection.)*

Because Great Lakes waters were so significant, aboriginal leaders had entrenched their fishing rights within land cession treaties of the mid-1800s. The Robinson treaties of 1850 with the Ojibwa of Lakes Huron and Superior, for example, permitted them to continue fishing in the waters of ceded territory except such sections that the provincial government might lease or sell to individuals or companies.[10] Ojibwa of northern Michigan, Wisconsin, and Minnesota sought similar safeguards in land cession treaties of 1837, 1842, and 1854. The 1837 agreement was typical. The Indians surrendered much of northern Wisconsin and east-central Minnesota while preserving their right to hunt, fish, and gather wild rice "upon the lands, the rivers, and the lakes" thus ceded "during the pleasure of the President of the United States."[11]

First Nations understandably and passionately defended their fisheries against illegal white encroachment as well as government programs for licensing and leasing. Canadian Indians claimed the right to fish in Ontario waters without regard to the white man's regulations. Trouble escalated in Ontario when the Crown, which assumed control of the industry in the

1850s, leased areas to non-Indian, commercial fishermen. The government claimed it was protecting the environment and public safety. Federal officials, who promised Indians the right of first refusal on fishing leases adjacent to their reserves, nevertheless granted most leases to nonnatives. Overfishing of the Great Lakes by these leaseholders soon threatened aboriginal communities.[12] In 1859, Saugeen chiefs urged fishery overseer William Gibbard to stop leasing their fishing islands, and the community again petitioned the Crown in the following year. But Gibbard persisted in issuing leases. In 1861, companies harvested twenty-five hundred barrels of fish worth ten thousand dollars.[13]

When spoken words and petitions failed, natives tried other remedies. Gibbard informed his superiors in 1863 that Indians had repeatedly damaged leaseholders' fishing stations. That year, on Manitoulin Island, protesters from Wikwenikong journeyed offshore to Lonely Island and ruined such a station. Gibbard's attempt to arrest the culprits failed, and as geographer Victor Lytwyn reports, the fishery overseer was "mysteriously murdered about a month after leaving the island."[14]

Commercial fishing by non-Indians intensified, and its impact hurt Great Lakes fish stocks. On behalf of the Wikwemikong Indians, William Kinoshaineg [sp?] warned the superintendent general of Indian affairs in 1881:

> If Indians and the white people fish together on the same ground, there will be too many fishermen altogether. The fisheries will become poorer and poorer every year. Finally the Indian will . . . [experience] misery and desolation. Formerly the Indian was the sole master of the land, the sole master of the fisheries. It was with his permission that the white man became landlord. The Indian took what he wished to use leaving the rest to the white man. Additionally, the Indians are confident and will continue to petition because of their knowledge of the important contribution of their ancestors to the British in their wars with the Americans. Our ancestors answered the King of England's call for help and protection. Our ancestors sacrificed their lives and shed their blood to defend the King of England.[15]

Four years later, visiting superintendent J. C. Phipps, stationed on Manitoulin Island, observed that pound nets set by commercial fishermen near native reserves had not only interfered with aboriginal families taking fish for their daily consumption but greatly reduced the overall amount of fish.

The previous summer, when Phipps sailed about the area to issue annuities, he was unable to buy any fish to feed his crew "so scarce had they become."[16] It is no wonder that Indians who had depended on the bounty of the Great Lakes for generations felt aggrieved and that the government's claim to manage Great Lakes fisheries in the Indians' best interest sounded hollow.

Access to off-reservation resources was also restricted south of the international border. The states of Wisconsin and Minnesota throughout the late 1800s hassled northern Ojibwa who fished in the waters of ceded territories. Federal agents repeatedly warned Indians that they must obey state fish and game laws the same as white citizens, "notwithstanding their treaty stipulations."[17]

Continual assertion of aboriginal fishing rights in the face of heavy-handed restrictions in both the United States and Canada documented the importance of this resource to reservation communities, north and south. The resultant Indian fishing "problem" at such places as Saugeen and Manitoulin also revealed the natives' willingness to defend treaty rights, with force if necessary. On a more peaceful plane, natives willingly adopted such new fishing technologies as large nets and deepwater boats and, when given the opportunity, competed with non-Indian commercial enterprises.

Finally, fishing history sadly showed that federal officials in both countries were more interested in opening Great Lakes resources to white businessmen and sportsmen than in properly guarding the resource interests of aboriginal peoples, with whom Washington and Ottawa had a trust relationship. The economic consequences hurt native communities well into the twentieth century.

Another key component of reservation Indian economies was hunting and trapping. Woodland game helped feed families, and animal pelts could be sold for cash. In 1877, Ontario natives marketed furs valued at $74,334. Twelve years later, the Hudson's Bay Company still staffed trading posts in the Lake Huron, Michipicoten, and Nipigon districts. Sudbury and Fort William were major Indian fur-buying and outfitting centers. These towns, situated along the recently completed Canadian Pacific Railway, helped to direct the flow of furs toward Winnipeg or Montreal, rather than northward via the traditional river system to Moose Factory and James Bay.[18] White Fish Lake families emerged from the bush each June, traded their furs at the Lacloche Hudson's Bay post, and promptly returned to their hunting grounds. Families from the Long Lake Reserve north of Lake Superior likewise relied heavily on hunting. Fur-bearing game was plentiful as late as the 1890s. Some of the best hunters, including widows with families to support, earned six hundred to eight hundred dollars annually through fur sales. During the summer months, family heads often worked ferrying store supplies for the Hudson's Bay Company.[19]

Even on southern reserves, such as Walpole Island, hunting remained an important part of the economy. When the superintendent general of Indian affairs wished to gather its band members late in 1885, presumably to vote on a weighty issue, Agent Alexander McKelvey informed Ottawa that many islanders were away hunting and working in the woods. They "always come home at Christmas," he noted, and might be assembled then "if the matter is pressing."[20]

Studies of Michigan's Little River Ottawa and Wisconsin's Menominee and Ojibwa document that hunting and trapping were also important, income-generating elements of aboriginal economies south of the international border. This was true as well in northeastern Minnesota. Lake Superior ice and bitter windstorms stopped Grand Portage Reservation families from fishing in 1879 and forced them into the interior between January and March to hunt. To the west, the Vermilion Lake schoolteacher in 1895 grumbled that native families left the reservation with their children in early September to hunt and trap and would not return until May. Hunting likewise remained central to the Fond du Lac Ojibwa.[21]

Another indicator of the ongoing importance of hunting and trapping was Indian insistence that treaties protected these rights. The 1850 Robinson-Huron and Robinson-Superior treaties guaranteed Canadian natives "the full and free privilege to hunt over the territory now ceded by them . . . as they have heretofore been in the habit of doing." In the United States, the Ojibwa treaties of 1837, 1842, and 1854 did the same. Like fishing, the implementation of state and provincial game laws greatly restricted native use of this resource.[22]

Gathering fruits, vegetables, and maple sap also contributed to family economies. Assignment to reservations did not stop this traditional activity any more than it halted hunting, trapping, and fishing. Throughout the period, white neighbors purchased large amounts of Indian maple syrup, wild rice, and berries.

Indian agents, missionaries, and schoolteachers stationed on Ontario reserves regularly complained about the absences of Indian families who left their homes in order to gather seasonal resources. In mid-April 1855, Deputy Superintendent Froome Talfourd informed Viscount Bury, superintendent general of Indian affairs, that a meeting with the Walpole Island chief and council would have to be postponed for another two weeks until community members returned from their sugar camps. Similarly, James MacKay, a schoolmaster at White Fish Lake, reported, in the summer of 1880, that just two children attended class when school opened in April. Only when families left their sugar camps did his student numbers increase to a daily average of seventeen. Some entrepreneurial Indians made money from these seasonal gatherings. Saugeen natives sold gentian roots for $2.25 per pound in the late 1800s. An Indian-gathered supply of ginseng worth one thousand dollars was shipped from Lake Simcoe in 1890. During a good season, Garden River families might each pick as many as seven bushels of berries per day, at $1.50 per bushel.[23]

Gathering remained important to native families in the United States, especially those located in remote, northern areas. Thus, while sugar making declined significantly on New York reserves because white lumber mills gobbled up stands of maple trees, collecting woodland products was central to native economies in Michigan, Wisconsin, and Minnesota as late as the 1890s. Aboriginal peoples devoted so much time to gathering berries, wild rice, and maple sap for local consumption and trade with whites that federal officials complained about the difficulty of maintaining spring school classes when so many youngsters had followed their parents on gathering expeditions. Recognizing this reality, the Indian Office approved La Pointe agent M. A. Leahy's recommendation that native children be granted a monthlong school vacation during sugar-making season. Besides maple sap, the forest products collected in great quantity by northern Wisconsin Ojibwa included wild rice, cranberries, blueberries, blackberries, raspberries, strawberries, and plums. The U.S. Census estimated that the amount of blueberries picked by Minnesota Ojibwa at Fond du Lac alone in 1890 was worth three thousand dollars.[24]

NEW INCOME SOURCES

Farming, gathering, hunting, trapping, trading furs, and fishing comprised only a part of reservation economies in the late 1800s. Thanks to expanding markets, native families developed new means of earning a livelihood. These ranged from the sale or lease of reservation resources, such as timber and minerals, to seasonal wage work for non-Indian neighbors. For emergency subsistence, aboriginal headmen sometimes looked to the Canadian and U.S. governments.

An especially attractive alternative for reservation families unable or unwilling to cultivate the soil was leasing their land. It provided a modest income while leaving parents and children free to pursue other activities. The pervasiveness of leases also stemmed from the determination of entrepre-

Ojibwa Indians gathering wild rice, ca. 1925. *(Courtesy Minnesota Historical Society.)*

neurial non-Indian neighbors to control reservation resources—from fertile farmlands to timber, minerals, fisheries, and railroad rights-of-way.

Leasing had immense appeal during the early reservation years, and mutually agreeable deals were struck throughout the Great Lakes basin. The situation in southern Ontario was revealing. By the mid-1870s, Mohawks on the Bay of Quinté Reservation leased most of their farms to whites. Extensive renting of native land also characterized the Rice Lake, Scugog, and Alnwick communities. At Six Nations, where the out-migration of young men reduced available cheap labor, widows and other shorthanded farmers had to lease portions of their land. Land rentals contributed $3,307.75 to the Six Nations' economy in 1898.[25]

Uncontrolled aboriginal leases alarmed federal officials for a variety of reasons. The Canadian Indian Department feared that reliance on leasing would cause young, able-bodied men to abandon farming and that their bad example would dishearten other tillers of the soil. Living idly on rent receipts instead of working hard would invariably lead to intemperance that damaged the entire family. Moreover, Indians who illegally leased their land rarely got sufficient rents. Then, if they tried to enforce the contracts, native families would have difficulties because the courts considered them minors. Finally, Ottawa objected to white leaseholders who stripped Indian lands of their timber and fertility and returned nothing to the soil.[26]

Renting aboriginal lands proved troublesome in the United States as well. A situation on Allegany Reservation is illustrative. Through a combination of sloppy bookkeeping and fraud, Agent T. W. Jackson estimated in 1888 that the Seneca had often not received one-tenth of the income they should have. From land leased by the villagers of Salamanca, the rents totaled about five thousand dollars; they should have been at least thirty thousand "if their affairs were properly managed." One leaseholder, a lawyer for the tribe, only paid two dollars annually to rent a deep lot with a fifty-foot frontage in the business district. The attorney had verbally promised the Seneca that when he built on the property, a room for their meetings would be provided free of charge. Yet this pledge, noted in the Seneca council minutes, was omitted from the signed contract. When the Indians tried to hold a council in the structure, the lawyer demanded a fee.[27]

Faced with such land problems in the field, the standard response by Ottawa and Washington was intervention to control the situation and insure that natives got the best land rents, that leaseholders paid promptly, that Indian recipients did not foolishly waste these funds, and that whites without licenses were deemed trespassers and expelled.[28] New leasing procedures still required that aboriginal residents approve all arrangements—either individually, for small plots of land, or in council, for large properties held in common. Reserves therefore retained some power over land leases.

This leasing policy brought prompt results in Ontario. In the 1880s, the Scugog agent seized crops grown illegally and only released them when white farmers pledged to fertilize Indian land properly and obtain Ottawa's permission before renting any more. The Indian Department also made inquiries regarding the suitability of tenants and investigated native complaints about delays in issuing leases. Despite some dissatisfaction among the Chippewa and Munsee of the Thames during the late 1800s, leaseholders improved a large portion of the reserve's swampland by clearing and ditching it and by erecting good fences.[29]

The sale of land ceded by earlier treaties was another income source for Canadian native communities. Again, this was done under federal supervision following guidelines set by the Indian Act of 1876. The marketing of surrendered aboriginal tracts carried at least two major benefits. First, the income funded Indian trust accounts, whose annual interest would help support native communities far into the future. Second, offering ceded Indian lands to Canadian pioneer families stimulated the country's expansion westward. To provide access to these disposable lands and help non-Indian settlers market their crops, Ottawa used monies from Indian land sales to construct colonization roads on the Bruce Peninsula and Manitoulin Island. The Indian Department excitedly noted in 1856 that land sales from the Owens Sound area had yielded one hundred thousand pounds. Ontario land sold for the benefit of Indians in 1877 totaled 43,813.31 acres and generated an income of $75,224.30.[30]

The Canadian Indian Department became, in part, an office of western land development. Aboriginal communities had the right to approve or disapprove of initial land cessions; after that, Ottawa set market prices and kept the real estate records. Income, though substantial, never went directly to native peoples; the Indian Department deposited land receipts in trust funds disbursed at its discretion. Ottawa's priority apparently was to get white settlers onto Great Lakes lands as fast as possible. Indian trust funds helped finance colonization roads, and so did bargain prices charged for ceded native land. On May 31, 1867, for example, by an order in council, the federal government reduced the sale price of Manitoulin Island land from fifty to twenty cents an acre to spur settler interest.[31]

Another economic opportunity for native communities was European and American tourists. Increasing numbers of them, supported by resort hotels, railroads, and steamship lines, traveled across the region and happily exchanged dollars for native goods and services.[32] The impact on both groups was an important part of Great Lakes history.

Tourists traveled to the Great Lakes for a variety of reasons. Some examined economic prospects for farming, mining, and town development; others were vacationing families, sportsmen, artists, and sightseers. Urbanites, who lived in an increasingly complex and chaotic environment, sought a more relaxed, outdoors experience free from some of civilization's restraints. The exotic homes, handicraft work, and seemingly carefree lifestyles of colorful aboriginal people captivated visitors.[33]

Reservation families generally did not write down their feelings about excursionists. Nevertheless, native responses indicated that, as in the past, they grasped the trade opportunities provided by this new wave of strangers. Glistening Great Lakes furs no longer obsessed non-Indians as they had for over two hundred years, but the two groups could still do business. In exchange for tourist dollars, local residents offered traditional handicrafts fashioned from local materials (mats, pipes, wooden bowls and ladles, skin bags, baskets), guides for interior excursions, and a variety of entertaining performances.

Tourist opportunities first impacted the Iroquois living near Niagara Falls. Business became so brisk that visitors could purchase crafts directly from local Indian women and children sitting "with their wares spread out before them" or in gift shops carrying a wider variety of native items, some from the American Southwest. Popular mementos included blankets, mats, baskets, decorated leather cases and miniature canoes, bows and arrows, toy papooses, and moccasins. Artisans decorated many of these items with colorful porcupine quills, beads, and sweetgrass.[34]

Vacation excursions later branched beyond Niagara. In Canada, those starting at Collingwood drew many customers. Once on board their steamer, passengers visited Indian reserves and settlements along the north shores of Lakes Huron and Superior as far as Fort William and Port Arthur. Entrepreneurial Indians came aboard at these stops to sell their wares, or passengers could disembark and explore the unfamiliar, frontier world. Juliette Starr Dana described one of the most popular and exciting attractions at Sault Ste. Marie in 1852 as follows:

> We got into a beautiful canoe with 2 Indians & went up the rapids or falls of Ste. Marie. They are a mile long, & interrupt the navigation between Lake Superior & the lower Lakes. The Indians standing in each end of the canoe first used their paddles or short oars, very quickly & on different sides, then as we got into foaming & boiling waters they laid them aside & took each a long pole & by long & vigorous pushes, propelled us between the immense boulders which through the clear waters we could see on all sides of us hardly below the surface. The whole fall is about 30 feet.
>
> The scene & its accompaniments was actually splendid. The rushing & foaming of the water, the tossing of our frail bark, the sun setting in gorgeous clouds directly before us, the lonesome melancholy looking shores & the imperturbability of the Indians who only broke silence occasionally in a few strange sounding gutturals. All made it an underlying memory henceforth inerasable. . . .
>
> At one place where the water was uncommonly fierce the savage before me turned & looked gravely in both our faces, as if to see how much courage we possessed.
>
> The descent was accomplished in four minutes although it had taken us an hour to go up. The principle [*sic*] labour is to keep the

boat from upsetting on the sharp rocks. . . . I would never advise any one to attempt it who did not possess strong nerves. There was such perfect calmness & self-reliance visible in our Indians that I could not feel the slightest approach of fear.

Sightseers arriving via steamer or rail recorded a variety of impressions about local Ojibwa people and their towns. Reactions ranged from curiosity about picturesque people who merely seemed part of the landscape to pessimism about the natives' future because of their apparent poverty and cultural backwardness.[35]

Outdoor adventure, like running the rapids of the St. Mary's River, rivaled the importance of souvenir craft exchange throughout the northern Great Lakes, where Ojibwa and Iroquois men became the entrepreneurs. Visiting explorers, fishermen, and hunters all needed native guides knowledgeable about the woods and waters, with bark canoes to carry them to North Country destinations. The money was good, too. By the 1890s, Indian boatmen taking fly-fishing tourists up the Nipigon River earned two dollars a day plus board and an additional fifty cents per canoe hire. Customers came from Europe, the United States, and Canada with handbooks listing the best Indian guides. Once parties journeyed into the interior and away from steamship and railway lines, greenhorn tourists saw their native guides from a new perspective; no longer just a colorful part of the scenery or a town curiosity, they were at home in the woods and commanded every part of the day's routine: packing and paddling canoes, portaging, setting up tents, and preparing meals.[36]

Besides guiding services and craft sales, natives entertained vacationers in unique ways. One was the powwow. No longer just a community gathering and a time to teach youngsters traditional dances and ceremonies, the pulsating powwow was redesigned to attract non-Indians. It offered native crafts, cuisine, and, as anthropologist Charles E. Cleland notes, "what the tourist expected of Indians: feather war bonnets, war dances, and Indian princess contests." Particularly popular among northern Michigan vacationers was a pageant based on Henry Wadsworth Longfellow's *The Song of Hiawatha*. The Grand Rapids and Indiana Railroad offered the show with an Indian cast drawn from U.S. and Canadian communities.[37] The bigger the North Woods resort business became, the greater was the demand for "real Indian" performers, mementos, and outdoor excitement. Tourism thus became a valuable part of the aboriginal economy and the economy of the entire region.

In quest of additional earnings to feed their families and to maintain eco-

Busy public dock at Walpole Island. *(Courtesy Wallaceburg and District Museum.)*

nomic as well as political independence, chiefs marketed reservation resources—forest products, minerals, fishing and duck-hunting leases—to nonnative neighbors. Vast timber holdings generated the most attention. Trees, which covered the undulating countryside like frozen green waves, had shaped historic aboriginal cultures and, by the late 1800s, triggered a lumber bonanza—first on ceded native lands and then on reservations. Struggling Indian communities for whom farming was not an economic cure-all, federal government officials, and nonnative entrepreneurs quickly grasped and tried to control opportunities created by the fierce, international demand for Great Lakes timber.

Valuable and attractive though it was, reservation timber was not free for the taking, either by Indians or neighboring, nonnative logging companies. Paternalistic Canadian and U.S. Indian departments, deeply committed to promoting aboriginal agriculture, worked hard to manage both timber harvests and monies they generated. Extensive reservation forests both impeded family farms and offered temptingly quick cash from unscrupulous white

Tourist boats at Walpole Island. *(Courtesy Wallaceburg and District Museum.)*

neighbors. Stealing native timber became a problem on both sides of the international border, as logging companies regularly swindled aboriginal communities.[38]

At times, Indians were part of the problem. In 1862, for example, William Spragge, deputy superintendent general of Indian affairs, noted how common it was for residents of the Moravian Reserve on the Thames River to sell logs to neighboring white sawmills against the wishes of the headmen. In the 1870s, the Ojibwa of Scugog traded wood for spirituous liquors and even bartered timber so that whites would chop Indian firewood. Meanwhile, in Wisconsin, wily white lumbermen near the Stockbridge and Munsee Reservation set up native logging companies headed by Indian front men who defrauded their own people, were deceived by their white partners, and ended up in debt. Eventually, native leaders objecting to these selfish practices called on federal Indian departments to stop the plundering of their forests. "Almost every post last winter," reported a field official stationed in Sarnia, "brought me letters from the Moravian tract

Dramatic portrayal of Hiawatha laying a deer at the feet of Minnehaha, 1901. *(Courtesy Archives of Ontario, image S 16353, acc. 10748.)*

complaining of parties who were trespassing and requesting me to come down and prevent it." Likewise, Tyendinaga Mohawk at the Bay of Quinté asked Ottawa to prevent non-Indian logging on the reserve.[39]

Soon after surveyors laid out reservation boundaries in the mid-1800s, Canada and the United States devised regulations to govern timber sales, guided by the Indians' need to generate income and white entrepreneurs' desire to get hold of native timber. Several factors shaped the new federal policies. As early as the 1860s, Ottawa feared that unless Indian trees were sold, they would be stolen, or the value of extensive dead and down timber would simply be lost due to decay. These valuable resources, like the soil that gave them birth, belonged to each reservation community as a whole and to their descendants. It was not considered right for greedy individuals, native or nonnative, to disregard long-term community welfare. The Indian Department, Spragge wrote, "very wisely claims a control which it will exercise for the good of the Indians in such [timber] matters and will look to the future while it takes care of the present." To do so, the government would license all timber cuts by Indians and non-Indians and then put out at interest the fees collected. Annual payments from these accounts would help support a variety of local projects, including farming and improved housing.[40]

U.S. officials took the same paternalistic approach to Great Lakes Indians and their reservation resources. Trees were the common property of each "tribe," and since the tribes were wards of Washington, their forests were governed by treaties and federal laws. Timber could only be harvested under an agent's supervision, with proceeds deposited "into the general fund for the benefit of the entire tribe."[41]

With these policy goals in place, the United States and Canada set up implementation mechanisms. Besides their other duties, Ottawa's agents must evaluate and report each Indian nation's timber holdings. These on-site bureaucrats, who theoretically best understood the vast number of aboriginal communities, were also expected to negotiate Indian consent to sale of their trees. Finally, the agents licensed and supervised logging operations, collected fees, seized illegally cut timber, and fined trespassers. By the 1860s, the Indian Department also appointed bailiffs to assist the agents in curbing illegal cutting and sale of reservation forest products.[42]

The U.S. Congress likewise restricted timber harvesting on America's Great Lakes reservations. Indian and non-Indian logging companies needed permission to cut "dead and down" or green, standing trees. Washington controlled whether these logs should be used for Indian building projects or might be sold on the open market. Government scalers cruised Indian forests and filed weekly reports on logging operations, including number of logs cut and banked from a particular parcel of reservation land, thousands of feet of green or "dead and down" pine harvested, totals scaled for a week, and amounts scaled to date. As in Canada, the local agent and his staff policed the reservations, apprehended trespassers, and levied fines.[43]

Indian residents did not sit idly by while others stripped lumber from their land. As with all matters concerning their communities, aboriginal leaders politicked to maximize opportunities for their people. That Indians were shrewd businessmen and businesswomen had been recorded since the days of fur trading, and this astuteness about the value of local resources persisted.

Both Ottawa and Washington recognized that aboriginal leaders in council must consent before license holders could log reservation land. To win over the chiefs, Canadian agents stressed that monies from the sale of timber would be invested and yield annual per capita payments. Generally, native governments surrendered forests only after their councils and the federal agents negotiated satisfactory terms for timber surrender. In 1869, the Walpole Island Ojibwa, Potawatomi, and Ottawa ceded their timber with the provision that all trees eighteen inches or less in diameter "be reserved for our own use." Islanders also wanted Deputy Spragge to visit the reserve, pay them part of their money immediately, and inform them in writing about the exact amount of their timber dollars to be invested. If loggers violated the terms of their permits (which they did in 1881 by cutting large white oak trees), Walpole chief J. G. Bird (Greenbird) complained to Ottawa. Like American Indian counterparts, Walpole entrepreneurs also obtained federal permits to log their own forests.[44]

Aboriginal leaders advanced their interests in the North Country, too. Manitoulin Island chiefs negotiated with the Indian Department in 1899 about the type and quantity of wood to be cut and sold by native logging crews. This included twenty-five thousand cedar railroad ties, ten thousand cedar posts, one thousand cedar sawlogs, and three hundred cords of poplar and spruce pulpwood. The Thessalon Reserve likewise spoke up in 1890 when it disliked the terms of their permit to cut pulpwood on the reserve. In such cases, the local agents usually forwarded aboriginal requests to headquarters, along with their recommendations.[45]

The Indian voice was thus heard, if not always complied with, by the Ottawa-knows-best Indian Department. When the seventy-six-member White Fish River community requested a permit to cut and market its timber, the department judged that tree stands were too small and scattered to implement the plan; instead, reservation timber should be ceded to the Crown and sold to benefit White Fish River. Chief James Nowagahbow was advised to present this better plan to his people.[46]

Though tense at times, timber negotiations between native nations and federal authorities in Washington and Ottawa were historically significant because of the value of reservation forests and the impact of timber sales on local communities. Logging payments fattened Indian trust funds, while logging operations created jobs for aboriginal workers: cutting trees, stacking them along riverbanks, floating logs to sawmills, and employment at the mills. Woods work included cutting and selling ties to railroads, firewood to passing steamboats, fence posts to farmers, and pulpwood to paper companies. An examination of lumbering on Wisconsin's Oneida Reservation and Ontario's Six Nations underscores the importance of this nonfarming activity to their economies and to the entire region in the late 1800s.[47]

Moneymaking timberlands of the Oneida nation proved a curse as well as a blessing. Throughout the last half of the nineteenth century, Indian entrepreneurs illegally logged these lands and grabbed quick profits from off-reservation lumber mills in Green Bay, Howard, and De Pere. This looting could not be stopped; natives held these resources in common, and the chiefs felt powerless to protect the public interest. By 1868, thieves had stripped the reserve of more than half of its marketable trees. In early February of that year, at the chiefs' request, Green Bay agent M. L. Miller visited some of the mills surrounding the Oneida. He discovered over one million feet of unlawfully sold logs. Mill owners refused to pay stumpage fees to the Oneida nation, and Agent Miller lacked authority to seize the contraband. The chiefs continued to pressure Miller to stop the plundering. He asked Washington to direct the U.S. district attorney to prosecute timber trespassers. The commissioner of Indian affairs promptly ordered the Green Bay agent to seize and mark all lumber cut on the Oneida Reservation, which he did. He also began legal action against one of the mill owners who most flagrantly encouraged Indians to strip their land of timber.[48]

In 1881, actions of the U.S. attorney for the Eastern District of Wisconsin, G. W. Hazelton, revealed a lucrative and illicit traffic in Oneida timber. This robbery, which had gone on for many years, had intensified during the winter of 1880–81. Deep snows trapped the agent at his Keshena headquarters and prevented him from patrolling the reservation. Timber thieves leaped at the opportunity like wolves scenting blood. So many Indians cut down trees and sold them at half value to neighboring mills that Hazelton could not track down all offenders. "If the Reservation can not be better protected from systematic thieving hereafter than it was last winter," Hazelton warned, "there will be no timber left on it [the Oneida Reservation] in five years." He arrested some lawbreakers for stealing and instituted civil suits against the most prominent, in order to recover the value of the timber and to alert others about the consequences of theft. Ultimately, twenty-six of the guilty parties paid $1,693.77 for the wood and legal costs.[49]

Timber trespass continued into the early twentieth century, yet the forest resources of the Oneida also contributed legitimately to their changing economy. Late in 1881, the commissioner of Indian affairs permitted the Oneida to cut "dead and down timber." This "produced a decided change for the better," the agent reported. "Nearly all the Indians that have been in the habit of hunting and loafing during the winter months are now working like colonists in the forest." By the following spring, Oneida businessmen had set up lumber camps and hired Indian loggers, whom they paid twenty-six to forty-five dollars per month plus board. A few years later, the local agent permitted would-be Oneida farmers to clear their land and sell marketable timber, as a way to stimulate agriculture and to sustain families until harvesting their first crops. Another income source was manufacturing hoop poles (circular wooden strips used to bind barrel staves). This, too, was done under the agent's supervision, to make sure that trees were not wasted and that the natives received a fair price for the poles.[50]

Oneida forests thus shaped the reservation experience and the economic development of the region. Quick, handsome profits attracted white mill owners, who freely purchased black-market logs for cut-rate prices. Many Oneida community members also disregarded federal regulations and used their nation's commonly held timber resources to advance their personal positions. The limited power of the federal government and even the Oneida chiefs to stop the timber raid also became clear. This was all part of the wrenching and momentous transition to Great Lakes reservation life as residents sought a workable balance between the old and the new.

Ontario's Six Nations likewise possessed a wealth of timber, which helped, along with agriculture, to drive economic development. Lumber companies with Iroquois contracts had removed most of the marketable timber from the Grand River Reserve by the 1860s. Two events then curtailed their activities. First, Deputy Spragge discovered that the Six Nations had received a "miserably insignificant" portion of these timber profits because of subterfuges, such as the lack of competitive bids. Second, the Indian council refused to approve further sale and export of reserve timber sorely needed by local farmers for building houses, sheds, fences, and barns to shelter their livestock and grain harvests. Frustrated lumber companies lobbied the Six Nations council with petitions from Iroquois residents requesting renewal of company contracts.[51]

When signatures failed to persuade policy makers, timber poachers preyed on the remaining stands of marketable trees. At times, they were abetted by shortsighted Iroquois families who preferred quick dollars from illegal timber sales to the hard work of farming. Federal officials and the Six Nations council had difficulty catching and successfully prosecuting the culprits. "At night, with a full moon," writes Sally Weaver, "timber was easily cut and hauled onto barges to be taken downriver for sale."[52]

A heated debate between the Six Nations council and local Indian superintendent J. T. Gilkison early in 1885 revealed the ongoing political and economic difficulties of managing the reserve's dwindling timber resources. At a February 10 meeting, a speaker announced that the council had again discussed the wood question. Gilkison then spoke at length about the importance of conserving what was left of their forest lands—"an inheritance and trust"—and appealed to the chiefs and warriors for their help. Gilkison wished that the council could carry the burden of forest supervision, but he believed that Indians would not report poachers. The Indian Act provided penalties for timber theft, and the responsibility for safeguarding Indian forests rested on him. Timber cutting could take place, Gilkison noted, but only if he issued a license. Even with help from forest bailiffs, some Indians abused their licenses or utterly disregarded them and continued their plunder. Gilkison asked the chiefs and warriors for a plan to combat this problem.[53]

The discussion intensified a few days later, when the council reported on their new policy for timber cutting, which allowed removal of dead wood from the reserve without a license and gave the council licensing authority for logging standing timber. Gilkison was astonished. What remained "of their once fine forests," he responded, was "now scarcely deserving the name of woods as it is difficult to find timber with which to frame a barn." He said that he would transmit their decision to Ottawa and await instructions. He also warned the council that his forest bailiffs would continue to prevent the removal of logs from the reserve. Guided by Canadian Indian law, he argued, he alone had authority to issue licenses at Six Nations. The council speaker responded that they did not need such laws; they had their treaties. Gilkison said, "Good night," and left. The issue was joined.[54]

Happily, by month's end, the parties hammered out a compromise. The council first accepted Gilkison's suggestion that a committee of six chiefs be appointed to work with him to decide on regulations for harvesting dead and green wood. On February 27, they presented a set of recommendations designed to protect the reserve's woodlands. Both the council and the Indian superintendent accepted them. The timber crisis was resolved.[55]

The Six Nations timber story in the late 1800s, like the situation at Oneida in Wisconsin, documented the fight among three contending powers to control this forest resource. The economic power of non-Indian lumber companies and the legal authority wielded by federal field officials were awesome; yet strong-minded aboriginal peoples fought—legally and illegally—to make the best use, in their judgment, of remaining timber stands. Eventually, most native leaders surrendered their forests in the face of intense pressure and promises of financial benefits for their people. Consequently, lumber mills gobbled up hundreds of square miles of Great Lakes forests during the last half of the nineteenth century. Initially, everyone seemed to benefit: laborers, farmers, town developers, government treasuries. Most believed that the bonanza would last forever. One skeptic was Chief Michel Dokis.

Chief Dokis's people had selected a sixty-one-square-mile reserve on the French River as part of the Robinson-Huron Treaty settlement. Their forests contained some of the most valuable timber in the Lake Huron region, an estimated forty-five million board feet of white pine. As Ontario's boreal forests receded with each passing year, lumber barons focused more attention on such remaining pockets as the Dokis Reserve. The Indian Department first tried to unlock it for loggers in the 1880s, in response to fourteen applications. Thomas Walton, the regional Indian superintendent, made the usual pitch to Chief Dokis about the financial advantages of surrendering his timber, as other reserves had, with the promise that investments would yield each community member at least four dollars annually. Dokis rejected the offer. Pressure on him intensified during the next two decades, with federal officials scandalously on the side of the lumbering interests and seemingly unable to grasp Dokis's desire to safeguard the timber for the long-term use of his people. Ottawa and its field officials dismissed Dokis's reasoning and disregarded his requests to keep government surveyors off Indian land. "The action of the Band in this matter exemplifies in a marked degree the incapacity of the Indians to manage their own affairs," Walton remarked in his usual patronizing fashion. Because of "the stubborn waywardness of one old man, their Chief," he argued, "they refuse to execute an act that would place all in most comfortable circumstances." The Indian Department showed a similar lack of respect for Dokis; more than once, Walton and the Indian Department tried to bypass him by holding a community-wide referendum on the surrender issue. Dokis's views still prevailed. Ottawa even failed to protect native lands from trespass and to provide fair compensation for these losses, despite the chief's complaints. Not until after Dokis's death in 1906 did Indian Department officials finally get the timber surrender they had desired for so long. By then, thanks to the "stubborn waywardess of one old man," writes historian James T. Angus, "Chief Dokis' descendents received . . . a very substantial $50 per person per month—not Walton's projected $4 per year," and "thus the Dokis Indians, then numbering 81 souls, became per capita the richest Indians in Canada."[56]

Adjusting to reservation life was tough enough for Dokis's people and other Great Lakes aboriginal communities, even if Ottawa and Washington had championed their interests. When federal officials seemed to be on the side of white developers, native communities became even more beleaguered. That they were not merely victims is illustrated by the Dokis story and the ways that they also fought to get just compensation for timber holdings and mineral rights.

The industrialization and urbanization of Canada and the United States in the late 1800s required Great Lakes copper, iron ore, and petroleum. The booming market for these minerals greatly affected aboriginal peoples, who had mined copper and collected oil from seepages since before European contact. Traditional native homelands contained extensive mineral resources, and the desire of entrepreneurs to exploit them precipitated the American La Pointe treaties of 1842 and 1854 as well as the Canadian Robinson-Huron and Robinson-Superior treaties.[57] Events at Mica Bay between 1847 and 1850 illustrated Canadian officials' determination to champion corporate resource extraction at the expense of aboriginal economic needs, despite their passionate protests.

The midcentury Great Lakes mining craze brought about extensive trespassing on Indian lands along the northern shores of Lakes Huron and Superior. Indian Department officials disregarded field agents' warnings and escalating native protests through petitions. In April 1846, Alexander Vidal arrived at Sault Ste. Marie to begin a mineral survey of the area. He reported to the commissioner of Crown lands:

> The Indian chief residing in the neighborhood and called Shinggwak waiting upon me this morning in company with the young hereditary chief Nab-na-ga-ghing and several other Indians for the purpose of claiming all the land here as their own. They say that the government have never purchased the land from them, and expressed their indignation at my having been sent to survey it, and more particularly at the government having licensed parties to explore the mineral region on the north shore of Lake Superior without consulting with them or in any way acquainting them with the intentions regarding it; indeed the old chief said that had they not been too few in number they would have prevented the party which has just gone up to explore.[58]

Paying no attention to aboriginal claims, the commissioner of Crown lands opened likely sites for sale and mining. The Quebec-Superior Mining Association production facilities at Mica Bay on eastern Lake Superior finally provoked a hard-hitting response from aboriginal leaders. Claiming they had never been paid for these mineral lands, Indians from the Sault Ste. Marie area occupied the mine and caused the owners to evacuate. Federal officials eventually arrested two chiefs and some of their followers, who were taken to Toronto and jailed. Both their Indian agent and the press called for leniency toward the Indians. They intended no disloyalty toward the British government. The executive council soon released them and, early in 1850, arranged for William B. Robinson to negotiate land cession treaties, including mineral rights, with Indian nations along the northern shores of Lakes Huron and Superior.[59]

Although elbowed off these most desirable mineral lands and onto restricted reservations, Indians still had to contend with outsiders who lusted for native resources "under the earth." Developers looking for marketable deposits of oil and ore first had to apply to the American or Canadian Indian departments, which, as was the case with lumbering, then sought contract approval from native councils.

Non-Indian newcomers to the Great Lakes in the late 1800s, whether tourists or moneymaking miners, fishermen, lumbermen, and farmers, sought more than the natural resources of reservation lands and waters. They needed the Indians' labor—to guide them throughout the region, to work on their boats and farms and in their mills and mines, and to grade railroad beds. The relationship was to become mutually beneficial, reminiscent of earlier fur-trading and military partnerships, except that native laborers in the late 1800s were clearly in an inferior economic position. Appealing seasonal opportunities, which often drew family members away from the reserves and the control of their agents, further frustrated the farming operations encouraged by Washington and Ottawa officials. The officials nevertheless seemed pleased when large numbers of Indians hired out to neighboring white farmers in New York and southern Ontario. At least native families were engaged in "civilized pursuits" and not off hunting and fishing or just lazing around. Indian agents rarely reported specific numbers of Indian farmhands except to say that there were "many," "a considerable number," or, in the case of Six Nations, "hundreds."

We know something of the lives the Indians lived off-reserve as seasonal rural laborers. White farm owners, though happy to hire these peaceful people of color with their distinctive cultures, worked their hired hands hard—"with the same maniacal rigour," notes Terry Crowley, "that they displayed in their own work habits." For agricultural laborers, this meant, according to Crowley, "fifteen-hour days, wretched working conditions, and condescending attitudes" from their employers, who often treated "their hands much as they do their teams." Ontario's seasonal farm laborers used for berry picking, hop picking, and flax pulling also contended with unsafe and unhealthy workplaces, little job security, and low wages.[60]

Only domestic service, with its confinement, round-the-clock responsibilities, and lack of privacy, was more demeaning. Female Indian workers often took these jobs and thus grappled with their own off-reserve challenges. One was the low expectation of Indian Department officials for its wards. By going out "as servants to the white people," the Lake Simcoe agent reported about native women in 1885, they are "learning habits which will be of advantage to them in the future."[61]

The lumber industry rivaled farming and domestic service as an employer of Indians during these timber boom years. Seasonal jobs proved plentiful and varied, from felling trees and driving logs down the cascading rivers of Ontario, New York, Michigan, Wisconsin, and northeast Minnesota, to noisy sawmill work and the loading and unloading of lumber at various port towns. For example, by the 1890s, most of the Mohawk men from Gibson Reservation supplemented their farm incomes with jobs at the Muskoka mills eight miles away. They departed after the planting season, leaving their wives in charge, and returned for haying time and harvest. At the Rama Reservation, young men were more committed to lucrative woods work, with jobs as raftsmen in the spring, in the sawmills in summer, and with lumber camps during the winter. Some rose to the rank of foremen. In the late 1890s, Garden River women did the wash for nearby lumber camps, which suggests that the industry's impact was not limited to the wages of males.[62]

Also remarkable about this time were the economic effects of a lumber mill on Wisconsin's Lac du Flambeau Reservation. J. H. Cushway and Company, which obtained a contract to harvest trees from Indian allotments, first built a sawmill on the reservation at a cost of nearly forty thousand dollars. Except for "the experts at work on the mill," reported the local Indian agent, members of the Lac du Flambeau community built the complex, and all who wanted work could get it. This included building a 2.5-mile railroad spur line of standard gauge to the mill. The rails alone weighed sixty pounds per yard. The main, two-story sawmill measured 136 by 46 feet. The wing or shingle mill was 46 by 32 feet and also two stories.[63]

Great Lakes natives earned additional wages on or near their reservations by working for road construction crews, for lake shipping and railway companies, as general laborers, and as Indian agency employees (government farmers, teachers at day schools, staffs of boarding/residential schools, interpreters, police, and the like). Those living near the international border, like members of Garden River Reservation, crossed it when necessary to find work. James M. McClurken's study of wage labor in two Michigan Ottawa communities revealed that by the end of the 1800s, many of these natives "made the greatest share of their living by laboring for non-Indians." Ottawa families most successful in obtaining this seasonal and low-paying wage work were those closest to transportation routes and concentrations of non-Indian populations.[64]

Whether the wages earned came from farms, sawmills, or jobs, these nontraditional income sources were sizable and had a major influence on reservation life across the Great Lakes region. In 1898, the Indian Department calculated that of the Six Nations' total income of $145,616.75, wages contributed $78,499.00. Wages were also impressive elsewhere in Ontario that year. At the Manitowaning Superintendency, for example, where hunting and fishing remained the primary moneymakers, take-home pay contributed $34,925 to an overall income of $237,648. At Fort William and Prince Arthur's Landing, another prime fishing and hunting area, Indians earned a total of $11,400 in wages and $56,095 from all sources.[65]

Without question, the growing number of Indians involved in wage work, plus the cash they earned, had produced major changes in reservation economies and cultures. Most aboriginal workers took entry-level jobs with neighboring farmers, the lumber industry, or other employers of seasonal labor. Earning, though seasonal and unpredictable, supplemented novice reservation farming or enabled other families to buy consumer goods and continue to follow hunting-trapping-fishing lifestyles. Most Indians still pursued a variety of jobs, yet with each passing year, a growing number became wage earners, and their economies changed from barter to money. Because these new economics linked the Indians' fates to those of their employers, twentieth-century economic problems of the Great Lakes hinterlands hit underskilled and undereducated native communities just as hard—if not harder.

Wage work produced consequences other than economic. Native families that purchased goods and services from stores no longer looked as much to woods and waters for sustenance. This altered their environmental views and led to the gradual loss of woodland skills and country food. Surroundings changed entirely when men and women moved into towns and cities to live and work. The consequences were not always positive. The U.S. Department of the Interior was upset in 1895 because of drunkenness among young Menominee men who sold their wage checks from logging to Shawano saloon keepers for two-thirds or half their face value. The inevitable brawls extended to logging camps and caused work stoppages. Hourly jobs also tended to be individualistic, thereby lessening an Indian worker's dependence on family, kin, and native nation. Wage work, largely seasonal, nevertheless helped struggling reservation families to survive. Some even prospered for awhile. But by encouraging acculturation, hourly work for pay off and on the reservations challenged aboriginal traditions—the old ways—with attractive new ones.[66]

FEDERAL SUPPORT

When both traditional and nontraditional economic efforts failed to provide enough support, Great Lakes reservation families turned to federal authorities for help. These authorities were obligated by law to care for Indian wards. In 1859, traveling artist Paul Kane captured something of the excitement sparked by government presents and annuity payments at two Indian gathering places. One was the village of Manitowaning on Manitoulin Island, where two thousand natives awaited the arrival of a boat carrying their gifts. As Kane observed, these included "guns, ammunition, axes, kettles, and other implements useful to the Indian." He wrote:

> The Indians assemble annually at Manetouwaning [*sic*] from all parts of the shores of Lakes Huron, Nipissing, and Superior, as well as from all the neighbouring islands. On the arrival of the presents, the Indians, male and female, accompanied by their children, immediately seated themselves in rows on the grass, each chief heading his own little band, and giving in their number and names to Sigennok [the principal chief], who here appears in his proper element, dividing the goods among them with great impartiality. He is really a very useful man. His voice is heard everywhere above the universal din of tongues, his native eloquence is unceasing, and seems to have the effect of allaying every envious and unpleasant feeling, and keeping all in good humour and proper order.[67]

The British government had offered Indians presents for more than a century in recognition of native loyalty and assistance during wartime and in return for land cessions. Gift distribution lists provide a rough local census and a window into aboriginal material cultures. Returns for Manitowaning in 1853, for example, documented an allocation of presents to 1,830 persons (thirty-nine chiefs, 570 warriors, 746 women, and 475 children), plus ten days of rations for all these families. Among the presents were thousands of yards of material (caddis [coarse woolen fabric, yarn, or ribbon binding], molton [a thick flannel], rateen [a thick twilled woolen cloth], irish linen, calico, domestic cotton), hundreds of point blankets, shawls, sewing needles and thread, 1,355 horn or box combs, awls, butcher knives, brass kettles, 1,290 pounds of tobacco, two flags, and hunting supplies (ball, shot, gunpowder, flints, and percussion caps).[68]

When Kane later visited the Menominee Reservation in Wisconsin, he also found a large assembly, of three thousand "anxiously awaiting the arrival of the agent with their money." The scene was noticeably different from Manitowaning. Because the Indians would be receiving money payments, a large number of merchants "collected, all busily occupied in the erection of booths for the display of their finery." Kane observed, "In about a week, the

Ojibwa annuity payment at La Pointe, Wisconsin, ca. 1860s. *(Courtesy Wisconsin Historical Society, image 48581.)*

bank of the river wore the aspect of a little town; the booths placed in rows, presented the scene of bustle and animation: the finery was, of course, all displayed to the best advantage on the outsides of the booths."[69] The importance of the federal governments' contributions to reservation economies as reflected in these two scenes, whether the agents brought presents or cash payments, continued throughout the rest of that century and into the next.

Monies and goods funneled onto reservations by the local agents came from several sources. One was treaty annuities, which were obligations, some for a set time period, agreed to by Ottawa and Washington in return for land surrenders. A second category—and by far the largest—was interest from Indian trust funds established with monies from the sale or rent of land, timber, minerals, and other reservation resources. (Ottawa and Washington took charge of aboriginal monies, depositing and investing them, because the Indians were their legal wards and considered incapable of managing their own affairs. This arrangement not only reduced aboriginal management opportunities but gave extraordinary financial and hence political power to the Indian departments and their field officials.) Comprising a third source of funds were irregular, special appropriations by federal legislative branches in response to a particular need, such as the failure of Indian crops due to flood or drought.

Federal administration of each Indian nation's accounts was complex and frustratingly bureaucratic, involving extensive white—not red—tape. To tap a community's own money for a worthwhile project, its council and the local agent must endorse a specific amount of money. This endorsement, in turn, had to be approved up through the federal chain of command. The enormous paperwork generated in carrying out the project was daunting. Data for each nation's accounts included funds on deposit and interest earned plus ongoing costs charged against the account. These included administrative costs plus emergency advances. Furthermore, Indian departments needed up-to-date census information in order to calculate local per capita payments. The 1875 interest monies divided among the Six Nations of the Grand River, for example, were $43,229, or $14.60 per person.[70]

Frequent disputes arose over who was an Indian—a community member—and thus entitled to share in annuities. Births and deaths altered census figures each year, but much more controversial were the rights of "mixed bloods," Indians living off-reserve, and newcomers from other reservations or nonrecognized aboriginal communities—some from across the international border. Federal agents regularly relied on the judgments of local chiefs and councils to resolve membership matters. For instance, La Pointe agent S. W. Campbell, in preparation for the 1900 annuity payment at Grand Portage, Minnesota, wrote ahead to ask that two chiefs obtain statistics on marriages, birth, and deaths so that Campbell could compile an accurate cash payroll.[71]

Controversies that swirled about the time of year for payments, their locations, and who should receive the disbursements for no-shows also indicated their significance to aboriginal families. Again, agency officials generally accepted the Indians' wishes about these questions.

Purchasing goods and then shipping them and monies to remote reserves was costly and further complicated payments. Yet the process, including certification of each annuity and trust payment received, underscored their importance. Green Bay agent E. Stephens apportioned the 1879 annuity goods and agricultural supplies to 145 Menominee family heads. Each of their signatures by the letter *X* was witnessed. Stephens also compiled a list of the items—boxes of axle grease, hoes, nails, plow handles, rakes, lumber, and the like—plus their quantities that each Menominee received. An interpreter, two witnesses, and Stephens then attested to the accuracy of the accounts. Finally, the agent verified that each recipient had labored on the reservation for himself/herself or the community in an amount equivalent to the value of annuity goods received.[72] Ottawa and Washington treated Indian annuity and trust funds so seriously because they were needed to promote a range of "civilization" programs, from Indian agriculture to education.

The L'Anse and Lac Vieux Desert Ojibwa of northern Michigan helped determine the use of their trust funds to promote farming. In response to the Indian commissioner's spring 1884 invitation, the natives met in council and voted on equipment and livestock (with a value of $998) that they wanted Washington to purchase for them. This included double wagons, breaking and ordinary plows, grub hoes, ox yokes, drag teeth, two yokes of cattle, and six milk cows. The secretary of the interior approved the request and deposited funds for the Michigan agent that December.[73]

Canadian Indian nations likewise voiced their wishes on using trust funds to aid agriculture. In March 1880, for example, the Six Nations council asked the superintendent general of Indian affairs to advance them money to buy seed for the spring planting. The next step, following a positive response from Ottawa, was for the council to appoint a committee to receive applications for seeds from individual farmers within the community. The committee included eight persons, each of whom represented a constituency: Mohawk, Seneca, Onondaga, Oneida, Lower Cayuga, Upper Cayuga, Tuscarora, and Delaware.[74]

Federally controlled Indian funds supported a wide range of initiatives besides farming. These included educational programs, paying off local shopkeepers and other creditors, salaries and pensions, and reservation improvements, such as upgrading roads and refurbishing a council house. Chief and council usually proposed these expenditures. No matter how modest the venture, it also needed the local agent's endorsement and the approval of the Indian department in Washington or Ottawa.

Considerable paperwork accompanied each bureaucratic step. In 1891, the Walpole Island Potawatomi council resolved to use one dollar of its funds to pay Joseph Otter for carpentry repairs to the council house. Agent Alexander McKelvey certified the document and forwarded it, along with a requisition on Potawatomi funds, to Ottawa. In a couple weeks, he received a one dollar check for Mr. Otter. To complete repair to the council house, Walpole Island also requested $2.50 to pay Joseph Wilson for lumber and forty-eight cents to pay the company of West and Davis for paint and nails. Such careful accounting procedures were just part of the story; federal officials insisted, too, that each reservation's requisitions promote Indian policy goals. Consequently, when the Canadian Wyandots requested approval in 1857 for two projects—fifty pounds to pay off debts and five hundred pounds to construct a sawmill—Deputy Superintendent General R. T. Pennefather turned them down. He reasoned that individuals should pay off creditors from their own annuities and that money for the mill would have to be taken from the principle of the Wyandot trust fund. The federal government, he said, "does not consider a speculation of that sort a proper investment of the funds entrusted to the government for the Indians."[75] Aboriginal wards might request how they wished to spend their own money, but the Crown knew best and exercised a veto power.

Emergency relief for native communities or needy individuals was another major use of federally controlled Indian monies. If a crisis were widespread, such as a crop failure due to drought or a killing frost, the agent requested and then distributed emergency provisions, seeds for replanting, and even cattle feed. When fires swept through native communities on Manitoulin Island and the north shore of Lake Huron, the Canadian government approved an expenditure of $550 for the local agent to purchase twenty barrels of flour, four barrels of pork, ten barrels of corn meal, one hundred bushels of Indian corn, thirty bushels of timothy seed, and one thousand pounds of rice.[76]

One of the largest efforts for emergency relief occurred early in 1890, following the U.S. Congress's appropriation of a relief fund of seventy-five thousand dollars for cold and hungry Great Lakes Ojibwa. The Indian Office instructed its agents to survey the reservations in person and, "based on actual facts," make a recommendation about goods needed. Meanwhile, Washington advertised in Chicago, Milwaukee, and Minneapolis newspapers, inviting bids for furnishing 225,000 pounds of flour, fifteen hundred barrels of pork, and seventy-five thousand pounds of corn meal. The La Pointe agent also reported a pressing need for blankets and protective clothing.[77]

Aged and infirm natives required ongoing care. Throughout the late nineteenth century, the Canadian Indian Department, responding to agents' reports, annually distributed blankets to reservation residents in poor health. In January 1890, for instance, J. C. Phipps at Manitowaning forwarded a list of thirty-one Indians in his superintendency that required winter assistance. He included their reserves, their ages, the reasons they needed help, and his recommended amounts for each, ranging from three to ten dollars. The total was $185. When necessary, the U.S. government provided relief for its reservations in the form of flour and mess pork among the poor. Both Indian departments used funds to assist off-reservation natives who needed medical attention, transportation, or other kinds of assistance.[78]

Micromanagement of aboriginal reservation finances created a bureaucratic nightmare for all concerned. Ottawa and Washington, constantly worried that their wards had become too dependent on annuity and trust payments, regularly issued directives that Indians must work if they were to eat. The Indian departments' control of native monies inevitably created quarrels and bitterness among individuals and reservation communities who did not understand the status of their accounts. To paternalistic administrators also fell the responsibility of a growing number of Indians not living on reservations. All these bedeviling responsibilities only grew over time and underscored that farming was not an economic panacea for Great Lakes reservations.

CONCLUSION

In 1996, the Royal Commission on Aboriginal Peoples reminded Canadians how poorly their federal government had championed aboriginal economies over the years.

> As for what were supposed to be their own lands—the reserves—Indian people found themselves under the control of government officials rather than their own leadership. Not only did the Indian department's stewardship of reserve lands and resources turn out to be abysmal, but the employment policies that were to be based on those lands and resources were mostly a failure.[79]

To a degree, the story of Great Lakes Indian non-farming activities during the second half of the 1800s confirms the commission's indictment. Both Canadian and U.S. governments regularly interfered when aboriginal families tried to find economic resources other than, or to supplement, commercial agriculture. These included traditional practices (fishing, hunting, trapping, gathering) and nontraditional ones (leasing land, catering to tourists, selling a variety of forest products, and earning wages from neighboring whites). Officials tried to control both Indian involvement in these enterprises and the monies generated, so that Ottawa and Washington could insure that Indians spent their earnings properly. Paternalism on both sides of the international border produced lackluster, languishing native economies increasingly snarled in white tape, excessively reliant on federal largesse, and increasingly deprived of off-reserve resources other than wage work for others.

Yet, at least for the late 1800s, the royal commission was incorrect to claim that "Indian people found themselves under the control of government officials rather than their own leadership." Native chiefs and councils regularly strove, using peaceful means where possible, to protect and control their economic resources and to accommodate the Indian Department only when necessary. For their part, individual Indian families decided independently just what their mix of economic activities would be—just as they had with farming. How can it be claimed that Washington and Ottawa controlled the livelihoods of Indians, especially in the north, when their agent rarely visited them and when they were gone from the reserve much of the year? Whether south or north of the international border, most natives certainly controlled their own lives and adjusted them, as they had since time immemorial, according to seasonal cycles and the inevitable quirks of nature. Moreover, when families left their villages for off-reservation work or to hunt, fish, and gather, they not only escaped their agents' and missionaries' supervision but, in the process, helped preserve their language, religion, family control of their children's education, and communal sharing, as well as the authority of clan chiefs and elders. To suggest that aboriginal peoples were mere victims imprisoned on desolate reservations is an injustice to them and a disservice to Great Lakes history in general.

To be sure, the challenge of preserving Indian autonomy was enormous, and the federal presence could be oppressive. Janet Chute and Deborah Anne Montgomerie have documented Garden River Reserve's fight to preserve its self-sufficiency with a seasonally integrated economy that did not rely wholly on farming. Rather than encourage reserve businesses, the department promoted increased dependence. Ottawa's direct aid was miserly, and officials regularly undercut aboriginal development plans by handing over their resources to outsiders.[80]

Such economic and political maneuvering became a pattern in dealings between natives and the Indian Department on a variety of issues across the Great Lakes. Aboriginal leaders and community members often protested against or disregarded unpopular and unwise federal policies. They sent lobbying trips to the nation's capital and used civil disobedience to communicate their views and hammer out agreements that safeguarded and opened opportunities for their people. Garden River Reservation chief Shingwaukonse spoke for many when he explained to the governor-general and the Canadian public the importance of husbanding reservation resources.

> The Great Spirit in his beneficence, foreseeing that this time would arrive when the subsistence which the forests and lakes afforded

would fail, placed these mines on our lands, so that the coming generations of His Red Children might find thereby the means of subsistence. Assist us, then, to reap that benefit intended for us.[81]

A particularly troublesome feature of federal supervision was the policy makers' persistent obsession that reservation Indians become farmers. In response to disappointing agricultural progress in the Great Lakes region and elsewhere, Washington and Ottawa tried a radical, new approach to Indian landownership: allotment. As is discussed in the next chapter, the consequences for native families proved unfortunate, and the pattern of reservation life was fundamentally altered.

{ 3 }

The Homeland Becomes a Checkerboard

Allotment and Location Tickets

The Indians' limited success of farming cash crops and performing nonagricultural work on and off reservations prompted Washington and Ottawa legislators to try new strategies. Otherwise, their hope for Indian community self-sufficiency and assimilation into the white mainstream would be unfulfilled. What came to dominate reformers' experiments in the late 1800s were the twin ideals of family-owned homesteads and citizenship. "The Indian people will not remain as a separate race among us, as the black race must," remarked Massachusetts senator Henry L. Dawes to a Friends of the Indian group.

> He is to disappear in the midst of our population, be absorbed in it, and be one of us and fade out of sight as an Indian. . . .You must give up the idea of keeping Indians together. You must, as soon as possible, spread them out into the community among the people. . . . Their blood, their sinew, their strength, are needed, and will help us.[1]

To stimulate this integration and replace Indian communal economic ties with a new appreciation for the value of private property, U.S. and Canadian Indian treaties and legislation pressured aboriginal families to select and improve modest-sized, private farm sites either on or off reservations. Their reward would be titles in fee simple. Freedom and equality also awaited those who followed the examples of white citizens. Such was the dream—and the promise.

Lucy Penaseway, a Michigan Ottawa widow, started down this path. First, she filed a homestead claim in nearby Traverse City; she then cleared some land, built a home for her four children, and planted strawberries and fruit trees. To sustain her family during the summer of 1876, Lucy took the youngsters to pick berries, which they sold in Traverse City. William Thompson, a shameless and opportunistic neighbor, took advantage of this hardworking, aboriginal farmer during her absence. He used bribery and a variety of legal shenanigans to get control of her property and destroy all trace of her improvements. Not until Lucy and her children returned from Traverse City did they discover their loss. Within five years, Thompson, like a jackal with a carcass, had stripped the holding of valuable pine timber. Then he abandoned it.[2]

White neighbors, rather than offering a worthy example to the Penaseway family, had robbed and betrayed them. The local Indian agent protested at length to Washington but without success. Ironically, the reformers' homestead plan ended up hurting, rather than helping, an enterprising native family.

Among the rapid changes that Great Lakes reservation communities faced during the last half of the nineteenth century, none was more disruptive to their economies and community cohesiveness than federal experiments with allotment (for American Indians) and location tickets (for Canadian First Nations). The pressure to focus on farming had been intense. Likewise challenging was federal regulation of resources, such as fisheries and timber. Yet nothing undermined native solidarity so much as disturbing their remaining homeland, the wellspring of their cultures and foundation for economic security.

How would aboriginal leaders north and south of the international border respond? Chiefs consulted, as they customarily did, with their people and sought a workable balance between the new and the old. Over time, some communities or community groups accommodated to the new federal programs as a way to protect and develop their natural resources. In doing so, they exhibited, yet again, both flexibility and a degree of control about making a living. Also playing active roles were those who refused to accept severalty because they believed it threatened their resources and traditions. Both groups met with varying degrees of success. Unfortunately, Lucy Penaseway's experience was not unique. Notable as well during the unfolding of allotment and enfranchisement were the persistent influences of Indians and their homelands on the Great Lakes region.

POLICY ORIGINS

Washington policy makers promoted allotment for several reasons. First, they continued a longtime dream of private landownership for native peoples that originated in colonial times. Massachusetts enacted the first Indian allotment legislation in 1633. Following the American Revolution, leaders of the early Republic, such as Henry Knox and Thomas Jefferson, advocated assigning Indians to small, individual tracts to encourage farming and general acculturation through a sense of personal possession. Federal officials at first implemented severalty in a piecemeal fashion. Article 8 of the 1817 treaty for Cherokee land cession, for example, included a severalty section and the promise of future ownership in fee simple for those "who may wish to become citizens of the United States." In some cases, as with the Wisconsin Brotherton in 1839, Congress simply legislated allotment with citizenship. By the 1870s, the Indian Office, the secretary of the interior, and the advisory Board of Indian Commissioners called for national severalty legislation. If Indian families had their own permanent homes, it was believed, they would be more inclined to horse-and-plow farming and to dissolve communal ties. Without severalty, Indians faced a bleak future. In an 1879 letter to Secretary of the Interior Carl Schurz, Ezra A. Hayt, commissioner of Indian affairs, remarked, "The experience of the Indian Department for the past fifty years goes to show that the government is impotent to protect the Indians on their reservations, especially when held in common, from the encroachments of its own people, whenever a discovery has been made rendering the possession of their lands desirable by the whites."[3] Native safety, "civilization," self-sufficiency, and citizenship all seemed to demand reservation allotment.

The U.S. experiment to individualize Great Lakes Indian land bit by bit began in 1854, when Lake Superior Ojibwa signed a treaty creating several reserves for them in northern Michigan, Wisconsin, and Minnesota. Article 3 of the agreement stated that

> the President may, from time to time, at his discretion, cause the whole [of each reservation] to be surveyed, and may assign to each head of a family or single person over twenty-one years of age, eighty acres of land for his or their separate use; and he may, at his discretion, as fast as the occupants become capable of transacting their own affairs, issue patents therefor to such occupants, with such restrictions of the power of alienation as he may see fit to impose.

Washington also included severalty provisions in the 1855 treaty with Michigan Ojibwa and Ottawa east of Escanaba and Keweenaw Bay on the Upper Peninsula and on the northwestern portion of the Lower Peninsula, including Beaver Island; in the 1856 treaty with the Wisconsin Stockbridge and Munsee; and in the 1864 treaty with the Michigan Ojibwa of Saginaw, Swan Creek, Black River, and the Au Sable band.[4] Allotment of Great Lakes reservation lands was thus well under way by the 1880s, when American policy makers decided that severalty should be a national Indian policy.

The most important advocates were the people who collectively called themselves the Friends of the Indian, which included such reform groups as the Women's National Indian Association of Philadelphia, the National Indian Defense Association, and the Indian Rights Association. These groups believed that Washington's Indian policy had failed miserably. Beginning in 1883, federal officials, educators, and delegates from Friends of the Indian met at Lake Mohonk, New York, each year to discuss reform efforts. Natives seemed demoralized by dependence on the government dole, followed too many of the old ways, and remained communal in their thinking. The reservation—"that hot-bed of barbarism," as John H. Oberly, commissioner of Indian affairs, called it—clearly was not preparing Indians for American citizenship. If aboriginal peoples were to be saved, the reservation system must be dismantled.[5]

The expectation was that Indian farmers working in cash crops with individual family tracts would learn how to compete in a market economy alongside their white neighbors. Allotment would also weaken tribal ties. Dawes, chair of the Senate Committee on Indian Affairs and a leading light at the Lake Mohonk conferences, headed the lobbying effort for a general Indian allotment act. What communal Indians lacked was "selfishness," Dawes insisted, "which is at the bottom of civilization." Besides reformers, severalty legislation was favored by white settlers, the railroads, and other entrepreneurs, because allotment would open up sixty million acres of Indian "surplus" land.[6]

Success came in 1887. The General Allotment Act, also known as the Dawes Act, authorized the president to assign 160-acre parcels to reservation family heads, eighty acres to single Indians, and forty acres to minors. To each allottee, the Indian Office gave a trust patent. The act also granted them and other Indians who abandoned tribal ways and "adopted the habits of civilized life" the "rights, privileges, and immunities" of other U.S. citizens. Following a quarter-century trust period, Washington would issue titles in fee simple to the new owners. Unallotted reservation lands would revert to the federal government and could be sold to non-Indians.[7]

That individual landholdings were a key to aboriginal improvement and economic self-sufficiency was also accepted by Canadian officials, even before Confederation in 1867. In the Gradual Civilization Act of 1857, the legislature acknowledged the desirability of fostering "the progress of Civilization among the Indian Tribes" and "the gradual removal of all legal distinction between them and Her Majesty's other Canadian Subjects." To that end, the act established a process for adult aboriginal males to become citizens. This included fluency in English or French, basic formal education, good moral character, and being "free from debt." Those who met these criteria would be enfranchised—admitted to the privileges of citizenship—and given small plots of land within their reserves. The Gradual Civilization Act disregarded native opposition to individualized land tenure. Thus it also signaled, according to historian J. R. Miller, that "Indian-government relations were changing dramatically" and moving "steadily from protection to compulsion and from cooperation to coercion."[8]

As in the United States, early Canadian treaties provided for individualized land tenure in a piecemeal fashion. An 1857 surrender by the Moravians of the Thames stipulated that reserved lands be divided into farm lots and that each family and their descendants be given written guarantee of the right of occupancy. A similar arrangement was made with the natives of Batchawana and Goulais bays in 1859. Likewise, Ottawa and Ojibwa chiefs of western Manitoulin Island agreed in 1862 to sell most of their portion of the island, to accept reserves on Manitoulin, and to reside within them on hundred-acre family plots.[9]

Following establishment of the Dominion of Canada in 1867, the new federal government put its own stamp on aboriginal policies inherited from Great Britain. The Indian Act of 1868 established that, in addition to other duties, the Canadian secretary of state would be the superintendent general of Indian affairs, charged with management of aboriginal lands and safeguarding of native peoples. That the natives would continue to be pushed in the direction of acculturation and civilization was emphasized in the next year by the Act for the Gradual Enfranchisement of Indians. It continued the enfranchisement process begun in 1857, which was designed in part to fragment the Indian homeland.[10]

In the 1876 Indian Act, a paternalistic Canadian government consolidated previous legislation and increased its everyday supervision of aboriginal affairs. A major goal was promoting enfranchisement and individual landholdings while still protecting the owners. It authorized the superintendent general to survey reserves into lots and to issue location tickets—deeds, in effect—to persons whom the "band" assigned to specific parcels. Henceforth, this property was not "subject to seizure under legal process" and could only be transferred to an Indian from the same community subject to the approval of the local council and the superintendent general. Ticket holders could not lease their land without the Crown's consent. The Indian Act also established a complex, three-year process by which males who resided on these lots might become enfranchised and obtain absolute title to their properties. Subsequent federal legislation in the 1880s and 1890s gave the superintendent general the power to allot reserve lands, thereby circumventing any local council that refused to assign tracts to community members or approve their leases.[11]

ABORIGINAL RESPONSES

When do-gooders came near, they so frightened American writer Henry David Thoreau that he ran for his life. The allotment program of the Friends of the Indians did not cause American Indians to bolt, but many were alarmed and ultimately resisted. Once again, paternalistic federal policy makers had not consulted with native leaders and simply dismissed the views of those fearing additional land loss. Tribal spokesmen, wrote historian Arrell Gibson, tried to explain "that reservations were bad enough, but allotment would be impossible." In 1886, a pessimistic Delaware chief, Charles Journeycake, commented to the Indian Defense Association about the many broken promises of land-hungry Americans:

> We have been broken up and moved six times. We have been despoiled of our property. We thought when we moved across the Missouri River and had paid for our homes in Kansas we were safe. But in a few years the white man wanted our country. We had good farms. Built comfortable houses and big barns. We had schools for our children and churches, where we listened to the same gospel the white man listens to. The white man came into our country from Missouri. And drove our cattle and horses away.

About the prospects of allotment farming following the Dawes Act, Shoshone chief Washakie summed up his thoughts by saying, "God damn a potato!"[12]

Enfranchisement also did not carry great appeal to Canadian aboriginal peoples. Many staunchly preferred to hold reserve lands in common and rejected outright the 1857 Gradual Civilization Act's attempt "to break them to pieces." Chiefs and their constituents willingly experimented with new ways to support their communities, including commercial agriculture and off-reservation employment, but they steadfastly refused to surrender tribal sovereignty and key traditions, such as communal landownership. Thus, between 1857 and 1876, only one Canadian Indian had jumped through all the enfranchisement hoops to become a full citizen. Forty-four years later, the number was just 250.[13]

Great Lakes native families echoed some of these national Indian sentiments about the prospects of private landownership. The New York Seneca council, for example, underscored the economic security that members got from their communal land system: "No Indian, however improvident and thriftless, can be deprived of a resort to the soil for his support and that of his family. There is always land for him to cultivate free of tax, rent or purchase price."[14]

Not all Indian nations and communities felt the same about severalty. In several cases, responses were mixed or openly favorable toward individual holdings. Those willing to try allotment had a variety of motives, such as control and sale of timber resources or protecting their improvements. One thing was clear during the closing decades of the nineteenth century: native leaders and community members freely expressed their views on national policies, worked diligently and creatively to protect aboriginal interests, and, in the case of Canada's enfranchisement program, refused to cooperate with unpopular federal initiatives.

On both sides of the international border, large numbers of Great Lakes Indian communities resisted the carving up of their communities into individual homesteads. In Wisconsin, Menominee Indian agents in the field and Washington administrators had pushed for allotment of the reservation since the mid-1800s. Yet both traditionalist and more acculturated Menominee opposed implementation of the Dawes Act. It was not the prospect of small farm plots that alarmed them; many accepted this facet of the Dawes Act. Rather, they feared loss of valuable timber resources that the Menominee could best harvest communally. The Dawes Act, they believed, would deny tribal rights to their forests and permit Washington to seize unallotted lands in order to sell them to non-Indians. Menominee opposition eventually prevailed. Allotment was avoided. In 1908, the Indian Office finally agreed to Menominee wishes and started construction of a tribal sawmill at Neopit.[15]

Likewise, on Walpole Island, chiefs and councilors opposed the issuing of location tickets that they thought would undermine the physical and cultural cohesiveness of their community. The large acreage that Walpole residents own collectively in the twenty-first century confirms their long-standing lack of enthusiasm for individualized property. Other Ontario communities, such as Garden River, resisted the enfranchisement program in order to prevent the breaking up of their reserves.[16]

The willingness of other Indians to experiment with new concepts of landholding and ways of making a living produced mixed reactions to allotment on some reservations. In 1881, an influential faction at Lac Court Oreilles, Wisconsin, objected to the allotment provisions of the 1854 treaty and, according to the La Pointe agent, were "opposed to every measure of civilization and progress," while two local chiefs were "good men" who supported the agent's civilizing efforts and stood up against "this disturbing element." Nine years later, twenty-five Lac Court Oreilles chiefs and headmen and a number of members petitioned the Indian commissioner in hopes of promoting reservation allotment under provisions of the 1854 treaty and the Dawes Act.

> We firmly believe that no new method nor measures are better adapted to ameliorate our present situation and supply our present necessities. We pray that the allotting of lands in severalty be continued under the several above mentioned approvals of the President.

Reserve allotment was but a means to an end, their Indian agent explained. Once families received parcels, they also hoped for permission to sell their timber. Proceeds, as supervised by the local agent or government farmer, would fund permanent improvements and help feed the natives while getting farms started.[17]

Individual ownership also triggered a nasty split among Wisconsin's Oneida in the 1850s and delayed implementation for forty years. The federal agent, land speculators, and one native group favored allotment. Division of the reservation, they argued, would lessen squabbling over the boundaries of improved farmlands and stop the plundering of commonly held timberlands. Moreover, reservation lands left over after allotment could be sold for the community's benefit. Despite these apparent advantages, those opposed were able to block the proallotment faction. The Oneida stalemate continued into the late 1880s, with opposing groups regularly bombarding Washington with petitions and delegations seeking political support. In May 1888, the "Great Father" (the president of the United States) was asked to protect the Oneida:

> against encroachments of the citizens of the U.S. and especially of our neighbors in Brown and Outagamie Counties, Wisconsin; for many

years various persons and parties amongst the Whites and Indians have been trying to obtain a foothold upon our Reservation, and to get possession of our land, and to induce us in some way, to nullify the Treaty by which we hold our Reserve; and now they have entered into a regular conspiracy with each other and with some discontented members of the tribe to have our land allotted in severalty in such a way as to allow us in a short time to sell our lots to white men; . . . now what we ask of our Great Father is simply his protection against these encroachments of his white children; if we are Indians we know enough to attend to our own proper business and we wish the Whites to do the same in regard to their proper business; we wish to have our treaty maintained in all its integrity; we ask to be allowed to live here in peace on this small spot under the same conditions as we have been living in the time past.

That same month, an Oneida group of councilors and headmen requested the U.S. commissioner of Indian affairs "to hasten the time for the allotments of our land in severalty." Petition signers contended "with a lawless and stubborn set of people" who did not hold offices yet had prevented the governing party from executing laws and regulations. The Oneida agent had recently failed to fashion a compromise between the two parties. The petitioners argued that this impasse should not be allowed to continue. If the federal government could not win over the opposition group, they asked, would not Washington at least apportion the lands of Oneida families who favored allotment and thereby "relieve, our troubles"? Yet another appeal to the Indian commissioner claimed that the reservation Oneida had "no laws or any rights to appeal to court and get justice." Along with division of their land, they sought the "rights, privileges, and immunities of citizenship" provided for allottees in the Dawes Act. Washington soon responded to these appeals and authorized Oneida allotment, thereby breaking the long-standing deadlock.[18]

Diverse feelings about individual landownership also characterized some Canadian aboriginal communities. Factions already existed within the Oneida community near London, growing out of their earlier purchase of reserve lands. Passage of the 1857 Gradual Civilization Act intensified these title issues as well as mismanagement charges against Chief Sickles. Indeed, "certain disaffected parties," reported the Oneida agent, intended to apply for enfranchisement, which was contrary to the general wishes of the community. The Oneida split was but a sign of broader, varied responses across southern Ontario. This was showcased at a Grand General Council meeting at Sarnia between June 25 and July 3, 1874. Among the delegates were representatives from Sarnia, Kettle Point, Rama, Walpole Island, Snake Island, Mud Lake, Alnwick, New Credit, Ojibwa of Muncytown, Moraviantown, Saugeen, Scugog, Cape Croker, Oneida, and Six Nations of the Grand River.[19]

The range of contradictory feelings on enfranchisement surfaced quickly. Speeches for and against the issue were notable for several reasons. One was the awareness of allotment experiences on both sides of the international border. Another was the acknowledgment of diverse skill and educational levels among reserve populations. Thus Sarnia's chief William Wawanosh remarked:

> It was high time that a certain number in each Reservation should be placed on a level with the whites. On looking over the Dominion he saw many of his race, who, on account of their education, industry, integrity and general knowledge, were competent persons to be enfranchised. While thus he spoke so encouragingly of some of his people, there were others, and they formed the majority, who did not possess the qualification necessary for enfranchisement; and he feared they would still remain, as they have in the past, in the capacity of minors. To enfranchise the unqualified Indian in Canada, he believed, would bring upon him the same disastrous results as it had done in Michigan and Kansas. This, he thought, could be avoided in Canada by making certain rules and regulations and he offered the following suggestions:—"That when an Indian wished for enfranchisement, his case should be considered in Council by his Tribe, or the Band to which he belongs, and if he is found to be a person possessing a fair education and general knowledge, industriousness, and bearing a good moral character, then his Tribe may petition the Government to grant a Title Deed to the lot of land which has been apportioned by the tribe to the enfranchised Indian. He is also to receive a portion of the principal money belonging to the Tribe; after which he is to be cut off entirely from any further privileges enjoyed by his Tribe." Chief Wawanosh concluded a powerful address by urging the Council to open a door to those ready for enfranchisement.

Chief John Henry, who represented the Ojibwa of the Thames, noted:

> Foreigners hailing from all parts of the world, and coming into Canada were made citizens at once; and he could not see why the

original owners of the soil were not elevated to this position. This, he thought, was one of the main reasons of the grand assemblage before him. He spoke of the Negro in the United States. As soon as he was emancipated, he began to fill important positions; and his voice was soon heard in the Legislative Assembly and in Congress. Chief Henry thought that we could never have peace until we opened a door to those yearning for enfranchisement. He coincided with the proposals offered by Chief Wawanosh, with the exception of cutting off the enfranchised Indian from any further participation in the annuities, etc. The annuity, he considered, was a birthright to the Indian and his family, whether he remained a minor or was elevated to the position of a citizen. Chief Henry also alluded to the great progress in civilization as having been made by the Indians in Canada during the last fifty years; it was only since that time we emerged from Paganism into Christianity. No other nation, he thought, could have made such progress in such a short time. Why then were we not citizens yet? It is for us to work for this privilege. We are here representing every tribe and most of the Reservations in Canada, and surely we ought to accomplish something towards the elevation and improvement of the Indian. He suggested the retention of the annuity by the enfranchised Indian and his family, for this reason: That it would prove a kind of link between himself and the Reserve to which he formerly belonged. If afterwards he was elected to sit in the Municipal Council or County Council, or was even elected a member of Parliament, he could thereby do a great deal for the good of his tribe.[20]

Those opposed to enfranchisement also took the floor to share their concerns. Chief Burning of Grand River warned that subdividing the reserve into hundred-acre lots would not accommodate all the Six Nations and New Credit families. Some would be "thrown out." Another spokesman did not like the idea of enfranchised individuals having to pay taxes on land that had been deeded to his people "for all time."[21]

The Reverend Abram Sickles of Oneida acknowledged these differences and proposed that the council "grant the privilege of enfranchisement to those wishing for it, and those opposed to it let them remain as we are now, as long as they wished." He proclaimed, "Let us hear each other," and listen they did. The Grand General Council approved a committee report favorable to enfranchisement, provided local chiefs and councils could approve enfranchisement applications and also control the location and size of the lots apportioned to enfranchised Indians.[22]

In summary, enfranchisement and allotment programs sparked strong feelings from aboriginal communities and their leaders. They understood that severalty and citizenship allowed the tentacles of Ottawa and Washington—of the "white man's way"—to reach into the heart of their reservations. How were native nations to preserve their sovereignty, control of their economies, and nurture traditional cultures if federal officials broke their homelands into pieces?

Many of these fears were validated as Canada and the United States began to individualize landholdings. Yet once again, this was not a tale of meek aboriginal compliance and victimization. Native families and community headmen tried in creative ways to control the implementation process—ranging from out-and-out resistance to boldly launching businesses on their new allotments.

IMPLEMENTATION CHALLENGES AND NIGHTMARES

Because they wanted to meticulously control their severalty programs while allowing only limited native input, the United States and Canada unwittingly created an implementation nightmare. Both the Dawes Act and the Canadian Indian Act set up extensive guidelines that offered numerous opportunities for bureaucratic mix-ups and misunderstandings by the Indians. Who was eligible for a private plot? How was the parcel to be selected and then properly recorded locally and at headquarters? What about leasing aboriginal lots and the rights of heirs prior to the granting of ownership in fee simple? Thousands of reservation allottees and their families, Indian councils, resident agents, and federal officials in Ottawa and Washington sought answers to these and numerous other questions during the late 1800s. The architects of the Dawes Act and the Indian Act intended to share their blessings of "civilization" and private ownership of land but instead placed a millstone around the necks of many disadvantaged aboriginal families.

On Great Lakes reservations, problems arose initially over who was entitled to own these valuable allotments. One troublesome facet of the eligibility issue was Washington's determination that it, rather than local councils, should be the final authority in creating reservation membership rolls. Nevertheless, consultation with local headmen regularly occurred. When George A. Morrison applied for allotments for himself and his family on Bad River Reservation in 1899, Agent S. W. Campbell informed Morrison that he must first convince the Indians in council that he belonged to the band and had "rights to benefits enjoyed" by them. Otherwise, said Campbell, "there will be no use for you to take any further steps in the matter." A year later, J. L. Prophet of Red Lake, Minnesota, inquired about his wife's rights at the Lac Court Oreilles Reservation. Campbell responded, "Allotments are made in open council and with the consent of the chiefs and majority of the tribe of Indians to which the allottee belongs." Uncle Sam remained the final authority, yet Indian communities retained considerable control over their membership and the severalty process.[23] Canada employed a similar system for determining allotment eligibility. Whether a native sought possession of a surveyed reservation lot or wished to become enfranchised, he or she must obtain the band's consent first and then the approval of the superintendent general of Indian affairs.[24]

Selecting a good plot of land, so critical to a family's economic well-being, involved complex procedures as well. The American version required that an individual apply for a particular tract of land, which perhaps encompassed improvements made or seemed fertile, was near water and firewood, or contained a good stand of marketable pine trees. If no other community member requested this parcel, the agent had the area surveyed and its boundaries marked. After the Dawes Act, the Indian Office no longer allowed reservation councils to rule on the acceptability of allotment applications. Canada's Parliament likewise modified the Indian Act in order to circumvent uncooperative chiefs and councils during reservation surveys and the assignment of individual locations.

Both federal governments also played dominant roles in determining the size of Indian family lots and in issuing land patents. In 1873, the Kettle Point community north of Sarnia requested that the Indian Department set aside parcels of one hundred acres for each family. Though pleased, Deputy Superintendent General Spragge recommended instead that the department approve fifty-acre allotments. This was done. The reservation was small, only 2,446 acres, and the Indian Department reasoned that good land must be preserved for an expanding future population and the possibility that members of the neighboring Sarnia community might legitimately wish to relocate to Kettle Point.[25]

Canada's control of location tickets was not foolproof. An inspector of Indian agencies reported from Rice Lake in 1905 that Indian agents and Ottawa had approved native allotment requests in such a haphazard manner that no reservation property was left for twenty-nine community members, over 40 percent of the total. Ownership of land was fundamental to enfranchisement, Inspector J. Andsell Macrae noted. Those without location tickets were "deprived of the rights of citizenship."[26]

South of the international border, federal officials also dealt with complex ramifications of allotment provisions in the La Pointe Treaty and the

Dawes Act. Washington issued trust patents, and allotments could be sold only with the consent of the president. Experience had taught the Indian Office that if titles in fee simple were given too soon, Indian men frequently bartered lands away at ridiculously low prices. Still, as at Rice Lake in Canada, allotment snafus surfaced regularly. In February 1881, the Indian Office advised the La Pointe agent that his predecessor had inadvertently created three allotments on the Red Cliff Reservation that overlapped ones earlier patented to other family heads. Their rights must be respected, Washington emphasized, but if they did not wish to occupy and improve their allotments, they might be disposed of to other, more industrious Indians "at a reasonable price." The Indian Office respected even the rights of absentee allottees who moved away from the reservations and made no improvements. Perhaps this was admirable, but at the same time, it prevented other local residents from using these neglected parcels.[27]

For all concerned, reservation allotment could be both a blessing and a curse. This became evident when U.S. Indian families and their agency overseers got involved with logging. In February 1893, Michael Brisette of Bad River Reservation sought permission to clear for farming purposes land patented to him. La Pointe agent William Mercer, who endorsed the request, estimated that the tract contained three hundred thousand feet of pine. The Indian Office granted this and hundreds of similar requests because the allotment policy was meant to encourage Indian farming.[28] Yet officials also feared that allottees would not receive a fair price for their timber, might squander the proceeds, and could fail to farm the cleared acreage. Washington therefore created elaborate, nightmarish procedures to control every aspect of reservation logging. The Indian Office justified these actions by asserting that allottees with trust patents did not have the right to cut and sell timber from their lands; legal title to this land remained with the federal government until it issued patents in fee simple to Indian family heads.[29]

A variety of factors powered what was to become a Northlands timber boom involving native families. First, they had to make a living, and if this meant selling standing timber on their allotments, men like Michael Brisette did so—perhaps as a prelude to farming. In the eyes of the Indian Office, one of the biggest roadblocks to commercial agriculture had been the magnificent pine and hardwood forests that enveloped the reservations and prolonged the traditional woodland culture. If their land were cleared of timber, Washington reasoned, then larger numbers of Ojibwa could cultivate the soil. Since annuities had expired in the mid-1870s, lumbering would also generate a new source of income. Thus, in 1882, the U.S. Department of the Interior granted Lake Superior Ojibwa allottees the right to cut and sell standing timber from their tracts under the supervision of the Office of Indian Affairs.[30]

Besides a sea of tree stumps rolling toward the horizon, the American reservation lumber boom left in its wake a massive pile of Indian Office paperwork. One culprit was the complicated contracting process. The average Indian allottee lacked the business experience, equipment, and capital to log his own tract. From the beginning, the Ojibwa contracted with experienced white lumbermen to dispose of their timber. These businessmen established isolated winter logging camps, built forest roads, hired dozens of high-priced lumberjacks, foremen, and cooks, hauled in provisions and other equipment with teams of oxen and horses, and cut and banked the timber on the driving stream. All camp expenses were charged against the contracted price paid to the landowners. If the logger managed well, the patentee received his fair net return for his timber. Yet the risks were his; the contractor escaped all costs of delivering banked logs, even those caused by accidents of weather. The Indian Office minimized the chance for loss by regulating native timber prices, insisting that only reliable and properly bonded contractors logged reservation lands, and supervising the camps so that the tribesmen were not exploited and so that whiskey was not sold to them. Bad River Indians also played a role in regulating their local contractor, the J. S. Stearns Lumber Company. During a tribal council meeting in May 1895, which Stearns attended, members chose a three-man business committee to study, each month, the fairness of logging camp hiring practices and prices charged at the company store. Any differences arising between the committee and Stearns would be adjusted with the help of the agent and the government farmer.[31] Commissioner J. H. Oberly's 1888 letter of instructions to the La Pointe agent about the Ojibwa of Lake Superior living on Michigan reserves revealed the huge paperwork that this process generated.

> Where an allottee holds a patent for his land, or his allotment has been approved by the President, *and you are satisfied that the sale of the timber on such allotments would be for the actual benefit of the Indian,* you will permit him to contract for its sale in the manner indicated by the Secretary, and in the accompanying form of contract. . . .
>
> Each contract should be accompanied by your statement showing the reasons why you believe the sale of his timber would result to the advantage of the Indian.
>
> A bond duly executed, with good and sufficient sureties, must accompany each contract.
>
> . . . You are again instructed to permit *no operations to be com-*

menced on any tract, until you receive notice of the approval of a contract covering the same.[32]

With Washington's supervision, the Lake Superior Ojibwa signed eighty-eight contracts with white lumber companies for the 1883 season. They harvested over forty-eight million feet of timber valued at more than $250,000. As I reported elsewhere, reservation logging peaked in 1888, "when 731 contracts for cutting and banking pine timber yielded 190,206,080 board feet which sold for $4.75 to $7.00 per 1,000 feet." My report continues:

> Between 1894 and 1922, the J. S. Stearns Lumber Company paid $6,813,373 for one and a quarter billion feet of timber taken from Bad River, and spent over a million dollars in wages for hundreds of Indian lumberjacks. The company mill at Odanah was eventually enlarged to a capacity of sixty million board feet a year. Stearns shipped thousands of carloads of lumber by rail throughout the Midwest.[33]

For Indian owners to benefit from allotment logging, several elements had to be secured. They included proper scaling of timber, foiling trespassers, and assuring that landholders spent timber proceeds properly—as determined by the Indian Office, not local natives. In 1895, the La Pointe agent drafted twenty-two rules for scalers. The rules applied to Lac du Flambeau allotments and were agreed to by Joseph H. Cushway and Company, which contracted to purchase the timber. Regulations instructed government scalers to measure, grade, and mark all cut logs before they were removed from an allotment. Scalers also numbered all logs, kept a watchful eye for trespassers, and maintained a "book of permanent record," which recorded all logs scaled, with their numbers, lengths, and type of tree for each allotment, "as called for in the contract." Weekly scaling reports in triplicate were submitted to the local agent. As a further safeguard, an inspector of scalers oversaw all their work.[34]

Indian Office paternalistic management of allottees' timber monies ensnared Uncle Sam in micromanaging reservation affairs, with predictable results. Initially, the La Pointe agent only managed the cash timber profits paid to Ojibwa landowners deemed incompetent. Beginning in the 1890s, because some Indians squandered their proceeds on whiskey, trinkets, and gambling, the Indian Office demanded that natives spend their money for permanent improvements on each allotment, such as building a house or pulling stumps in preparation for planting, or to support the education of allottees. "The experience of this Agency for a number of years, demon-

Logging on the Lac Court Oreilles Reservation, 1909. *(Courtesy Wisconsin Historical Society, image 39615.)*

strates conclusively that the Indians are not proper custodians" of large sums of money, wrote La Pointe agent Matthew A. Leahy in 1890.[35]

Ironically, Washington's management of each allottee's logging account trapped Indians as well as local agents in a maddening thicket of paperwork and personal relationships. The experience of Andrew Skinaway from Bad River Reservation was illustrative. In October 1895, he visited the Ashland agent to complain that his father-in-law, Tom Condecon, and his wife's brother had been meddling in Skinaway's affairs. Condecon, who seemed to be after all his daughter's logging money so he could set up his own business, had already obtained an order for one hundred dollars signed by his daughter, Maggie. Skinaway insisted that without the interference of his in-laws, with whom he lived, he and Maggie would get along fine. His intention was to use both their logging monies to build a house and move away from her parents. Skinaway requested that the agent not recognize the money order that Maggie gave her father. Agent William A. Mercer, determined to support Skinaway, ordered the Bad River agency farmer to advise Maggie to work with her husband and build their house. He argued that this would be the best use of her money and that her "husband should come before the father or brother." The farmer, Mercer advised, should tell Maggie's relatives that the Indian agency would not tolerate their interference in the domestic or business affairs of Andrew and Maggie.[36] How did the La Pointe agent become a personal financial manager and marriage counselor? The Indian Office assumed it knew what was best for aboriginal peoples in all circumstances: private and public, individual and reservation-wide.

By the 1890s, with the purpose of "protecting the Indian against himself," a paternalistic Uncle Sam doled out monthly allowance checks worth $10 to Ojibwa allottees. This course of action was dreadfully time-consuming. In June 1899, for example, the La Pointe agent forwarded 108 checks for distribution by the Bad River agency farmer. The agency office at Ashland maintained financial records for each allottee, who was entitled to know his or her credit balance. Should a native wish to withdraw a large sum from the account in order to build a home or make farm improvements, application must be made to the local agent, who forwarded it to Washington with his recommendation.[37]

Predictably, some allottees felt frustration because they could not control their own economic resources. Daisy M. Whiteside explained to the La Pointe agent that she did not understand when she signed her lumber contract "that the balance of forty dollars ($40) was to be paid in niggardly installments of ten dollars ($10) per month, or whenever your fancy dictated." Whiteside continued:

> I think I am quite capable of using any money lawfully mine. . . . Please understand Mr. Campbell, you are not dealing with an illiterate savage. . . . I have reached my majority and am a citizen of the United States and I demand the rights and privileges of one. . . . I am ill and need the money, not only for present expenses, but for medicines I have had, and the small amount you say you will send me would certainly not pay my bills. . . . Kindly send me the full amount of forty dollars ($40) as I refuse to accept anything but that amount. If you do not do so, my Masonic friends have informed me that they will interfere in my behalf and appeal to Washington.[38]

Besides introducing these control issues, large-scale logging changed the lifestyles of many Indians who worked in logging camps or on allotment farms. Their profits enabled them to buy good farm machinery and afford comfortable houses. Some Ojibwa purchased logging equipment and contracted to harvest their neighbors' timber. Because of reservation logging, Agent James T. Gregory predicted that reservation Ojibwa would never return to their former hunting-gathering-trapping ways of life. Secretary of the Interior William F. Vilas reported to the U.S. Senate in February 1899, "The removal of the pine from lands belonging to Indians in severalty is no more to be deplored, if they have enjoyed fair compensation for its value, than the clearing of forests everywhere before civilized improvement."[39]

Lake Superior Ojibwa cultural "progress" was great; but allotment timber money, which amounted to $428,221.41 during the winter of 1887–88, promoted dependence as well as "civilized improvement." Agent Gregory warned that if logging income were ever cut off, the Ojibwa would suffer greatly. When the Department of the Interior suspended timber sales in 1899 because of irregularities, Congress had to appropriate seventy-five thousand dollars in relief funds for reservation families.[40]

For years, besides the mixed blessings created by allotment logging monies, other challenges bedeviled allottees, native leaders, and Indian Office personnel who oversaw reservation affairs. Early in June 1893, the Bad River council questioned the La Pointe agent about the Sam Denomie family. Denomie, after disposing of the timber on his eighty-acre tract, left Bad River in 1887 and acquired 160 acres of Michigan land. He then sold the timber off that parcel for five thousand dollars. Over the years, he also had two wives from the L'Anse Ojibwa community of Michigan and fathered six children. In 1893, Denomie wished to live again at Bad River. This puzzled the council. What were the rights of Denomie, his wife, and his children to obtain allotments and other benefits of Bad River membership? By the end of the month, the commissioner of Indian affairs answered the council's many questions.[41] There must have been considerable staff time involved just to satisfy the allotment concerns of one native community about one of its members. La Pointe Agency correspondence revealed many similar, equally complex, and time-consuming issues revolving around allotment. These included the guardianship of minors' tracts, leasing, rights-of-way for railroads, the rights of married couples with allotments on different reservations, and the recourse for families who did not like their allotments and wanted to exchange them for others.

ALLOTMENT OF ABORIGINAL LANDS BY 1900

In 1881, Secretary of the Interior Carl Schurz observed, "The greatest danger hanging over the Indian race arises from the fact that, with their large and valuable territorial possessions which are lying waste, they stand in the way of what is commonly called 'the development of the country.'" Developers of the Great Lakes region, which included lumber interests, "civilizing" Indian agents, and entrepreneurial natives, thus championed severalty. Particularly striking were figures for Lake Superior Ojibwa. In August 1900, after more than thirty years of Indian Office support for allotment, La Pointe agent S. W. Campbell reported the figures listed in table 1. There was also a flurry of activity to the east, on Michigan's Keweenaw Bay, where government officials created 679 allotments on the L'Anse Reservation between 1875 and 1930.[42] The surveying and division of the Menominee, Stockbridge, and Oneida reservations were considerably slower, as revealed by the 1890 census figures in table 2.

To the north, in Canada, reservation response to individualized landholdings was lukewarm. Some natives, like those at Port Arthur, favored location tickets that could settle disputes over property lines and enable parents, as undisputed owners, to pass possessions on to children.[43] Still, community surveys went slowly, as suggested by the figures from the summer of 1888 in table 3.

Events on Walpole Island and New York Seneca reservations showed that resistance to severalty could be spirited and long-term. Agent Alexander McKelvey reported from Walpole in 1884 that some young islanders wished to obtain forty-acre family farms and had applied to the council for location tickets. Chief and council seemed inclined to comply but eventually bowed to the opposition of older Indians and would not confirm the grants. In the

TABLE 1. Allotments for Lake Superior Ojibwa Reservations, August 1900

Reservation	Allotments	Acres
Bad River	662	51,884.02
Red Cliff	205	14,166.01
Lac du Flambeau	458	36,634.32
Lac Court Oreilles	702	54,862.13
Font du Lac	450	30,296.73
Grand Portage	304	24,191.31
Total	2,781	212,034.52

Source: Agent S. W. Campbell to CIA William A. Jones, August 5, 1990, AR, CIA 1900, 409.

TABLE 2. Number of Unallotted Acres on Menominee, Stockbridge, and Oneida Reservations, 1890

Reservation	Unallotted Acres	Square Miles
Menominee	231,680	362
Stockbridge	11,803	18.5
Oneida	65,608	102.5

Source: U.S. Bureau of the Census, *Report on Indians Taxed and Indians Not Taxed,* 619.

following year, the agent observed that it was "almost impossible for a young man to get a piece of land on the island." McKelvey proposed that the government undertake a modestly expensive procedure of survey and lot assignment for prospective farmers. He argued that those needing wood for fuel, fencing, or building could then obtain it within their properties and that this would put an end to the helter-skelter and wasteful current system and also encourage young men to stay on the reserve and farm. Though sympathetic, the Indian Department acknowledged the local council's power to grant these plots and suggested that the Walpole agent convene a general meeting of residents and have all adult males vote on whether to survey the island and divide it into lots. In 1886, the chief, secretary, and three members of council measured and marked off a forty-acre plot for William A. Elias, who desired a location ticket for island land he had already cleared. Even this near fait accompli did not bring council assent, so powerful was the opposition of "a few of the old men." McKelvey claimed that the council and the majority of islanders favored the general allotment of land but dared not stand up against "these old Pagans." As the chief explained it, they did not want any "innovation," and "it was better to let Indians be Indians." Faced with such opposition, McKelvey was powerless. He felt particularly sorry for young men who wanted to get land of their own in order to farm: "If they go and squat on a piece of land some of these old fellows at once claim that they have a prior right. And I know of one young man who made a start for a home three times and was driven off each time."[44]

Meanwhile, to the east, in New York State, many members of the Seneca nation similarly battled to preserve communal Allegany and Cattaraugus reservation lands against the allotment juggernaut. Like so many aboriginal peoples, these Iroquois had no tradition of viewing land as a commodity

TABLE 3.   Location Tickets Issued to Canadian Agencies, Summer 1888

Agency	Population	Location Tickets Issued
Alnwick	232	70
New Credit	240	2
Ojibwa and Muncey of the Thames	583	233
Moravians of the Thames	281	85
Cape Croker	391	2
Rama	236	1
Ojibwa of Georgina Island	128	40
Golden Lake	79	15
Mohawk of Gibson	109	37
Sucker Creek	107	25

Source: List of Agencies with Location Tickets Issued, enclosed with Circular, July 23, 1888, NAC, DIA, RG 10, Red Series, vol. 2425, title 87762 (microfilm C-11218).

that could be owned by individuals and sold to outsiders. Early opposition to severalty had exempted them from Dawes Act provisions, but powerful local and state forces conspired to break up their holdings. The Seneca fought against a variety of proallotment pressures from influential land, railroad, and mining companies that hoped to open up thousands of reservation acres for development. Missionaries, Indian policy reformers, and a number of local Seneca politicians also pushed for private landownership. Indian rights advocate Philip C. Garrett, for example, likened the Seneca reservations to "cancers in the midst of the body politic" and accused the Iroquois of clinging to communal land "because they want barbarism and not civilization." But the antiallotment Seneca were not alone; powerful, non-Indian supporters included Bishop William D. Walker, attorney John Van Voorhis, and Senator Matthew Quay. Historian Laurence M. Hauptman argues that without their help, "the Senecas undoubtedly would have lost their lands, the linchpin of their cultural identity." Hauptman's complex, in-depth study of the Allegany and Cattaraugus reservations also focuses on the internal struggle among three native political groups whose fortunes were intertwined with battles for or against allotment.[45]

Allotment controversies in upstate New York, on Walpole Island, and elsewhere across the Great Lakes were full of meaning. Many Indians and non-Indians became involved, from local aboriginal families and their councils to nearby lumber interests and policy makers far away in Ottawa and Washington. The debate among all parties was so intense because vital issues of policy and resource development were at stake. Through it all, Indians were very much a part of the decision-making process—as they always had been.

CONCLUSION

During the summer of 1876, seventeen Canadian Ojibwa reserves sent a total of sixty-seven delegates to a grand council held at Saugeen Reservation. They unanimously voted to express their "gratitude to the Honorable D. Laird, Superintendent General of Indian Affairs and to other members of the present Dominion government for the Indian Act of 1876 passed at their last session." They also expressed their "hope to see the Indians of Canada devoted and benefited by the enfranchisement therein permitted" and added that they had "no doubt that many of our people will avail themselves of its advantages."[46] The resolution, perhaps prompted by political courtesy, was a poor predictor of the future yet mirrored the optimism felt by many about the Indian Act and the Dawes Act.

American policy makers, reformers, and land developers were hell-bent on breaking up reservation holdings into individual family tracts. Theoretically, this would weaken tribal ties and enable horse-and-plow Indian farmers to compete in a market economy with nonnative neighbors. Indian holders of trust patents (in the United States) and location tickets (in Canada) could ultimately obtain both citizenship and land patents in fee simple. Some parties understandably rejoiced over the Indian Act and the Dawes Act.

The response of native peoples, who, for the most part, had not been consulted about either act, was mixed. On occasion, the legislation produced nasty, community splits. The unanimous support of the 1876 resolution of the grand council proved hollow as large numbers of Great Lakes Indians resisted all attempts to break their communities into pieces. Others willingly experimented with new concepts of landownership, especially if it protected their improvements and gave them a mechanism to harvest resources, such as timber, and to clear land for commercial farming. Allotment successes, with attendant consequences, were particularly notable among the American Lake Superior Ojibwa. By 1900, federal officials had surveyed and assigned 2,781 allotments encompassing 212,034.12 reservation acres. Reportedly, many families had abandoned hunting and fishing for a living and taken jobs in the lumber industry. Some even used pine profits to establish their own lumber businesses. Additional families bought new homes and farm machinery with dollars generated by the sale of timber from their allotments. The situation in Ontario was noticeably different. Twelve years after the Indian Act, Ottawa had issued significant numbers of location tickets only for the Ojibwa of the Muncey and Thames and for the Moravians of the Thames.

Whether the landholding changes were far-reaching or modest, Indian community leaders and family units significantly controlled the process, through individual decisions to cooperate with federal policy implementers or oppose them. True, some long-range consequences of severalty support hurt native reservations—economically, environmentally, politically, culturally—but these could not all be foreseen. Those who, like Lucy Penaseway, tried to support their families by taking up homesteads were the same sorts of persons who experimented with newfangled farming practices and wage work. Aboriginal choices were limited and filled with uncertainty and controversy. Yet the freedom to make choices existed: natives could resist the new or adapt institutions and practices to the "white man's way" of making a living.

Great Lakes Indian experiences with allotment and location tickets must have disappointed reformers and federal policy makers. The Dawes Act triggered some resistance as well as extensive loss of Indian lands and timber resources without producing widespread economic self-sufficiency through commercial farming. Likewise, the Canadian system of location tickets met much local resistance. Actually, the entire Indian Act, of which enfranchisement and these tickets were a part, became a notorious source of abusive, misguided federal power over Great Lakes native communities well into the next century. On both sides of the international border, it was a disturbing and oft-repeated story: white do-gooders and frontier developers separated Indians from even more of their homeland and, in the process, weakened their cultural ties, economies, and political defenses.

Another facet of the story was how reservation breakups impacted the Great Lakes economy and environment. Aboriginal land was quickly acquired by non-Indian settlers and developers. Subsequent timber harvests from these areas as well as native parcels fueled the lumber industry, water and land transportation companies, and a building boom throughout the Great Lakes and the Great Plains. The "Big Cut" of timber also changed the environment forever. Clearing aboriginal lands for fencing and farming destroyed the forest habitat and the traditional economic resources it provided. Dams, sawmills, and shipping facilities fouled and redirected once-pristine watercourses.[47]

By the 1890s, severalty had fostered only modest agricultural success. The Lake Superior Ojibwa farmed only 2,865 of their allotted 212,034.52 acres. Agents optimistically pointed out that increasing percentages of reservation men labored in "civilized pursuits." The Indian Office also hoped that allottees would use these wages and profits from timber sales to improve their homesteads and purchase farm machinery. But having large numbers of self-sufficient, commercial farmers remained only a hope.[48]

On the American side of the Great Lakes, perhaps the most negative consequence of Washington's severalty program was lost reservation land. Helen Hornbeck Tanner writes that at every stage of the process—from allotment selection and receipt of trust certificates to presidential land patents—"interference came from land speculators, loan sharks, lumbering interests, and aggressive settlers, at times working in collusion with Indian agents and the federal land offices." The Indian Office had implemented severalty among the Ottawa and Ojibwa of the upper Great Lakes since the mid-1800s, with the result that "close to 90 percent of allotted reservation land passed rapidly into non-Indian possession, usually before patents were received."[49] The case history of Lucy Penaseway and William Thompson illustrated how unscrupulous and opportunistic neighbors could get control of aboriginal lands and how allotment could harm, rather than help, enterprising natives. To the west, in Wisconsin, Indian allotments were often forfeited when taxes went unpaid. "A Wisconsin county tax sale notice can be mightily confusing when you do not understand ownership to begin with," writes Charles F. Wilkinson, "when you have never heard of taxes, and when you speak only Chippewa." By the 1920s, Wisconsin's Oneida also lost most of their lands and, with them, their tribal government, replaced by town and county systems. What became of the landless Indians in Minnesota, Wisconsin, Michigan, and Indiana? Often, they formed villages on remaining parcels or "Indian towns" adjacent to white urban areas. Yet as they congregated in these places, as Cleland notes, band integrity and the authority of chiefs and elders began to break down.[50]

Further south, land loss characterized the Indiana Miami as well. In 1872, Congress authorized allotment of the Meshingomesia Reserve in order to promote assimilation into the white mainstream and commercial farming on grants that ranged from 77 to 125 acres. Miami owners did not have to pay taxes and could not sell their land until January 1, 1881. After that, the allottees became citizens and could put their land on the market. Historian Stewart Rafert describes the subsequent disaster for the Meshingomesia Miami. Twenty-two years later, they owned only 1 percent of the original reserve. For the Miami, rather than "an advance toward civilization . . . it was instead a descent into poverty and the destruction of tribal culture."[51]

C. Joseph Genetin-Pilawa has authored an excellent Great Lakes comparative study of American and Canadian Indian experiences with allotment and enfranchisement. Focusing on the experiences of Bad River, Lac du Flambeau, Walpole Island, and Six Nations, he documents how individual family holdings initially stimulated both farming and the timber industry. Genetin-Pilawa also argues persuasively that the "implementation and administration of the policies by the federal officials [in the long run] not only impeded economic development on the reservations but forced Native people into an even more marginal position." Ironically, allotment and enfranchisement were supposed to encourage capitalism among aboriginal peoples. Instead, the consequences of misguided paternalism emanating from Ottawa and Washington were increased land loss and Indian dependence. Genetin-Pilawa underscores the similarities of American and Canadian policies and their administration. When faced with corruption and mismanagement by local officials and timber companies, native peoples tried valiantly, with letters and petitions, to bring these misdeeds to the attention of higher-level federal officials.[52] Just as with their farming and non-farming activities, Great Lakes aboriginal roles were anything but passive as they struggled to protect their core territories and traditions.

Unfortunately, the same self-righteousness and misunderstanding that shaped governmental and do-gooder attempts to change the way Great Lakes Indians made their livings also typified battles to control the Indian mind and soul. These campaigns are the subject of the next two chapters.

{ TWO }

Battling for the Mind and Soul

{ 4 }

The Education Crusade

Humorist Mark Twain, an astute observer of the American scene, once wrote, "Soap and education are not as sudden as a massacre, but they are more deadly in the long run." Schoolteachers, backed by federal officials and mainline churches, expected to have that sort of impact on Great Lakes aboriginal students and, through them, on entire reservation communities. Not content with restructuring native economies, Canadian and American policy makers who were bent on bringing their wards into the mainstream proposed to change the inner Indian. "The time for fighting the Indian tribes is passed," remarked President Merrill Gates of the Lake Mohonk Conference in 1891. He went on, "We are going to conquer the Indians by a standing army of school-teachers, armed with ideas, winning victories by industrial training, and by the gospel of love and the gospel of work." Once again, Indians became an object for alteration. This time, the thinking was that children must modify their behavior, whether in a day school or boarding school.[1]

The new form of warfare, which turned classrooms into battlegrounds, created momentous change within reservations and drew into the fray native leaders, parents, pupils, schoolteachers, missionaries, Indian agents, and other federal officials. The fierce struggle extended into the next century. Control of reservation minds was at stake. For centuries, Great Lakes aboriginal families schooled their children in the ways of the woods and waters and how to deal with European newcomers who came to trade and fight and settle. Parents oversaw this educational process prior to the reservation years, and they found any alteration of this system—of subjects studied and values learned—both alarming and appealing.

Few doubted that education was vital to the future of Great Lakes reservations. Aboriginal leaders and parents believed that only skilled and knowledgeable young people could sustain community populations, provide necessary foodstuffs, preserve their identities and traditions, and protect their families from external dangers and loss of sovereignty. To do so, it was necessary, as it had been for over two hundred years, to interact with the newcomers; they had the tools and skills and power that Indian survival required. Perhaps, it was thought, government schools would provide these benefits. For some natives, it seemed worth a try, provided they could control the process and safeguard core values. Also hopeful, Canada and the United States committed considerable energy and monies to Indian schools, but with a different agenda, linked to the historic policy of "civilizing," Christianizing, and assimilating native families—not to preserving reservation sovereignty and traditions. Federal education policies in both countries were tied as well to promoting economic self-sufficiency through farming and to inculcating capitalist values. Thus the time was propitious for a blossoming of Great Lakes reservation schools. Only time would tell what would result from the differing agendas of natives and newcomers.

AMERICAN AND CANADIAN EDUCATION PROGRAMS

A mixture of motives and opinions buttressed Washington's education program for reservation Indian wards across the country. Policy makers and idealistic reformers wholeheartedly believed that aboriginal cultures offered mainstream Americans nothing of value and must be destroyed if Indian families were to become "civilized" and survive. Thomas Jefferson Morgan, commissioner of Indian affairs, admitting that "this civilization may not be the best possible," argued that Indians "cannot escape it and must either conform to it or be crushed by it." Hiram Price, an earlier commissioner, concurred with the prognosis that it was "either civilization or extinction." This sense of urgency was characteristic of the education program. The post–Civil War years were marked by a concurrent sense that the time was right for reform. Since the 1600s, Europeans and then Americans had promoted formal education for Indians. Congress created the Civilization Fund in 1819, and with assistance from Christian churches, Washington created a network of Indian schools. Yet only a small percentage of youngsters lived with their families in permanent villages and attended classes. By the 1870s, there was reason to believe that more children could be educated; the Indian Wars appeared nearly over, most native nations were confined to restricted reservations, and the United States was committed to a peace policy toward aboriginal peoples. Based on these perceptions, America's leaders felt an obligation to act on behalf of its wards. Education also promised to be an effective weapon in the "civilization" arsenal because it targeted children, who could be molded more easily than their parents. That Congress agreed was suggested by its escalating appropriations for Indian education—from $100,000 in 1870, of which the Indian Office only spent $37,597, to $2,277,557 in the 1893 fiscal year.[2]

North of the Great Lakes, paternalistic policy makers and reform groups concerned about the fate of reservation families likewise looked to education as a powerful assimilation tool. It promised to elevate the "savages" from a state of helplessness and economic dependence to a position as self-reliant, "civilized" members of Canadian society. Indeed, since the 1830s—when Sir George Murray, secretary of state for the colonies, established a policy of "civilization" for aboriginal peoples—British and, later, Canadian officials envisioned reservation communities that contained not only houses and barns and gristmills but schools that would offer the training needed for commercial agriculture and other proper pursuits.[3]

As in America, a shared set of beliefs buttressed Canadian Indian education policy. Ethnocentric Christian missionaries as well as federal officials dismissed aboriginal belief systems and practices. They were deemed not only different but backward and an absolute hindrance to the elevation of native peoples, who must be treated, in their present condition, as incompetent and childlike government wards. Yet these peoples were considered inferior culturally, not intellectually. Indian children and their parents were believed to be educable in the ways of Western civilization, and it was thought that this must be accomplished as soon as possible, even if it required coercion. Otherwise, the rapid western expansion of newcomer settlements into aboriginal homelands would doom native communities.[4]

Such enthusiasm for Indian education on both sides of the international border produced a rapidly expanding network of schools for children of all ages. Prior to the 1870s in the United States, Uncle Sam had delegated this responsibility mainly to Christian churches; then, during the closing decades of the nineteenth century, the federal government appropriated sufficient funds to establish its own school system. Washington built and operated two types of facilities. Much like the small primary schools attended by the youngsters of American citizens, reservation day schools introduced Indian boys and girls to basic academic subjects as well as U.S. history, values, and institutions. The Indian Office also hoped that the information conveyed by teachers in day schools would impact students' parents. Later, when Indian mothers and fathers were seen as conservative deterrents to their children's education, Washington created boarding schools both on and off the reservations, to have more control over the upbringing of Indian boys and girls and to weaken that of parents. Attendance data reveals the federal government's commitment to this educational program plus the response of reservation families. Besides the increase in Indian education appropriations between 1870 and 1893, 20,522 native students attended classes by century's close, at twenty-five off-reservation boarding schools, eighty-one reservation boarding schools, and 147 reservation day schools.[5]

Meanwhile, the Canadian government, equally committed to aboriginal schooling, created its own extensive educational system. It, too, emphasized both day and residential school experiences, although Ottawa relied much more on Christian denominations to staff and administer these government-sponsored facilities. Reservation day schools, by far the most numerous, lost favor throughout the last half of the 1800s, because federal officials believed that students' association with their parents at the end of each school day and during the summers undermined the assimilation process. Boarding schools promised to break the hold of dead-end, traditional ways and to equip boys and girls better for sedentary farm life on individual plots of land. By 1893, there were seventy-eight Indian day schools in Ontario—more than double the number from 1869. They enrolled 2,310 children. The boarding/industrial schools had also grown, from one to four.[6]

Figures for Canada and the United States document the governments' desire to school native children as a means of speeding up the "civilization" and assimilation process. Great Lakes aboriginal leaders and parents, aware that they must make economic adjustments in order to survive on their reservations, likewise appreciated the importance of learning from the newcomers. Just as with Ottawa's and Washington's plan to transform native economies, considerable cooperation occurred between reservation families and federal officials, but there was also sizable resistance when parents learned what was happening in the day and boarding schools. Indian education—a battle for the minds of aboriginal young people—thus became part of an ongoing, high-stakes struggle of give and take between native peoples and newcomers, the struggle over the future of reservation life.

CONTROL OF SCHOOLS

Critical issues, such as control and funding, had to be resolved if the schools were to function effectively. Many were established by Christian missionaries, who initially dominated Indian education. Following Canadian Confederation, the federal government decided to work through existing Anglican, Methodist, Presbyterian, and Roman Catholic schools and churches. In part, this was because their workers exercised much local influence. The powerful Anglicans, for example, maintained eight schools on the Six Nations Reserve by the mid-1800s and, at times, even helped shape Iroquois council decisions. The struggle among churches to control certain reserves and their educational subsidies flowing from Ottawa indicates that much was at stake educationally and in other realms. This "sharp, bitter struggle," writes J. R. Miller, "generated reams of correspondence, not to mention oceans of gall, among both representatives of the churches and agents of the government." He continued, "For those not satisfied with the catcalling between Catholics and non-Catholics, there were sometimes the howls of those who opposed any federal funding of church agencies."[7]

Missionary teachers determined to transplant new value systems also exercised much influence on Great Lakes reservations within the United States. The federal government, as in Canada, contracted with the churches to carry part of the burden of educating Indians. Help consisted of monies to build schools, land grants for each structure, and per capita subsidies for pupils. These facilities continued to supplement the growing number of federal day and boarding schools until the 1890s, when Congress terminated church contracts.[8]

As important as missionary teachers were, both federal governments retained the overall legal responsibility for civilizing and assimilating aboriginal children and their families. The policies of Ottawa and Washington, their school subsidies, their field supervisors, and, in many cases, their own classroom employees became vital to the formal instruction of reservation young people. In Canada, the Indian Department's control of aboriginal funds meant that in order to pay a teacher or upgrade schoolhouse facilities, each band council must formally request to use its own money. If this request were authorized at the highest level by an order in council, Indian authorities still had to document each penny spent, according to strict, federal accounting practices. When educational responsibilities in the field were delegated to religious organizations, Ottawa still demanded quarterly reports on official forms showing school attendance and documenting student progress.[9]

Uncle Sam's educational role was roughly similar. If a native nation like the Menominee wished to appropriate part of its trust fund to clothe youngsters and support their schools, the Indian Office expended these monies as requested. Washington also paid per capita subsidies for aboriginal pupils attending Wisconsin schools operated by religious groups. In New York, where the state took a great deal of responsibility for Indian education, seven of its superintendents of public instruction oversaw thirty-one Iroquois schools by the late 1870s. Included was a boarding facility, the Thomas Orphan Asylum, established in 1855 on the Cattaraugus Reservation.[10]

Shared responsibility for native education eventually became the norm in both Canada and the United States. Initially, their governments jockeyed for power with religious organizations. The compromises they hammered out benefited both parties. Federal officials saved substantial funds by allowing the churches to operate many schools; in turn, the missionary work of the churches was subsidized and recognized as an important facet of the Indian "civilization" process.

Reservation leaders and families, it must be remembered, also played an important role in education funding and policy making. Involvement was based on a general recognition that the white man's schools would teach native communities important and practical skills needed to survive economically, culturally, and politically. Indians certainly were not interested, writes historian John Milloy, "in a curriculum designed to assimilate their children." Letters from concerned parents and Indian councils about education issues thus poured into local agents' offices and included requests for government support, sometimes for schools already operating and paid for by Indian reserves. The Oneida of the Thames, well aware that their children needed to learn the three R's, built three schools by the early 1880s and paid the teachers' salaries for years before asking Ottawa for assistance. The Oneida, Walpole Island, and the Ojibwa and Muncey of the Thames also worked in conjunction with the Church of England to fund day schools. At Bay Mills in northern Michigan, where parents had earlier refused to send their children to school, they paid a teacher's salary in the early 1880s and promised to send between twenty-five and thirty students to the school if the Indian Office would resume its aid. Conversely, aboriginal leaders not pleased with their children's schooling demanded changes or cut their subsidies from trust funds. This was the case in the mid-1800s, when New Credit, Ojibwa and Muncey of the Thames, Sarnia, and Walpole Island wrote to terminate their support of industrial schools.[11]

The Six Nations on the Grand River showed more initiative and control than any other Great Lakes reserve. Chiefs started committing monies to education in 1877, and the Iroquois school board soon began a building campaign and fashioned instructional policies. Community leaders identified sites for schoolhouses, drafted building plans, evaluated tenders (bids), and submitted annual reports to the Six Nations council. Within a decade, students were attending thirteen reserve schools.[12]

DAY SCHOOLS

Scholars have devoted much attention to boarding schools and their impact on aboriginal children as well as entire reservation populations.[13] Yet the role of day schools should not be neglected; many more Indian boys and girls attended these widespread institutions than residential ones. Also, parents as well as chiefs and councils exercised far greater influence over local day schools.

By the mid-1890s, Great Lakes native children attended seventy-seven reserve day schools within Ontario. This far-flung network, like the aboriginal population, was concentrated in the warmer southern regions, where farming and permanent villages were common. Six Nations of the Grand River supported ten such schools, while aboriginal communities along Lake Superior's north shore and their Indian agent struggled to maintain one viable school per reserve. Throughout the province, schoolhouse numbers had grown considerably over time as Indian, federal government, and church policy makers focused on the importance of education for reservation youngsters. Support for the building program also came from Indian fathers and mothers who, like parents everywhere, wanted their children to be able to walk to a nearby school.[14]

Each day school's agenda reflected the goals of its founders and directors. The Canadian government's Indian School Fund paid portions of teachers' salaries, but it was the Anglican, Methodist, and Catholic churches—drawn by the opportunities for "civilizing" and Christianizing native pupils—that built many of the schoolhouses and staffed their classrooms. Growing numbers of schools greatly increased these costs. The Methodist Church of Canada had a network of fifteen Ontario Indian schools by 1890, for which it paid half of the teachers' salaries as well as all expenses for furniture and building repairs. When the church sought to relinquish the responsibility, Ottawa calculated that the day schools' total annual cost was $4,550.[15]

A third player in the drama of the day school was the local Indian community. Its funds, authorized by council, also helped to cover school expenses, such as building construction and maintenance plus teachers' salaries. At Six Nations, a board of trustees oversaw the nine schools funded by the New England Company, a nondenominational, Protestant missionary organization. The board's composition reflected local constituencies and included three members appointed by the chiefs, the local Indian agent, the resident Anglican clergyman, and the principal of the Mohawk Institute. Aboriginal parents formed the most powerful reserve group; they decided whether or not their children would even attend a neighborhood day school.[16]

South of the international border, day schools also dominated the educational program for Great Lakes Indian youngsters. Twenty-five such facilities stood on the New York Iroquois reservations in the mid-1880s, and another ten operated in Michigan. Children from each of the major Lake Superior Ojibwa communities in northern Wisconsin attended local day schools, as did boys and girls on the Oneida, Stockbridge and Munsee, and Menominee reservations. Fond du Lac, Grand Portage, Bois Forte, and Vermilion in northeastern Minnesota had similar schools.[17]

In October 1890, Ontario's Thessalon Reserve asked that a teacher be assigned to its school. Indians wanted a mixed-blood or native instructor, and because it was a Catholic community, Ottawa authorized the priest at Wikwemikong, Father Hebert, to make the appointment. In early November, Agent J. C. Phipps, upon learning that the schoolhouse was not complete, urged Thessalon to finish the floors, install glass windows and a stove, provide a supply of cordwood, and build the school desks as well as a partition for the teacher's living quarters on the upper floor. Meanwhile, the appointed teacher, Victoria Wakigigig, had boarded a steamer and was en route to Thessalon. A month later, eleven boys and thirteen girls attended classes and used books sent by the Indian Department. But the teacher still did not have slates, copybooks, ink pens, pen holders, and ink pellets. Workers also lacked the five hundred feet of lumber to build seats and desks for the students and partition off the teacher's second-floor apartment. It was a bumpy start, but Thessalon families finally had their own school.[18]

Finding a teacher was not always accomplished as promptly and smoothly as at Thessalon; several parties had to be pleased with each appointment, including the instructor. At nonsectarian day schools in Ontario, the Indian Department appointed teachers after reviewing certificates of moral character and academic competencies and seeking input from aboriginal community leaders. The latter seemed appropriate since Indian funds helped to support these institutions. Sometimes the federal government delegated appointive powers to local authorities. Thus, in 1875, the New Credit council selected for each of its schools three-member boards of trustees with the authority to appoint teachers. In the 1880s and 1890s, Ottawa allowed South Hastings County officials to select teachers for the four Tyendinaga schools.[19] If, however, a church had founded a school and initially staffed it, the department's policy was to share the cost of teachers' salaries while permitting church officials to make staff decisions. These teachers reported to their missionary societies instead of the Indian agents, which left the agents uninformed about school matters.[20]

Because these were Indian schools—partially funded, built, and attended by reservation people—their wishes about teachers carried weight. Over the years, a mixture of Indians and non-Indians staffed most day schools, with a few exceptions. Six Nations, Walpole Island, and Nawash (Cape Croker) usually hired natives from their own communities. Along the remote shores of Lake Superior, mixed bloods often conducted classes.[21] Whatever the staff choice, one theme dominated: community control. The preferences could be as diverse as the many moods on the Great Lakes. Thus, in 1878, the majority of West Bay parents on Manitoulin Island demanded a white teacher and "would not send their children to school to be taught by an Indian teacher." A few years later, other Manitoulin families at Sheshegwaning refused to accept a teacher appointed by the Indian Department, and the school closed by default. When the standoff continued into the next school year, the local agent unfairly blamed the parents for not caring about their children's education.[22]

Not all teacher troubles were between natives and the Indian Department. Far to the east, on the Bay of Quinté, the prospect of hiring a woman teacher from their own reserve precipitated a nasty, internal struggle. Each school district annually elected a two-person school board of trustees that, with the local missionary, managed school matters. Trustees appointed teachers subject to Indian Department approval and the Tyendinaga council's requisition for a teacher's salary. That the trustees possessed fundamental authority became clear in 1860 when a young teacher from the reserve, Catherine Loft, applied for a job. The trustees opposed her even though the missionary member of the trustees favored Loft, as did the local agent and the superintendent general of Indian affairs. The local county board of public instruction even certified Loft as a teacher, but the two elected Indian trustees were adamant. When the agent appealed to the Tyendinaga council, it, too, opposed Loft, claiming that controlling the boys in schools was a man's job and that Loft did not have a good command of the English language. Thus Loft's candidacy failed.[23]

The imbroglio was not without meaning. Education was clearly an important matter, and the Tyendinaga residents demanded an annual election of school officials. The Indian Department might dispute the trustees' decision on Loft, but their jurisdictional authority, confirmed by council, was ultimately respected. The young teacher, though unsuccessful in this endeavor, nevertheless represented how much a determined Indian scholar might achieve. Obtaining a school certificate "is highly creditable to her," Agent W. R. Bartlett wrote to the Tyendinaga council, adding, "and it ought to be gratifying to you to find one of your own band thus taking advantage of the means of education provided by the Mohawks and by perseverance and study to qualify herself for a school teacher."[24]

Rather than thwarting the desires of a teacher applicant, as at Tyendinaga, a much more common experience was a community's inability to attract and keep a good teacher, who must deal with the challenges of isolation, a low or modest salary, and culture shock. At remote Grand Portage, Minnesota, the teacher in 1888 was the only federal employee on the reservation. Such circumstances resulted in empty schoolhouses and a high turnover of instructors. C. Skene, the visiting superintendent for the Parry Sound area, lamented:

> Although there are four good school houses on the reserves and the teachers are each paid $250 a year, I regret to say that several of the schools were closed for a great part of the year for want of teachers. The Indians are very anxious to have their children educated, and pay the teachers as liberally as they can afford, yet I find it impossible to obtain teachers. I have taken every means possible, by advertising and writing to obtain teachers, yet I am disappointed.

Such frustration, argues Peter Schmalz in his history of southern Ontario Ojibwa, prompted the hiring of Indian teachers instead of whites ("qualified or not").[25]

The demand for credentialed teachers and evaluation of their classroom performance increased over the years, even for the more isolated northern schools, and officials in both Washington and Ottawa came to appreciate the importance of adequate salaries. By the 1890s, from Tyendinaga in the east to Fort William and Grand Portage in the west, school inspectors filed detailed reports about teachers, their students' courses of study and academic progress, and the adequacy of school buildings. Evaluations were not always positive, and officials regularly replaced teachers for incompetence. The Walpole Island situation was particularly promising by century's close. Lambton County school inspectors liked what they observed each month about the three native teachers, and the children's parents seemed pleased as well with the staff and the pupils' educational progress. The well-supplied schoolhouses were kept "clean, warm, and comfortable."[26]

These buildings, as well as curriculum, student achievements, and parental involvement, were important parts of reservation day school history across the Great Lakes. School buildings, such as the new one at New Credit Reserve in 1892, stimulated education and reflected local values. Built in the center of the reserve, the New Credit schoolhouse was "a fine red brick building, with white brick facings" and, according to the Indian Department, was as well-equipped inside as any "first-class country school-house." Community members planted the grounds with ornamental trees. They also paid for the teacher, caretaker, and all school supplies. School physical improvements at New Credit immediately boosted the enrollment from thirty-nine to fifty-two and the average daily attendance from 13.5 to 36. The 1869 Gradual Enfranchisement Act had granted Canadian chiefs and councils the right to construct and maintain such schoolhouses and other public buildings, subject to the federal government's approval. Thus, when a new school seemed needed on Walpole Island in the late 1880s, the Ojibwa chief and council became a building committee and, with the local agent, located a site and solicited bids from two construction firms. It was also common for reserves to share building costs with the Indian Department; parents provided the lumber and labor, while Ottawa furnished nails, boards, shingles, window sashes, glass, and locks. Like their Canadian counterparts, the buildings of the U.S. Indian day schools were fundamental to the educational process. Among the Lake Superior Ojibwa, each of their frame buildings was valued at between seven hundred and eight hundred dollars and had room for about thirty-five students. A wood-burning stove provided heat, though there was no indoor plumbing. Teachers' quarters were either attached to the school or found nearby.[27]

Inside reservation day schools, the course of study was designed to give native children a practical education and to prepare them for citizenship as envisioned by Canadian enfranchisement legislation and the Dawes Severalty Act. In 1889, besides the course of study found in most country schools (reading, writing, spelling, English grammar and composition, arithmetic, and geography), Commissioner Morgan encouraged Indian schools across the country to teach patriotism. Both U.S. and Canadian policy makers also discouraged the use of aboriginal languages in day schools.[28]

As important as teachers, buildings, and curriculums were, schools needed large numbers of native boys and girls in order to meet the educational goals of aboriginal and federal government policy makers. Yet one of the day schools' most distinguishing characteristics in the late 1800s was low attendance rates. Reservation education plans, like federal economic policies, suffered from realities when put to the test.

Records kept by teachers revealed their limited impact on native youngsters whose parents were unwilling to give up seasonal mobility and send

Indian day school near Hayward, Wisconsin, ca. 1880. *(Courtesy Wisconsin Historical Society, image 55936.)*

their children to classes. The numbers of school-age children on the reservations compared to those enrolled in 1895, shown in table 4, were particularly revealing. Especially low enrollments at the northern Minnesota reserves (the last three listed in table 4) suggested that parents and children still spent much of the year hunting, fishing, and gathering off their reserves. Ontario figures during the last half of the century also showed limitations for day schools. On the Six Nations Reserve, created in the late 1700s, its five

TABLE 4. Number of School-Age Children on Reservations Compared to Number Enrolled, 1895

Reservation	School-Age Children	Enrollment
Red Cliff	170	155
Lac Court Oreilles	275	179
Bad River	140	117
Fond du Lac	235	46
Grand Portage	94	20
Vermilion Lake	203	60

Source: Agent W. A. Mercer to CIA Daniel M. Browning, April 1, 1895, NARA, GLR (Chicago), OIA, La Pointe Agency, LS; Agent M. A. Leahy top CIA Thomas J. Morgan, August 29, 1892, AR, CIA, 18792, 518.

schools enrolled only 150 out of 400 eligible children in 1858, and 1876 data from all Indian schools in the province showed 1,669 enrolled out of 2,781.[29]

Likewise enlightening were the low average daily attendance numbers compared to student enrollments. As table 5 shows, reports over time from representative Ontario reserves showed increasing enrollments but continually troublesome absentee rates. Of the 1,669 enrolled Ontario Indian students, only 773 attended regularly in 1876.[30]

School participation on American Great Lakes reserves was also disappointing according to several snapshot views. An 1884 study of New York documented that 514 native students out of an estimated youth population of 1,034 showed up for classes consistently. Two years later, investigator Alice Fletcher noted that the average daily attendance of the estimated one thousand Indian boys and girls of Michigan was 127. Fletcher found the same disappointing situation on Wisconsin and Minnesota reservations that same year.[31]

Indian children avoided day schools for a variety of reasons. Some who still could not speak English as late as the 1890s must have been put off by the prospect of classroom recitations. Parents did not force the hesitant and were accused by federal officials of not supporting their educational efforts and of generally being too lax in disciplining children. Still, if the teacher created a friendly and accepting classroom, native children would come. At Walpole Island in the 1870s, one of the schools taught by a local teacher had good attendance, while another with a white teacher languished. When an

TABLE 5. School Enrollment and Attendance on Ontario Reserves for 1880, 1883, and 1895

Reserve	Year	Enrollment	Average Daily Attendance	Percentage
Six Nations	1880	336	130	38.7
	1895	398	198	49.7
Walpole Island	1880	97	47	50.5
	1895	121	61	50.4
Mohawk of Gibson	1883	15	8	53.3
	1895	26	13	50
West Bay	1883	22	8	36.4
	1895	41	14	34.1
White Fish River	—	—	—	
	1895	14	9	64.3
Garden River	1880	23	14	60.9
	1895	69	38	55.1
Red Rock/Helen Island	—	—	—	
	1895	24	13	54.2

Source: AR, DIA, 1880, 1883, 1895.

aboriginal instructor took over the latter, attendance improved considerably. Parental dependence on their children for economic help remained the most serious detriment to their formal education. So widespread were these absences that teachers periodically had to close the schools.[32]

As was so often the case in Great Lakes native history, the newcomers and their policy makers had to adjust to these realities. Some Indian agents and teachers modified the vacation schedule to better coincide with seasonal harvest times. Other officials argued in favor of boarding schools, which would insure student attendance and quarantine them from "savage" family influences. Additional strategies included the inducements of hot lunches for the children and the advocacy of compulsory attendance. An 1894 amendment to the Canadian Indian Act permitted the federal government to require school attendance. South of the international border, in 1891, Congress ordered that every school-age child who was in good health and a member of an Indian group under the special protection of the U.S. government must go to school. Teachers in the day schools could now call on Indian police to track down truants.[33]

For aboriginal children who attended regularly or even sporadically, reservation day schools unquestionably impacted their communities. Inspirational teachers contributed a great deal. In the early 1890s, Miss Hattie Taylor at the Rama schoolhouse won praise for motivating pupils to take an interest in their work, while at Sarnia, Miss Walsh affected "marvelous" changes in attendance and filled her building each day. Rice Lake children and their parents reportedly loved and respected the local teacher, Miss Malard. Students with a thirst for formal education also helped to make the day schools a limited success. A young Moraviantown man with such a desire obtained a book, learned how to read in the evenings by firelight after long days as a lumberjack, and then enrolled at the local day school. In 1891, a graduate of the Alnwick Reserve's Alderville School was the first to pass the high school entrance examination. Other determined youngsters included a number from the Mohawk Bay of Quinté (Tyendinaga) Reservation who attended high school in Deseronto.[34]

Day school attendance figures showed that boys usually outnumbered the girls by as much as a third, perhaps because parents felt that men, rather than women, would be the ones who mainly interacted with white neighbors and thus needed the skills that schools offered. The aggregate report for the ten Six Nations schools in 1880, for example, showed 190 males enrolled and 145 females.[35] The course of study for both sexes was similar. (It was the boarding schools that emphasized gender separation—in curriculum as well as living quarters, the dining hall, and even the playgrounds.) Exceptions would be Catholic day schools, such as those at Wikwemikong and Fort William, which maintained separated facilities for boys and girls.

The parents of the children in day schools played a much bigger role in their education than is generally portrayed. Certainly they were not powerless victims, hopelessly standing by while their children were dragged off to school by brutish white civilizers. Many native fathers and mothers supported their local day school with monies and encouragement and vigilant supervision of teachers. Even parents who disliked a teacher or the school exercised considerable influence by withholding financial support, lobbying their council, or refusing to send their youngsters off to classes. One family attitude, often unreported, was parental hostility caused by teachers' offensive disrespect for aboriginal students, families, and cultures. Historian Carol Devens's *Countering Colonization* helps readers to grasp the alienation some native women felt toward the schools and Christian churches. Both institutions threatened the mothers' management of their daughters' education. Teachers and missionaries also seemed bent on turning boys and girls against their own aboriginal lifestyles. For these parents, the classroom became a battleground.[36]

Criticism of Indian mothers and fathers as well as efforts to change their points of view did not come just from Ottawa and Washington. When community members at Six Nations Reserve opposed the schools, individual members of the school board encouraged them to meet with the board and discuss grievances. By the mid-1890s, each teacher was required to visit the homes of children who did not attend regularly. Meanwhile, to the west, on the Moravians of the Thames Reservation, the council kept watch on school absentees and established a fine of five cents per day for parents whose children missed classes "without good cause."[37]

This sort of pressure could only come from councils favoring day schools and supported by many reserve families. In the mid-1800s, Six Nations chiefs encouraged the establishment of day schools by various missionary groups but insisted they be built only where families wanted them. Opposition of the longhouse people was respected. Thus the impressive complex of day schools grew on the reserve, even though proeducation parents still took their children out of classes at planting and harvesting time.[38] Likewise, the Walpole Island council and parents worked cooperatively with the Indian Department to expand its school system. In July 1889, the council and Agent McKelvey agreed that children sorely needed a third school. The two existing buildings were filled to capacity with eighty boys and girls, thereby preventing attendance of additional youngsters (there were 172 persons of school age in the agency). Furthermore, many potential students lived too far away from the current structures. The solution seemed to be a new facility close to the neglected children. The Indian Department authorized McKelvey to ask the chiefs to call a general council, and at the meeting on July 31, those attending talked over matters fully and voted unanimously in favor of establishing another school. Participants also gave the chief and council authority to select a site, agree on a design, and seek bids from contractors. McKelvey sought Ottawa's approval for all these steps, since reservation land and the expenditure of Indian monies were involved. The process moved along quickly, and by late November, the school was built and the keys were obtained from the contractor; a teacher was approved in December. The agent reported in March 1890 that "nearly every seat is occupied" and that nearly half the young scholars were attending school for the first time. The new building had "a larger attendance of scholars . . . than at either of the others." Clearly, support for Walpole's day schools was strong, from chief and council, parents, the Indian Department, and attending boys and girls.[39]

Involvement with day schools also subjected families, via their school-age children, to intensive acculturation. By century's end, federal officials advocated regular classroom attendance for all aboriginal youngsters. No longer could mothers and fathers wander at will. New jobs, permanent homes, and children in school tied them to the reservation and drove another wedge between them and the old woodland ways. On Walpole Island and other Great Lakes reserves, a workable, educational partnership thus developed between community members who supported day schools and newcomers who promoted Indian "civilization."

Still, there was discontent about the rate of "progress" and the shortcomings of day schools. In 1887, A. Sutherland, general secretary of the Missionary Department of the Methodist Church, pointed out a number of them. Not surprisingly, they included irregular student attendance, parental apathy regarding their children's education, difficulty obtaining qualified teachers, the lack of school inspectors and examinations, and negative reserve influences, such as avoidance of the English language. Dislike of reservation influences surrounding students of day schools was also voiced by Secretary of the Interior Schurz: "With the exception of a few hours spent in school, the children remained exposed to the influence of their more or less savage home surroundings, and the indulgence of their parents greatly interfered with the regularity of their attendance and with the necessary discipline." Canada and the United States took steps to get at the hindrances Sutherland identified. By century's end, federal officials, in conjunction with native leaders, worked hard to curtail truancy, and inspectors regularly visited day schools. Their reports detailed the strengths and weaknesses of school buildings, instructional materials, local teachers, and student learning. Yet the Indian day school was "under the best of circumstances, attended with unsatisfactory results," lamented the Canadian Indian Department. Thus persuaded, large numbers of Canadian and American educators and policy makers turned to boarding schools as a way to get aboriginal children away from the "savage home surroundings" identified by Schurz and Sutherland.[40]

BOARDING SCHOOLS

With good reason, scholars have devoted much attention to the network of Indian boarding schools that developed during the last half of the nineteenth century and continued into the twentieth.[41] They had an enormous impact on generations of native students and their home communities, including the Great Lakes region.

In 1897, the deputy superintendent general of Indian affairs clearly summarized Canada's goals for its native boarding schools. Separation from "home influences" would permit a quicker and more thorough "inculcation of the habits, customs and modes of thought of the white man." At the same time, aboriginal cultures—"all that exists in common between them"—could be washed away. The half-day system and Christian churches that administered the schools were vital elements of the plan to transform aboriginal youngsters. The latter would promote the students' religious conversion, thereby refining and enriching their character, while dedication of half the school day to training in manual skills would allow graduates to take up residence on individual plots of land and earn a living within the mainstream Canadian economy. Indian leaders from southern Ontario initially helped support these institutions with annuity monies, not because they wanted cultural modification or assimilation, but because their people needed schooling.[42]

American reformers embarked on a parallel campaign for boarding schools. In July 1890, exasperated La Pointe agent Matthew A. Leahy informed the commissioner of Indian affairs of his agreement with the Lac Court Oreilles Reservation's request for a boarding school for their children. The most recent census showed that they had 309 school-age boys and girls, yet during the most recent school quarter, only 177 were enrolled, and their average attendance was 106. Leahy argued that boarding schools not only would provide Lac Court Oreilles youngsters with clothing, food, and shelter but would "retain the children within the influence of the teachers." Such views about the benefits of boarding schools had been expressed for years. Ezra Hayt, commissioner of Indian affairs, noted in 1877, "The exposure of children who attend only day-schools to the demoralization and degradation of an Indian home neutralized the efforts of the schoolteacher, especially those efforts which are directed to advancement in morality and civilization." Founded in 1879, Captain Richard Pratt's Carlisle Indian School in Pennsylvania became the model for a national network of government off-reservation facilities, thanks to glowing reports about its successful teaching. Especially promising was Pratt's outing system, which placed advanced students on nearby farms to enhance their manual labor training as well as social skills and proficiency in the English language. In 1884, Secretary of the Interior Henry Teller reflected a widespread belief when he said, "The greatest agency for the civilization of the Indian is the manual-labor school. Indeed, I do not think I shall be far out of the way if I say the only agency for that purpose is the manual-labor school."[43]

Such high hopes led Washington and Ottawa to create a far-flung complex of boarding schools. America alone had twenty-five during the last two decades of the nineteenth century. Canadian natives, who enrolled in only three such government-funded institutions in 1883, attended twenty-two industrial and fifty-three boarding schools by 1907. Many were located within the Great Lakes region. Among the Iroquois on U.S. reservations, the Philadelphia Society of Friends supported a boarding school at the Allegany Reservation that housed forty-five students in 1900, while the Thomas Orphan Asylum, established by the State of New York in 1855 on the Cattaraugus Reservation, enrolled 130 that year. Across Lake Erie, in Michigan, boarding schools operated in the towns of Mt. Pleasant, Baraga, and L'Anse by century's end. Next door, in Wisconsin, the Indian Office funded off-reservation schools at Tomah and Wittenburg plus residential institutions on Menominee, Oneida, and Lac du Flambeau lands. Two additional schools drew support from the Catholic Church: one among the Menominee and another at Odanah on the Bad River Reservation. In remote northeastern Minnesota, a government school at Vermilion Lake housed and taught Ojibwa children from nearby reserves.[44] Residential schools likewise dotted the Ontario countryside at various times during the last half of the 1800s, including Mount Elgin (at Muncytown), the Mohawk Institute (Brantford), Alnwick Industrial School (at Alderville), Wikwemikong Industrial Schools on Manitoulin Island (one for boys and one for girls), Shingwauk Home at Garden River (for boys), the Wawanosh Home (for girls—part of the Shingwauk complex), and the Fort William Orphanage. The extensive records generated by these Canadian and American institu-

Graduates of Mohawk Institute. *(Courtesy Library and Archives Canada, image C-085134.)*

tions have allowed historians to look at both school operations (teachers and staff, buildings, curriculum, student life) and the reactions to them by native students, their parents, and community leaders.

The ambitious plans of boarding schools placed an enormous burden on all involved, including the parents, who must bid adieu to their children, and the youngsters, who adjusted to living away from home in a strange institution. Moreover, boarding schools faced momentous challenges if they would care for and transform aboriginal children. Early in the twentieth century, the Mount Elgin principal wrote:

> We were under no illusion what ever as to the difficulties of the task awaiting us—the business management of a thousand acre farm, the purchase and sale of all the live stock connected therewith, the judi-

cious expenditure of approximately $25,000 per annum in wages, food, clothing, fuel, light and many other things incidental to the life of the school. Add to these the final responsibility for the health, happiness and discipline of at least 120 boys and girls in residence, the selection of suitable officers and teachers, and the blending of all these varied interests into something like a happy and suitable community life, and we have a job quite big enough to tax the energies of any one man.[45]

South of the Lakes, the Bureau of Catholic Missions, under contract with the Indian Office, administered Saint Joseph's Indian Industrial School on the Menominee Reservation starting in 1883. Washington withdrew financial support in the late 1890s, but a few years later, it sanctioned the use of Menominee trust funds to pay school expenses. Like the Mount Elgin principal's responsibilities, those of Saint Joseph's were extensive and outlined in much detail by successive government contracts. To understand the life of aboriginal boys and girls in boarding schools, one must examine each facet of school operations as addressed in these contracts, from the teaching staff and physical plant to curriculum and student experiences.[46]

In his history of Canadian Indian residential schools, J. R. Miller judged that the overall performance of teachers was inadequate, though there were "many gifted and dedicated instructors in various institutions at different times." Government, missionary, and school officials too often hired instructors with not enough professional training. This was excused at times because interviewees had an evangelical zeal. The shallow pool of applicants and their subsequent mediocre performance in the classroom also reflected the boarding schools' shoestring budgets, their inability to pay the staff more than a pittance, and their general unattractiveness as teaching posts. The frequent turnover of disenchanted hires further undermined a staff's success. One beacon in this otherwise gloomy picture was the willingness of Mount Elgin and the Mohawk Institute to hire some aboriginal teachers and staff. Often, they were former students of boarding schools.[47]

The array of employees and their yearly salaries at American boarding schools is suggested by Tomah Indian Industrial School's 1896 report of rates of pay by position:

superintendent	$1,400
farmer	720
disciplinarian and engineer	720

carpenter	720
matron	660
principal teacher	660
teacher	540
teacher	600
laundress	500
cook	500
seamstress	560
clerk	600
assistant seamstress	480
assistant matron	480
night watchman	240
assistant cook	300
assistant cook	300

As in Canada, American teachers and staff received lower salaries than similar employees of public schools. Historian Philip Huckins writes that workers in boarding schools "traveled to remote areas, were cut off from family, had to occupy poor housing, and were often given insufficient rations to eat." Those who labored at Catholic institutions, such as Saint Joseph's, sometimes fared even worse. With the hope of uplifting the "pagan" Menominee and leading them to a better life, sisters and brothers "taught at Saint Joseph's without pay" and "cooked, cleaned and cared for students 24 hours a day for years."[48]

The boarding schools' campuses reflected educational goals of white administrators and policy makers. The outbuildings supported the students' out-of-the-classroom activities and usually included stables and barns for housing livestock and storing tools, agricultural equipment, harvested crops, and a church. Boys and girls spent most of their waking and sleeping hours in a large main building that included dormitories, quarters for "officers," an infirmary, classrooms, playrooms, a kitchen, and a dining hall.[49]

The curricula at boarding schools, like other aspects of aboriginal education and federal policy in general, was designed to transform backward Indians and refused to recognize anything worthwhile in their cultures. Zealous administrators, such as Pratt at Carlisle, went about their tasks with hard-nosed efficiency. A case in point was the processing of new students, which almost immediately traumatized them. School officials cut their hair,

Indian boarding school in Tomah, Wisconsin. *(Courtesy Wisconsin Historical Society, image 38080.)*

washed and dressed them in stiff white man clothes and heavy work shoes, often gave them new "Canadian" or "American" names, and, in all cases, marched the children off to learn the school's militaristic daily routine. Dormitory, classroom, mealtime, and playground life dictated by the bell had begun—and never would be forgotten. Errant boys and girls faced harsh punishment. The general goal of all activities was to teach aboriginal youngsters to live and later work as Canadians or Americans. Children thus celebrated all national and religious holidays, attended regular church services, learned patriotic and folk music, and were encouraged to play the same games that non-Indians enjoyed, from marbles and parlor games to tobogganing, skating, baseball, soccer, cricket, and basketball. The classrooms focused on the same academic subjects as their courterparts in day schools, with even more emphasis on English as the language of instruction. Not surprisingly, the downplaying of native culture and history—anything to which students could relate—increased their sense of alienation and disinterest. The half-day system further undercut academic progress. Children accordingly spent either the morning or the afternoon learning practical skills away from their desk and providing free labor, thereby helping the schools cut costs. The boys' tasks included farming and also trade skills, such as carpentry, harness making and shoemaking, blacksmithing, printing, masonry, and

Girls in the Oneida Indian school laundry room. *(Courtesy Milwaukee Public Museum, image A-621-4C.)*

caring for machinery. The European model of separate spheres for the sexes dictated that female students not only be physically separated from the males but learn homemaking skills. These included cooking, baking, cleaning, washing, ironing, dressmaking, knitting, and simple nursing. Such vocational training, argues J. R. Miller, created a "buckskin ceiling" that produced native students with mediocre academic skills and proficiency in manual labor best suited to serving the needs of well-to-do whites.[50]

The boarding schools' fanatical emphasis on students speaking English deepened the trauma felt by sensitive native boys and girls. In the mid-1880s, J. D. C. Atkins, U.S. commissioner of Indian affairs, wrote that English was "good enough for a white man and a black man [and] ought to be good enough for the red man"; after all, it was "the language of the greatest, most powerful, and enterprising nationalities beneath the sun." The Canadians, of course, concurred. In the 1990s, their Royal Commission on Aboriginal Peoples, after assessing the system of boarding schools, concluded that it had been "balanced on the proposition that the gate to assimilation was unlocked only by the progressive destruction of Aboriginal languages." Both federal governments eventually ordered the suppression of all non-English communication. Too often, the means employed were excessively harsh.

They ranged from denying privileges to cutting off girls' hair and physical punishment. The reward system used by Shingwauk was an exception to such callousness. Each week, the boys and girls received individual allocations of buttons. They had to surrender one whenever a teacher or fellow student overheard the use of Ojibwa, and at the end of the week, those with the most buttons received a prize of nuts. "Not a word of Indian is heard from our Indian boys after six months in the institution," remarked a proud Reverend Wilson.[51]

Overviews of the experiences of Great Lakes Indians in boarding schools must be presented with some hesitation because they were so diverse. Each boarding school had unique characteristics, and these varied over time because of a headmaster's administrative style as well as fluctuating federal and church policies and financial support. Furthermore, the length of stay varied enormously, as did children's ages and reservation affiliation. The situation at Tomah Indian Industrial School in September 1895 is illustrative. The fifty-one female students, whose ages ranged from three to eighteen, represented six reservations, in the following numbers:

Oneida	3
Ojibwa	39
Winnebago	4
Menominee	3
Stockbridge	1
Sac	1

The eighty-one male students were affiliated with seven reservations, in the following numbers:

Oneida	5
Winnebago	13
Ojibwa	59
Stockbridge	1
Menominee	1
Brotherton	1
Sac	1

The scope of the boys' ages was five to eighteen.[52]

Notwithstanding these variations, some generalizations may be offered about boarding/residential schools. The transplantation from tender and caring reservation homes, where parents rarely used physical punishment, to seemingly harsh and inhospitable institutions must have upset children of all ages. How could supervisors ever replace parents? First, there was a painful separation from nurturing parents, which usually began with a lengthy ride by boat, railroad, or horse-drawn conveyance to the boarding school. New arrivals next faced a physical alteration. Educators believed that Indians on the road to "civilization" must look and dress the part by reflecting the dominant society's hair and clothing standards. For this reason, school officials loved before-and-after pictures of this surface transformation. Mainstream Victorian beliefs about proper gender roles also turned the students' world topsy-turvy. The education of girls was deemed especially important; they would become the civilizing agents for future Indian families. Yet whenever possible, the schools kept boys and girls separated—in the dormitories, at mealtimes, on the playground, and during vocational instruction.[53]

Though more vulnerable than reservation parents, boys and girls in boarding schools expressed their views about the authoritarian school routine and, like their parents, should not be viewed as helpless victims. Over the years, student complaints centered on the lack of emotional nurturing, poor food and clothing, and inadequate supervision, which allowed staff and students to inflict physical, sexual, and emotional abuses. Particularly upsetting was the restriction on students' home visits. This was understandable from the perspective of the schools, given the reason for their establishment: to separate youngsters from the ways of their parents and community. The resultant family hardships surfaced regularly when parents and their children petitioned for more time together or when parents withdrew their sons and daughters from the boarding schools. The Reverend Wilson, for example, regularly complained about aboriginal parents "not allowing the children to remain a sufficient time with us." So serious was the problem that, in 1891, Shingwauk eliminated summer and Christmas holidays at home for students. A couple years later, federal legislation required that Canadian Indian children be sent to boarding schools for uninterrupted periods.[54]

Boys and girls thus restricted—and at times unhappy—protested in a variety of ways, ranging from noncooperation in and out of the classroom to stealing food, arson, and running away. Deliberately set fires plagued both Shingwauk and Mount Elgin. Whether simply homesick or rebellious over confinement to the boarding school and living life by the bell, significant numbers of students were expelled, ran away, or failed to finish their course of study. Of the seventy-eight Shingwauk girls enrolled between 1874 and

1882, only twenty-two stayed for either four or five years. The Reverend Wilson did not give up on them or the boys without a battle. In the spring of 1878, when three boys turned up missing, Wilson went after them—all the way to Walpole Island. One of the lads was a favorite preparing to be a teacher. After hiding out in a swamp until he could talk with the boy, Wilson convinced him and the other two to return to Shingwauk. Besides engaging in hot pursuit, school officials and Indian agents also deterred "runners" by assessing parents for the expense of tracking them down and for school property, such as clothing, taken by truant children.[55]

The responses of parents and other community members to boarding schools were mixed (like so many of their relations with nonnative neighbors), ebbing and flowing over time in response to changing reservation circumstances and the policies of particular school administrators. Illustrative of these attitudinal swings is the early history of Mount Elgin. Its founder was an Ojibwa Methodist minister, Peter Jones, who visualized a native-run boarding school that would help students to retain their aboriginal identities while instructing them in skills needed to protect their remaining land base and survive alongside non-Indian newcomers. Jones traveled extensively in Canada and England to raise the necessary funds to start his school on the Ojibwa of the Thames Reserve. Mount Elgin opened in 1849. Circumstances then conspired to shatter Jones's dream. Ill health led to his replacement by a non-Indian minister, and henceforth the Mount Elgin administration and curriculum produced a gradual reduction of Indian support.[56]

The favorable attitudes of many Wisconsin Indians documented an important component of parental feelings about boarding schools. Mary S. St. Martin wrote to the Tomah superintendent in March 1897 that she was coming to visit her two daughters next month. She said she planned to bring a dress for one of them and was glad to learn they enjoyed the skating and sliding. Mary would also bring her youngest child, Nellie, who was three and already wanted to attend Tomah. A couple years earlier, the U.S. Department of the Interior reported that the well-run Tomah school should be expanded; many Indians from the area wished to attend, but there was not enough room.[57] Even more impressive was the Menominee Reservation's support of Saint Joseph's. In the mid-1890s, when Congress cut off support for parochial boarding schools, Menominee families petitioned Washington to allow them to use part of their timber trust fund to finance Saint Joseph's. The reservation's wishes eventually persuaded Washington to approve tribal funding on an annual, contractual basis.[58]

Parents were not always so supportive, and those with complaints used several strategies to get their way. In the early 1860s, the Sarnia and Walpole

St. Joseph's Industrial School, Keshena, Wisconsin. *(Courtesy Marquette University, Sacred Heart Province Franciscan Records.)*

Island reserves sought to discontinue their financial support of the Mount Elgin Industrial School. Its program was not teaching aboriginal youngsters the skills they needed: farming, carpentry, blacksmithing, shoemaking, and other "mechanical occupations." Community leaders preferred instead to use their funds to upgrade local day schools with better teachers and buildings. At times, fathers and mothers from northern reserves objected that their children did not need to learn such trades; they were required at home to hunt and fish and help support their families. Parents lodged additional complaints about their children in boarding schools having to work too hard, about sickness and mortality, and about the poor food.[59] Mrs. Alice Tredo, living in the Duluth area, wrote to the La Pointe agent:

> When I spoke to you about the government schools, you told me that the Lac Du Flambeau School was a very nice school.
> So therefore I took your word and I sent six of my children there, but you never mention to me that the children were starving in that

school. Corn-meal-mush for every meal, a person soon gets tired of. When they never see sugar or butter on there [*sic*] bread. And they only see meat for dinner, and it smells that bad that they can not touch it.

When the children goes to the table they all start to cry, that they are starving.

I suppose when you go to that school, they have every thing fine and nice, because they know just about what time you are to be there.

If they keep on with such board, I will be obliged to send for the children. I will not see my children starve, they are not acostom [*sic*] to going with out butter or sugar on the table....

My oldest boy ran away from there, because he was starving. With nine milking cows, I am sure they could have butter on the table twice a day. They do it in other government schools in the East.... My boy says there is plenty of good things cooked but it goes to the Employes [*sic*], that the poor children never sees any of them....

I suppose he [the superintendent] thinks because the children are Indians that a dry piece of bread is good enough for them, but I will let him know that they have just as fine a mouth as he has. My boy said that they put a pie on the table, and it is not fit for any body to eat.[60]

Parents voiced their displeasure in such formal complaints to Indian agents, school officials, and missionaries. Sometimes, reservation groups signed petitions that were forwarded to administrators and policy makers. Cutting off financial support was an option for the reservations that helped fund boarding schools, such as Sarnia, Walpole Island, and Menominee. Unhappy fathers or mothers might withdraw their youngsters—with or without a school's permission. Indian agents' files contained many reports of these parental "kidnappings" and some parents' threats of legal action unless the schools returned their children. Teachers understandably did not want families to remove boys and girls partway through the academic year, but generally the U.S. and Canadian Indian officials acceded to parental requests. An exception was Washington's "Browning Ruling," which was in force from the mid-1890s to 1903 and was intended to prevent parents from moving their children from one boarding school to another. Local agents and school officials also had the authority to keep children in school against their parents' wishes and even to deny students home visits. As the guardians of Indian children, wrote Commissioner Thomas Jefferson Morgan, the

Girls at Lac du Flambeau School. *(Courtesy Wisconsin Historical Society, image 55938.)*

government was justified in using such power, for "we do not think it desirable to rear another generation of savages."[61]

Although boarding schools provoked mixed responses from reservation families and, later, from white policy makers, these institutions unquestionably shaped the educational history of Great Lakes native peoples. On the positive side, students who spent time at boarding schools usually acquired useful knowledge, ranging from proficiency in the English language and vocational skills to a better understanding of the dominant Canadian and American cultures. Yet as the years passed, the general feeling of most involved, except for diehards like Richard Pratt, was of disappointment with this educational experiment. Boarding school costs seemed too high to Ottawa and Washington, and too many students retained their Indian identities and returned to home communities—went "back to the blanket"—instead of following the assimilation paths envisioned by the Gradual Enfranchisement Act and the Dawes Act. The goal of Pratt and other supporters of boarding schools "was never attained," writes Francis Paul Prucha, who explains:

> The system on which he had placed his hope was rejected. His basic assumption that it was possible to eradicate completely the culture of the Indians and assimilate them as European immigrants were assimilated into American society was a questionable one and could not have been accomplished without great human cost. His importance lies not in promoting this impossible dream, but in his part in awakening public opinion to the capabilities of the Indians and in mobilizing forces to promote their education.[62]

Canadian historian J. R. Miller attributed the shortcomings of residential schools to "underfunding and excessive reliance on missionary staffs." The results were "a failure to provide rudimentary academic instruction effectively and problems such as excessive workloads for students, poor diet, and inadequate care by overworked staff. Physical punishment was common in most schools, and in some both sexual and physical abuse were frequent."[63]

Without question, Great Lakes aboriginal communities were affected by the experiences of some members who returned from boarding schools with helpful insights and skills. Alumni also brought back troubles. They carried an inner tension that plagued some for the rest of their lives and impacted the lives of their children and grandchildren. With feet in both worlds, yet fully accepted by neither, many former students felt trapped in limbo. Some never got loose and, writes James Wilson, "sank into apathy, alcoholism, and despair, helping to create a cycle of abuse, dependency, and self-destructive behavior that still haunts Native American communities today." Another disappointment for Great Lakes natives, Robert Cleland notes, was that many boarding schools, such as Mount Pleasant, prepared them "not for assimilation into middle-class America, but as laborers in American fields and factories," ready only "to enter American society on the ground floor, as agrarian laborers and domestics."[64]

The legacy of boarding schools in Canada was mixed and equally dark. "Certainly there were hundreds of children who survived and scores who benefited from the education they received," concluded the Royal Commission on Aboriginal Peoples. The commission went on to explain:

> There were teachers and administrators who gave years of their lives to what they believed was a noble experiment. But the incredible damage—loss of life, denigration of culture, destruction of self-respect and self-esteem, rupture of families, impact of these traumas on succeeding generations, and the enormity of the cultural triumphalism that lay behind the enterprise—will deeply disturb anyone who allows this story to seep into their consciousness.[65]

CONCLUSION

The obligation felt by Ottawa, Washington, and many Christian evangelists to "civilize" and assimilate Indian boys and girls produced far-flung networks of schools whose influence on reservation peoples was momentous. Also striking, beneath the surface, were the similarities of these educational programs: the use of day and boarding schools, partnering with religious organizations, curricula, problems experienced with native students and their parents, and adjustments to such field realities as low enrollments and truancy. By the 1890s, Uncle Sam's infatuation with day and boarding schools had lessened, and a new hope emerged that by enrolling reservation youngsters in nearby public schools, the exposure to mainstream culture would be more effective in "civilizing" them than either of the Indian-only schools. Ottawa held on longer to the option of boarding schools and continued to contract with religious groups to administer the institutions long after the United States abandoned such partnerships. Yet it was the similarity between white American and Canadian policy makers that made the Great Lakes education story distinctive. They shared a common belief that formal schooling of Indian youth was a powerful integration tool—indeed, a universal panacea for all kinds of social and economic problems on the reservation.

A focus by writers on the harmfulness of boarding schools plus absenteeism in the day schools has obscured much of the positive Indian response to both types of schools. Many families and community leaders, north and south of the international border, believed in the importance of some formal education for their youngsters, though their agenda was not always the same as the white newcomers. Indians pressured or at least allowed the federal governments to establish schools in their midst—twenty-five among the New York Iroquois alone in the mid-1880s. Natives often helped finance construction and then maintained the structures. A school board at Six Nations on the Grand River set educational policy. Some schools had aboriginal teachers. Over the years, Indian parents sent thousands of their children to day schools as well as boarding schools. As in any community, not everyone supported the local schools, and ideas changed over time as well; families became disenchanted with schools or came to the realization that formal education was necessary. Many parents, especially up north, regularly took children out of class so they could help with off-reservation hunting, trapping, fishing, and gathering. Whether fathers and mothers supported or resisted the day and boarding schools, they exercised far more control over the influential educational process than heretofore given credit. The same may be said of the children, whose resistance to the procedures of boarding schools at times bedeviled administrators and who even terminated operations by burning buildings. True, boarding schools crippled some children emotionally—making them unable to function well in either the Indian and white worlds—but the continuing support of such boarding schools as Saint Joseph's and the desire of so many Wisconsin Indian parents to get their children enrolled at Tomah, for example, cast a more positive light on relationships between Indians and boarding schools.

The overall plan of policy makers, Indian agents, missionaries, and schoolteachers to transform Great Lakes natives through their children did not succeed any more than had earlier programs to transform aboriginal economies. The fault lay once again in unrealistic and ethnocentric goals; the unwillingness of federal governments, despite their sense of urgency, to commit enough funds for a long enough period; and the unanticipated unwillingness of Indian families and community leaders to be pushed around like pawns on a chessboard. Instead, the Indians supported those schools and school activities that they believed benefited students and the reserves. School programs that did not were ignored, just like federal government requests that all reservation residents become commercial farmers. Some families tried formal education, and some did not. Nearly all kept their options open and refused to accept totally any culturally transforming program coming out of Washington or Ottawa. Though hard pressed and in need of new skills and new approaches as they faced a challenging future, Great Lakes Indians continued to keep a hand on the tiller and direct, as best they could, the course of their lives.

Educational and economic programs were not the only ones to blow across the bow, disturbing and challenging native communities. The exhortations of Christian evangelists stirred up menacing waves, as they had been doing for over two hundred years on the Great Lakes. Their hope was to save the Indian souls and ready them for assimilation and citizenship within Canadian and American societies. Like the soap and education to which Mark Twain referred, "salvation" had the potential to be poisonous.

{ 5 }

Traditional Spirituality versus Christianity

Finding a Balance

"*Brother, the Great Spirit has made us all;* but he has made a great difference between his white and red children"—so Seneca chief Red Jacket once informed a visiting missionary to New York's Buffalo Creek Reservation. Red Jacket continued: "Why may we not conclude that he has given us a different religion according to our understanding; . . . Brother, we do not wish to destroy your religion, or take it from you; we only want to enjoy our own."[1] Christians nevertheless continued proselytizing across the North American frontier. For four centuries, they helped shape relations between Indians and non-Indians. Missionaries mattered. They dwelt among aboriginal peoples, studied their languages, and spread the Gospel—albeit with limited success. Protestant and Catholic evangelists taught thousands of native children in rustic schoolhouses as part of a "civilization" program endorsed by the Canadian and American governments.

Not surprisingly, reservation families and community leaders responded to these profound religious challenges with the same discernment and remarkable creativity they showed in secular areas. The goal, as always, was to defend their cultural traditions and independence. To do so, natives sought a workable balance between the new and the old, between accommodation to changing circumstances—such as the preachings of evangelistic Catholics and Protestants—and protection of their peoples' resources and traditions. Chiefs and counselors realized quickly, for example, that missionaries brought with them considerable power, ranging from spiritual influence to political, which could help safeguard the reservations. Native responses to preachers of the Gospel were usually negotiated, varied from community to community, and defied easy generalization, much like their reactions to federal economic and educational initiatives. Two things were certain: Great Lakes Indians continued to shape their own history and that of the region, and the international border made very little difference in native responses to the Christian missionaries.

NATIVE SPIRITUALITY

"If you pull on the thread of 'Native American religion,'" writes historian Joel W. Martin, "you end up pulling yourself into the study of Native American culture, art, history, economics, music, dance, dress, politics, and almost everything else.... One thing always leads to another when land, religion, and life 'are one.'" Whether practiced among southwestern Hopi or Great Lakes Ojibwa and Iroquois, aboriginal spirituality was an integral part of everyday life and guided all aspects of behavior, from village organization to marriage and burial customs. Belief that their homeland was a sacred gift from the Creator required Indians—if they would prosper—to be respectful stewards of the waters and woods. In turn, they would grant power and wisdom about the living world.[2]

Anthropologist Charles Cleland reminds us that Great Lakes Indians did not believe their living world was governed by "physical laws and predictable relationships." Rather, for these hunter-gatherers and farmers, the earth was a place of great support and guidance, but it was also capricious, mysterious, and, at times, frightening. Hard work and well-honed skills did not insure survival, for aboriginal peoples were not the only inhabitants of their natural world. Neighbors included the spirits of deceased family members; spirits associated with nearby plants, animals, waters, and fish; and the more distant spirits of the high-flying eagle, sun, and moon. The Indians' symbiotic relationship with their spirit-filled surroundings shaped their concepts of time and space. The Mississaugas of the Credit River, for example, viewed time as a seasonal cycle. They gave calendar months and even places names that reflected recurring activities, such as *seegwum* (the spring season of the rising sap) or *machickning* (a fishing place). Another example of homeland bonding was respectful treatment of spirit-filled plants, animals, rivers, and lakes. Great Lakes Indians especially venerated bears, who were skillful hunters and could "turn the tables" on humans and make them the prey. Feared, admired, intelligent, and the possessors of several human qualities, bears had great spiritual powers in the eyes of native peoples. Ojibwa connectedness to their environment was particularly close; they believed that bears and other animals often changed themselves into humans.[3]

Aboriginal author Basil Johnston affirms that Christian missionaries and other Euro-Canadians and Euro-Americans misunderstood the spirituality of Ojibwa people. Newcomers "took it for granted that aboriginal people, being of simple heart and mind, believed in the presence of little spirits in rocks, trees, groves, and waterfalls, much as the primitive peoples of Europe believed in goblins, trolls, and leprechauns." The Ojibwa word *manitou* meant much more than spirit. Johnston's exposition includes "mystery," "essence," "substance," "supernatural," "invisible," and "godlike." Manitou, he writes, "refers to realities other than the physical ones of rock, fire, water, air, wood, and flesh—to the unseen realities of individual beings and places and events that are beyond human understanding but are still clearly real."[4]

In the mysterious Great Lakes spirit world, nonhuman forces operated within every facet of nature, from humble plants and animals to the awesome Great Lakes and giant heavenly bodies, such as the sun and the moon. Spirits were not always friendly toward those living in their midst. This prompted Indians to spend considerable time and resources trying to appease spirits and acquire some of their power. "Traffic with these spiritual powers, like contact with electricity, was dangerous but nevertheless essential to success," writes historian John Webster Grant, who further explains, "Religious practice, therefore, had to do mainly with gaining the favour of the spirits, avoiding offence to them, and showing due appreciation for the benefits they bestowed." One must resist sweeping statements about these ceremonies and traditions for placating spirits, for they varied among Indian nations, bands, and individuals. But without question, religious observances permeated the historic behavior of Great Lakes aboriginal peoples, and if hungry families were to be fed, they must maintain respectful, reciprocal relationships with slain animals as well as crops harvested from the fields. In short, religious rituals and beliefs were vital to the everyday lives of native peoples because the ability to connect with the spirit world was the most important of all.[5]

The path to power provided several options. Working alone, individuals might perform a vision quest, make tobacco offerings, or sing special songs to spirits of the animals and fish. After killing an animal, the hunter respectfully thanked its spirit for the sacrifice and tried to treat its body with respect. Dreams were sought because they conveyed messages needed for success while hunting and on the warpath.[6]

In their perpetual quest for religious power and preservation of harmony with the natural world, Great Lakes natives also sought help from the shaman (medicine man). Such persons, villagers believed, had extraordinary ability to communicate with the spirit world or to understand the healing properties of plants. Sick persons sought the shaman's services. So did those who needed a mediator with the spirit world, perhaps because of violating a taboo, or those who wanted to know what the future held for a war or hunting party. Their insights made shamans high-ranking community leaders, and they did not look kindly on Christian missionaries, who threatened to displace them.[7]

Part of the passionate quest to connect with the spirit world involved participation in communal ceremonies that included singing, dancing, and drumming. For Great Lakes Algonquian speakers, the Midéwiwin (Grand Medicine Society) brought members together to promote good health by means of visions, proper personal conduct, and lengthy instruction in the medicinal properties of plants. The society incorporated many of their individual relations with spirits into a set of religious ceremonials conducted by an organized priesthood.[8]

The religious practices of Iroquoian peoples, who also sought power through medicine men, vision quests, and soothing plant and animal spirits, displayed some distinctive elements. For example, they paid great attention to dreams. "They were believed to reveal hidden desires or to foretell calamities," writes Grant, "and their messages had to be acted out if the desires were to be fulfilled or the calamities averted." Iroquoian speakers had been farmers for hundreds of years, and over time, their ceremonies reflected the shift away from hunting-gathering lives. Bigger, more permanent villages allowed for more sizable ceremonies. These centered on the agricultural calendar and featured feasts and other rituals that coincided with planting and harvesting the fruits of their fields. Distinctively Iroquoian communal practices also included religious associations that cut across clan lines and the periodic cleansing and reburial of deceased relatives' bones in mass graves.[9]

Whether Iroquoian or Algonquian, native peoples maintained a constant dialogue—comprised of songs, fasts, sacrifices, ceremonies, and prayers—with the shifting spiritual forces of the Great Lakes. "For people who felt like this," writes Martin, "the spiritual drama never stopped." But it could be radically altered. By seizing most of the Indian homeland, Canadian and American newcomers interrupted the centuries-old dialogue between Indians and that portion of their natural world. In addition, Christian missionaries attacked aboriginal religious beliefs and practices. Thus began a new chapter of the spiritual drama.[10]

EARLY CHRISTIAN EVANGELISTS

Because present-day Canadian and American societies extol cultural diversity, it is difficult to imagine an earlier time when the Friends of the Indians and other policy makers appeared less open minded. They envisioned homogeneous homelands full of educated, self-sufficient, Christian citizens. Native peoples could be part of the mix, provided they abandoned their backward, pagan ways.

What convictions, especially those held by church leaders and their missionaries, buttressed the ethnocentrism of this earlier age? Fundamental to their evangelism was the evangelists' confidence that their religion was superior to aboriginal spirituality. Noble Indians were considered rational human beings and not biologically inferior, but it was believed that their misguided cultures, geographically isolated from advanced Western civilization, had to be replaced—by force if necessary—in order for the Indian to survive. Two other assumptions were part of the paternalistic mix. Missionaries, who went into the field with little firsthand knowledge of aboriginal communities, had faith that they could Christianize and civilize them within a few decades and that Indians would willingly cast off traditional ways.[11]

Canadian and American missionaries' impact was intensified, writes historian C. L. Higham, because they "were like cogs in a large machine." Higham explains, "While they pursued the missionary societies' goals, the missionary societies acted as liaisons with congregations and governments, and supplied missionaries with policies, financial and spiritual support, a plan for conversion, and a structure for communication." Nationally in Canada, most Protestant missionaries to the Indians were affiliated with the Anglican, Methodist, and Presbyterian churches. In the United States, Methodists and Presbyterians shared reservation evangelical work with Congregationalists and Baptists. Missionary societies—governed by boards of clergy as well as business leaders and politicians—recruited, trained, and dispatched hundreds of missionaries to sites worldwide. Most were men, although women grew increasingly important as supporting wives, helpers, and educators. Once missionaries reached the field, church organizations built and outfitted the first Indian churches and schools. Federal governments later shared part of this burden. News from the field also flowed back through missionary organizations and was disseminated by their printing houses. The *Missionary Herald* of the American Board of Commissioners for Foreign Missions in Boston, for example, had a circulation of 16,241 in 1860 and was read by perhaps 292,000 Presbyterians.[12]

Missionary societies and their field agents employed a two-fold strategy to save aboriginal peoples from extinction and transform them from unproductive pagans to self-supporting Christians. One approach was to bring native communities "under the influence of the Gospel." This would not only lead to personal salvation but help promote the natives' integration into the Canadian and American mainstreams. A second approach was to teach Indians about "civilization," particularly horse-and-plow agriculture. This, too, fostered assimilation and built on the Indians' desire for occupational training and financial assistance. Missionary strategies thus tied in nicely with long-standing governmental economic and educational programs. Not surprisingly, a partnership developed between these two "civilizing" agencies.[13]

Church organizations envisioned wonderful things happening on frontier reservations when this model was implemented. After the construction of schools and churches, Indian converts would grow in number and eventually take on leadership roles within their congregations. At the same time, members who had taken up commercial farming would be self-sufficient and able to support their own church and school. Some Christians would likely feel called to the ministry in order to serve their own or other native reserves. At this point, the original missionary could move west or north to another community and start the same type of conversion process until the entire West had been "saved" and "civilized."[14] For evangelistic Easterners, it was an exciting, though idealized, picture.

Whatever one thinks about crusading Christian churches, there is no question that their Great Lakes missionaries in the nineteenth century faced considerable challenges and played key roles on aboriginal reserves. At first, it was the utter isolation that was so daunting. When the Reverend Edward F. Wilson visited the Sault in 1869, he found that Mr. and Mrs. Chance were in charge of the Garden River mission. The complex included a mission house and log school. They "felt they were indeed in the land of the Indian, far away from civilization." Other difficulties included the language barrier and native families' frequent absences from home villages while hunting, trapping, gathering, and fishing. Added to these obstacles was perhaps the toughest of all: convincing the Indians to adopt Canadian and American ways of life as well as the Gospel message. Besides regular church attendance and financial support, these ways included wearing white man's clothes, new standards of personal and household cleanliness, enrolling children in school, and abandoning polygamy. Missionaries understandably faced stiff opposition from at least three groups: dissenting reserve members; other Christian denominations; and fur traders, such as the Hudson's Bay Company, whose economic interests would be hurt if Indians abandoned the hunt. Also disruptive to the church's work was the rapid influx of non-Indian settlers and Indian fears that they might be uprooted from their reserves.[15]

Faced with such obstacles, dedicated missionaries revealed personal qualities that gained them some remarkable successes. Fundamental was their faith in the Gospel message and concern for the souls of aboriginal peoples. The Reverend Wilson wrote of his continued belief "that it is God's will that every wandering sheep should be sought out and, if possible, be brought into the Good Shepherd's fold." Such beliefs and their love of people enabled church workers to endure frontier isolation and the physical work needed to build mission stations and care for their families, suffer through extremes of Great Lakes weather, and study native languages. Certainly another key to their achievements was a willingness to listen and learn from the Indians and other locals—about the land, its waters, and the complexities of their life ways. To survive, these "excellent men, the learned pastors of the Canadian mission," wrote German geographer Johann Georg Kohl after an 1855 visit to the Sault, "are always obliged to appropriate some of the life and acts of the Canadian Voyageurs." Kohl continued:

> They understood how to steer a canoe, guide a Mackinaw bark, and get ready the dog-sledge. They are good sailors, and wear water-boots and South-westers suited to the swamps and rainy and stormy climate of their widely extending and desolate parishes, so far as is feasible without entirely abolishing the clerical costume.[16]

The ability of missionaries to surmount the Great Lakes challenges produced a number of Christian conversions and also made them influential reservation residents. Above and beyond their spiritual duties, evangelists continuously urged local Indians to adopt the white man's more "progressive" ways. Missionaries who lived on the reserves sought to model this behavior and regularly lent a hand. They taught the children, advised aboriginal farmers, often provided medical assistance, and got involved in local political affairs. Church workers interpreted and advocated for Indians in their dealings with federal governments.[17]

The most observable and impressive measure of missionary activity was the number of Christian churches that dotted the Great Lakes reservations by the late 1800s. The Methodist Church, among all the denominations at work, launched the most successful evangelical campaign. The conversion in 1823 of Peter Jones (*Kahkewaquonaby*, or "Sacred Feathers"), a mixed-blood Mississauga, led to the planting of churches across Upper Canada from the Bay of Quinté to the Sault. Some pastors were native. Jones was later joined by other aboriginal missionaries and church workers, including George Copway, George Henry, Peter Jacobs, Allen Salt, Henry Steinhauer, John Sunday, and Catherine Sunegoo Sutton. Meanwhile, Church of England priests, supported by the Society for the Propagation of the Gospel in Foreign Parts, maintained a strong ministry among the Six Nations on the Grand River Reserve. Mohawk worshipers belonged to the oldest Protestant church in Ontario. Members brought from New York's Mohawk Valley a Bible and silver communion service presented by Queen Anne. Anglican missionaries also labored at the Bay of Quinté and northwest as far as Manitoulin, the Sault, and Michipicoton by the end of the century. Moravian missionaries continued their ministry among the Delaware at the village of Fairfield.[18]

Protestant churches were not alone in their concern for Indian souls. The Roman Catholic Church was especially influential on the north shores of Lakes Huron and Superior starting in the 1830s. When Michigan's northern Ottawa migrated to Manitoulin Island in order to avoid America's Indian removal program, priests came to work among them. From there, evangelists pushed south into Georgian Bay and as far as Walpole Island and Amherstburg. Others created parishes to the west between the Sault and Fort William.[19]

By the 1890s, a remarkable array of churches dotted fifty-five of the fifty-six Canadian reserves. From the Bay of Quinté in the east to Walpole Island in the south and Lake Nipigon in the northwest, groups of Christian Indians regularly worshiped together. Many reserves had more than one church. In 1896, Six Nations, for instance, had seven Anglican, three Methodist, five Baptist, and one Plymouth brethren. The total number of Great Lakes Canadian Indians "acknowledged and claimed as being" Christians, compiled by church workers and Indian agents in 1895, was also impressive: 16,245 out of a population of 17,907. That year's census listed 1,366 as "pagan." They generally lived in the remote north, where hunting, trapping, and gathering were still necessities and kept roving native families from close contact with missionaries and Indian agents. Six Nations, with 835 "pagans" in 1895, was the major exception to this distribution. Concerned enumerators must have seen Grand River as a hotbed of hidebound "traditionalists."[20]

South of the international border, American missionaries also established numerous reservation churches. A synopsis of evangelical work among the Six Nations of New York and in northern Michigan and Wisconsin with Algonquian peoples, shown in table 6, testifies to the importance of these committed Christians.

Clearly, these churches were an important presence in Indian country.

The Gospel message had fallen on fertile soil and was responded to positively by many Great Lakes Indians. Church growth was also a tribute to the work of dozens of valiant missionaries.

One such evangelist was the Reverend Asher Wright. He personified the dedication of missionaries among the New York Iroquois and helped explain the relative success they achieved. Following graduation from Dartmouth College, Wright worked for forty-three years among the Seneca, particularly those on the Cattaraugus Reservation. He translated into their language a book of hymns and parts of the New Testament. "He is said to have been the only male missionary," writes church historian Joshua Bolles Garritt, "who ever acquired anything like a satisfactory knowledge of the Seneca language." He also gave his services as a physician gratis, supplying the Seneca with medicines that he bought with his own modest salary. Helping to establish an orphan asylum was part of the ministry of Wright and his wife. According to Garritt, she was her husband's "companion in labor through

TABLE 6. Churches on Great Lakes American Indian Reservations, Late 1800s

State	Reservation	Churches	Denomination	Membership Data Available
New York	Onondaga	3	Protestant	47
	Tonawanda	3	Protestant	94
	Allegany	2	Protestant	131
	Cornplanter	1	Protestant	39
	Cattaraugus	3	Protestant	170
	Tuscarora	2	Protestant	238
Michigan	Isabella	4	Protestant	288
		1	Catholic	12
	L'Anse	1	Catholic	
		1	Protestant	75
Wisconsin	Menominee	3	Catholic	
	Oneida	1	Protestant	
	Lac du Flambeau	1	Catholic	
	Lac Court Oreilles	2	Catholic	
		1	Protestant	
	Bad River	1	Protestant	
		1	Catholic	
Minnesota	Fond du Lac	1	Catholic	
	Grand Portage	1	Catholic	

Source: Data for New York are from U.S. Bureau of the Census, *Report on Indians Taxed and Indians Not Taxed*, 476–77. Data for Michigan are from ibid., 332–33. Data for Wisconsin are from Green Bay Agent D. H. George to CIA, August 28, 1900, AR, CIA, 1900, 403–5; Green Bay Agent Charles S. Kelsey to CIA, August 28, 1891, AR, CIA, 464–65, 617–26; LaPointe Agent to CIA, January 26, 1888, NARA, GLR (Chicago), OIA, RG 75, LaPointe Agency, LS. Data for Minnesota are from U.S. Bureau of the Census, *Report on Indians Taxed and Indians Not Taxed*, 353–54.

these years of service" and had an even better fluency in Iroquois, which enabled her to carry on her husband's ministry after his death in 1875.[21]

Meanwhile, on Walpole Island, neither Methodists nor Catholic evangelists had much success until the Anglican bishop of Toronto appointed the Reverend Andrew Jamieson, a University of Edinburgh graduate, to this mission in 1845. Modest achievements testified to his determination, perseverance, patience, respect, and genuine concern for the native community. Jamieson was ill-prepared for setting up a Walpole mission when he arrived in July with his wife and three children. He was the only non-Indian on the island and unable to communicate verbally with its inhabitants. The federal government had recently built a little church. Assuming there must be parishioners, Jamieson rang the bell on Sunday, arranged the seats, and waited. Nobody came. The scene was repeated the next few weeks, then Jamieson closed up the building. There "were Indians all around" the church building, but they "were all Pagans, thoroughly satisfied with their own beliefs and they did not care to leave wigwams to listen to the white missionary."[22]

Rather than forsake his post, like earlier missionaries to Walpole, Jamieson shifted strategies. He obtained an interpreter and went out among people "to draw their attention to the things that belonged to their peace." Reflecting the ethnocentric white mind-set of the day, Jamieson saw a community beset by superstition, intemperance, and indolence. "They were very poor," he judged, "living in bark wigwams." Of visits to each leading man of the island, Jamieson said:

> I would go to his place at the time appointed, most likely under a tree near his wigwam. There he would be seated on the ground with his women around him with painted faces feathers in their hair and tomahawks by their sides. Laying down on the ground some tobacco—the usual method of approaching the wild Indian smoking would commence. After a little I would rise and address them through my interpreter.

After eighteen months of such meetings and regular visits to native homes, Jamieson's gentleness and kindness were rewarded; two adult islanders asked to be baptized. Jamieson reopened the church, and other community members—"by twos and threes"—accepted Christianity. "The earnestness of these early converts was undoubted," Jamieson reported, "for they had to sacrifice much in following their convictions of duty." This included verbal and physical abuse from their "pagan" relatives and neighbors.[23]

Church on Walpole Island. *(Courtesy Wallaceburg and District Museum.)*

During the closing decades of the century, the fruits of Jamieson's labors were evident. The congregation built its own church, complete with an organ, using money sent from England. Each year, his parishioners contributed to the diocesan mission fund. "It is a matter of wonderment to me that they can give so much for the majority of them are still poor," Jamieson noted, "but they make it a point to set apart a certain portion to the service of God." Jamieson's effectiveness as a priest increased in part because he learned the local native languages and no longer needed an interpreter. One member of the congregation remarked: "We are so thankful you can now speak to us in our own tongue. We now know that which we hear comes actually from yourself. Sometimes we have been perplexed and bewildered and could scarcely believe that what we heard from the Interpreter was the true meaning of what you said." That life was not easy on the reserve was suggested in Jamieson's 1885 correspondence.

> Walpole is very low and is almost on a level with the river and full of swamps and marshes. The parsonage stands on one of the lowest spots, hence malaria during the summer and autumn was constantly around it. Shortly after I pitched my tent here I was taken down with bilious fever and remained on the sick list for months. And long after, exposure to the north wind, or any extra exertion would bring on chills and fever. But, thank God, that is a thing of the past, as I am now in robust health and have been so for many years. I am now acclimated. During our stay on the island we always dreaded July, August and September, the sickly months of the year and rejoiced to feel the first frosts in October and November. . . . Often at times we were obligated to have a smudge at each side of the table while sitting at breakfast. Our island was often called mosquito point. Moreover we had other visitors from the swamp in the shape of snakes of different kinds. I have frequently killed them in our parlour. The copperhead and the rattlesnake are on the island. Of these I have killed several and on one occasion, my daughter, a child of 13 years killed a rattlesnake with 8 rattles within 3 feet of our door.[24]

Like the Wright family on the Cattaraugus Reservation, Jamieson and his wife provided medical services for Indians and promoted farming as well as the formal education of their children. Following Jamieson's death in 1885, the Reverend John Jacobs, a native Anglican pastor from Rama Reserve, continued Jamieson's work. Jacobs was succeeded by the Reverend Simpson Brigham from Walpole Island, whose parents, Ziba and Elizabeth, Jamieson had baptized, as well as their six children.[25]

At Sault Ste. Marie, another Canadian, Anglican priest Edward F. Wilson, personified the Christian evangelists' belief that their work must not be limited to spiritual conversion. He labored for twenty-five years among the Ontario Indians and focused his work on educating the young. Wilson hoped that they and their parents might abandon "pagan" beliefs and lifestyles and learn the skills necessary to earn a living like the white newcomers. Between 1868 and 1871 he worked closely with an interpreter and trained Indian catechists for reserves in and around Sarnia. Then the church

The Reverend Simpson Brigham (*center*) of Walpole Island. *(Courtesy Wallaceburg and District Museum.)*

called him north to the Garden River Reserve. Its chief, Shingwauk, had urged the Anglican bishop in Toronto to send Wilson to them, with the hope that "before I died I should see a big teaching wigwam built at Garden River." Support from local Indians and Anglican Church donations enabled Wilson to build Shingwauk School at the Sault, an institution that housed and instructed Great Lakes Indian children for nearly a century.[26]

Wilson's extended efforts at educating native youngsters reflected a widely held belief among clergymen and church policy makers that Christian conversion and the Indians' salvation must be accompanied by general instruction in the ways of the Canadian and American mainstream. Therefore, the influence of church workers on Great Lakes reserves was not limited to church buildings, worship services, and Sunday school classes. Acting as unofficial Indian agents, Catholic and Protestant missionaries and their associates constantly moved about the reservations, modeling proper behavior and urging natives to "take up the plow," send their children to school, build permanent homes and outbuildings, fence their land, abstain from alcohol, dress like whites, lead healthy lives, and generally adopt the roles

Methodist church of Sarnia Reservation, 1908. *(Courtesy Archives of Ontario, image C 7-3, 1470).*

played by white husbands and wives. Missionaries were powerful agents of change, and the reservations would never be the same.

Brian S. Osborne's study of Methodist missionaries among the Mississauga earlier in the century is illustrative of how pervasive the church's influence could be. At the urging of church leaders, including Peter Jones, the Mississauga relocated to Grape Island in the Bay of Quinté and created a model village. The agricultural and Christian calendar regulated every aspect of the residents' lives, from seasonal planting and harvesting to maintaining their homes and properties. Equally demanding were the church gatherings at least three times a day for worship, prayer, and Christian education. Change was also required within the home, as the responsibilities of children, mothers, fathers, and grandparents were realigned to fit a Methodist ideal for family life. New hygienic standards became part of this package as well.[27]

This urging of Christian converts to surrender their woodland traditions, live in permanent villages, and accept "civilized ways" was not the same as repression or colonialism. In his biography of Wilson, historian David Nock notes that the humanitarians disparaged reservation superstition and barbarism, yet what they "wished the Indians to achieve was exactly the goal that many European immigrants have set for themselves in their quest for a new life in North America." Nock further explains:

> Wilson dreamed of a future "when the present barrier between the white and Indian population will be broken down, and one in language, one in pursuits, tastes, ambitions and hopes, they will join on equal terms in building up this great country." The aim of the humanitarians was not to keep the Indians in subjection.[28]

That church workers got involved in local politics and helped fashion public perceptions of native peoples was further evidence of their influence. Equipped with firsthand knowledge about reservation conditions, missionaries felt obligated to inform Canadian and American officials about policies that worked well and those that should be modified and abandoned. When mission-sponsoring organizations, such as the Episcopal Church, the American Board of Commissioners for Foreign Missions, and the Society of Friends, joined the lobbying effort, the church voice became a powerful one. During President Ulysses S. Grant's peace policy, Protestant denominations worked cooperatively as never before and considered themselves partners in championing Indian rights and formulating American reservation policy.[29]

Historian C. L. Higham describes in detail how nineteenth-century Protestant missionaries stirred Canadian and American public interest in native peoples. This enabled evangelists to raise money for their work and to help shape popular images about Indians. Interestingly, as missionaries' thoughts changed about aboriginal character—from noble to wretched to redeemable—the missionaries incorporated their views into lecture tours, wide-ranging correspondence, and scholarly publications. Politicians and bureaucrats in both nations as well as the general public listened to church workers' thoughts on Indian matters. As Higham explains, because missionaries crossed back and forth across the international border to make speeches, they "helped to meld Canadian and American images of Indians into one slowly evolving image that remained central within these societies for years."[30]

Missionaries played political roles where policy decisions mattered the most: on Great Lakes reservations. As influential local residents, they owned or had the right to use land within the community. They had the blessing of federal authorities and seemed to speak for them. At the Sault and Walpole Island, Anglican priests had special legitimacy because they were invited by local chiefs. Missionaries also earned their status by supplying important services to Indian families: education of the youth, care for the sick, and Christian sacraments to mark life's most important waypoints. Some missionaries, such as Edward Wilson, lobbied local councils to support particular initiatives, such as starting a school. Too much embroilment in local politics could, of course, destroy an evangelist's power base. Chiefs called on trusted pastors to interpret and mediate at councils with government officials or to draft community petitions to federal authorities. One missionary, Peter Jones, became a chief at the Credit Reserve, and Andrew Jamieson was the Indian Department's official representative at Walpole Island.[31]

Clearly, missionaries and their church sponsors helped shape reservation history during the late 1800s, and any assessment of Christian influence must take into consideration the harvest of these sowers of the Word. In some cases, the harvest seemed bountiful, the converts and number of Christian churches numerous. But were the conversions true and enduring? To address this important question, native responses to Christian missionaries must be examined in some detail.

NATIVE RESPONSES

Great Lakes Indians listened politely to Christian evangelists. That was the native way. Yet fathers, mothers, chiefs, and children were just as discerning as they had been with Indian agents, schoolteachers, traders, and others who urged Indians to abandon traditional ways of thinking and behaving. Rarely was a community's decision unanimous toward any of these proposals. There were differences of opinion, mixed motives, and personal positions—all of which fluctuated over time.

Six Nations reservations illustrated these complexities on both sides of the international border. Sally M. Weaver notes that the split between Christian and non-Christian dated from the 1780s, when missionaries preached the Gospel in New York villages. Did religious differences alone activate and sustain this division? This was certainly not the case among the New York Iroquois, as reported by the Bureau of the Census in 1890.

> Leading Indians who have returned to their pagan associations admit that they did not gain what they expected in the way of influence or position when they "joined the christians." Both terms have a political meaning among the Six Nations. Members of the christian party are not of necessity christian at heart. Neither are members of the pagan party necessarily of pagan faith.

Examinations show that the social and political relations are so commingled that the real number of converted Indians is but vaguely determined.

Enumerators also cautioned, "The mere statement of the value of church buildings and the number of church members of each organization does not afford an entirely sound basis for testing their real influence and progress."[32] Clearly, native responses to Christian evangelists were significant yet diverse and difficult to measure—even at one place, the New York reservations, and one point in time, 1890.

The variation in native responses to Christian evangelists through the years makes generalizations tricky. During a thirty-three-year period, for example, Protestant missionaries established stations in northern Michigan at Grand Traverse Bay and Little Traverse Bay as well as Middle Village. Dozens of Indian families attended church services and sent their children to a day or boarding school. Nearly 150 officially joined the church before memberships declined and the mission was abandoned in 1871—another victim of the winds of change sweeping the Great Lakes. Missionaries blamed Indians' disinterest in education and subversive "Romanists." Aggressive white settlers, far more disruptive, elbowed natives off their land. Those remaining were too scattered to support a church and fearful of removal to beyond the Mississippi. Still others ceased to live as Indians and became Michigan citizens.[33]

Why was aboriginal reaction to Christianity so prominent and complicated—in northern Michigan and elsewhere on the Great Lakes? "How could it be otherwise?" writes Joel W. Martin; it was associated with "new peoples, technologies, markets, and ways of living." Martin continued:

> The story of the spread of Christianity among Native American peoples is a complicated tale with many unexpected twists and turns, outright reversals, and sudden breakthroughs. More than anything, it is a story of contradictions. Because Christianity's spread in the New World is associated with both horrible and wonderful things, it has elicited contrary, even contradictory, responses from American Indians.[34]

Reservation residents found Christianity appealing for a variety of reasons. For some, the reason was the similarities between the new religion's teachings and traditional spiritual beliefs. Or perhaps the Gospel's emphasis on equality spoke to their social and spiritual yearnings. For these Indians, Martin writes, there was "no insurmountable contradiction in being Native and Christian." Others saw new political and economic opportunities in conversion. Professed Christians would probably receive more assistance in educational and economic development from the dominant culture. Christian chiefs could more effectively champion their people's interests with local Indian agents, influential missionaries, and policy makers in Ottawa and Washington.[35]

Three examples from Wisconsin reserves document a strong commitment to Christian church support—and control. When the Menominee agreed in the mid-1850s to live on a reservation, chiefs established separate villages that reflected their religious beliefs. Professed Christian communities that thus developed on the east side of the Wolf River strongly supported local churches. Because they also accepted the federal government's "civilization" program, these Menominee generally sent their children to schools, adopted citizens' dress, and tried horse-and-plow agriculture. Several years later, at Bad River to the north, the work of the Catholic Church was clearly important to the Ojibwa. Early in 1898, 125 Ojibwa petitioned the Indian Office to use two thousand dollars of their tribal timber monies to help build a new Catholic church on the reservation. Considerably more is known about Wisconsin Oneida church members, because the Reverend W. G. Miller published memoirs about the Oneida mission twelve miles northwest of Green Bay. As the elder (or "Big Missionary," as he was called), Miller spoke at an 1850 quarterly meeting. In his memoirs, he describes the aftermath.

> This done, I took my seat. . . . The business must now be done in a strong language, and in the method of the red man. After sitting in absolute silence for some minutes, the head Chief of the Nation, "Big Jake," as he is called, being one of the Stewards, turned to a brother on his right and spoke a few words, and received a reply. Then turning to another, he did the same and thus continued to address each personally until all had been consulted. At intervals there were long pauses, indicative, as I judged, of the gravity of the matter to be considered. At the end of an hour the Council had completed its work. The Chief then arose in a very dignified manner, but without ostentation, and, calling to his aid an interpreter, proceeded to reply to the opening address. He began his speech by expressing thanks, on behalf of himself and people, that the "Big Missionary" had come once more to see them. He next referred to the good work that had been performed by the Missionary [the Reverend Henry Requa], and the special blessing of God upon his people. And in conclusion, he reported

the items of business they had considered, and the action taken in each case. If anything further was desired at anytime, it was always presented in a most respectful manner. In this case it was represented that they needed some repairs on the Church, and a bell, and they desired that the Missionary might be permitted to go abroad and raise the necessary funds. Permission was granted, and the Missionary, taking several fine singers of the nation with him, went to New York, Boston, and other places, and secured the needed help.

At the close of the public services came the hand shaking. The Missionary understood the matter and detained me in the Alter for a moment. Commencing with the ladies and ending with the children, every person in the Church came forward and shook hands with the Elder....

... On his [the Missionary's] return with bell, the people were overjoyed. For the first week after it was hung in the steeple, it was kept going, almost night and day. The friends came from every part of the reservation, and no one was satisfied until his own hand pulled the rope.[36]

Examples of fervent native commitment to Christian churches also abounded in Canada at this time. Congregational members and even some local councils committed monies to build and remodel churches and even replace those destroyed by fire. They helped to fund and construct parsonages. Some communities hired native sextons and pastors. The expanding numbers of churches and regular attendance of faithful members also testified to the seriousness with which many Indians took their conversion to Christianity.

Reasons for accepting missionaries and, ultimately, baptism varied from a chief's perception that political and economic benefits might follow to genuine, individual conversions. Studies of the Mississauga, Walpole Island, and Garden River reserves illuminate this process. Brian S. Osborne admits that the Kingston/Bay of Quinté Mississauga's turn to Methodism in the 1800s was a complex matter and happened at a critical juncture. The influx of white settlers took most of the band's land base, disrupted traditional ways of life, and caused serious social and health problems. In the face of destitution, their own religion appeared unable to avert it. Many Mississauga turned to Methodism, whose missionaries promised native listeners a better life—salvation materially as well as spiritually. One child whose family accepted Methodism reported happily: "In the wigwam I was cold and hungry. Now we have plenty to eat, and live in good houses like our white friends." Some Mississauga converted because native preachers offered testimonials and pointed out similarities between traditional beliefs and those of the Methodists.[37]

Similarly, at Walpole Island and Garden River, astute chiefs understood the threat caused by growing numbers of white neighbors and the necessity of accommodation. In the best interest of their peoples, native leaders tried to control the unavoidable missionization and to encourage evangelists from churches that could best promote their reserves. Probably for political reasons, Walpole Island chased out the Jesuits and invited an Anglican missionary. Benefits could flow from a church so cozy with the Canadian government. Chief Peterwegeshick specifically requested a "black coat teacher" for his people. At Garden River, Chief Shingwauk, equally perceptive about the Church of England, adopted a similar plan. According to the Reverend Wilson, by the 1830s, the chief was bewildered by the many religions offered to him when he was still a "pagan," so "he and his father and other Indians journeyed 300 miles in a canoe and walked another hundred miles till they got to Toronto." They went to visit the "Great Chief [the lieutenant governor of Upper Canada], Sir John Colborne, and asked his advice as to what they should do about religion." Colborne told them that the country belonged to the queen, that he belonged to the queen's church, and that he thought loyal Indians "ought to belong to the Queen's church, too." So Shingwauk and his party "returned to Garden River and ever since were faithful members of the Church of England."[38]

The dedication and persuasiveness of Jesuit missionaries in northern Michigan and Wisconsin and of Andrew Jamieson on Walpole Island also inspired Christian conversions. La Pointe agent W. R. Durfee reported in 1881 that priests had proselytized with "untiring zeal and energy" for many years, "with the result I should estimate that seven eighths of all of what are called Christian indians in this agency are communicants of the Catholic Church." Durfee continued:

> I have personally known of their traveling hundreds of miles on snow shoes in midwinter through pathless forests to hold services in the indian language in isolated parts of their district. They seem to have a faculty, whether personal or through the rites and ceremonies of their church, of reaching the indian nature to which no other denomination can approach.

Walpole Indians likewise responded to qualities they admired in Jamieson as well as to the Gospel as he preached it. Jamieson showed respect for native people and their ways. He was tolerant and patient with prospective converts rather than hounding them. He and his wife visited Indians in their homes and generally sought to befriend them. Eventually, he could write: "The leading chief is a firm and fast friend of mine.... I have often invited the chief men to dinner. And on the first of this month a party of Indians about forty in number sat down to dinner in my house." Another attribute that attracted Walpole families to him was Jamieson's willingness to learn the Ojibwa language. He not only preached in their tongue but interpreted for them and generally was their advocate with the world outside the reserve.[39]

That a number of Walpole Islanders internalized the Gospel message was noted over the years in Jamieson's correspondence. Together, these natives attended and helped to finance an Anglican church on the reserve. True, those who attended church regularly were not large in number. Between 1862 and 1884, when Jamieson supplied congregational statistics, the number of church members grew from 400 to 450 in a community whose numbers increased from 750 to 850. Church members who worshiped regularly proved considerably less—between 100 and 115—yet their dedication seemed solid. Jamieson wrote that it is "by their sacrifices of money which they cheerfully make for the cause of Christ that we see the value that they put on their religious privileges." He reported:

> In June last of their own accord they proposed to make certain improvements in the interior of the church which required an outlay of $50 to be paid the end of September—but fever broke out among them during the sultry heat of August and September. I feared they would not be in condition to carry out their designs and improvements would not be carried out. There was some delay, but the promised amount was handed in—the last dollar paid November 1st. Remembering it is hard for them to get their bare necessities of life, it shows their love for the Gospel real and practical.
>
> We had an interesting time at Christmas. The Indians made the preparations, cleaning the church and decorating it with evergreens. Certain parties told them the decorations were needless, uncalled for that there was nothing in the word of God to sanction them. One of the Indians replied that he was a poor Indian, but he could read and he had read in the Gospels that the multitude took branches of trees and even their own garments and spread them in the way when their Lord and Master was passing—that Jesus found no fault but com-

mended them for so doing and in my opinion our Savior would not be displeased at our humble efforts to adorn this church at this particular time.

Indian commitment to their Walpole church was demonstrated again in 1878, when they decided to pay the expenses of two delegates to attend the diocesan synod in London, Ontario. Meanwhile, the Island's Potawatomi, like the Anglicans, had outgrown their first church by 1884 and, with their Methodist missionary, had built a second.[40] The personal behavior of Indians highlighted in Jamieson's correspondence suggests as well a deep commitment on the part of some church members, though it is impossible to know exactly how many.

Meanwhile, at the Sault, the evangelism of Garden River converts was also noteworthy, as was their expectation that fellow Christians, especially federal officials, would help safeguard native minerals, timber, fish, and other resources. Following Shingwauk's baptism in the 1830s, fellow believers regularly interrupted their winter hunts to journey to the Sault, where they enrolled their children at the mission school and listened to the Reverend William McMurray preach. Impatient with the priest's limited ministry on the St. Mary's River, Shingwauk's son, Ogista, and a companion obtained supplies and carried the Gospel message to the north shore of Lake Superior. Assistance came from a Hudson's Bay Company factor, George Keith, who provided free transportation for Ogista's party. An impressed Keith was "amazed at the knowledge they have acquired of Christianity." The Indians "behaved in every respect with the greatest propriety," wrote Keith, adding, "I am persuaded the seeds they have sown will bring forth fruit to repentance and reformation." Ogista's zeal indeed blossomed; chiefs at Pic River and Michipicoten requested that missionaries be sent to their reserves. McMurray also reported that Lake Superior Indians who were headed east to receive government presents lingered at the Sault in order to attend his services. These he increased to three on Sunday and two during the week. "They [the Indians] hold religious meetings among themselves, on such days as they do not attend to me," the delighted priest reported.[41]

Like the Walpole Island chiefs, who recruited Jamieson to advocate for their interests,[42] Garden River tried to protect its natural resources with the help of fellow Christians. Because they loved God, Shingwauk's followers felt they should be respected and protected by Canadian law. The chief enlisted local missionaries to petition religious organizations as well as the federal government about Christian natives' grievances and plans for economic development.[43] Thus did Garden River and Walpole Island believers look to Christianity to help save their lands as well as their souls. Missionaries, like Indian agents and fur traders, served as both cultural brokers and patrons.[44]

The mixing of Christian and traditional beliefs and practices was likewise common. Historian Sheldon Krasowski, in his study of Walpole Island's response to the Reverend Jamieson, notes that church members "participated in pagan ceremonies" and that "peoples described as pagan sat on the Walpole Island council and made a living by farming." Proportions of old and new religions varied among individuals and changed over time. Still, historical sources reveal that this blending occurred frequently and involved compatible features of customary spirituality and Christianity. The practice of the Ojibwa vision quest, for example, resembled Methodist faith in guidance by the Holy Spirit. Likewise, for Iroquois farmers, traditional planting and harvest celebrations echoed those of the Anglicans. Another blend occurred among Indians who accepted the Gospel but refused to be restricted to farms month after month. They preferred to follow traditional, seasonal rounds of hunting, trapping, fishing, and gathering. Still others led a settled life and accepted the Christian faith yet, to observers like the Reverend Wilson, remained superstitious. About those in the Sarnia area, Wilson wrote, "They never seemed to lose altogether their faith in witchcraft, especially in that form by which it was believed that certain persons had power to cause sickness or misfortune to others." Janet E. Chute, Shingwauk's biographer, comments on the personal balance he was able to keep between Christian and traditional beliefs—a belief system that became "a cultural legacy, maintained by his descendents." Certainly, his balancing of new and old—supporting the local Anglican church while also participating in time-honored ceremonies associated with conjuring and the Midéwiwin—was far from rare. Not until Shingwauk was close to death did he destroy his religious belongings, comprised of "papers and birch-barks, and painted dreams, dances, and songs," as described by Ogista.[45]

In native communities where missionaries served, the ends of the religious spectrum were formed by aboriginal people who rejected the missionaries, on the one hand, and fellow community members who accepted the Gospel message, on the other. Opponents' numbers varied from reservation to reservation yet remained significant in some areas as late as 1890. Reasons why they rejected Christianity were rarely spoken; families just stayed away from mission churches. Historic encounters with Christians had certainly turned some North American Indians against the Gospel message. European nations, under the banner of the cross, had warred against aboriginal peoples, tried to dominate their everyday lives, and driven many from their homelands. Representing themselves as God's chosen people, Canadians and Americans had turned Indians against Indians and taken their children away to boarding schools where they were taught to dislike their native heritage. This was not the entire story of encounters between natives and Christians, but there was enough white hypocrisy, colonialism, and suffering to close many Indian minds and ears to evangelists. Later, reservation conditions caused some families to seek strength in the old ways—long hair, Indian languages, sacred ceremonies, vision quests—and to cling more firmly to them no matter what the church and state said. In the tradition of Handsome Lake and the Shawnee Prophet, beleaguered natives also turned to shamans in hopes that new, powerful prophecies might provide the power needed to preserve their communities.[46]

Missionaries particularly threatened shamans and native women. Carol Devens's work has focused on their resistance to colonization. Medicine men understandably opposed evangelists, who tried to unseat them from positions of great influence. Less obvious, but just as menacing, was the new, subordinate role that the church advocated for women. Their position would be greatly reduced both as economic partners and as guardians of traditional ways. Moreover, the church wanted their children to be schooled, purged of Indianness, and reformed by white teachers. Mothers' vital roles would thereby be subverted and marginalized. No longer would they transmit culture to their daughters. Instead, mission schools, Devens writes, would direct girls "away from the world of the native woman, away from the autonomy and prestige of females in traditional life, and toward the responsibilities of Christian womanhood with its emphasis on female piety, domesticity, submissiveness, and the patriarchal nuclear family." Husbands, though also expected to abandon past practices, could retain important positions as community leaders and family providers. Christian churches urged them to become family heads rather than partners with their wives.[47]

Developments on a few reservations, like those of the New York Iroquois, epitomized the presence and importance of Christian opposition. The Iroquois, "of all American Indians, have best preserved their traditions," wrote census enumerators in 1890. Of the 3,976 Iroquois on the Onondaga, Tonawanda, Allegany, Cattaraugus, and Tuscarora reservations, only 701 were communicants or church members. Among the Onondaga, 426 out of 494 (86.2 percent) adhered to traditional ways, especially the clan chiefs, whose position was threatened by the Christians' call for a popular election of leaders. Longhouse Iroquois generally lived in separate settlements on each reservation, further signaling the seriousness of their disagreements with Christian Indians.[48]

Meanwhile, on Michigan's Isabella Reservation, where the Christian opposition numbered only 7 percent of the population, the Ojibwa nevertheless held "festivals and war dances," dressed in traditional garb preserved for such occasions. Like Iroquois "pagans," these Ojibwa families lived near one another. So did seventy-five traditional Ottawa and Ojibwa further north, in a remote and forested section of Mason County. Preferring to live "as far from civilization as possible," they spoke little English, declined to farm, kept their children at home, used herbal medicines rather than seek a white medical doctor, and maintained long-standing spiritual beliefs and practices. Their numbers were not as impressive as the numbers of Iroquois, but these non-Christian Michiganders were equally hard-core.[49]

The situation was not much different across Lake Michigan, in Wisconsin, as shown in table 7.

Those Menominee who rejected the missionaries' call to convert withdrew west of the Wolf River to isolated parts of the reservation, where they tried to keep alive traditional ways; they continued to garden, gather, and hunt and refused to send children to the white man's schools or to wear his clothes. Seclusion was still no guarantee of harmony, and disagreements arose about whether to follow Midéwiwin ways or the newly introduced Dream Dance (or Drum Dance).[50]

Conservative Menominee learned of the Dream Dance during the summer of 1881 while hosting Potawatomi, Winnebago, and Ojibwa visitors. They, too, opposed Christianity and the federal government's civilization program for Indians. Drumming, singing, praying, and the encouraging speeches of elders were all part of a Dream Dance "song service." These rituals, first revealed to a Sioux woman and containing Christian as well as aboriginal elements, appealed to Menominee seeking supernatural power so they could preserve the old ways. Quite the opposite response came from Green Bay agent Ebenezer Stephens; he was worried about the hubbub and the dancers' "War whoops." They also neglected their farm duties, and his Indian police could not (or would not) disperse the intertribal dancing. Even threats to withhold their annuities proved ineffective. Christian Indi-

TABLE 7. Non-Christian Wisconsin Indians, 1890

Reservation	Numbers	Census Takers' Comments
Menominee	ca. 300	"pagans"
Lac Court Oreilles	ca. 800	"The pagan Indians adhere very tenaciously to their old customs."
Lac du Flambeau	590	"This reserve can be called the stronghold of Chippewa paganism."
Bad River	ca. 320	"pagan"

Source: U.S. Bureau of the Census, *Report on Indians Taxed and Indians Not Taxed*, 621, 624–25.

ans denounced the Dream Dance at a meeting with Stephens, while admitting that some of their number had joined. Washington finally sent troops from Fort Snelling. Their stay was brief. They encountered only peaceful Indians, perhaps calmed by the army's arrival. Though the Indians were nonviolent, the impact of the Dream Dance—that summer and well into the twentieth century—was undeniable. Some traditional Menominee regarded its ceremonies as a new prophecy and founded the Zoar settlement in order to follow its ways and fend off the outside world. Other "pagans" integrated the Dream Dance into the Midéwiwin.[51]

Like the Zoar Menominee, some Ojibwa and Winnebago withdrew from Washington's gaze and the acculturating tendencies of Christian reservation inhabitants. At Old Village on Lac du Flambeau, for example, Ojibwa found the isolation they wanted in order to hold fast to Midéwiwin and Dream Dance teachings. Wisconsin Winnebago continued to practice their ceremonies of the war bundle and medicine lodge, as they, too, hunkered down against encroaching whites and the winds of change sweeping their homeland. In the late 1800s, when word was brought from Nebraska of the new peyote religion, or Native American Church, some joined up. It promised followers a better life while retaining their Indian identity. First, they had to give up the old ceremonies as well as smoking and drinking. Then, with the help of peyote, they could be rehabilitated spiritually. From Winnebago country westward, many versions of the peyote religion evolved, but whichever interpretation was followed, participation in the "all-night ritual involving songs, prayers, and consumption of the sacred plant . . . had a powerful effect on its participants, healing bodies and spirits," writes Joel W. Martin, who further reports, "Confirmed alcoholics stopped drinking, sick children revived, and almost everyone felt closer to the sacred powers." Like the vision quest, peyote produced many unpleasant experiences followed by feelings of euphoria and strength.[52]

The largest and most powerful Canadian "pagan" group was at Six Nations of the Grand River and numbered 630—18.4 percent out of a population of 3,425 in 1890. This reversed the situation that had existed early in the century, when non-Christians far outnumbered converts. Here, as with the New York Iroquois, longhouse followers strove to preserve time-honored customs, including social organizations, a confederacy government, Six Nations languages, and vital ceremonies. Thus, in 1885, during the Midwinter Ceremony, participants sacrificed a white dog, whose body they adorned with red spots, ribbons, feathers, and a wampum string. Smoke from its burning body and from tobacco rose through the longhouse roof, carrying up the community's thanks as well as its sins.[53]

Church on Kettle Point Reservation. 1909. *(Courtesy Archives of Ontario, image C 7-3, 1890.)*

To the west, on the Oneida Reservation, a core of fellow Iroquoians struggled as well to preserve longhouse traditions in the face of Christian challengers. The intensity of the spiritual tug-of-war was revealed in 1858. Two Oneida chiefs, the Reverend Mr. Sickles and Moses Skyler, journeyed to the Indian Department in Toronto with a report about dissolution of the local Church of England congregation. Prophets had visited the reserve claiming that the white man's Bible was suitable for him but not Indians, who must revere their old gods. Many adults accepted this message and started dancing as they used to before accepting the Gospel. Do you mean that these dancers are no longer Christians, a federal official asked Sickles and Skyler? They answered, "Yes."[54]

Non-Christians also were noteworthy at Sarnia, Kettle Point, and Walpole Island. Krasowski's study of Walpole resistance to Jamieson's ministry, for example, argues that even membership in his church did not signify abandonment of traditional native customs and beliefs. Between 1862 and 1884, membership averaged four hundred, yet those worshiping regularly were only a quarter of that number. (Jamieson attributed this to the islanders' persistent travels to hunt and fish and gather. These fruits they supplemented by farming.) Krasowski thus calls into question the community's conversion to Christianity and commitment to follow "civilized" ways.[55] Here, as well as on several other Great Lakes reserves, resistance to Christianity and the white man's "civilization" program showed that native people exercised a degree of control over their spiritual as well as their temporal lives.

CONCLUSION

Thoughts expressed in a 1914 publication of the Missionary Education Movement of the United States and Canada revealed the thinking of late Christian evangelists who toiled among Great Lakes Indians in the nineteenth and early twentieth centuries: "Give the Indian time to 'think white'—to catch the incentive and to achieve the goals which the paleface prizes—and he will make good."[56] Transforming Indian beliefs and thinking patterns was an enormous challenge, but dozens of church workers devoted their lives to saving Indian souls and instructing them about white ways. Missionaries certainly mattered. They confronted and assaulted long-standing native beliefs and practice, both individual and corporate. These included prayers, fasts, sacrifices, songs, and ceremonies. Evangelists made a significant and long-lasting impact on reservation families. This put church workers on a par with other white change agents, such as Indian Office officials, traders, settlers, and schoolteachers.

Native decisions about Christian conversion, writes historian Elizabeth Graham, must be seen against changing historical circumstances of the mid-1800s: "the encroachment of white settlers on Indian hunting grounds and the disappearance of game, debilitating drunkenness which left the Indians in debt to the traders and bereft of all their possessions, the high incidence of sickness and death resulting from contact with the white population and liquor."[57] Prompted as they were by mighty forces, Indian reactions to Christian churches proved remarkably discriminating, just as they had been with Indian agents, schoolteachers, and others who urged them to make top-to-bottom cultural changes. There was no pell-mell rush either to accept the Gospel or reject it. Rather, aboriginal responses ranged across a spectrum, from enthusiastic acceptance of Christianity to outright denial. Decisions also fluctuated over time. Why? Because it was the Indian way to decide individually and each day how they would keep a spiritual balance in their lives.

After rejecting Jesuit missionaries, Walpole Island's relationship with the Reverend Jamieson's family illustrated both Indian control of their reserve and the important, mutually beneficial connection between a missionary and his flock. The priest and his wife, besides preaching the Gospel, helped educate the children, provided medical care, and studied the Indians' ways and their language. Jamieson advised chiefs and headmen and acted as a local Indian agent by representing their interests to the Canadian government and the general public. He clearly gave much to the community, and in response, many local natives gave much of themselves to him and his church. That his story was replicated on dozens of reservations north and south of the Great Lakes showed that missionaries mattered. At a stressful time, they offered something important that could help Indians protect their homeland, many of their fundamental values, and their distinctive role in the region's history.

The same was true for politics, the subject of the next chapter. With Ottawa and Washington demanding that Indians change their political structures, aboriginal families and their communities were determined to exercise as much independence in governance as they did in making a living, educating their children, and relations with the spirit world. They were autonomous communities that reacted to a changing world in ways that seemed to serve them best. "How could it be otherwise?" writes Joel W. Martin.[58] Such was the way of their forefathers who dealt with French fur traders and British redcoats who encroached on the Great Lakes country. Indians canoed through history with hands on the paddles, guiding their own destiny.

{ THREE }

Who Shall Rule at Home?

{ 6 }

Reservation Politics

The Challenge of Shared Governance

Canadians bent on "civilizing" the Indian, which included a proper governance of their communities, exuded optimism in the late 1860s and early 1870s about progress made. The Reverend Andrew Jamieson reported, for example, that when he first arrived on Walpole Island, "the Indian Councils I attended were very different in character to the ones I have attended of late years." He explained:

> Then there was much smoking confusion and often much drunkenness. Now, although the smoking continues the proceedings in Councils are marked by a wonderful degree of quiet order and decorum. Then it was necessary for me to do all the writing, take down the speeches as they were delivered and finally put them in a proper shape for the eye of the Governor General. *Now,* I am present simply as a spectator. The Indians do their own writing and draw up memorials to the gov't themselves whilst I simply affix my name to the document as a witness that they have been drawn up in full Council.[1]

Politically, much was the same on other Ontario reserves, according to the Indian Department. "Many of the bands exercise nearly all the powers of municipalities, and are being rapidly trained to self-government," observed the 1872 annual report, which continued,

They have their own Council Houses, which often resound with bursts of natural eloquence, or are enlivened by displays of mother wit and shrewd good sense; they maintain their own agents, doctors, and schoolmasters; and their general intercourse with the Department, with rare exceptions, are courteous, intelligent and reasonable.[2]

Canadian and U.S. policy makers expressed such delight because each nation believed that changing traditional Indian governance practices was essential to the natives' acculturation, economic self-sufficiency, social integration, and, ultimately, citizenship. Neither Ottawa nor Washington showed any lack of resolve in this matter. Thomas J. Morgan, U.S. commissioner of Indian affairs, warned in 1889: "The Indians must conform to 'the white man's ways,' peaceably if they will, forcibly if they must.... They can not escape it, and must either conform to it or be crushed by it."[3] Morgan spoke for federal officials on both sides of the international border who were prepared to intrude on tribal governments and forcibly transform them just as they had tried to revamp reservation economies, educational practices, and spiritual beliefs and practices. The scenario was ripe with irony, for although the stated goal was Indian independence, the political regulations and restrictions emanating from Washington and Ottawa foreshadowed, like a sticky spider's web, ensnarement and wardship.

Once again, Indian families and community leaders faced a crisis: conform or be crushed. This they understood, particularly those on the southern reserves that witnessed the white juggernaut all around them. Yet how much compliance should there be? Their right to home rule in the manner they chose was basic to reservation self-determination and security of their homelands, basic to their identity as native peoples. Freedom and sovereignty were fundamental to the future of their children and their children's children. Once again, the challenge was to find a workable balance between the new and the old, between accommodation to changing circumstances and protection of their people's core resources and traditions.

At this mid-nineteenth-century turning point, Indians fortunately brought to the task hundreds of years of experience in self-government, adjusting to changing circumstances, and dealing with menacing neighbors. More recently, they had negotiated partnerships with French, British, and American pioneers. Confinement to reservations in the mid-1800s, however, had greatly reduced aboriginal powers. Newcomer nations no longer needed Great Lakes Indians as military allies or economic partners, and whites had already acquired most of the native homeland. Indian communities thus faced greater challenges than ever before as they fashioned, individually and in conjunction with other reservations, new political relationships with Canada and the United States.

TRADITIONAL GOVERNANCE

Governmental structures of aboriginal families, villages, bands, clans, nations, and confederacies stemmed from the common need to deal with internal and external quarrels and to regulate the use of local and regional resources. Diverse, constantly evolving systems of rules and regulations, along with enforcement mechanisms and leadership offices, characterized the Great Lakes region. Environmental variations within the basin likewise contributed to this kaleidoscope of political systems. For example, New York's corn-fed Iroquois occupied permanent villages within a mild climate zone. Their politics were multileveled and complex. In contrast was the loose and informal organization of the hunter-gather Ojibwa on Lake Superior's chilly north shore. They moved about in small bands and family units from season to season. Early contact with European newcomers stepped up the rate of adaptive political change. Indians not only faced stiffer challenges but experienced outside interference with traditional governments. Native political structures also shared some striking similarities. In part, this was because of environmental similarities, such as warmer climates south of the lower Great Lakes. Other factors included shared problems and the spreading of political practices through trade and intermarriage. A third distinctive feature of historic Indian governments was their degree of success. Despite the awesome challenges they faced before and after contact with Euro-Canadian and Euro-American newcomers, Indian bands at no time became the mere puppets of outsiders.[4]

Fundamental to Indian governance were the functions of autonomous individuals, families, and clans. In the nineteenth century, countless problems came from the unwillingness of federal officials to accept this reality and from their determination, in many cases, to impose hierarchical structures. The principle of personal liberty infused all aspects of Great Lakes aboriginal culture—from child rearing to religious beliefs, economic activity, and politics. Neither family members nor chiefs could compel an individual to act in a certain way. What gave cohesion to society, observed one Canadian study, was "an equally strong sense of responsibility to the community," seen in the practice of sharing. These two forces were not contradictory; individual rights and responsibilities were "viewed as serving rather than opposing collective interests." Individual autonomy thus promoted "a strong spirit of egalitarianism in communal life." The spheres that commonly governed individual behavior were families and clans. They ruled on membership issues and resource use. They educated children about their responsibilities. They dealt with adult wrongdoers.[5]

That political units were difficult to define added to the complexity. Villages, in response to changing circumstances, periodically calved off new units or fused with other groups. Tribes also evolved along different paths. By the late 1600s, for example, the large Potawatomi community in Wisconsin atomized and expanded around the southern end of Lake Michigan. By 1800, families clustered in more than one hundred villages, each with a headman "who holds himself independent." All considered themselves Potawatomi, yet anthropologist James A. Clifton finds no evidence of regional divisions, such as subtribes or bands. The Menominee chose a different route. The precontact clan and village system gave way by 1830 to nine modest-sized bands.[6]

To focus the will of a community composed of such independent units was the role of chief and council. Whether a Menominee band chief or a Potawatomi village headman, their leadership qualities historically had included success on the warpath and on the hunt. A medicine man's closeness to the spirit world likewise helped him shape village thinking. After contact with the newcomers, Indian leaders needed prowess in fur gathering and trading. By the mid-1800s, these skills gave way to oratorical and diplomatic ones, as well as to the ability to lobby and obtain annuities from federal officials.[7]

Chief selection varied from one Indian nation to another. One might earn a position, such as that of war chief, or inherit it. Iroquois clan mothers managed the choice of their chiefs. Whatever the process, autonomous villagers looked for charismatic, experienced leaders who had demonstrated wisdom, generosity, humility, commitment to community traditions and ideals, and attentiveness to public opinion. Chiefs who did not listen would be removed—Iroquois clan matrons called it "dehorning"—and could be killed.[8]

Councils provided a place for male adults to air views and set policies on issues of local interest (such as the regulation of farming, hunting, and fishing) and beyond (war and peace, for example). Some bands and villages permitted women to participate in open discussions about the general welfare. Several factors contributed to the emergence of a consensus joining together individual points of view. Persuasive orators played an obvious role, but so did careful listening to the perspectives of others. Patience and respect must also be present, as well as the avoidance of confrontation during the lengthy consensus-building process. Finally, shared community history and strong kinship ties enabled agreements to surface.[9] The selection and duties of councils, like the qualities looked for in chiefs, adapted to changing circumstances.

Such challenges, be they preserving a Great Lakes balance of power or forging a trading alliance, required chiefs periodically to represent their community and its interests at national gatherings (of Iroquois or Ojibwa chiefs, for instance) or at international meetings with other Indian nations or delegates of the French and British governments. Later, newcomers also came from Ottawa and Washington, representing rapidly expanding entrepreneurial nations bent on clearing the forests and planting farm communities from the Atlantic to the Pacific. Indian governance systems especially bothered these agents of empire, and the result was a frontal assault on yet another cherished set of Indian traditions, another destabilizing blow at Indian reservations that was reminiscent of programs to overturn aboriginal economies, educational systems, and spiritual traditions.

THE ASSAULT

A number of factors provoked the attack on traditional Indian politics in the late nineteenth century. American reformers disappointed with President Grant's peace policy regarded reservations as a barrier to cultural change rather than a refuge for beleaguered native families. The reservations' consensus-style government systems and the inability of chiefs to command obedience contributed to the painfully long process of reaching a binding agreement and to the sluggish rate of "progress" in economic development, education, and abandonment of "paganism." The political assault was also intended to both undermine the power of independent-minded traditional or hereditary leaders and get residents used to local political institutions that they would find outside the reservation. An attack on Indian political independence got additional support from aggressive land developers; they liked any policy change that promised to open Indian lands for settlement by a rapidly expanding, frontier population. Decidedly different than these entrepreneurial motives were those of American and Canadian social engineers. Although they, too, pushed for abandonment of reservations and their traditionalist tribal governments, it was with the goal of elevating and assimilating aboriginal peoples and thereby creating a homogeneous citizenry. Cultural conformity should be expected of the Indian, not just of European and Asian immigrants. How would this be done? It was thought that those in the Canadian and American mainstreams, who believed they represented higher stages of cultural development, must guide those at lower levels—whether they liked it or not.[10]

In the same spirit, acts of Parliament and the U.S. Congress sought to substitute their visions of proper local government for the long-standing practices of native communities. The rewards for Indians who gave up their cultures would be citizenship, voting rights, and protection of the law—the crowning achievements of this assimilation process. Only with citizenship, wrote reformer Helen Hunt Jackson in her influential *A Century of Dishonor*, would law protect the Indians' property and their rights to "life, liberty, and the pursuit of happiness."[11]

Between 1857 and 1890, a series of Canadian laws confined Indians to the legal status of minors and made the federal government their guardians, with the power to oversee every aspect of reservation life. This legislation weakened the position of reservation leaders and generally curtailed native sovereignty. Indians would be considered no longer as distinct peoples with rights to self-government, which had been the case since the Proclamation of 1763, but as individuals subject to the Crown. Its Indian Department would supervise the selection of chiefs and councilors. Parliament would decide which powers local officials could exercise. It would impose a municipal model of government and then oversee all native actions. Gone would be the practice of nation-to-nation negotiations. In its place, a client people would be guided by the Crown's gatekeepers: resident Indian agents.[12]

Legislation from the late nineteenth century spearheaded the Canadian attack on traditional aboriginal politics, beginning with the 1857 Gradual Civilization Act. It established the goal of transforming Indian wards into citizens and laid out an enfranchisement process that disregarded tribal political autonomy. The act defined who was and was not an Indian and blatantly discriminated against the rights of Indian women and children. In 1869, two years after Confederation, the Gradual Enfranchisement Act directly interfered with reservation self-government. It gave the Indian Department the power to force a municipal-style government on aboriginal communities, which included the election of chiefs and councilors. Federal legislation not only denied the vote to Indian women but gave the Indian Department the right to depose chiefs. Responsibilities accorded to band councils were fairly minor and included building schools and maintaining roads and bridges. The 1869 act likewise denied reservation councils the power to enforce their bylaws. Henceforth, the reservations would not be truly self-governing. They were to become mere shadows of their former political independence, with the Canadian government reserving the right to confirm all legislation from the band councils.[13]

Historians agree that the 1876 Canadian Indian Act was partly a consolidation of earlier legislation. Additionally, it was far more detailed in asserting the federal government's control of reservation affairs, including the political. The "overall effect," observed a royal commission more than a century later, "was ultimately to subject reserves to the almost unfettered rule of federal bureaucrats. The Indian agent became an increasingly powerful influence on band social and political matters and on most reserves came to dominate all important aspects of daily band life." Thus Ottawa became progressively more pushy, rigid, and paternalistic. Sir Hector Langevin explained why this was necessary during the parliamentary debate on the Indian Act: "Indians were not in the same position as white men. As a rule they had no education, and they were like children to a very great extent. They, therefore, required a great deal more protection that [sic] white men." Clearly, Canada sought to establish colonial reservation governments that would do the Indian Department's bidding rather than be an independent voice for the interests of aboriginal people.[14]

Legislation in the 1880s and 1890s further strengthened the Indian Department and weakened band governments. The 1880 Indian Act, for example, prevented reservation governments from controlling money gained from land surrenders or resource sales. During the next couple of years, the power of Indian agents greatly increased as well; they became administrators of aboriginal justice systems, with the same authority as off-reserve magistrates and justices of the peace.[15]

Such blatant interference in the political affairs of reservation communities, all in the name of civilization and protection, similarly characterized the U.S. government during this period. Earlier in the century and guided by the Supreme Court's decision in *Worcester vs. Georgia* (1832), Washington recognized Indian sovereignty within their homelands—the right to exercise legislative, regulatory, and judicial responsibilities. (Canada, however, did not acknowledge Indian sovereignty and, as noted earlier, only delegated limited political authority to chiefs and councils.) The vulnerability of American Indian self-government lay in the pronouncement of the U.S. chief justice John Marshall that Indian nations were also "dependent" on the federal government. Over time, Uncle Sam's determination to "civilize" and assimilate them, even if force were needed, reduced the Indians' status from protected sovereign nations to wards. Indian agents usurped local government responsibilities, managed the community's economic resources, and supervised acculturation programs—from farming and allotment to education. Many agents employed Indian police forces to enforce the white man's laws and to stamp out traditional Indian ways, such as marriage and burial customs.[16]

As in Canada, the United States implemented this politically intrusive program with a barrage of legislation and executive orders. Particularly devastating to Indian sovereignty was Congress's 1871 decision to no longer recognize tribes as independent powers with whom it "may contract by treaty." Henceforth, the House and Senate simply legislated policies and programs—with or without native consultation. In that year, Washington also seized considerable economic control of Indian homelands by forbidding reservation residents to enter into contracts without the approval of the commissioner of Indian affairs and the secretary of the interior. The federal government further weakened Indian leaders by granting enormous power to local Indian agents. They, rather than chiefs, distributed annuities and rations to families. They, rather than chiefs, controlled the new Indian police forces, whose charge was not only to maintain order but to enforce the agents' "civilizing" programs. The established political order was further damaged when Indian police, who answered to the agent, cut their hair, wore non-Indian clothing, took the census, settled on allotments, suppressed traditional religious ceremonies, and sent children off to boarding schools. Although Indian judges appointed by the federal government could fine and jail local offenders, Congress's Major Crimes Act of 1885 required a trial in federal courts for reservation cases involving such offenses as murder, rape, and burglary. Two years later, the Dawes Act, discussed in chapter 3, delayed full citizenship rights and legal protections until an Indian allottee had received a patent in fee simple after twenty-five years.[17]

Despite their paternalism and rigid regulation of Indian affairs, Washington and Ottawa regularly consulted chiefs and councils. Clearly, these headmen were not just the handmaidens of federal officials, ruling indirectly for them rather than for native people. For that reason, the political actions of chiefs and councils must be examined. What were their relations with local agents and with Indian offices in the national capitals? What issues triggered the most creative native initiatives, and how did aboriginal leaders promote the interests of their people?

GREAT LAKES INDIAN INITIATIVES

Each Great Lakes Indian community responded in a unique way to the powerful internal and external pressures that it faced during the second half of the nineteenth century. Still, a few generalizations can be made. Local chiefs and councils realized they must at times accommodate the demands of aggressive, resourceful Washington and Ottawa policy makers and their field officers. The result was a governing partnership between Indian headmen and federal officials. Together, they staged elections for reservation officials; set and approved their salaries; and grappled with critical, everyday resource issues, such as allotments, leases, fishing rights, and tribal membership. Political cooperation enabled chiefs and councils to preserve much of their homeland and their identity as Indians and to keep a hand on the tiller of their fate as they sailed into the twentieth century. To portray Indian leaders largely as victims of oppressive colonial powers is to disregard the fruits of these hard-won, productive partnerships with federal officials.

Though cooperation was a dominant political theme, it could not mask the underlying, natural tensions between Indian councils and federal bureaucrats at all levels. Native communities regularly challenged and refused to do the bidding of assimilationist Indian agents and policy makers. Resourceful chiefs and headmen, defenders of reservation interests as they saw them, pressed federal officials to abandon or modify many of their programs. When unable to persuade a local Indian agent, chiefs deluged Washington and Ottawa with petitions. Native delegations carried complaints directly to national capitals. They used missionaries as advocates and hired attorneys to defend native rights. They partnered with other reserves to strengthen their messages. In short, aboriginal politicians understood the white man's political system and used it for Indian ends. One thing was certain: Great Lakes Indians were just as assertive politically as they were in matters of religion, education, and making a living.

Another corrective to the notion of federal political dominance was suggested by Canadian agent William Van Abbott in 1894. He only visited the Michipicoten and Big Heads on Lake Superior once a year.[18] Otherwise, these isolated and independent bands directed the activities of their own families and villages, free from Ottawa's interference. How different their situation was compared to southern Indian communities. They regularly contended with aggressive white neighbors, missionaries, schoolteachers, and resident agents—all of whom had a finger on daily reserve affairs.

One more political generalization emerges from the record: the loyalty of Great Lakes natives to the United States and Canada during times of political crisis. Historian Laurence M. Hauptman's Civil War study, while acknowledging that individual Indians historically joined war parties for a variety of reasons, argues:

> Most Iroquois see themselves as citizens of their own Indian nations, not New York or the United States. They generally perceive themselves as Indian allies of the United States going to war to help as part of treaty obligations. In the Civil War era, the president was seen as the Great Father, however fickle and unreliable, protecting Indians from mercenary interests of their enemies.

Large numbers of New York Indians thus joined the military in the 1860s and fought to preserve the Union. In Wisconsin, men representing nearly 10 percent of the total Oneida community volunteered for army service. Their tradition of loyalty stretched back to the American Revolution and was continually emphasized in dealings with Washington officials before and after the Civil War. Of the 120 Menominee men who fought for the Union, about one-third died.[19]

The same spirit characterized Canadian reserves, whose leaders rarely lost an opportunity to underscore their historic loyalty to the British Crown (particularly during the War of 1812) and Indian willingness to shed blood again if called on. These thoughts permeated petitions sent to the Canadian seat of government as well as speeches made to visiting dignitaries. In one such speech in August 1874, Six Nations chief Jacob General reportedly addressed the governor-general and the Countess of Dufferin at the Six Nations council house.

> He reminded His Excellency, that when British supremacy on this continent was in peril, their Indian forefathers shed brooks of blood on behalf of the English nation, and, if the services of the Six Nations were ever required again, in defense of the British flag, they would be willing to risk their lives as their forefathers had done. The Six Nations, had confidence in the treaties they had with the English Government, none of which had ever been violated.

Expressions of native loyalty abounded that day. Decorating the road to the reserve, four arches proclaimed a Six Nations' welcome to the royal guests. An Indian band played "God Save the Queen." A royal salute was fired. Another band greeted the dignitaries with "Rule Britannia." The assembled crowd numbered about five thousand, and the speakers' platform was strikingly arranged with flags, ensigns, a carpet, and scarlet chairs. As the governor-general and countess proceeded to the dais, "flowers were thrown in their Excellencies path, by Indian maidens, the audience rose, and a number of children sang the National Anthem."[20]

CHIEFS, COUNCILS, AND INDIAN AGENTS

Expressions of aboriginal loyalty and partnerships with Canadian and American federal governments required a recognized Indian leadership—chiefs and councilors—who could mobilize and then express their constituents' political wishes. Diversity, once again, characterized community affairs. Selection of chiefs and council members were a case in point. Some reserves, like Six Nations in Ontario plus the Tonawanda Seneca and Tuscarora of New York, retained their councils of hereditary chiefs throughout the late nineteenth and early twentieth centuries. More often, Indians modified traditional political patterns to meet changing circumstances. Thus, when some Oneida of the Thames chose to follow the Handsome Lake religion, they also established their own chiefs' council—an alternative political structure to the traditionally chosen council of, by then, Christian chiefs. Other reserves elected some or all of their officials. At Wikwemikong on Manitoulin Island, for instance, residents settled political differences by recognizing two life chiefs and electing seven other chiefs and councilors. Finally, in response to federal pressure or dissatisfaction with the status quo, several native reserves adopted an elective system for choosing their leadership. Thus the Allegany and Cattaraugus Seneca of New York, disillusioned by the land sales of hereditary chiefs, proclaimed a republican form of government in 1848.[21]

With the election of more and more reservation councils, another political pattern emerged. Both Washington and Ottawa became acknowledged political partners when it came time to vote. Local Indian agents and their superiors set the day for balloting, helped determine which males could participate, certified the election, officially recognized officeholders, and even retained the power to depose chiefs.

Notwithstanding a guiding—and, at times, interfering—federal hand, local American and Canadian chiefs and councils exercised broad and important powers in conjunction with Washington and Ottawa. A representative incident illustrates this political collaboration. In 1899, the L'Anse and Lac Vieux Desert bands of Lake Superior Ojibwa voted in open council to expend $993.50 of their funds to repair the local school and to purchase agricultural equipment, supplies, and livestock. The council then composed a supply list, which it forwarded to Washington through a local disbursing agent. Though the Indian Office had to approve the requisition, it represented a grassroots initiative and judgment about local needs.[22]

Councils like L'Anse and Lac Vieux Desert exercised power in a variety of ways. Historian David Beck's study of Wisconsin's Menominee leaders documents how they facilitated decision making and championed reservation interests while wrestling with a paternalistic Uncle Sam. His agents tried to dominate local politics; they presided over council meetings, set agendas, and decided whether or not to recommend a request to headquarters in Washington. Menominee chiefs and councils nevertheless refused to play this subservient game.[23] If they wished to discuss an important issue at a meeting, they did so. If an agent did not endorse a decision and forward it to the Indian commissioner, native delegations repeatedly bypassed the agent and carried their requests to Washington. Beck notes as well that Menominee agents at times filed misleading reports about council proceedings. Historically, they were arenas for hammering out a tribal consensus, yet agents pictured them as unproductive struggles between young radicals and older traditionalists.

The ability of the Menominee to coalesce politically in defense of their interests was never more clear than in 1871. Congress, at the urging of one of its members—Oshkosh lumber tycoon Philetus Sawyer—proposed to sell part of the reservation. Washington would implement the plan only if the Indians acquiesced. Although considerable disenchantment existed about the economic development of their homeland, particularly its timber resources, those attending the council meeting in March expressed a united opposition to further land sales. Two months later, the council, with over two hundred in attendance, offered an alternate scheme to selling either reservation land or its timber to white lumbermen. The Menominee proposed to harvest their own timber. Such a creative consensus even persuaded their agent, who excitedly informed the Indian Office that his charges would get much more money by marketing their own timber and could use the profits to support local farming.

Meanwhile, in Canada, chiefs and councils likewise maneuvered skillfully and doggedly to advance the welfare of their people in the face of a paternalistic Indian Department and aggressive white developers. That Walpole Island politicians, for example, became increasingly adept at managing their own affairs and dealing with the federal government became clear to the Reverend Jamieson, whose observations introduced this chapter. Six Nations council meetings during the late 1800s likewise reflected the Indians' ability and desire to control their own affairs, as well as their recognition of the necessity of dealing effectively with federal officials. The frequency of these gatherings depended on the press of business and might be called either by the chiefs or the local agent. The sessions usually lasted several days while a consensus was sought on a variety of agenda items.[24] A federal official was supposed to chair council meetings; in reality, the chiefs guided proceedings through an orderly agenda and allowed the agent, with the help of an interpreter, to speak when appropriate. The agent also kept minutes, which were forwarded to Ottawa for sanctioning or follow-up questions. Twenty-seven chiefs plus the speaker attended the meeting on June 16, 1885, and deliberated on a variety of items, ranging from ownership of land and road maintenance matters to approving payment of bills.[25]

Chiefs from Six Nations Reservation reading wampum belts. *(Courtesy Library and Archives Canada, image C-085137.)*

Headmen like those at Six Nations represented their people's interests and sought to find ways to reconcile them with the demands of Washington and Ottawa. Federal officials also had to work this rough, middle ground. Effective ones not only understood but respected aboriginal political procedures. Thus, in 1855, when the salary of old chief Joshua Wawanosh became an issue, the Indian Department initially decided to question elders of the Sarnia Reserve separately. Deputy Superintendent Froome Talfourd soon learned that it would be better to follow Indian custom in such important matters and convene a general council, which expressed a unanimous wish to increase the chief's salary. The governor-general later approved the pay raise, knowing that Sarnia wanted it.[26] Twenty years later, when Cape Croker's chiefs and principal men dismissed Chief William Macgregor as well as another person who served as secretary and interpreter, the Indian Department pointedly reminded them of its prerogatives. Once a chief's selection was endorsed by the superintendent general, only he could remove the officeholder, and he could only do so after a charge had been filed. Moreover, Cape Croker could not elect a new chief until the Indian Department sanctioned the election, which must be held with the local Indian agent present.[27]

Besides selecting local leadership, councils and the Indian Department cooperated on many money matters, such as setting salaries for chiefs and the growing number of reservation employees. In the mid-1800s, the payrolls mainly included chiefs; then, with growing responsibilities for resource development and protection, Indian governing bodies started hiring—from their own funds—secretaries, treasurers, interpreters, policemen, forest bailiffs, school officials, and others. In 1885, for instance, Six Nations had fifty pathmasters to superintend roadwork.[28]

Canadian and American federal officials, who held all Indian funds from land and resource sales in interest-bearing accounts, insisted on approving all disbursements in advance. They then made sure that these monies were expended properly. The process smacked of paternalism, but the theme of political cooperation again prevailed. Walpole Island was illustrative. From the 1850s to century's end, chief and council first authorized money for a particular project, be it large or small. (Relief monies approved in December 1882 totaled $161 and ranged from $48 "to build a small house for an old person" to $4 to help a widow.) The local agent certified each council resolution. Next, the islanders completed requisition forms specifying to whom monies from their trust funds should be disbursed and for what services. Ottawa reviewed the requests and made necessary payments. Last, the Walpole agent certified that "the articles have been received, the services performed, and that the prices are fair and just."[29]

Meddlesome though this financial procedure was, it showed significant respect for Indian input, including in personnel matters. In 1859, when charges were preferred against Six Nations interpreter Peter Smith for taking bribes, stealing, and "habitually misinterpreting," the Indian Department responded judiciously and respectfully. First, it sent an investigator to gather facts. Then, before expressing a judgment about Smith's guilt or innocence, the governor-general asked the chiefs to assemble and listen to the evidence obtained by the department's fact finder and to allow Peter Smith to speak in his defense; after Smith had left, the council would make a judgment. A large majority decided he was guilty, whereupon the department could confirm the decision, knowing it acted justly and according to the reserve's wishes.[30]

Such productive political relationships required close cooperation between reservation councils and federal agents. Yet Indian correspondence from the period and current scholarship reveal much tension and dissatisfaction about day-to-day dealings on the local level. At times, Indians had serious complaints about federal appointees. Beck's study of the Menominee underscores both a fundamental lack of trust and disgust with Washington's paternalism and ethnocentrism. Beck cites a government official who noted in 1870 that the Menominee "have little confidence in Agents: they look upon all employees [of the federal government] as so many leeches, who live off the money belonging to the tribe." The official emphasized, "I know they have no respect for an Agent, now." Beck also cites five Menominee leaders who complained about their agent in 1884, because he failed to appear at the reservation as promised with monies needed from their logging fund. "This plainly shows the way he looks at us," the writers commented bitterly, explaining, "He looks upon us as mere brutes and does not care a particle for this people. He would rather see us doomed to death." The Menominee were not alone in this harsh judgment. As Beck reports, Secretary of the Interior Samuel J. Kirkwood received an irate letter from Judge Sam Ryan of Appleton, Wisconsin, who protested about how the Indians were regarded and treated: "They are really, as a tribe, qualified for citizenship, and yet each succeeding agent seems determined to treat them as barbarians."[31]

Leaders of Canada's New Credit Reserve also had trouble creating an effective political partnership with their agent. In 1859, Chief Joseph Sawyer and twenty-three others advised the Indian Department about the many shortcomings of newly appointed agent James McLean. He acted in an arrogant manner and regarded local Indians as "inferior beings, ignorant and perfectly insignificant." Too often, he dismissed native requests and evidenced little interest in the community's welfare. "We cannot," wrote the petitioners, "endure him any longer. As you [the Indian Department] desire the prosperity—the welfare and happiness of our people—the preservation of peace and unity among us, you will not turn a deaf ear to the wishes of our people."[32]

Battling Ottawa and Washington was difficult enough even when petitioners spoke authoritatively with a resolution from a band council. At other times, reservation factionalism weakened their political clout. Serious differences of opinion within the political leadership were to be expected. Politics could not help but reflect mixed Indian responses on a variety of fronts, including horse-and-plow agriculture, formal education in government schools, and the call of Christian church bells. The challenge to change was not new; Indian cultures had been evolving long before Europeans invaded North America. But the reservation years of the late 1800s brought intense pressure for rapid adjustment by a people embattled on greatly restricted homelands. Usually, there was not enough time to talk over the array of options—from cooperation to resistance—and to forge a new community consensus. Loosed from the moorings of the past, Indian decision makers grappled as best they could with the barrage of new problems and new opportunities.

That political differences at times jelled into factions was clear from events on several reservations, including those in Wisconsin. Historian Robert Bieder points out that although some reservation residents took extreme positions as either traditionalists or favoring accommodation, the majority were more fluid and pragmatic. Their goal of "getting on with life" required picking and choosing from both customary practices and the ways of the white man. Their mixed family economies reflected this reality—this shuffling, writes Bieder, across "blurred ideological divisions in their struggle to survive." Politics simply mirrored this reality. Voters on all reservations shifted from one bloc to another depending on the issues, be they minor or momentous. They did not lack ambitious politicians. "No ward politician, seeking small offices, a little patronage, and the control of public funds," observed U.S. census takers in 1890, "can more shrewdly manipulate voters or pledge small favors for votes than the ambitious Indian chief."[33]

The Canadian reserve leadership, facing similar external challenges, was just as likely to divide on their response. At Six Nations, for example, those who favored hereditary leaders wrangled for decades with those favoring an elected council. The Mississauga of Alderville who favored acculturation had an ongoing struggle with more conservative members. Even religious affiliation could be a source of community partition, although one often found a struggle for political power beneath these badges. Missionaries quickly learned that if they got caught up in these controversies, their evangelical effectiveness was damaged At Sarnia, even Indian agents—ardent champions of the Church of England—got mired when they backed an Anglican faction against Chief Waywaynosh and his Methodist supporters.[34]

INFLUENCING FEDERAL POLICY MAKERS

Another indicator of the importance of Great Lakes aboriginal politics was intertribal cooperation. It took various forms. On Manitoulin in 1864, chiefs from both the ceded and unceded portions met in council. Wah-ka-ke-zhik, speaking for the eastern communities that had refused to sign the 1862 treaty, warned his brethren who surrendered much of western Manitoulin that their white neighbors would soon control all the best jobs: "To you, my friends, will be given the lowest meanest work to do as servants—such as, carrying water, cutting up wood, cleaning stables, making baskets, etc." Furthermore, he argued that there would not be enough land for their children, since the Indian population was increasing in numbers. Wah-ka-ke-zhik called for a reunification of the island's Indians: "We should eat out of one dish." This was why his people were determined to hold on to their part of the island. Chief Wai-she-guon-gai, who spoke for reserves on the western part of the island, disagreed with this prognosis. His communities, too, were concerned about the future and their children; that was why they signed the treaty and trusted the whites to treat them well. The chiefs tactfully agreed to disagree. The Indian Department, on the other hand, was upset that the chiefs even held councils. The following year, when they gathered from the mainland and the Bruce Peninsula to discuss how "to get back the island" (Manitoulin), Deputy Superintendent General William Spragge instructed his agent at Manitowaning to inform the Indians firmly that the department refused to recognize their gathering because it was not sanctioned beforehand and because no department representative presided over the assembly. Agent Charles J. Dupont was also told to warn the eastern Indians that they should not meddle in the affairs of native islanders who signed the 1862 treaty and whose interests were now different.[35]

Less impromptu than these meetings was the ongoing Grand General Council of Ontario. It met on a different reserve every two years during the last half of the 1800s and included nearly all Canadian Great Lakes Ojibwa bands. A band could send one delegate for every hundred members. In 1886, a Sarnia Reserve council selected its three representatives and one from Stoney Point for the grand council. Sarnia also appropriated forty dollars from tribal funds to pay their traveling expenses and board. Following a meeting, the grand council published both its minutes and its constitution. The latter embodied procedures for its conferences and the duties of officers to be elected at each gathering. The council's purpose was to discuss issues and advocate those measures that "would bring about civilization in the truest sense of the word to those Indians whom they represented."[36]

As with the gathering of Manitoulin Island bands, the meetings of the Grand General Council provoked revealing responses from the Indian Department, which historically preferred to keep native bands divided. As early as 1851, when Beausoleil asked the department for barrels of flour and pork so that the reserve could help host a council, it triggered a tough response. Robert Bruce, the superintendent general of Indian affairs, said that he did not encourage grand councils. He maintained that tribal councils alone should direct local affairs and that participation in intertribal gatherings diverted them "from more profitable pursuits" and cost too much money. Still, the superintendent general did not totally reject the request; the Indians, he decided, must formally request assistance and outline the business items on the council's agenda.[37]

Ottawa eventually allowed band funds to subsidize grand councils and even sent observers—at the Indians' request. In June 1896, the observer was

Inspector J. Macrae, who proceeded to Cape Croker as ordered. He was to witness only and say nothing that might bind the department. Macrae's report, filed the next month, was an enlightening supplement to the council's published minutes. First, the delegates, who included some young "and really clever members," impressed Macrae with their decorum, good sense, and wisdom. The orderly speeches were "intelligent, occasionally eloquent and well marked with moderation." Those with opposing opinions treated each other with "the utmost courtesy." Second, Macrae observed, the printed council minutes did not reveal the significance of these deliberations. Delegates, familiar with the Indian Act and its several amendments, debated some of its provisions and showed an impressive understanding of Indian interests. So struck was Macrae that he extolled the grand council's usefulness for all parties. It was not Ottawa's enemy; on the contrary, while discussing points of law and policy, the assemblage displayed faith in the federal government's good intentions and a "willingness to abide under its guidance." Participation in the council also gave Indian representatives a "more enlarged understanding," which they carried back to their home reserves.[38]

The Indian Department came to take seriously the actions of grand councils. In June 1900, the delegates at Wikwemikong urged Ottawa to choose its Indian agents more carefully and not to appoint men who were known alcoholics. In response, the department asked the council to furnish names of the agents referred to so that the matter could be investigated. It also admitted, in a letter to the grand council, that past agents had indeed been removed from office for inappropriate and unlawful behavior. The document listed four such persons, with their offenses.[39]

Meanwhile, the Iroquois Confederacy continued to function on both sides of the international border, though its former sphere of influence—intertribal and international affairs—was greatly restricted. At Six Nations in Ontario, the chiefs became a recognized, local governing organization, while intermarriage increasingly blurred tribal borders within the reserve. The New York story was different. Neither Washington nor Albany recognized the confederacy's political authority, and the Allegany and Cattaraugus Seneca operated as independent political units. Still, the confederacy was not totally obsolete; it revived intertribal cooperation when it championed New York Iroquois land claims and, in 1898, won a two-million-dollar settlement.[40]

Claims against the U.S. government likewise prompted the Ojibwa of Lake Superior to work more closely together. Late in 1895, reservations sent delegates to meet at Bad River, where they agreed to hire attorneys to help get the monies Washington owed them because of 1854 treaty commitments.

Cooperating reservations later signed contracts with local lawyers as well as a Washington law firm.[41]

For Indian political leaders determined to protect and advance their communities' interests, hiring attorneys and working intertribally were but two strategies employed. Another was outright resistance. As noted in earlier chapters, individuals simply refused to cooperate with federal officials. Corporate resistance occurred when reserves refused to accept an electoral system for choosing their leadership or other types of outside interference in their political affairs. Janet E. Chute and Deborah Anne Montgomerie have documented the Garden River experience. The former recounts how, in the 1880s, the Garden River and Batchewana bands implemented with some success a policy of passive, unified resistance. The goal was to stop Ottawa's use of Indian capital funds without their consent. Such fierce independence had a history. Twenty years earlier, the local Anglican missionary and the Indian Department disapproved of the personal behavior of Chief Ogista—"a wily, destitute man"—and desired to replace him with his brother, Buhkwujjenene. But Garden River would have none of it; so federal officials had to accept Ogista's continued leadership. "While this incident shows that the Department was involved in choosing which leaders would represent the band to the Department," Montgomerie writes, "it also illustrates the constraints on departmental action."[42]

Rather than choose outright resistance to Ottawa and Washington, a more common native approach was to consult with local agents and try to influence the thinking of distant policy makers. Thus, in 1859, Oshkosh and twenty-nine other Menominee chiefs invited their agent to a council. It began with an opening ceremony; then native leaders voiced a series of complaints, which they hoped the agent would send to the Indian commissioner. Confinement to a reservation was part of their predicament. Also, they claimed that annuity "money passed through too many hands before it reached them, and that a part of it was thus lost to them." Oshkosh, who spoke of these injustices for an hour following the lesser chiefs, noted diplomatically that the "Great Father" (the U.S. president) could not be aware of the Menominee problems—or else, such was the implication, he would not permit them. The council asked the agent to carry their concerns to Washington, along with a richly decorated peace pipe. As the years passed, tribal headmen continued to champion their cause through local agents. In April 1882, for example, three Menominee visited the agency to complain about the excessive prices of a local trader compared to those charged elsewhere. They also heard that the trader had gone to Washington and were afraid that he schemed to get their logs and "take advantage of us in an underhanded way." In this and other cases, Indians were quick to voice their concerns and clearly were aware of off-reservation conditions that affected their interests. Resolute chiefs regularly compelled local agents to investigate complaints and report findings to the Indian commissioner.[43]

Canadian headmen likewise used their agents to help redress grievances. Chiefs often asked them to pass on a complaint to the superintendent general. In 1859, the Sarnia council believed a recent act of Parliament infringed on their fishing rights guaranteed in earlier treaties. Agents also became fact finders. Several members of the Alderville band accused Chief John Simpson and Secretary John Rice of drunkenness in 1860. Visiting superintendent W. R. Bartlett agreed to go to their reserve and decide whether enough evidence existed to recommend removal of the officeholders.[44]

Chiefs repeatedly bypassed local agents if they did not trust them or wanted to sway policy makers. Indian councils made their voices heard in several ways: petitions, memorials, and letters; lobbying among white friends; hiring attorneys; and sending delegations to national capitals. Aboriginal peoples, as noncitizens, obviously lacked political clout. But they were a population to be taken seriously. Their history had been intertwined with that of Euro-Canadians and Euro-Americans for over two hundred years. Native peoples also had treaty rights and valuable land.

Numerous Indian petitions, memorials, and letters preserved in Ottawa and Washington archives show the intensity and shrewdness of political leveraging. Likewise revealed are issues that dominated the agendas of chiefs and councils. Wanting their agent removed, for instance, was the reason fifty-eight Wikwemikong heads of families and warriors petitioned the "Great Chief" (superintendent general of Indian affairs). They cited evidence that the agent "hates and despises the Indians": he called them refugees from America, refused to receive them at his home, made Indians miserable, and provided no service to them. "We will never have any more to do with him," the authors concluded. Similarly, at Sarnia, fifty-one chiefs, headmen, and warriors added credence to complaints about Chief David Wawanosh by jointly asking the Indian Department to remove him. As Mississauga historian Michael Ripmeester reports, the Mississauga of Alderville used a petition when faced by a removal threat from non-Indian settlers. Their skillfully worded message to the Canadian government read, in part:

> We have always relied upon the friendship and kindly feeling of the British Government and we have been fostered and protected by the Government. We have ever been faithfully and loyally attached to the Kings and Queens of England—We have shed our blood when the

War cloud covers the land of the British Lion for the defense of British rights and possessions and we are always ready to take up arms and defend our beloved Sovereign Queen Victoria.

Ripmeester interprets their petition as an act of resistance—a political weapon: "By acknowledging a subordinate role, by stating a need for protection, and by recounting their continued loyalty and service to Britain, the Mississaugas are, in effect, both reminding the Indian Department of a long-standing relationship and requesting that the government continue to uphold it." In the end, Canadian officials bowed to Mississauga intransigence and abandoned plans to relocate them two hundred kilometers to the north.[45]

So numerous did these delegations become that the Canadian Indian Department issued a circular in 1874 condemning the practice of sending them as too costly (the traveling expenses of deputations were taken from Indian funds) and as taking up too much of the superintendent general's time. Henceforth, the government would only receive these groups if they had been officially appointed by the band in council and if their visit was preapproved by Ottawa.[46] Nevertheless, natives continued to lobby, with some success, at the seat of power.

The Six Nations' sojourn in 1870 was remarkable. It began when a speaker in council objected to the 1869 Indian Act; its effect, he felt, was devastating to the Six Nations Confederacy, even though the Indians had been long-term allies of Great Britain. Moreover, he complained, the Canadian Parliament had not consulted with the Indians about possible consequences. The Six Nations wanted the continued authority to govern themselves with "their own well tried usages and customs" rather than the Indian Act's proposed municipal model. Because the reserve could not accept such legislation, the council decided to send six persons, including an interpreter, to present its views to the government.[47]

That spring, when Chief N. H. Burning's delegation arrived in Ottawa, they met first with the superintendent general of Indian affairs, John Howe, and then with the House of Commons. Howe asked the native group what they disliked about the Indian Act. They began by showing him wampum belts "handed down from past ages," one of which portrayed a chain of figures representing a treaty between them and the British government. The implication was clear; as loyal allies, they should have been consulted about legislation impacting Indian people who were quite able to govern themselves. At the end of the hour-long interview, the superintendent general conceded that representatives of the Six Nations should have been given a

Six Nations Indian superintendent and several chiefs. *Standing, left to right:* John Hill, Josiah Hill, William Wedge, Nicodemus Porter; *sitting, left to right:* David Thomas, Jasper Gilkison (Indian superintendent), David Hill. *(Courtesy Woodland Cultural Centre.)*

chance to express their views in Parliament. This satisfied the delegation. The House of Commons speaker and members received them cordially as well. The speaker, while accepting the gift of a carved cane, "expressed his earnest wish to be of any service in his power to the Six Nations."[48]

In 1879, an intertribal lobbying group from Garden River, Batchewana, and the northern Lake Huron reserves also journeyed to Ottawa to present their concerns directly to policy makers. These included the discontinuance of presents, the general lack of respect for historic alliances, and the Crown's unconcern for treaty obligations. In short, Great Lakes natives saw themselves as historic partners, not as mere clients of the Indian Department. The superintendent general of Indian affairs, wishing to discourage the mission, denied them funding; but they obtained it from the grand council. Undeterred by a threatened rebuff at the Indian Department, assertive delegates got a meeting with the governor-general, Lord Lorne. Had this not been possible, they proposed sailing to England to lay grievances before the queen. The satisfaction given by Lord Lorne made this unnecessary. He listened to complaints about the proposed allotment of native reserves; then he assured aboriginal leaders that the Crown had not forgotten its special relationship with native nations, and he promised to meet soon with band chiefs. Historian Janet E. Chute describes how Chief Ogista at Garden River used this new relationship with Lord Lorne, who visited the reserve in July 1881, to fight an Indian Department scheme to get control of the reserve through another land cession.[49]

Resourceful aboriginal lobbying continued, despite departmental roadblocks, because Toronto and Ottawa were seats of power where records were kept and policy formulated. In the mid-1880s, the Christian Island council appropriated funds to send their chief and secretary to Toronto to search the records of the Crown lands office. A local missionary, William Elias, accompanied them. The party took a boat to Penetanguishene and, from there, traveled by rail to Toronto, where they consulted with and ultimately hired George Ritchie, a local lawyer, to assist with their research on land surrenders. The council later paid for another trip to Ottawa, where the delegation met with the deputy superintendent general of Indian affairs. He gave them permission to see all the department's papers on land surrenders. Yet as late as 1890, federal officials fussed because a delegation of Manitoulin Island chiefs proposed to visit Ottawa. The local agent deemed it "unnecessary" and "wasteful," while the deputy superintendent general, L. Vankoughnet, tried to check such visits by deducting their costs from the annuity monies of individual delegates. Still they came.[50]

Indians south of the international border likewise understood the power of a petition. Sometimes, it was delivered personally; at other times, it was mailed to the Indian Office or to politicians who might act on it. In July 1868, twelve Menominee chiefs, headmen, and warriors implored Congressman P. Sawyer to stop the unlawful removal of forest resources from their reservation and the general mismanagement of agency finances. Many community members could not read and write; thus, they wanted Washington to appoint a neutral person to assist them with business affairs. In the previous month, Menominee chiefs had journeyed to the nation's capital and presented a detailed report of grievances. Now, they hoped that Sawyer could prod the Indian Office to take action. He endorsed the July petition and forwarded it to the Indian commissioner. In the spring of 1900, the Bad River Reservation, aware that a bill affecting them was being debated on Capitol Hill, likewise had their agent contact legislators and forward a petition expressing Indian wishes.[51]

Menominee politicked continuously during the last half of the nineteenth century. Clearly, they understood Washington's treaty obligations, were aware of bills brought before Congress that touched Indian interests, and were prepared to take their case to lawmakers and central administrative offices—even if forbidden to do so by their agent and the Indian commissioner. Though remarkable, the Menominee campaigns were similar to those of other Great Lakes native communities.[52]

Tribal leaders lobbied on the state as well as national levels. In 1869, chiefs and headmen thanked Wisconsin secretary of state Thomas J. Allen for providing introductory letters to influential Wisconsin politicians in Washington. Building on Allen's sympathy, the Menominee asked if he would "take our whole affair [treaty claims] in hand," for which "we would be willing to reward you accordingly." But their eyes were usually on the nation's capital. There, they sought proper compensation for the treaty of 1854, which they considered a swindle forced on them. Until a Menominee delegation journeyed east to meet with the Indian commissioner, wrote their agent in 1868, "they will never be fully satisfied." Indeed, he noted, "this business can be better accomplished in Washington, away from the throngs of old traders and others who might and no doubt would interfere injuriously in any treaty or agreement made with them." That such political activity occurred for many years was confirmed by the Menominee agent, who gave letters of introduction to a delegation in 1890. Somehow, they had found out that a bill to sell their pine timber was before Congress, and they insisted on making their views known directly to lawmakers. A "large number of the Menominees can write and are able to defend their rights," the agent pointed out, adding, "I know that the Indians took up a collection among themselves, amounting to $424.13, which I did not consider any of my business, as they have for the past fifteen years, protested the sale of their Pine timber on the stump and sent delegations to Washington *several* times, always getting the money by collection among the tribe."[53]

Some lobbying trips proved successful. In 1887, the Shawano Businessmen's Association sent a representative to promote passage of a bill giving the businessmen access to reservation timber. A Menominee group followed him to Capitol Hill to protest such legislation. Washington responded by sending its own special agent to Wisconsin. He spent twenty days looking into the possible consequences of the bill; then he filed a devastating report about the economic harm that would be done to Indians if Congress enacted such a law.[54]

Sometimes, aboriginal peoples pressed their case off the reservation through intertribal cooperation. Such an opportunity arose in 1860, when the Prince of Wales visited Canada. The Indian Department arranged for His Royal Highness to meet Great Lakes native delegates but warned them and their agents about who to send—two chiefs from each band—and how they should behave. Superintendent Richard T. Pennefather wanted "only respectable men" and maintained that they "must distinctly understand that no business will be transacted nor must any remarks be made upon the policy of the government towards them." Reservation leaders, keenly aware of this unique opportunity to underscore Crown obligations to its historically loyal Indian subjects, agreed to meet the prince. That summer, delegations of at least eighty chiefs traveled via steamboat and at federal government expense to Sarnia. They honored His Royal Highness and, at welcoming performances, received commemorative medals bearing Queen Victoria's image. Indians in traditional garb attracted public attention and affirmed their cultural distinctiveness. To the colonial secretary, the Duke of Newcastle, they also presented petitions outlining Indian grievances over land rights, treaty promises, and the behavior of the Indian Department. Six Nations chiefs later met with the prince at Brantford.[55] Once again, Great Lakes Indian politicians showed, like those before them who had negotiated with Europeans and Americans, that they could creatively and vigorously support the interests of their people.

REPRESENTATIVE ISSUES

Besides examining Indian political strategies used to advance their interests, it is also revealing to look at issues that drove reservation politics during the late 1800s. Some, like Menominee objections to the 1854 treaty and concerns about timber sales, have already been discussed. Also worrisome were money matters—such as leases and fishing rights—and local government structures. In each case, chiefs and councils seemed keenly aware of community needs and targeted those for which it was worth fighting.

Canadian chiefs were frequently on the defensive against settlers and developers who sought control over such reservation resources as timber, fisheries, mineral deposits, and fertile farmland. Yet the Indians had a potent, political weapon: the federal government insisted that land surrenders and leases were valid only if native communities consented. Council meetings in the late 1800s thus devoted much time debating these issues. In the process, they maintained considerable control of their future.[56]

The Alderville, Sarnia, Walpole Island, and eastern Manitoulin Island bands exemplified important politicking over money matters. Michael Ripmeester's Mississauga study underscores that this community exercised political independence in dealing with missionaries and Indian agents, especially when their land base was at issue. They repeatedly denied requests to cut timber and cede portions of their reserve. "A particularly significant instance of refusal involved the planned removal of the Mississaugas to a new reserve two hundred kilometers to the north," writes Ripmeester, who notes that their refusal "to buckle under pressure . . . demonstrates active manipulation of power structures." Equally astute was the Sarnia council. In 1856, when their agent sought to obtain water frontage needed by the Great Western Railway, the headmen talked it over for several hours and then agreed on terms to offer to the Indian Department. These terms included naming the price (nine hundred pounds), requesting to appoint one of the arbitrators if the price were to be fixed by negotiation, and asking that band members receive per capita cash payments. The Indian agent, calling the price exorbitant, predicted that Sarnia would never get the money. A few years later, their frontage on the St. Clair River was again a subject of debate. Mr. E. Younghusband requested to buy or lease four to five acres in order to construct an oil refinery. Two chiefs and forty-five principal men heard the proposal and learned of the endorsement by the superintendent general of Indian affairs. This time, Sarnia balked. Some members of the Progress Party were amenable to leasing river frontage for building wharfs or manufacturing plants, but all in attendance unanimously rejected the prospect of a smelly oil refinery.[57]

A meeting between Walpole Islanders and Indian Department representatives in 1895 clearly revealed the importance of local decision making, the reserve's determination to control its resources, and lingering hostility toward the department. At issue was Ottawa's desire to obtain surrenders of island timber, sand, and shooting privileges over its leased marshes. Local agent McKelvey, assisted by James J. Campbell, fully expected Walpole's leadership to be cooperative when the council was convened in the mid-morning. Within an hour, interested band members arrived and increased the assemblage to a hundred persons. Speakers hostile to any more surrenders dominated the debate, which lasted until 10:30 p.m. and won over most of the crowd. Their arguments included a desire to preserve timber resources for future generations and the belief that they could make more money by selling sand themselves. Additional feelings motivated community members. "I was forced to conclude that the spirit of antagonism to the Department," Campbell reported, "has not had time to wear off, . . . that those interested in the past in obtaining surrenders from these Indians have made a practice of bribing some of the principal men to use their influence in their favor." Federal officials, such as Campbell, might have seen the council as an example of "unreasoning obstinacy," but it is more likely that Walpole Island understood its interests and acted wisely, not out of wrongheadedness.[58]

Suspicion of hidden motives also affected negotiations between eastern Manitoulin Island bands and Ottawa. In the mid-1870s, the Ontario government offered a loan of $1,880 to bands living on unceded land, part of a provincewide program to help fund such public improvements as roads and schoolhouses. Nevertheless, at a council held at Wikwemikong to explain fully the loan's purposes, the Indians rejected it by a large majority, fearing that the government was underhandedly trying to buy their land. Local agent J. C. Phipps tried to convince the Indians that they should have confidence in his department, which was concerned about their welfare. But historical memory was too strong, and the chiefs exercised their power to turn down the loan. That the story did not end here is illuminating. A month later, in July 1877, the paternalistic lieutenant governor-in-council brushed aside local objections and approved the payment of $1,880 to the island's reserves. Though regularly browbeaten and overruled in this manner, Indian councils across the Great Lakes nevertheless continued to define and articulate native interests and to do battle with whatever forces threatened them.[59]

Likewise exemplary was the independent-mindedness of Minnesota's Bois Forte Ojibwa. During the summer of 1888, their chiefs and headmen conferred with Indian agent J. T. Gregory, who sought consent to a railroad right-of-way through their reservation. He explained the financial benefits and Washington's desire to strike a deal. Nevertheless, after "due deliberation," the band "refused to give their consent under any consideration whatsoever" and stated "that this decision was final."[60]

Another issue that continually appeared on council agendas in the late 1800s was band membership. Much was at stake. As marginalized people with limited resources, Indians understood that bloated membership rolls meant less sustenance to share. Paring down these lists increased benefits. In 1899, when George A. Morrison applied for a family membership at Bad River Reservation, La Pointe agent S. W. Campbell informed him that he must first satisfy the local Indian council that he belonged to the community. Only then could he hope to gain access to their rights and privileges. Further north, in Minnesota, matters were complicated by Canadian Indians who had intermarried with Grand Portage and Vermilion Lake members yet also drew benefits from across the boarder. Again, it was local councils that listed such persons, and they asked Washington to either drop them from Minnesota rolls or add them. Membership rolls likewise created extensive debates each year at the Six Nations council in Ontario. Following deliberations in January 1870, for example, it added twenty-one persons to the roll and removed fourteen. Decisions were anything but simple. Because Phoebe Maracle reportedly married a white man, the Indian Act required that she lose her native status. But the council speaker argued against such action. Six Nations had never been consulted in fashioning this act of Parliament; thus it refused to recognize the law and intended to keep the young woman on the membership list.[61]

Great Lakes Indian councils also comprehended the economic value of their historic fishing rights and campaigned vigorously to protect them. As early as 1859, when Sarnia learned about an act of Parliament which interfered with fisheries on Indian land, its council directed their Indian agent to remind his government that its action violated treaty rights guaranteed by Great Britain. The reserve would "not give up their fishing grounds but retain them & use them as usual."[62] They did this for several decades to come, while battling both the Indian Department and the Department of Marine and Fisheries.

Natives also fought hard to preserve their forest resources. Battle lines extended from reservation logging roads used by timber thieves to the halls of Congress nearly a thousand miles away. During the 1860s, a Menominee watchdog committee oversaw white companies with permits to cut "dead and down" timber, and the Menominee council quickly informed the Indian Office if these loggers cut green, standing trees. The council also petitioned the Indian commissioner in the early 1870s for permission to harvest their own timber. Once permission was obtained, Menominee politicked regularly to make sure that their people received the best price for their logs and that local traders did not siphon off proceeds by charging native customers inflated prices.[63]

Menominee vigilance continued. In 1889, five chiefs and headmen traveled to Washington to help shape congressional thinking about the sale of Wisconsin Indian pinelands. In October 1890, the Menominee nation accepted provisions of a federal act of June 12, 1890, regarding the sale of their timber.[64]

Ojibwa leaders bent on making a success of agriculture regularly requested—or demanded—help to which they were entitled. In 1878, for example, three Red Cliff chiefs complained about the lack of support promised by the 1854 treaty. One recalled that the "Great Father" had urged the Indians to live on their new reservation and cultivate the soil. If they did, he would assist them. Instead, one chief grumbled that he had had to buy his own cattle and farm tools. "We want this provision of our Treaty complied with," he demanded. Another headman lamented that his people had no tools with which to build farmhouses. "My young men are willing to work and cultivate and till the soil," he explained, emphasizing that Washington must then stick to its promises. Ojibwa were also not always happy with the local government farmer. A number of Bad River residents protested against the reappointment of W. G. Walker in 1895. They brought "grave charges of irregularities" about land allotment to families. The petitioners wanted one of their own capable men appointed to the position. Such preferential hiring had been promised at the time of the treaties. The Bad River objections brought a favorable response from the commissioner of Indian affairs, who replaced Walker.[65]

Attempts by Ottawa and Washington to impose new political systems on aboriginal reserves further complicated their efforts to protect local resources and generally chart their communities' future. Federal officials in both nations advocated a municipal model of government, with elected Indian councilors and a mayor (or chief). This not only weakened the clans' powers to select leaders but gave Canada and the United States supervisory power over reservation decisions. Native reactions to these schemes differed considerably. The choice to accept or reject an elective system could be messy and divisive and could drag on for years. Yet local debates illustrated each reservation's determination to control its own destiny.

In the United States, the perceived inability of Great Lakes chiefs to deal effectively with a variety of challenges—from economic and educational to religious and political—prompted changes in government structure. In 1848, the Allegany and Cattaraugus Seneca of New York did away with their traditional chiefs and created a federal republic complete with a written constitution that provided for an annually elected council. Wisconsin Oneida, likewise disenchanted with their hereditary council, changed to an elected one in the early 1870s.[66] The drive to modify neighboring Menominee politics came mainly from Washington. Its reforms—reservation police and courts controlled by Indian agents—undermined local autonomy. By century's end, the Indian Office had persuaded several traditional chiefs to surrender their authority.[67]

Similarly, the Canadian push for political reform came mostly from federal officials bent on greater local control in order to accelerate the Indians' "transformation from the status of wards into that of citizens." Early willingness to accept a municipal model of government was strongest among the bands of southern Ontario who were most bombarded by nonnative influences. William Plummer, central superintendent, thus reported in 1881 that most reserves had "an elective Council presided over by a chief." On the Bay of Quinté at Tyendinaga, for instance, Sampson Green, head chief, presided over a council made up of seven other chiefs—all chosen at an election supervised by Plummer and approved by the Indian Department. Less than two decades later, forty-two Great Lakes bands used an elective system to pick political leaders.[68]

Reservations could not always shift overnight from traditional to publicly chosen councils. Sometimes, the transition was gradual, as at Walpole. Its experience was notable partly because it illustrated a native community's political adaptability to changing circumstances. The resultant governmental change revealed as well Ottawa's wish to control native decision making and the Indian Department's conviction that its charges could not conduct their own public business. The opening wedge for federal influence was provided in 1863 by Chief Peterwegeshick, whose reported public drunkenness caused Ottawa to dispatch local agent Froome Talfourd to gather facts about the chief and also to propose a new governmental structure, according to which Walpole's council should consist of five men of "mature judgment and good character" who could read and write. The Indian Department would appoint three persons recommended by the agent in consultation with the local missionary, Andrew Jamieson. Band members would elect two others. The local agent, according to the plan, "would of course be the head of the council when present," with "all special subjects [important reserve issues] to be submitted for his supervision." Talfourd convened a band council as directed, heard testimony about Peterwegeshick's behavior, and urged those assembled to accept the Indian Department's design for a new council. The agent reported that Walpole voted overwhelmingly to accept the scheme, agreed to pay modest annual salaries to council members, and elected two of their own to serve.[69]

Two additional observations should be made about Walpole's change in government. First, its early move toward an elected council predated the 1869 Gradual Enfranchisement Act and the 1876 Indian Act, both of which called for an elective system. Second, despite Ottawa's flagrant encroachment on Walpole sovereignty, its newly structured council refused to be a puppet. Instead, it fought shrewdly and steadfastly to protect their reserve homeland and further the interests of band members.[70]

Although an elective system generally prevailed on Great Lakes reservations by the early twentieth century, some communities balked at accepting such newfangled institutions, despite intense federal pressure. American and Canadian officials, self-righteous and blind to the worth of traditional native cultures, attributed these rejections to childish stubbornness and distrust.

Six Nations of the Grand River was the largest reserve that resisted pressure to change its traditional and autonomous government. Although nearly all Ontario aboriginal communities surrendered to an elective system by century's end, Six Nations kept its confederacy council until Ottawa locked their chamber doors in 1924 and no longer recognized the right of hereditary chiefs to rule. Indians had provoked this action. Since the late 1800s, deep division characterized Six Nations. "Progressives," who favored formal education, Christianity, and social status attained by achievements and wealth, sought to remove their hereditary chiefs and set up an elective system. To this proacculturation "party," the old leadership represented outdated longhouse and confederacy traditions. Adherents also lacked the proper schooling to be effective champions during challenging times. As factional lines drew tighter and the atmosphere became charged with emotion, the council found it increasingly difficult to achieve consensus. This division plus an unfavorable federal investigation about conditions at Six Nations prompted Parliament to disband the confederacy council.[71]

The complex and disputatious political scene on the Grand River was replicated in other Great Lakes Indian communities. Generalizations are all the more difficult because of local structural changes—some rapid and some incremental—as well as evolving federal policies about Indian governance. Scattered refugee Indian settlements added another layer of complexity. In America, for example, they included Indiana Miami, Ottawa in the northwest corner of Michigan's Lower Peninsula, and Potawatomi in the extreme southern and northern parts of the state. Except for the Miami, Uncle Sam did not even recognize them as political entities in the late 1800s, and in 1897, the Indian Office terminated tribal status for the Midwest Miami.[72] Nevertheless, self-governance was as important for these "unofficial Indians" as it was for Six Nations, Walpole Island, and the Menominee.

CONCLUSION

Three developments around the turn of the century exemplified the continued significance of Great Lakes Indian politics. The Six Nations council, still composed of hereditary chiefs, responded to rapid changes on and off the reserve by adopting a full set of written bylaws. The hope was to strike a balance between the age-old customs of Iroquois country and the dynamic, intrusive Ontario Province, with whom Indians regularly interacted. It was an Indian solution to a pressing local challenge. To the west, Moravians of the Thames took similar steps. Their council enacted rules and regulations requiring parents to send youngsters to school. Their community not only accepted the value of formal education but took political action to promote it.[73] Meanwhile, Garden River battled continually to protect and develop its reserve. When neighboring developers at Sault Ste. Marie petitioned the prime minister to end the reserve system so they could get access to Garden River, its council launched a counteroffensive. A Garden River delegation journeyed to Ottawa in 1906 and successfully defended reservation boundaries, although a subsequent order in council permitted a railroad the right-of-way through the reserve. Another four years of lobbying and bargaining yielded more safeguards for Garden River. Its council had shown, once again, the importance of proactive Great Lakes Indian politics. Native reservations were not powerless. Nor did they behave like hapless victims. The Garden River story demonstrated, Janet E. Chute observes, that the "encroachments of modern capitalist society would come only so far, and no farther."[74]

Indians responded to these encroachments in diverse, ever-changing ways and with much political savvy. Political initiatives were also of profound importance in protecting their core territories and values, just like their reactions to federal programs that tried to refashion native economies, formally educate their young, and eradicate long-standing spiritual beliefs and practices. Because of federal pressures, many native communities accepted an electoral system. Others continued with hereditary clan chiefs. Walpole chose a middle ground, with its leadership being a mixture of elected and Ottawa-appointed councilors. Such political decisions could be divisive and drag on for decades, but they were usually Indian decisions.

Chiefs and councils on both sides of the international border, no matter how selected, did not become mere puppets of federal bureaucrats. Chiefs understood local interests and desires—from membership issues to the apportionment of homeland resources—and championed them creatively and persistently while using their available resources. Indian politics were complex and disputatious, but they mattered. Indians had political experience. They had treaty rights. They had protocols that must be followed. All who dealt with them knew this, including federal officials, politicians, educators, missionaries, and developers seeking access to valuable reservation resources. American and Canadian Indian leaders frequently created effective governing partnerships with local agents and their superiors. Yet if headmen differed with an agent or disapproved of a policy he tried to enforce, natives knew how to use the white man's political system toward their own ends. They cooperated intertribally. They hired attorneys. They bombarded bureaucrats and legislators with letters, petitions, memorials, and personal visits. Federal officials regularly browbeat and overruled native councils and delegations, but not always.

By 1900, the well-laid plans of Washington and Ottawa to shape the future of Great Lakes Indians—to transform their governments into handmaidens of acculturation and assimilation—had failed to a significant degree. Federal legislation in both countries weakened the powers of chiefs and councils, and intrusive Indian agents demanded and obtained a powerful voice in reservation affairs. Yet it was also clear that, despite Indian marginality, factionalism, and a colonial status, their leaders remained keen interpreters of reservation interests and, with some success, championed the self-determination and sovereignty of their people. In doing so, they helped shape the course of Great Lakes history. Indians showed remarkable resilience, adaptability, and diversity in their politics, just as they did in other spheres of Great Lakes reservation life. Though no longer masters of their fate, chiefs and councils played a critical role—during their own day and as heroes for later generations.

Conclusion

Moccasins in the Mainstream

In 1893, Chief Simon Pokagon, a sixty-three-year-old Michigan Potawatomi, spoke at the Chicago World's Columbian Exposition. His words carried the authority and the pain of one who endured both Indian removal and the ordeal of reservation life.

> We have no spirit to celebrate with you the great Columbia Fair. . . .
>
> Where these great Columbian show-buildings stretch skyward, and where stands this "Queen City of the West" *once* stood the red man's wigwams. . . . All [the resources of the region] were provided by the Great Spirit for our use; we destroyed none except for food and dress; had plenty and were contented and happy.
>
> But alas! The pale faces came by chance to our shores, many times very needy and hungry. We nursed and fed them, fed the ravens that were soon to pluck out our eyes and the eyes of our children. . . .
>
> The cyclone of civilization rolled westward; the forests of untold centuries were swept away; streams dried up; lakes fell back from their ancient bounds; and all our fathers once loved to gaze upon was destroyed, defaced, or marred, except the sun, moon, and starry skies above, which the Great Spirit in his wisdom hung beyond their reach. . . .
>
> As the hunted deer close chased all day long, when night comes on, weary and tired, lies down to rest, mourning for companions of

the morning herd, all scattered, dead, and gone, so we through weary years have tried to find some place to safely rest. But all in vain! Our throbbing hearts unceasing say, "The hounds are howling on our tracks." Our sad history has been told by weeping parents to their children from generation to generation. . . .

We never shall be happy here any more. . . . We only stand with folded arms and watch and wait to see the future deal with us no better than the past.[1]

The period following the War of 1812 was certainly hellish for Great Lakes aboriginal peoples. They were no longer needed as military allies and fur-trading partners by Great Britain and the United States, whose rapidly expanding populations in the region coveted Indian resources. One by one, Iroquoian and Algonquian nations ceded most of their homeland and either relocated west of the Mississippi River or, by the 1850s, accepted small reservations scattered throughout the Great Lakes basin. Ontario lands included fifty-six such parcels; in the United States, there were twenty-five. By 1870, officials estimated the native population at 41,500.[2] During the reservation years of the later nineteenth century, it made little difference whether Indians lived north or south of the international border drawn on the water. All were buffeted by the "cyclone of civilization" driving westward and northward: white farmers and laborers, entrepreneurs, a transportation revolution with an attendant market revolution, federal policy makers and their coercive field agents, plus evangelistic schoolteachers and missionaries.

In response, Canadian and American Indian community leaders as well as individual families valiantly and creatively defended their cultural traditions, economic and political independence, and reservation homelands. Chiefs and councils, drawing on long-standing traditions of mutual respect and cooperation with non-Indians, sought a workable balance between the new and the old, between accommodation to changing circumstances and protection of their peoples' resources and traditions. There was no monolithic native response to the exercise of power wielded by government agents, schoolteachers, and missionaries; rather, Indian groups and individuals responded in various ways, ranging from accommodation to resistance, and made use of the resources available to them.

Their story is worth telling. Great Lakes reservations were important battlegrounds where Indians fought peacefully to protect what was left of the old ways. Here, too, aggressive Canadian and U.S. frontiersmen sought control of remaining native resources. Other newcomers, hoping to save the Indian from extinction, worked diligently to "civilize" and ready reservation families for absorption into the mainstream. The outcome of these struggles helped shape the future of both sides of the watery, international border.

RECONSTRUCTING THE INDIAN

In January 1998, the Canadian minister of Indian affairs, Jane Stewart, apologized for misdirected Indian policies of the past. Speaking for her country, she said:

> We are burdened by past actions that resulted in weakening identity of Aboriginal peoples, suppressing their languages and cultures, and outlawing spiritual practices. We must recognize the impact of these actions on the once self-sustaining nations that were disaggregated, disrupted, limited or even destroyed by this dispossession of traditional territory, by the relocation of Aboriginal people, and by some provisions of the Indian Act. We must acknowledge that the result of these actions was the erosion of the political, economic, and social systems of Aboriginal people and nations.

Two years later, the U.S. Bureau of Indian Affairs made a similar statement.[3]

Indian legislation was so detrimental that it is difficult to grasp how federal policy makers and others of goodwill, such as missionaries and schoolteachers, could have been so blind—so ethnocentric. But they were. How could bureaucrats and Christian churches believe that it was in the interest of Indian children to separate them from their parents? Yet it was done.

Lawmakers, humanitarian reformers, and many Canadian and American citizens campaigned for two goals during the last half of the 1800s: transformation of "savage," reservation Indians into "civilized" citizens; and maximum control of their Great Lakes homeland, with its valuable fish, timber, minerals, and fertile soils. Many motives, some self-serving, propelled government policies and programs toward native peoples. Fundamental was the conviction in both countries that inferior aboriginal cultures based on hunting, gathering, fishing, and subsistence farming must be replaced. Otherwise, their families could not survive within an industrial, agricultural, and capitalist market system. When Indians walked the "white man's road"—that is, embraced white values and behaviors offered to them on white terms—they would become self-sufficient citizens accepted without bias in the more "advanced" Canadian and American societies.

To implement such cultural transformations, both federal governments enacted legislation and formulated detailed procedures for dealing with native wards. The Canadian approach, like the American, was characterized by "the raw intrusiveness of the instruments of policy used by the state in Aboriginal matters," as noted the Royal Commission on Aboriginal Peoples in 1996. The commission went on to report, "These policy instruments did not seek only to influence or guide, as is the case in many other areas of public policy; rather, they invaded Aboriginal peoples' lands, traditions, lives, families and homes, with a cradle-to-grave pervasiveness that other Canadians would have found utterly intolerable if applied to them."[4] North and south of the international border, federal policies promoted a large-scale reduction of Indian landholdings and the confinement of Indians first to halfway houses called reservations and then to family-sized tracts. Once these programs were in place, local Indian agents, government farmers, schoolteachers, and missionaries launched their respective cultural assaults on captive audiences. For Canadian citizens, the 1876 Indian Act and subsequent modifications embodied both their goals for aboriginal peoples and the unbridled power given to the Indian Department over everyday reservation life. Its officials, for example, could determine whether a person ceased to be an Indian because of marriage or acquiring an education. For Indians living on American reservations, the Dawes Act tore at the fabric of their communities by giving Indian agents enormous control over the native land base—from the assignment of allotments to supervision of their incomes from sales of lumber and other commodities. Perhaps the ultimate expression of this high-handed and coercive acculturation was found in Canadian and American residential schools, which literally walled Indian children off from their parents.[5]

Federal policies and programs for aboriginal peoples, including those on Great Lakes reservations in the late 1800s, were grounded in a series of questionable assumptions. First, if these "pagans" became "civilized," Canadian and American citizens would accept Indians into the mainstream. Policy makers also believed that Indians would quickly realize the need to abandon out-of-date, traditional ways and embrace programs designed to upgrade their economies, education of the young, religious beliefs, and political systems. Finally, for recalcitrant native wards, federal agents would have sufficient power to force a cultural transformation.

The assumptions soon crashed into cold reality. The "Indian problem" was not going to disappear according to plan. Indians refused to abandon their cultures wholesale. They would not be wards or pawns on the chessboard of Great Lakes history. Instead, native communities insisted on respect and consultation. They were also determined to retain a degree of control over their cultures, their reserves, and their futures.

ABORIGINAL RESPONSES

"It is a sad day for the Indians when they fall under the assaults of our troops," commented Richard H. Pratt, founder of the Carlisle Indian boarding school. "But a far sadder day is it for them," he continued, "when they fall under the baneful influences of a treaty agreement with the United States whereby they are to receive large annuities, and to be protected on reservations, and held apart from all association with the best of our civilization. The destruction is not so speedy, but it is far more general."[6]

On the contrary, reservation life neither destroyed Great Lakes Indians nor turned them into helpless victims—wards of the Crown or Uncle Sam. The Indians drew instead on ancient traditions of creative adaptation to changing circumstances in order to fashion new lives on a restricted land base, where they maintained their identity as Indians and refused to accept the white man's way of life completely. On the reserves, they pursued their interests using strategies of accommodation, evasion, or outright resistance. Here, they either controlled everyday life or—in the case of education and politics, for example—shared authority with nonaboriginal officials.

The task was not easy. Factionalism regularly strained community harmony. Issues varied according to time and place and occasionally appeared petty. Lines of division most often occurred between groups white observers called "conservatives" and "progressives." The former clung more steadfastly to traditional ways of feeding their families, educating their children, interacting with the spirit world, and governing their homeland. Progressives felt it wiser to dip their moccasins in the mainstream—to experiment with the ways of white neighbors, to compromise, to share authority with federal officials. Michael Ripmeester's study of Alderville First Nation and Robert E. Bieder's *Native American Communities in Wisconsin, 1600–1960* underscore the significance of these divisions.[7]

Reservation history was even more complex than this two-sided model. Families placed themselves at many points along the conservative-to-progressive spectrum, and through the years, members shifted points of view and practices in response to changing circumstances. To picture native people frozen in time, rigidly adhering to one point of view, is inaccurate and a disservice to nineteenth-century Great Lakes Indians and their descendants.

While trying to build a future, reservation families and their chiefs and councils confronted obstacles besides factionalism. At times, their restricted land bases and the necessity of finding new ways to support themselves resulted in poverty and associated problems, such as poor housing and the spread of tuberculosis and other communicable diseases. Embattled natives also experienced second-class status and a loss of power in a region that had once been theirs. Expansive, non-Indian neighbors continually breached reservation boundaries in search of marketable resources to which they felt entitled. Canadian and American officials were charged with protecting aboriginal interests but instead restricted their off-reservation hunting and fishing rights and sought increasing statutory control over the everyday lives of Indians. Local agents, farmers, schoolteachers, and missionaries likewise worked to destroy all vestiges of Indian traditional ways. With the exception of remote northern bands, Great Lakes reservations became battlegrounds to control the Indians' purse strings, minds, and souls.

Confrontations did not have to be so contentious. As early as the 1840s, the Reverend Peter Jones, a Methodist convert and Mississauga chief, advised the government that his people could achieve equal membership in Canadian society only if the government provided four guarantees: Indian ownership of their homeland, sufficient farmland to sustain native families, access to good schools for the children, and enjoyment of the same civil rights as fellow Englishmen. "May the time soon come," he averred, "when my countrymen will be able to walk side by side with their white neighbors and partake in all the blessings and privileges enjoyed by the white subjects of her most gracious Majesty the Queen!" Unfortunately, notes Jones's biographer, the government "moved in the opposite direction," with the result that for their first fifty years, reservations became zones of contention about treaty rights, land claims, freedom of religion, cultural integrity, and political sovereignty. Instead of valued, self-supporting citizens, Indians became government wards and a people of two worlds. "Despite good intentions [of the "civilization" policy]," writes Charles E. Cleland, "the last half of the nineteenth century was almost as difficult for Great Lakes Indians as the first. Although they did achieve their major objective in dealing with the United States, that is, the right to remain in the Great Lakes region, they found the new order difficult and frustrating."[8]

Making a living was a case in point. As white neighbors gobbled up off-reservation resources, resourceful native peoples adjusted in ways necessary to feed themselves and preserve community autonomy. For hundreds of aboriginal families, especially in the south, this meant a major commitment to horse-and-plow agriculture. The decision seemed reasonable; the land could support farming, and their communities had strong horticultural traditions. Canada and the United States also offered technical assistance. In addition, nearby markets beckoned for the Indians' surplus crops. Indian families that focused on plow agriculture altered gender roles, housing, day-to-day living (including diet), and relationships with the local Indian agent and non-Indian neighbors. There can be no doubt that agriculture is a key to understanding Great Lakes reservation adaptation and survival in the late 1800s.

Adherence to more traditional economic ways—seasonal hunting, gathering, and fishing—though evident in the south, still typified the northern reserves in both Ontario and the American Great Lakes states, where the climate and soil were much less hospitable to growing crops. Nonfarming activities included two kinds: Indians fed their families by continuing seasonal practices and by developing new income sources, such as leasing land, tourism, timber sales, and off-reservation employment created by the rapid growth of new industries and towns. Indian workers and their homeland resources played vital roles in Great Lakes business operations during the late 1800s, thereby continuing long-standing traditions of mutual respect and cooperation with non-Indians, traditions that reached back to the days of fur trading.

The limited success of reservation farming in cash crops and of nonagricultural economic initiatives prompted Washington and Ottawa legislators to try new strategies. The twin ideals of family-owned homesteads and citizenship dominated reformers' experiments. The response of Great Lakes native peoples was mixed. Large numbers of aboriginal families resisted all attempts to break their communities into pieces. Others willingly experimented with new concepts of landownership, especially if it protected their improvements and gave them a mechanism to harvest resources, such as timber, and to clear land for commercial farming. Whether the landholding changes were far-reaching or modest, Indian community leaders and family units significantly controlled the process.

The same held true for the education of their children. Many families and community leaders, north and south of the international border, believed in the importance of some formal education for their youngsters. Native communities pressured or at least allowed federal governments and churches to establish schools in their midst. Indians often helped finance construction and then maintained the structures. Some schools had aboriginal teachers. Over the years, reservation parents sent thousands of their children to day schools as well as boarding schools. As in any community, not everyone supported the local schools, and ideas changed over time as well. Some families became disenchanted with schools. Others came to the realization that formal education was necessary.

Federal policy makers and missionaries worked diligently to save Indian souls as well as to instruct the children in white ways. Church workers confronted and assaulted long-standing aboriginal beliefs and practices, both individual and corporate. Indian reactions to Christian churches proved remarkably discriminating. There was no pell-mell rush either to accept the Gospel or to reject it. Rather, aboriginal responses were once again noticeably mixed and subject to fluctuation over time. Each individual—not a missionary or Indian agent—decided how to keep a spiritual balance in life. Perhaps the most observable and impressive measure of missionary activity was the dozens of Christian churches that dotted the Great Lakes reserves by the late 1800s.

American and Canadian assaults on native government systems were meant to speed up the slow and expensive acculturation process. A series of Canadian and American laws between 1857 and 1890 attacked the powers of chiefs and councils, confined Indians generally to the legal status of minors, and made the federal governments their guardians, with power to oversee every aspect of reservation life. Once again, the aboriginal response surprised federal officials. Indian politicians—experienced, resolute, patient, astute, and resourceful—accepted the need to accommodate aggressive and powerful bureaucrats and legislators, and the result was a governing partnership in the field. If chiefs and councils did not trust local agents or wanted to sway policy makers, native voices were expressed via petitions, memorials, letters, lobbying among white friends, hiring attorneys, and sending delegations to Washington and Ottawa. Despite Indian marginality and factionalism, their leaders remained keen interpreters of reservation interests and were taken seriously.

Though state, provincial, and international boundary lines theoretically divided the Great Lakes region, waves of change between 1850 and 1900 battered both sides of the border. Triggered and shaped by these momentous developments, American and British (later Canadian) Indian policies were almost indistinguishable. This is not at all surprising. Great Britain founded and greatly influenced the early history of both Canada and America, especially their Indian policies and administrative apparatus. Because both nations dealt with many of the same Indian tribes in the Great Lakes basin, both the reservation challenges they presented and the proposed solutions to these problems inevitably overlapped. For these reasons, it makes sense to think of Canadian and American Indian policies and administration during the early reservation years as parallel stories within the Great Lakes basin. Documentary evidence is scarce about direct communication between the federal Indian offices in both countries, except to suggest that they were aware of situations across the border. In January 1870, for example, the U.S. counsul at Fort Erie, F. N. Blake, described for the secretary of state, Hamilton Fish, the management of Indian affairs in British America. Blake's report detailed conditions on Great Lakes reservations—from census figures and educational facilities to Blake's personal observations of a Six Nations council meeting. Blake also outlined the role of local Indian agents and British laws pertaining to natives. Congress subsequently published Blake's report as a House miscellaneous document.[9]

Likewise similar were native reactions in Ontario, Minnesota, Wisconsin, Michigan, and New York. What differentiated Canadian and American reservations was not federal government policies and their administration in the field. Rather, it was geography and demographics—and understandably so. Developments on the southern Iroquois reservations at Grand River and in New York State, for example, were remarkably similar during the late 1800s. They had fertile soil and strong horticultural traditions and were surrounded by non-Indian settlers. Markets beckoned to aboriginal families who tried commercial farming and who learned mainstream skills, such as speaking, reading, and writing the English language. Likewise, the deep-rooted traditions of the Iroquois Confederacy prevented Canadian and American federal agents from dominating reservation politics. In contrast, commercial farming was not a realistic alternative for Indians assigned to remote and chilly reservations, whether north of Duluth, Minnesota, or Sault Sainte Marie, Ontario. They had little contact with non-Indian neighbors or Indian agents and could still support themselves with a seasonal harvesting of wild nature's bounty.

Other factors besides geography helped reduce the significance of the Canadian-American border for reservation people. One was the border's permeability during this time period. Iroquois from New York and Ontario regularly visited distant relatives and were aware of local happenings north and south of the Great Lakes. The same was true for the Ojibwa of southwest Ontario and southern Michigan, for the Ottawa of Manitoulin Island and Michigan's Upper Peninsula, and for the Ojibwa of Grand Portage, Minnesota, and what is today called Thunder Bay, Ontario. Native peoples of the Great Lakes, like their non-Indian neighbors, shared too much in the way of history, economic ties, religion, educational goals, and political traditions to be hermetically separated by a boundary drawn on water. Philip Curtis Bellfy's study of the Anishnabeg of the Lake Huron borderlands argues persuasively that during their nearly four hundred years of interaction with Euro-Canadians and Euro-Americans, native peoples moved freely throughout the upper Great Lakes, even after establishment of the international border in 1783. So-called Canadian and American chiefs even signed treaties on both sides of the border. Shingwauk, for example, lived and fathered children on both sides of the St. Mary's River. Bellfy notes that "by marriage he had formed alliances that stretched from Little Current on the east end of Manitoulin Island through Sugar Island and Sault Ste Marie and on to L'Anse in the central portion of Michigan's upper peninsula." Native missionaries, such as Peter Jones, John Sunday, and William A. Elias, evangelized among their people on both sides of the border.[10] Thus the most striking characteristics of regional Indian history during the late 1800s were the similarities in Canadian and U.S. Indian policies and in the ways reservation people dealt with schoolteachers, missionaries, and the agents sent out from Ottawa and Washington.

THE YEAR 1900: MOCCASINS IN THE MAINSTREAM

Because Canadian and U.S. governments confined Great Lakes natives to scattered reservations and pummeled them with strikingly similar acculturation programs, it was no surprise that a half century of this treatment left Indians poised between two worlds. Indian agents, assisted by a resident staff of teachers and missionaries, directed "civilization" programs and supervised all facets of native life, from farming and timber harvests to school curriculum and tribal governments. Indian traditional lifestyles and beliefs understandably eroded while tribal bonds loosened due to lack of contact among the bands. Once the proud, influential proprietors of a vast Great Lakes homeland, aboriginal nations had, to a degree, been marginalized and modified. Most families, especially in the south, lived on reservations in permanent frame or log houses and earned their living either by farming or from wage work close to home. Gone were the distant expeditions to trapping grounds, isolated trading posts, and enemy encampments. Other features of their traditional cultures had been replaced. Many reservation natives regularly attended local Christian churches. Schools enrolled a significant number of Indian boys and girls who dressed, like their parents, in white men's clothes. A powerful mainstream tugged forcefully at Great Lakes Indians with offerings of the good life, if only they would let go of the past. Internal struggles between "progressive" and "conservative" factions suggested to outsiders that their future as unique, independent communities was in doubt.

American Indians of the Great Lakes nevertheless maintained an important presence in 1900. The census that year showed the following populations:

New York	5,257
Pennsylvania	1,639
Ohio	42
Indiana	243
Illinois	16
Michigan	6,354
Wisconsin	8,372
Minnesota	1,658 (in the "arrowhead" counties of Carlton, Cook, Lake, and St. Louis)[11]

Census takers in 1890 judged New York Iroquois to be "self-sustaining and much farther advanced in civilization than any other reservation Indians in the United States."

> On all the reservations crimes are few, stealing is rare, and quarreling resulting in personal assault, infrequent. . . . They are shown to be as law-abiding as the same number of average white people. . . . The growth of self-reliance is especially noticeable. This tends to greater diffusion of agricultural products, better homes, and clothing.
>
> There is scarcely any poverty among the Six Nations.

The Tuscarora Reservation, for example, with a population of four hundred tribal members plus forty-one Onondagas and twenty-three whites, supported three Christian churches with a membership of 238. English speakers numbered 343, and 292 could read as well. Farmers cultivated forty-two hundred acres. "It would be difficult to better balance, settle, and utilize a tract of this size than has been done in its development," remarked Henry Carrington, a contemporary observer, who added:

> Nearly the entire land not reserved for timber has been put to use. . . . The whole reservation is under fence, the chiefs enforcing a rule that every land owner shall maintain a fence at least 4 feet high. . . . [The Tuscarora] have also developed fine orchards of peach and apple trees to the extent of 269 acres. These have been carefully trimmed and kept in good bearing condition.[12]

Meanwhile, to the west, on Michigan's Lower Peninsula, moderately acculturated Indians were distinguished by extensive land loss. In the rush to integrate them into the state's mainstream, the federal government's allotment scheme lacked adequate safeguards—in effect, throwing them "to the wolves." Lands were lost and federal services abruptly withdrawn. Scattered native families, many of them landless, survived through their inherent pluck and adaptability. Living along the banks of rivers and on the shores of Lake Michigan, they played service roles or supplied labor for minimal pay instead of living as the coequal, self-sufficient farmers envisioned in 1855. For them, life on the new reservations did not last long, unlike the experiences of Lake Superior Ojibwa and the natives of Canada and New York, whose land bases were more secure.[13]

With moccasins clearly in the mainstream, the Ojibwa of Keweenaw Bay on the Upper Peninsula numbered 850 and lived mainly in the towns of Baraga, on the west side, and L'Anse, on the opposite shore. All wore "citizen's dress," half held membership in Christian churches, 750 knew enough English for everyday conversation, and 500 could read. Labor in "civilized pursuits" provided all their support, according to Indian Office records.[14]

That Wisconsin's Bad River band found itself in two cultural worlds during the decade of the 1890s was evidenced by the presence of two factions, the "progressives" and the "non-progressives" or "vagabonds," as the La Pointe agent dubbed them. The latter opposed clearing reservation land, farming allotments, and any other "civilized industry." This conflict was also evident each Fourth of July, when tourists at Ashland, Wisconsin, took a special train to Odanah to see their neighbors, in native garb, celebrate the national holiday with a traditional war dance and lacrosse game. Yet reservation cultural change was obvious everywhere. Out of a population of 645, all wore white man's clothing, 575 could read, 500 could speak English, and 95 percent supported themselves with "civilized" jobs. Church membership of 455 testified to the enduring effect of Leonard Wheeler's missionary work.[15]

Conditions in central Wisconsin echoed those of the northern part of the state, New York, and Michigan. Initial adjustments to life on the widely scattered reservations had been made. Although the Indians were not thriving, their adaptability and fortitude at least enabled them to survive the transition and establish permanent homes on restricted land bases. Campisi and Hauptman have noted in their study of the Oneida, for example, that the nation as a whole had feet in both their old world and the new one of the white man. Horse-and-plow farming gradually supplanted traditional methods. Some families used the English language and attended Christian churches. Native leaders shared political control of their communities with U.S. government officials. Increasing factionalism reflected the Oneida nation's gradual and cautious movement into a new era.[16]

Menominee family whose dress shows a life in two worlds. *(Courtesy Wisconsin Historical Society, image 55932.)*

Oneida Indian women in mainstream dress, ca. 1900. *(Courtesy Wisconsin Historical Society, image 55923.)*

Ojibwa log house, well, and wigwam frame reflect the old and the new on Lac Court Oreilles Reservation. *(Courtesy Wisconsin Historical Society, image 3958.)*

Even at remote Grand Portage Reservation, Ojibwa dress and buildings show the mainstream's influence, ca. 1885. *(Courtesy Minnesota Historical Society.)*

Even Minnesota's Grand Portage Reservation, far to the north, near the international boundary, had altered its long-established ways by century's end. Residents wore "citizens' clothes." Some claimed to be Christians. Many lived in comfortable cabins, whitewashed and shingled. Stoves provided heat as well as a cooking surface, while cellars stored homegrown potatoes and other vegetables. Census takers observed in 1890, "In the cabins of some of the more advanced families may be found clean towels, a looking-glass, clock and table, and in two or three instances a sewing machine."[17]

A reporter for the *Ashland Daily News* understood that the Indians of the Great Lakes, already a people of two worlds, were indeed on the verge of another new era in their history. "Ashland people will probably never again be offered the opportunity of seeing so many Indians who still retain their old customs," he noted on September 11, 1896, when a special train brought to town ten coaches filled with Indians from nearby reservations who had come to help celebrate a visit of Buffalo Bill's show. He continued,

> The old leaders are yearly passing away, the new generation taking their places are being educated with a view of making them industrious citizens of the United States, and soon the reservations in this

vicinity will be converted into flourishing agricultural communities, whose residents will be indeed educated, civilized and progressive citizens of the United States.[18]

The newspaper's optimistic description of these Lake Superior Ojibwa was echoed at century's end by Indian Department reports about Canada's Great Lakes Indians. Reporting from Rice Lake, for example, Inspector J. Ansdell Macrae pointed out that native families were in "close touch with their white neighbors." Children even attended the same school, located on the reserve. The band was "comfortably housed," and those who farmed appeared prosperous. Yet there were also negative aspects, which Macrae candidly documented and which illustrate that these Great Lakes Indians were poised between two worlds. Only one-third of the families engaged in agriculture. They cultivated 488 acres of the reserve's 1,860-acre total. Other persons earned a living mixing customary pursuits (fishing and rice gathering) with wage work for non-Indian neighbors. The children's routine reflected this trend. Parents enrolled just over half their boys and girls in school.[19]

Like other reserves in the well-populated and warm "banana belt" of southern Ontario, Six Nations and Walpole Island revealed a close contact with nearby non-Indians and their institutions. Frame and log houses, churches, and school buildings dotted both reserves. Horse-and-plow agriculture had become an economic mainstay by 1898. The value of Six Nations farm implements and vehicles was $28,898.00, with livestock and poultry assessed at $48,575.00. Walpole figures for the same were $8,857.00 and $17,903.00. Enumerated sources of income also showed the importance to Indians of nonfarming activities within the Ontario economy, from wages received to money earned from fishing and hunting.[20]

Although the white population thinned out further to the north, the influence of its market system, Indian agents, missionaries, and teachers was pervasive. Aboriginal families realized they had little choice but to step up their adaptation to the Euro-Canadian world. Yet they generally held on to their native identities, overwhelmingly choosing to maintain band membership over enfranchisement.

This middle position could be seen across the upper Great Lakes by the end of the 1800s. The 398 enrolled members at Cape Croker Reserve in Bruce County, for example, owned one hundred log or frame houses. The local agent valued their personal property at $68,200. All claimed to be Christian: two-thirds Methodist and one-third Roman Catholic. Three day schools offered classes for the young. Their income sources remained mixed and included fishing (the catch was valued at four thousand dollars annually), wage work, land rentals, and hunting. Ottawa was especially proud of the agricultural progress. With only 65 percent of the nearly sixteen-thousand-acre reserve fit for farming, families had cleared five thousand acres, cultivated fifteen hundred, and fenced five hundred. They built fifty barns and fifty-six horse stables. The value of livestock, poultry, and farm equipment totaled $13,500.[21]

Conditions at the twenty-five-thousand-acre Garden River Reserve on the Saint Mary's River also reflected this economic and cultural give-and-take. Two schools (one Protestant and another Roman Catholic), three churches (Anglican, Methodist, and Roman Catholic), and an array of log and frame houses testified to Euro-Canadian influence among the Indian population of 431. The reserve contained valuable timber and mineral resources. Yet the short growing season, with killing frosts on either end, limited motivation to farm. Native families still tried. Using an impressive variety of livestock and farm implements, they cleared and cultivated twelve hundred acres, on which they grew mainly potatoes and hay. Men mainly supported their families with traditional fishing plus wage work for white entrepreneurs as guides, lumberjacks, and boatbuilders. Women helped by selling crafts, doing laundry at lumber camps, berry picking, and manufacturing maple sugar.[22]

Even the remote Fort William and Nipigon bands modified customary ways in response to the winds of change in the late nineteenth century. The former reserve contained just over thirteen thousand acres and was home to 245 Ojibwa. They, too, developed a mixed economy, which included farming and wage work plus the usual berry picking, fishing, hunting, and trapping. A Catholic priest and five Sisters of St. Joseph attended to the educational and spiritual needs of the reserve. All but seventeen Indians professed to be Christians. The 465 members of the Nipigon band lived at the seventy-five-hundred-acre reserve at Gull Bay as well as on Jackfish Island, near a Hudson's Bay trading post. Hunting remained a major occupation, while families experimented with farming and sought jobs with tourists and other non-Indian employers. There was a school on Jackfish Island, and the Indian agent counted 178 Roman Catholics among the band members. The rest he deemed to be "pagans."[23]

The first fifty years of Great Lakes reservation life had not prepared native families to become self-sufficient, respected citizens of either Canada or the United States. Nor did all of them wish to be. Nevertheless, north and south of the international border, the process of adjusting to the white man's cultures, begun in the early 1600s, had accelerated tremendously. Most aspects of Indian lives had noticeably changed. The Indians' moccasins were in the mainstream by 1900 and would continue to be during the next century.

The concentration of native populations on reservation islands also deepened their environmental footprint. Permanent dwellings, outbuildings, farm fields, fences, and roads characterized much of the local geography, especially in the south. Further north, timber harvesting, commercial fishing, and some mining altered the forests, inland streams, and the Great Lakes themselves. Likewise, Indian schools, churches, lumber camps and mills, and villages sprinkled across the region changed the landscape. The ecological impact of aboriginal families was extended even further by those who worked off-reservation in nearby towns, lumber mills, and farms.

"NEITHER RED WARRIORS NOR WHITE FARMERS"

Federal government goals for their Great Lakes Indian wards were the same as for aboriginal peoples elsewhere across Canada and the United States. When Canada obtained the Hudson's Bay Company lands in 1869, it intended to "civilize" its new Indian wards by using the same methods that had "operated so beneficially in promoting settlement and civilization among the Indians" east of Lake Superior. Thus, writes J. R. Miller, the pattern of Indian Department interference and coercion was repeated, "in all its ugly detail," with the tribes of western Canada. Central to the process, as it had been for the Great Lakes, was the reservation, with its paternalistic Indian agents, schoolteachers, and missionaries.[24]

Strikingly similar was the American approach to its aboriginal wards beyond the Mississippi once the Indian Wars were over and the tribes assigned to reservations. "Thousands of them are yet in a state of childhood," wrote T. J. Morgan, commissioner of Indian affairs, in 1891. They "are living in the twilight of civilization," he said, "weak, ignorant, superstitious, and as little prepared to take care of themselves as so many infants." Because America was a great and powerful Christian nation, Morgan continued, it would treat all these wards with "paternal care" and protect them "'against further decline and final extinction' and their estates from waste and destruction." He advised, "When the Indians shall have become citizens of the United States this paternal control will cease."[25]

When implementing these goals nationally, the U.S. and Canadian governments used methods employed earlier on Great Lakes reservations. The key strategy was encouraging Indian farming. Without agriculture and a fixed residence to feed and house Indian families, noted the Canadian Indian Department in its 1898 annual report, "neither churches nor schools nor any other education influence can be established and applied." The report went on to say that farming "inculcates furthermore the idea of individual proprietorship, habits of thrift, a due sense of the value of money, and the importance of its investment in useful directions." Washington agreed, even though many western tribes lacked agricultural experience and were confined to reservations with poor soil, inadequate rainfall, or growing seasons so short that "it would be a difficult matter," noted the commissioner of Indian affairs in 1886, "for a first-class white farmer to make a living."[26]

Other lines of attack for modifying Indian ways of life across North America were the breaking up of reservations into family tracts and the formal education of native youngsters. Views expressed over the years by American commissioners of Indian affairs were harshly negative toward Indian families. It is no wonder Washington felt the need to send children off to boarding schools and separate them from their parents, whose homes were considered "a fire-damp of heathenism, ignorance, and superstition that will extinguish all the flames of intelligence and virtue that have been kindled by contact with civilization." Unless Indian education became a priority, the Indian Office argued, the American people will be "perpetually supporting them [Indians] as idlers and drones." Congress responded in major ways to such pleas. In 1880, it had appropriated only seventy-five thousand dollars to support Indian schools. Fifteen years later, the expenditure was $2,060,695, and the educational network had grown to include nineteen off-reservation boarding schools, seventy-five reservation boarding schools, 110 reservation day schools, and sixty-two institutions (operated by churches or secular groups) with whom the federal government contracted. In the 1890s, Washington also required that all Indian children attend school. Those who did numbered more than twenty thousand by the close of the century.[27]

The Canadian assessment of "pagan" aboriginal cultures and of the need to remove and uplift the youth in order to equip them for mainstream society paralleled the thoughts and the actions of American neighbors to the south. First, the Indian Department felt a moral obligation toward native people—a "sacred trust with which Providence has invested the country." The key to improving their social and economic lives—"the permanent elevation of the race"—was educating the youth. This could only be achieved by altering the views of parents. They were not inclined to force their children to do anything and also feared that their boys and girls would be lost to them if they attended the white man's schools and took on a different set of values and spiritual beliefs. Only parents who were in close contact with non-Indian neighbors on the southern reservations agreed to send their children to schools. The most effective schools, reasoned the Indian Department, were residential facilities that separated the child from "the deleterious home influences." As in the United States, the nationwide number of Canadian Indian schools grew rapidly during the closing years of the century. In 1889, school-age aboriginal children numbered 15,835. Classroom enrollments were as follows: 5,759 attended 215 day schools, and 700 attended 16 boarding schools.[28]

Finally, likewise reminiscent of their approach to Great Lakes Indians, the United States and Canada each sought to speed up the "civilization" and integration process by altering native political systems and attacking tribal sovereignty from coast to coast. North of the Great Lakes, the Indian Department systematically tried to replace hereditary rulers with elected chiefs and councilors, thereby hoping to infuse "that spirit of individuality without which no substantial progress is possible." American policy makers could not agree more. We want the Indian to "say 'I' instead of 'We,'" reported the commissioner of Indian affairs in 1888, and " 'This is mine,' instead of 'this is ours.' "[29]

That American and Canadian aboriginal families would recognize the need to adapt to changing circumstances during the late 1800s seemed a foregone conclusion to federal policy makers and reformers of goodwill. The Indian "can not sweep back with a broom the flowing tide," remarked a commissioner of Indian affairs in 1888, explaining:

> The forests into which he ran whooping . . . have been felled. The game on which he lived has disappeared. The war-path has been obliterated. He is hemmed in on all sides by white population. The railroad refuses to be excluded from his reservation—that hot-bed of barbarism. . . . The Christian missionary is persistently entreating him to abandon paganism. Gradually the paternal hand of the Government is being withdrawn from his support.[30]

It was thought that the Indians of North America would surely see these realities and place their moccasins and themselves fully in the Canadian and U.S. mainstreams.

Yet native peoples never quite saw the world the way Euro-Canadian and American officials and reformers did. In the United States, Indians beyond the Mississippi fought 1,065 military engagements rather than surrender their homelands and traditional ways and be confined to restricted areas. In the end, they became reservation Indians as did the Canadian tribes west of the Great Lakes. But the situation rankled. It was not helped by altruistic reformers and Indian agents, with their battery of intrusive programs, including farming instruction, allotment of the land, formal education of the young, and interference with traditional ceremonies and political practices. Natives of the prairies, plains, mountains, and deserts not surprisingly developed various strategies, like their eastern counterparts, to cope with these new conditions—strategies that neither Washington nor Ottawa anticipated. One thing aboriginal peoples had in common, besides their suffering and stubborn determination to remain Indians and control their lives, was a profound sadness about losing so much of their homeland. Sounding much like Red Jacket from an earlier time, Chief Little Raven of the Southern Arapaho spoke for many Indians of the West:

> Long ago the Arapahoes had a fine country of their own. The white man came to see them, and the Indians gave him buffalo meat and a horse to ride on, and they told him the country was big enough for the white man and the Arapahoes, too.
>
> After a while the white men found gold in our country. They took the gold and pushed the Indian from his home. I thought Washington would make it all right. I am an old man now. I have been waiting many years for Washington to give us our rights.[31]

Indians who resisted the white man's acculturation program were a formidable force and acted from reasonable motives. The white man's broken promises, which so troubled Little Raven, also undermined Indian faith in Washington's various reservation initiatives. In 1881, for example, when Sitting Bull ended his Canadian exile and surrendered to the commander at Fort Buford in Dakota Territory, he spoke with disdain about accommodationists and reservation life: "I do not wish to be shut up in a corral. It is bad for young men to be fed by an agent. It makes them lazy and drunken. All agency Indians I have seen were worthless. They are neither red warriors nor white farmers. They are neither wolf nor dog."[32]

Traditional ways of life still beckoned for many western reservation residents determined to keep such customs alive—from courtship practices and polygamy to clan ceremonies and sacred rituals, such as the Sun Dance. Parents withheld their children from government schools and their cooperation from Washington officials who would change aspects of the old ways. Such resistance in turn triggered coercive responses from federal officials. For instance, in 1890, because the Hopi would not send their children to boarding schools, the Indian Office, demanding that a set number of boys and girls enroll each year, sent army troops to collect them. Native resistance provoked even more extensive action from Congress. During the 1890s, it authorized compulsory school attendance for Indians and also permitted the

Indian Office to withhold annuity money from parents who would not send their children off to be educated. Washington later discovered, ironically, that boarding schools empowered some graduates by giving them the tools—particularly the ability to read and write English—to oppose more effectively the forces designed to Americanize their reservations.[33]

As in the Great Lakes region, Indians west of the Mississippi opposed many federal programs and did so in ways unanticipated by the Indian Office. Historians have written extensively, for instance, about how the so-called Five Civilized Tribes and many of their native neighbors in the Indian Territory, west of Arkansas, worked cooperatively to stop the allotment of their lands in the late 1800s. Another form of resistance was refusal to give up religious rituals, such as the Sun Dance, which the Indian Office deemed "pagan" and tried to stamp out. Instead, natives who were determined to keep important ceremonies spiritually alive took them underground or modified them in order to fool federal watchdogs. This desire to preserve the old ways helps explain Indian receptiveness to the Ghost Dance and to such prophets as Smoholla and Skolaskin.[34]

Just like in the Great Lakes basin, western reservation experiences were not just characterized by native resistance. Accommodation was also a theme. For these aboriginal leaders and their followers, military resistance seemed futile, as did the dream of restoring traditional ways of life. A more realistic approach, they felt, was to make the best of reservation life. This included cooperating with federal authorities, taking up farming, adopting "citizens's dress," attending a Christian church, and sending their youngsters to school in order to better understand white ways and obtain useful cultural tools.

Even those who had militarily resisted homeland loss and confinement—such chiefs as Geronimo, Red Cloud, Sitting Bull, and Joseph—eventually realized that they must make their peace with reservation life. Chief Joseph expressed these feelings in 1879: "When I think of our condition my heart is heavy.... I know that my race must change. We can not hold our own with the white men as we are. We only ask an even chance to live as other men live.... Whenever the white man treats an Indian as they treat each other, then we will have no more wars."[35] Like Potawatomi chief Simon Pokagon, they judged that putting their moccasins into the American mainstream was necessary. Yet they could still be Indians and still be critical, when warranted, of Uncle Sam's treatment of reservation people.

Clearly, then, the Great Lakes reservation story of resistance and accommodation was replicated a bit later in the 1800s by Indians west of Ontario and beyond the Mississippi. Each family, based on its circumstances in a given year, decided what it needed to do to survive as Indians and to prosper. In doing so, the Indians asserted the power to shape their own future, despite the sometimes oppressive forces of intrusive federal agents and their associates as well as the ever-present greed of some white neighbors for native land and resources. To portray freedom-loving, hardworking, adaptive, and creative Indian people during this period as helpless victims who no longer played important roles in Canada and the United States does a great injustice to history.

BURNED ON THE BOTTOM OF THE MELTING POT

The Chicago World's Columbian Exposition, at which a sad Chief Pokagon spoke about the loss of Indian homeland, attracted twenty-five million visitors. Exhibits trumpeted industrialization's triumphs, including electric lightbulbs, long-distance telephone calls, and the phonograph.[36] The rapid growth of America's cities and big businesses during the previous half century not only generated a variety of alluring consumer goods and services but catapulted the nation onto the world stage as a major economic and military power.

The costs of this sea change were high—and not just for Indian people. Rural and small-town newcomers to the city, whether native-born or foreign-born, struggled to adjust to the weird and wonderful rhythms of urban life and to the changing nature of factory work. Products once created by individual, skilled craftsmen were churned out on assembly lines by wage earners. The U.S. and Canadian federal government were not directly responsible for these developments, nor were they entirely to blame for the difficulties endured during this era by urban workers, women, immigrants, African Americans, and African Canadians. These groups, like the native peoples of the Great Lakes, were shaken by massive, international forces far beyond their control.

Ambivalence characterized the response of the American and Canadian publics to these changes. They were disturbed by many aspects of industrialization and urbanization and by the large number of foreigners who disembarked on North America's shores to keep the assembly lines humming. Nevertheless, for Americans, writes historian Glenn Porter, this new order "met the central needs of an increasingly materialistic society," and "most simply accepted the costs because the benefits were so appealing."[37]

Romantics and social engineers, who visualized America and Canada as melting pots in the late 1800s, pressured all residents to accept mainstream values and ways of living and to become an amalgamated people. Such was the ideal. Ironically, while national leaders summoned everyone into the mainstream, social and economic structures kept less fortunate groups—workers on assembly lines, women, immigrants, blacks, and aboriginal peoples—in disadvantaged and exploited positions. They got burned on the bottom of the melting pot.[38]

The industrial expansion of Canada and the United States required an army of skilled and unskilled factory laborers. The fruits of their production were unevenly distributed, however. Unskilled workers, whose large numbers often kept wages at the subsistence level, had little job security. Despite "all the traditional celebrations of the rising standard of living and the fruits of plenty in the American economy," writes historian Eric Arnesen, "poverty remained a chronic, often inescapable feature of working-class life." Much like the scattered Great Lakes reservations, diversity on the factory floor—including skilled and unskilled workers, native-born workers and immigrants, males and females, whites and nonwhites, Protestants and Catholics—prevented laborers from promoting reforms with a single voice. Out of 27.6 million American workers in 1900, only one million belonged to unions. In that year, the Canadian labor movement was also small and fragmented. Much as native people relied on communal support in order to cope with reservation life, urban factory workers turned to fraternal organizations as a social safety net to help with the costs of illness and the deaths of loved ones.[39]

Women's labor increasingly helped fuel the growth in cities and industry, yet they, too, remained at the bottom of the melting pot. Ambitious American and Canadian females suffered a double dose of injustice; they earned less than men, they endured legal discrimination, and those trying to make it on their own in towns and cities were among the poorest residents. Race, ethnicity, class, marital status, and location helped shape female experiences. Women on Canadian farms were a case in point. The nation's census takers regularly refused to recognize females as workers, despite their prodigious contributions in the home as well as in the gardens and fields. Moreover, family customs and laws worked against women starting their own farms or inheriting land. Beyond the family farm, work for females was limited to domestic service on another farm or teaching school for a salary less than that paid to men. It is no wonder so many young, rural women sought additional opportunities in the city. There, though, employers and landlords took advantage of them as well as the daughters of immigrant families.[40] Diversity, the inability to vote, and poor pay all worked against women as they struggled to cope, like reservation peoples, with the challenges of life in the late nineteenth century.

A third group of disadvantaged persons who made their homes in Canada and the United States during this era is immigrants. They came chiefly to find jobs, and their large numbers had a major impact on both industrial and urban development. Between 1866 and 1900, 13,259,469 arrived in the United States, most without skills or much money. More than eight hundred thousand were French Canadians who, like Great Lakes native peoples, were not adverse to crossing an international border in pursuit of economic opportunity. Immigrants, also like many reservation residents, constantly moved within cities, experimenting with new ways to make a living, adjusting to mainstream social structures, and simultaneously holding fast to traditional customs, including languages and mutual aid societies.[41]

One of the most obvious links between aboriginal and immigrant histories is the discrimination newcomers experienced from native-born Americans and Canadians. Motivated by a number of fears, especially economic and social, they turned on coworkers and neighbors. Treatment of Chinese newcomers was the most blatant case. First attracted to American goldfields and construction work on the transcontinental railroad, Chinese in the United States numbered approximately 125,000 in 1882. In that year, national anti-immigration sentiment led to passage of the Chinese Exclusion Act, which marked the beginning of a restrictive trend designed to keep out the "wrong" kinds of people. Like others with distinctive cultures and skin colors, Chinese families tended to live together in urban areas, such as San Francisco and Los Angeles, where they established supportive institutions and preserved much of their culture.[42]

Asian immigrants fared no better in Canada. The Canadian government recruited sixty-five hundred Chinese workers to help build the Canadian Pacific Railway, even though many whites intensely disliked the newcomers. John A. Macdonald, Canadian prime minister, justified his labor policy to a Toronto audience: "Well they do come and so do rats. I am pledged to build the great Pacific Railroad in five years, and if I cannot obtain white labour, I must employ other." Not surprisingly, Chinese workers were abruptly let go upon the railway's completion. That was not all. Ottawa quickly moved to choke off further Chinese immigration by imposing a fifty-dollar head tax in 1885, increased to five hundred dollars in 1904. Chinese already in Canada, unwanted by mainstream society and unable to bring families over to join them, created their own reservation-like existence in urban Chinatowns.[43]

Most native-born Americans and Canadians of African origin shared a similar fate as providers of cheap labor when needed but otherwise confined to a segregated, second-class status. Whether the place was Victoria, British Columbia, in the 1860s, Nova Scotia throughout the 1800s, the American

South after the Civil War, or northern American cities by the turn of the century, the story was much the same. South of the Mason-Dixon Line, for instance, African American families were no longer slaves but became enmeshed in a sharecropping agricultural system that often led to indebtedness and poverty. Like Great Lakes Indians, many Southern blacks went looking for wage work, and their diaspora led to the planting of distinctive and separate enclaves in towns and cities throughout the nation. Like other migrants and like immigrants and reservation Indians, they adjusted to new circumstances in such special spaces, while fostering traditional institutions and values.[44]

Aboriginal peoples clearly shared many experiences with other oppressed groups in Canada and the United States. Together, they faced the challenges of "going with the flow" of a rapidly changing, discriminatory, capitalistic mainstream in the late 1800s. They made a living for their families and used similar techniques to preserve their identities and traditions. That was not all. The grit and creativity and resilience of urban laborers, women, immigrants, blacks, and Indians—all of whom faced white, male intransigence—foreshadowed a continuing struggle for equality in the next century.[45]

Nevertheless, the story of Great Lakes aboriginal peoples in the late 1800s was in many ways unique. The entire region had once been their homeland, before they were confined to reservations. They had distinct cultures and a unique historical relationship with Great Britain, Canada, and the United States. Indians had treaty rights. Federal legislation and court decisions acknowledged Washington's and Ottawa's ongoing obligations to Indians as well as their unusual legal status.

EPILOGUE: THE VIEW FROM INDIAN COUNTRY

During the early years of the twentieth century, Great Lakes Indians sustained themselves with great difficulty on marginalized reservations. The burden of history was heavy—and troublesome: the loss of homeland, the rapid influx of non-Indians, decisions made about how to live alongside disapproving neighbors, and the ensuing tribal factionalism. Also oppressive was the continuation of harmful federal programs and public attitudes toward native peoples. The consequences, not at all surprising, included weak aboriginal economies, substandard housing and health conditions, and low education levels. Population estimates did not change markedly between 1870 (41,500 persons) and 1900 (40,864).[46]

The slow rate of acculturation and economic competitiveness, despite expensive efforts of local Indian agents, teachers, and missionaries, deepened the historic ambivalence toward Indians. The Canadian and American publics still showed some respect and concern for aboriginal wards and held high the goal of assimilation. Yet the failure of national "civilization" programs for the reservations fed latent racism and undercut the belief that Indians were capable of social integration as equals in Canada and the United States.[47]

Despite the physical separation and poverty experienced by many Great Lakes Indians in the early 1900s, white influences continued to penetrate and modify native communities as they had for nearly three hundred years. South of the international border, the Menominee experience was noteworthy. With a population of 1,736 in 1916, their reservation, like so many below Lakes Superior and Huron, became an island amid a rising white sea that was alluring as well as ominous.[48]

First, modern transportation and communication multiplied the ties between Menominee families and the outside world. In 1906, a railway crossed the reservation. Its depot at Neopit linked the new lumber mill to markets across the country. Telephone and extended postal services followed, and by the early 1920s, two state highways crossed Menominee country. These developments prompted population shifts: one involved families drawn to jobs at the Keshena Indian Agency or to seasonal logging and lumbering work at Neopit; the other was a scattering of community members to off-reservation employment opportunities. Indian dress, housing, and diet also reflected the influence of white neighbors. The majority of Keshena residents, for example, lived in log or frame structures with board floors. Because of the scarcity of game, the Indians' meals included salt pork, chicken, gravies, pastries, coffee, and tea. More traditional foods, still obtainable, were enjoyed: fish, berries, maple sugar, and, to a limited degree, products of the hunt. Reservation families neglected farming in favor of jobs in lumbering camps and sawmills; still, Menominee women cultivated gardens and produced beadwork and basketwork for sale.[49]

Pervasive as the dominant society seemed to be in Indian country, historian Frederick E. Hoxie reminds us that native leaders across America still "talked back to civilization." The nation's economic, political, and cultural power was enormous and could not be denied. Yet Indians remained troubled by the mainstream's refusal to accept minority peoples as equals and by America's apparent inability to distribute its great wealth more equitably. Such shortcomings were reason enough for Indian communities to resist total assimilation. They sought a middle ground instead, by preserving their unique identities, local political control, and vital aspects of traditional cultures. By "talking back to civilization," Indians of the Progressive Era not only buttressed their own generation, Hoxie argues; they "helped define, preserve, and even stimulate faith in 'Indianness' for the remainder of the twentieth century."[50]

The Indian call to resist being swept away by the American mainstream was all the more important because Washington policy makers and Christian evangelists persisted in their acculturation program well into the 1900s. Its characteristics were many: ethnocentrism bent on culture replacement, suffocating paternalism characterized by constant intervention in reservation affairs while refusing to listen to Indian voices, continued allotment and loss of Indian land, and the resultant marginalization and dependence of Uncle Sam's wards. Treating aboriginals as individuals rather than tribal members and trying to control every aspect of their lives ended up trapping them as well as Indian Office bureaucrats under piles of paperwork. When reservation families did not show rapid "progress" according to plan, some pessimistic policy makers and reformers came to doubt their long-established belief that native peoples could be assimilated as equals. Others, like John Collier, tried to reverse the Dawes Act philosophy that individualized economic pursuits on the reservation.[51]

The scene in Ottawa and on Canadian reserves was strikingly similar to America's, as it had been during the previous half century. In part, this was not surprising, given the parallel economic development of the Great Lakes basin north and south of the international border. Southern Ontario, like the American Upper Midwest, became an urbanized and industrialized corridor dotted with farms. To the north, agriculture thinned out in favor of forestry, mining, fishing, and catering to sightseers. Reservation Indians had little choice but to take subsidiary roles as farm laborers, mechanics, domestic servants, and tourist attractions in support of the dominant society. Native families that became marginally self-sufficient delighted federal officials because they bolstered Ottawa's overall program of Indian "civilization" and assimilation. "I want to get rid of the Indian problem," wrote the deputy minister of the Indian Department, D. C. Scott, in 1920, so that Indians will be "able to take their position as British citizens or Canadian citizens, to support themselves, and stand alone." Scott explained:

> That has been the whole purpose of Indian education and advancement since the earliest times....
>
> ... Our object is to continue until there is not a single Indian in Canada that has not been absorbed into the body politic, and there is no Indian question, and no Indian Department.[52]

Canadian bullying strategies to achieve these goals also persisted well into the twentieth century. One was enfranchisement. Historian J. R. Miller describes various means by which, prior to 1940, the federal government tried, with "gross political interference," to impose full citizenship and strip Indian families of their status and treaty rights. Likewise, residential and day schools continued to denigrate native ways and to impose the dominant culture on Indian boys and girls. A third example was the unremitting federal assault on aboriginal governments, with their hereditary chiefs and, in the case of Iroquois communities, influential clan mothers. Ottawa's goal was compliance with the Indian Act's municipal government model. Indian Department officials, by deposing selected "life chiefs" or imposing an elective system for choosing chiefs and councilors, hoped to get reservation councils more sympathetic to the economic, educational, and spiritual plans of the department.[53]

By the 1920s, doubts arose in Canada, as they did in the United States, about hard-line government programs. Indians had not become self-supporting Canadian citizens in large numbers. Indeed, they seemed more than ever isolated and mired in poverty. Some church groups lost faith in the residential schools' ability to acculturate native children. Cost-conscious federal bureaucrats similarly questioned whether the reservation system, with its extensive farm programs, missions, and schools, was "civilizing" native families. Another reason to doubt Canada's policy of cultural repression was the rising tide of aboriginal political protest, which, J. R. Miller points out, would ultimately be the dominant voice calling for change.[54]

What characterized America's Indian policy during the first two decades of the twentieth century was its continuity. Such policy makers as Indian commissioner Francis E. Leupp might restructure their field offices and upgrade personnel, but Washington retained the long-standing goal of forcibly assimilating Indians into American society as educated, self-supporting, individual landholders who had cast off tribal affiliations. Once assimilation was accomplished, Uncle Sam would finally be rid of his "Indian problem." The public had few objections to the status quo; reform fervor had faded since the heady days of the Dawes Act, and other citizens held varied views about natives, including an unrelenting desire to exploit their resources. Historian Arrell Gibson's 1980 indictment of Washington still rings true:

> Occasionally Congress passed a statute which was modestly protective of Indian rights, and now and then a federal tribunal would render a decision in favor of Indians. However, for nearly three decades

of the new century, the federal government as primary trustee for Native American rights and property was basically indifferent to its charge.[55]

The response of American Indians to these developments was once again noteworthy. Determined to control their lives and communities during the gloomy early decades of the twentieth century, natives continued to adjust creatively to ever-changing circumstances. They supported their families by using resources on and off the reservations: hunting, fishing (some of it commercial), trapping, gathering, farming, logging, hosting tourists, and seasonal work as day laborers and domestic servants. They also preserved their identities as aboriginal peoples and brought forth "Red progressives": young leaders "schooled in American ways, united for the first time by a common language, English, and aware of the challenges confronting their people"— young leaders who championed their interests and the sanctity of reservation homelands. In short, native peoples had agency, to use the modern parlance, and they endured.[56] Still, the works of Charles E. Cleland, Robert E. Bieder, and other scholars remind us that Great Lakes Indians constantly battled poverty as jobs in the lumber industry declined (the Menominee Reservation was an exception) and competition with white farmers became increasingly difficult. The strength of aboriginal communities was also sapped by overcrowded and unsanitary living conditions, high rates of tuberculosis and smallpox, debilitating factionalism, exploitive non-Indian neighbors, and suffocating Washington bureaucrats during the early twentieth century.

Wisconsin reservations were representative, with some communities surviving better than others. The beleaguered Oneida coped each day with the consequences of the Dawes Severalty Act. They came under the jurisdiction of local governments as traditional chiefs lost their authority. Town and county officials, like their Michigan counterparts more than half a century earlier, levied taxes on Indian allotments, and lack of cash to pay these assessments or ignorance about monies owed led to the loss of all but a few Oneida farms by the 1920s. This drove adults in search of employment into nearby Milwaukee and Green Bay, where they had to adopt many of the white man's ways in order to survive. The experiences of their children in schoolhouses staffed by non-Indian teachers who imparted the history and skills of the dominant society also made it difficult for native families clustered in cities or on remnant Oneida lands.[57] Laura Kellogg, a tribal member who attended white educational institutions and later championed the ways of her people, lamented that it did not have to be this way.

When we stop to think a little, old Indian training is not to be despised. The general tendency in the average Indian schools is to take away the child's set of Indian notions altogether, and to supplant them with the paleface's. There is no discrimination in that. Why should he not justly know his race's own heroes rather than through false teaching think them wrong? . . . Now I do not say here that everything he has natively is right or better than the Caucasian's. Not at all, but I do say that there are notable qualities and traits and a set of literary traditions he had which are just as fine and finer, and when he has these, for the sake of keeping a fine spirit of self-respect and pride in himself, let us preserve them.[58]

During the first two decades of the twentieth century, the Indian Office also targeted the Ojibwa of northern Wisconsin for acculturation programs, especially economic development. The results were mixed. Implementation of the allotment program continued to break up communal reservation lands into eighty-acre family tracts to be used for timber sales and farming. By 1910, most available Indian lands were apportioned and occupied "more or less" by allottees. Each received a trust patent, which restricted sale of the land for twenty-five years—unless there was a good reason for early termination of the trust period, such as the acknowledged competency of an Ojibwa owner. By the late 1920s, about half at Bad River and four-fifths at Red Cliff had received patents in fee simple through certificates of competency. Their future seemed bright. Ojibwa allottees could use monies from the sale of their timber to establish permanent homes, improve their farms, and work for economic self-sufficiency. Such was Uncle Sam's hope. Though there was a certain logic to it, this dream almost always foundered on the rocky realities of frontier economics: reservations unsuited for agriculture, white acquisition of Indian farmland (by means of purchase, leasing, or outright fraud), and nationwide depressions that destroyed family farm profits.[59]

In between these Ojibwa homelands and what was left of the Wisconsin Oneida Reservation were the Menominee. They fared better than most of the state's aboriginal peoples, because of an independent, self-sustaining lumber business. Carlisle School graduate Reginald Oshkosh, the son of a traditional chief, contended that his people should be more than mere employees of prosperous white timber companies that profited from reservation resources. He said that they must become "independent and self-supporting" and "terminate our relations as wards of the Government."[60] Opportunity knocked in July 1905. A cyclone blew down between twenty and thirty

Ojibwa council lodge at the 1906 Wisconsin State Fair introduces visitors to their Indian neighbors. *(Courtesy Wisconsin Historical Society, image 6912.)*

million log feet of trees. If they were not cleared and sawed into lumber within two years, the wood would rot, yet federal government regulations prevented the Menominee from salvaging more than 17,500 board feet. The local Indian superintendent, taking Uncle Sam's usual approach to reservation assets, proposed selling the fallen trees to non-Indian companies from Oconto and Oshkosh. This plan was derailed by influential Wisconsin senator Robert M. La Follette's interest in the situation. He convinced Congress to build a tribal sawmill using Menominee trust funds and to allow the Indians to cut and sell their own timber. This approach would create more Indian jobs and greater Indian profits than merely selling their downed trees. Congress's consent in 1908 included a requirement that the U.S. Forest Service oversee the Menominee lumber operation to make sure that Indians harvested trees annually on a sustained-yield basis. The town of Neopit soon grew up around a mill built on the Wolf River.[61]

Whether working for financial independence, like Menominee lumbermen, or greater control of other reservation affairs, Indian peoples contin-

Menominee Reservation sawmill. *(Courtesy Wisconsin Historical Society, image 24938.)*

ued to play an important role in the Great Lakes story during the rest of the twentieth century. How they did so is the subject for another study. The early 1900s suggested that it would be a time of persistent challenge and change. At no time in the past—and, one suspects, at no time in the future—would they permit domination by the white man. Great Lakes aboriginal people were determined to endure and to survive as Indians, inspired, perhaps, by the following words of a nineteenth-century Ojibwa leader:

> As there are many species of plants, birds, fishes and animals, each one with its own peculiarities, so there are different kinds of men, each one with its own blessings from the Great Spirit. We are not fools. We have our wisdom given to our Ancients by the Great Spirit, and we shall cling to it.[62]

Non-Indians who surrounded the reservations in the early twentieth century assumed that their neighbors would soon vanish into the mainstream; so, too, did Ottawa and Washington policy makers. A century later, we realize how wrong they were. Native Americans and Canadian First Nations, employing resistance and accommodation strategies and with help from gener-

Having experienced the mainstream, veterans of World War I return to the Lac Court Oreilles Reservation. *(Courtesy Wisconsin Historical Society, image 35070.)*

ations of new leaders, have regained much numerical, cultural, and political strength. The legacy of the early reservation years was indeed powerful.

When the Red Power movement of the 1960s exploded onto the American and Canadian stages, it drew guidance and strength from native leaders of the past. Some were battlefield commanders, such as Sitting Bull and Geronimo. Others were astute and resourceful Great Lakes chiefs and councils and clan mothers, protectors of their homeland and champions of their people by peaceful means during the years 1850–1900. They kept alive the dream of economic self-sufficiency, of self-determination, of Indian identity and sovereignty, and of their historic right to unimpeded border crossings—from one end of the Great Lakes basin to the other. Red Jacket, Tecumseh, Peter Jones, Shingwauk, and Pokagon would be pleased.

Notes

ABBREVIATIONS

AR	Annual Report
CIA	Commissioner of Indian Affairs
DIA	Department of Indian Affairs
GLR	Great Lakes Region
LR	Letters Received
LS	Letters Sent
NAC	National Archives of Canada (Ottawa)
NARA	National Archives and Records Administration (Washington, D.C.)
OIA	Office of Indian Affairs
RG	Record Group
SGIA	Superintendent General of Indian Affairs
WIHC	Walpole Island Heritage Centre

PREFACE AND ACKNOWLEDGMENTS

1. Kingston, *Western Wanderings, or A Pleasure Tour in the Canadas,* 2 vols. (London: Chapman and Hall, 1856), 1:160–71.

2. Environment Canada et al., *The Great Lakes: An Environmental Atlas and Resource Book* (Chicago: Great Lakes National Program Office of the U.S. Environmental Protection Agency, 1987), 3.

3. Berton, *The Great Lakes* (Toronto: Stoddart Publishing Company, 1996), 20.

4. Nixon, Special Message to the Congress on Indian Affairs, July 8, 1970, in *Public Papers of the Presidents of the United States: Richard Nixon, Containing the Public Messages, Speeches, and Statements of the President, 1970* (Washington, D.C.: Government Printing Office, 1971), 565.

INTRODUCTION

1. Red Jacket, "Address to White Missionaries and Iroquois Six Nations," http://www.americanrhetoric.com/speeches/nativeamericans/chiefredjacket.htm (accessed March 23, 2007).

2. Victor P. Lytwyn, "Waterworld: The Aquatic Territory of the Great Lakes Nations," in Dale Standon and David McNab, eds., *Gin Das Winan: Documenting Aboriginal History in Ontario; A Symposium at Bkejwanon, Walpole Island First Nation, September 23, 1994*, Occasional Papers, no. 2 (Toronto: Champlain Society, 1996), 14; Margaret Beattie Bogue, *Fishing the Great Lakes: An Environmental History, 1783–1933* (Madison: University of Wisconsin Press, 2000), 4.

3. Environment Canada et al., *Great Lakes*, 17; Helen Hornbeck Tanner et al., eds., *Atlas of Great Lakes Indian History* (Norman: University of Oklahoma Press, 1987), 2–3; Selwyn Dewdney, *The Sacred Scrolls of the Southern Ojibway* (Toronto: University of Toronto Press, 1975), 162–67.

4. Edmund Jefferson Danziger, Jr., "Historical Importance of Great Lakes Aboriginal Borders," in Jill Oakes et al., eds., *Aboriginal Cultural Landscapes* (Winnipeg: Aboriginal Issues Press, 2004), 2.

5. Tanner et al., *Atlas of Great Lakes Indian History*, 4–5; Royal Commission on Aboriginal Peoples, *Report of the Royal Commission on Aboriginal Peoples*, vol. 3, *Gathering Strength* (Ottawa: Minister of Supply and Services Canada, 1996), 11–22.

6. Tanner et al., *Atlas of Great Lakes Indian History*, 4–5, 18–19, 22–23; Royal Commission on Aboriginal Peoples, *Report of the Royal Commission on Aboriginal Peoples*, vol. 2, *Restructuring the Relationship* (Ottawa: Minister of Supply and Services Canada, 1996), 780–85; David W. Penny, *Great Lakes Indian Art* (Detroit: Wayne State University Press and Detroit Institute of Arts, 1989), 11–12.

7. Tanner et al., *Atlas of Great Lakes Indian History*, 59–60.

8. Charles E. Cleland, "An Overview of Chippewa Use of Natural Resources," in James M. McClurken, comp., *Fish in the Lakes, Wild Rice, and Game in Abundance: Testimony on Behalf of Mille Lacs Ojibwe Hunting and Fishing Rights* (East Lansing: Michigan State University Press, 2000), 8–9.

9. Edmund Jefferson Danziger, Jr., *The Chippewas of Lake Superior* (Norman: University of Oklahoma Press, 1978), 10–11; Diamond Jenness, *The Ojibwa Indians of Parry Island: Their Social and Religious Life* (Ottawa: J. O. Patenaude, 1935), 7–9; Robert E. Bieder, *Native American Communities in Wisconsin, 1600–1960: A Study of Tradition and Change* (Madison: University of Wisconsin Press, 1995), 23–24, 32; Emerson S. Coatsworth, *The Indians of Quetico* (Toronto: University of Toronto Press, 1957), 5–6.

10. Neal Ferris, "Continuity within Change: Settlement-Subsistence Strategies and Artifact Patterns of the Southwestern Ontario Ojibwa, A.D. 1780–1861" (M.A. thesis, York University, 1989), 263–64; Edward S. Rogers, "Northern Algonquians and the Hudson's Bay Company, 1821–1890," in Rogers and Donald B. Smith, eds., *Aboriginal Ontario: Historical Perspectives on the First Nations* (Toronto: Dundurn Press, 1994), 322–25.

11. Danziger, *Chippewas of Lake Superior*, 13–16; Priscilla K. Buffalohead, "Farmers, Warriors, Traders: A Fresh Look at Ojibway Women," *Minnesota History* 48 (Summer 1983): 241; Coatsworth, *Quetico*, 16–18.

12. Jenness, *Ojibwa Indians of Parry Island*, 10–16; Bieder, *Native American Communities*, 23, 30–32; Rogers, "Northern Algonquians," 317–20; Coatsworth, *Quetico*, 8, 10–11, 19–27; Ferris, "Continuity within Change," 262–63, 267, 269–70.

13. Danziger, *Chippewas of Lake Superior*, 16–20; Coatsworth, *Quetico*, 43–53.

14. John Webster Grant, *A Profusion of Spires: Religion in Nineteenth-Century Ontario* (Toronto: University of Toronto Press, 1988), 9–10; Danziger, *Chippewas of Lake Superior*, 16–20; Jenness, *Ojibwa Indians of Parry Island*, 18–28, 79–89.

15. Danziger, *Chippewas of Lake Superior*, 16–20; Jenness, *Ojibwa Indians of Parry Island*, 47–53, 60–68, 75; Coatsworth, *Quetico*, 43–53.

16. Danziger, *Chippewas of Lake Superior*, 23–25; Phillip Bellfy, "Division and Unity, Dispersal and Permanence: The Anishnabeg of the Lake Huron Borderlands" (Ph.D. diss., Michigan State University, 1995), 62–64; Coatsworth, *Quetico*, 5; Bieder, *Native American Communities*, 24–25; Rogers, "Northern Algonquians," 323, 325.

17. Tanner et al., *Atlas of Great Lakes Indian History*, 26–27. For a brief history of the league, see Elisabeth Tooker, "The League of the Iroquois: Its History, Politics, and Ritual," in Bruce G. Trigger, ed., *Handbook of North American Indians*, vol. 15, *Northeast* (Washington, D.C.: Smithsonian Institution, 1978), 418–41. In *The Ordeal of the Longhouse: The Peoples of the Iroquois League in the Era of Colonization* (Chapel Hill: University of North Carolina Press, 1992), Daniel K. Richter tries to provide a detailed Iroquois history from an Indian perspective.

18. John Bartram et al., *A Journey from Pennsylvania to Onondaga in 1743* (Barre, Mass.: Imprint Society, 1973), 58–59; William N. Fenton, "Northern Iroquoian Culture Patterns," in Trigger, *Handbook*, 303; Richard Aquila, *The Iroquois Restoration: Iroquois Diplomacy on the Colonial Frontier, 1701–1754* (Detroit: Wayne State University Press, 1983), 32; Barbara Graymont, *The Iroquois in the American Revolution* (Syracuse, N.Y.: Syracuse University Press, 1972), 9–10; Royal Commission on Aboriginal Peoples, *Report of the Royal Commission on Aboriginal Peoples*, vol. 1, *Looking Forward, Looking Back* (Ottawa: Minister of Supply and Services Canada, 1996), 52.

19. Harmen Van den Bogaert, "Narrative of a Journey into the Mohawk and Oneida Country, 1634–35," in J. Franklin Jameson, ed., *Narratives of New Netherland, 1609–1664* (New York: Charles Scribner's Sons, 1909; reprint, New York: Barnes and Noble, 1959), 141; Father Joseph François Lafitau, *Customs of the American Indians Compared with the Customs of Primitive Times*, ed. and trans. William N. Fenton and Elizabeth Moore, 2 vols. (Toronto: Champlain Society, 1974), 2:16, 69–70; Fenton, "Northern Iroquoian Culture Patterns," 302, 306; Aquila, *Iroquois Restoration*, 32; Graymont, *Iroquois in the American Revolution*, 9; Royal Commission on Aboriginal Peoples, *Report*, 1:52.

20. Fenton, "Northern Iroquoian Culture Patterns," 309–11; William N. Fenton, "Structure, Continuity, and Change in the Process of Iroquois Treaty Making," in Francis Jennings, ed., *The History and Culture of Iroquois Diplomacy: An Interdisciplinary Guide to the Treaties of the Six Nations and the League* (Syracuse, N.Y.: Syracuse University Press, 1985), 10.

21. Lafitau, *Customs*, 1:70, 341–47, 358; Reuben Gold Thwaites, ed., *The Jesuit Relations and Allied Documents: Travels and Explorations of the Jesuit Missionaries in New France, 1610–1791*, 73 vols. (New York: Pageant Books, 1959), 43:265; Graymont, *Iroquois in the American Revolution*, 17.

22. Johannes Megapolensis, "A Short Account of the Mohawk Indians, 1644," in

Jameson, *New Netherland,* 178–79; Fenton, "Northern Iroquoian Culture Patterns," 306–7; Graymont, *Iroquois in the American Revolution,* 12–13.

23. Thwaites, *Jesuit Relations,* 15:155; Elisabeth Tooker, *Ethnography of the Huron Indians, 1615–1649,* Bureau of American Ethnology Bulletin 190 (Washington, D.C.: Bureau of American Ethnology, 1964), 58–60; Bruce G. Trigger, *The Children of Aataentsic: A History of the Huron People to 1660,* 2 vols. (Montreal: McGill-Queen's University Press, 1976), 1:32, 34.

24. Lafitau, *Customs,* 1:113–14; Graymont, *Iroquois in the American Revolution,* 10.

25. Fenton, "Northern Iroquoian Culture Patterns," 314; Aquila, *Iroquois Restoration,* 32; Lafitau, *Customs,* 1:294–99.

26. Aquila, *Iroquois Restoration,* 32; Lafitau, *Customs,* 1:70, 292.

27. Lafitau, *Customs,* 1:292–93.

28. Aquila, *Iroquois Restoration,* 32–34; William N. Fenton, "The Iroquois in History," in Eleanor Burke Leacock and Nancy Oestreich Lurie, eds., *North American Indians in Historical Perspective* (New York: Random House, 1971), 131, 139.

29. Aquila, *Iroquois Restoration,* 30.

30. Red Jacket, "Address to White Missionaries and Iroquois Six Nations."

31. Brown quoted in Randall White, *Ontario, 1610–1985: A Political and Economic History* (Toronto: Dundurn Press, 1985), 110.

32. Robert Bothwell, *A Short History of Ontario* (Edmonton: Huntig Publishers, 1986), 52–53, 98–99.

33. U.S. Bureau of the Census, *The Seventh Census of the United States, 1850* (Washington, D.C.: Robert Armstrong, 1853); U.S. Bureau of the Census, *Census Reports Volume I, Twelfth Census of the United States, Taken in the Year 1900, Population Part I* (Washington, D.C.: U.S. Census Office, 1901), xviii, 443–80.

34. Rogers, "Northern Algonquians," 333–35; Kenneth Norrie and Douglas Owram, *A History of the Canadian Economy* (Toronto: Harcourt Brace Jovanovich, 1991), 240–41.

35. Barry, *Georgian Bay: The Sixth Great Lake* (Toronto: Clarke, Irwin and Company, 1968), 75–76.

36. William Ashworth, *The Late, Great Lakes: An Environmental History* (Detroit: Wayne State University Press, 1987), 65.

37. For a discussion of northeastern Indian removal, see Francis Paul Prucha, *The Great Father: The United States Government and the American Indians,* 2 vols. (Lincoln: University of Nebraska Press, 1984), vol. 1, chap. 9. In "Disunity and Dispossession: Nawash Ojibwa and Potawatomi in the Saugeen Territory, 1836–1865" (M.A. thesis, University of Calgary, 1997), Stephanie Louise McMullen discusses how the arrival of hundreds of American Potawatomi impacted one Canadian area.

38. James Morrison, *Aboriginal Peoples in the Archives: A Guide to Sources in the Archives of Ontario* (Toronto: Archives of Ontario, 1992), 4–5; Tanner et al., *Atlas of Great Lakes Indian History,* 164–65.

39. Treaties with the Ottawas and Chippewas of the Sauking [Saugeen] and Manitoulin, August 9, 1836, and October 6, 1862, in Canada, *Indian Treaties and Surrenders, from 1680 to 1890,* 2 vols. (Ottawa: Brown Chamberlin, 1891), 1:112–13, 235–37; Royal Commission on Aboriginal Peoples, *Report,* 1:156–58, 467–68.

40. Canada, *Indian Treaties and Surrenders,* 1:147–52; Royal Commission on Ab-

original Peoples, *Report,* 1:158–59; Bruce W. Hodgins and Jamie Benidickson, *The Temagami Experience: Recreation, Resources, and Aboriginal Rights in the Northern Ontario Wilderness* (Toronto: University of Toronto Press, 1989), 32–34; Deborah Anne Montgomerie, "Coming to Terms: Ngai Tahu, Roberson County Indians, and the Garden River Band of Ojibwa, 1840–1890; Three Studies of Colonialism in Action" (Ph.D. diss., Duke University, 1993), 230–36.

41. U.S. Consul F. N. Blake to Secretary of State Hamilton Fish, January 6, 1870, in *Report on the Management of Indians in British America by the British Government,* 41st Cong., 2d sess. (1870), H. Misc. Doc. 35, serial 1433, 33; AR, CIA, 1869, 25.

42. AR, DIA, 1869, 25; Peter S. Schmalz, *The Ojibwa of Southern Ontario* (Toronto: University of Toronto Press, 1991), 176; Elizabeth Graham, *Medicine Man to Missionary: Missionaries as Agents of Change among the Indians of Southern Ontario, 1784–1867* (Toronto: Peter Martin Associates, 1975), 31, 44.

43. Blake to Fish, January 6, 1870, in *Report on the Management of Indians,* 2–6; AR, DIA, 1869, 25; Sally M. Weaver, "Six Nations of the Grand River, Ontario," in Trigger, *Handbook,* 528; Graham, *Medicine Man to Missionary,* 30.

44. Petition of Oneida of Canada Delegates Abraham Sickles and Moses Brown to the President of the United States, May 11, 1864, enclosed in Charles E. Mix (who received the petition at a grand council meeting in New York) to CIA William P. Dole, June 21, 1864, NARA, OIA, RG 75, LR, New York Agency (microfilm M-234, roll 590, frames 263–68); AR, DIA, 1869, 25; Deputy Superintendent General Froome Talford, Statement [about the condition of] Indians under His Superintendency, September 1, 1857, NAC, DIA, RG 10, Field Office Records, Western (Sarnia) Superintendency, Deputy Superintendent General's Office Letterbook, 1846–59, vol. 585; Schmalz, *Ojibwa of Southern Ontario,* 177.

45. AR, DIA, 1869, 25; Talford, Statement of September 1, 1857; Memorandum on Case of Peter C. Clark, One of the Wyandots of Anderdon, William Spragge, [1868], NAC, DIA, RG 10, Ministerial Administration Records, Deputy Superintendent General's Office, Reports on Indian Affairs, 1862–68, vol. 722, 413–14 (microfilm C-13412); 413–14; Nin-Da-Waab-Jig, *Walpole Island: The Soul of Indian Territory* (Walpole Island: Nin-Da-Waab-Jig, 1987), 64; Schmalz, *Ojibwa of Southern Ontario,* 176–78; Dean Jacobs, "'We have but our hearts and the traditions of our old men': Understanding the Traditions and History of Bkejwanong," in Standon and McNab, *Gin Das Winan,* 1, 9.

46. AR, DIA, 1869, 25; Graham, *Medicine Man to Missionary,* 39–40.

47. AR, DIA, 1869, 25; Florence Murray, ed., *Muskoka and Haliburton, 1615–1875: A Collection of Documents* (Toronto: Champlain Society, 1963), lviii, 120–23; Schmalz, *Ojibwa of Southern Ontario,* 178.

48. Census figures drawn from AR, DIA, various years, and from Murray, *Muskoka and Haliburton,* lviii.

49. Blake to Fish, January 6, 1870, in *Report on the Management of Indians;* Agent C. L. D. Sims to SGIA, September 1, 1899, NAC, DIA, RG 10, Manitowaning Agency Letterbook, vol. 10525, August 25, 1899–February 14, 1900, 54–66 (microfilm C-15253); SGIA William McDougall, Memorandum on Negotiations for Surrender of Manitoulin Island, November 3, 1862, NAC, DIA, RG 10, Ministerial Administration Records, Deputy Superintendent General's Office, Reports on Indian Affairs, 1862–68, vol. 722, 74–79 (microfilm C-13412).

50. Census of 1857 by Visiting Superintendent of Indian Affairs George Ironside, NAC, DIA, RG 10, Superintendency Records, Northern (Manitowaning) Superintendency, Statement of Indians Entitled to Annuities, 1846–57, vol. 621, 194–98 (microfilm C-13391–92); W. R. Wightman, *Forever on the Fringe: Six Studies in the Development of Manitoulin Island* (Toronto: University of Toronto Press, 1982), 21–22.

51. Census of Indians for Annuity under the Robinson Treaty for the Year 1877, Northern Superintendency, First Division, by Visiting Superintendent of Indian Affairs J. C. Phipps, March 1, 1877, NAC, DIA, RG 10, Deputy Superintendent General's Office Letterbook [from Northern (Manitowaning) Superintendency], 1876–77, vol. 547, 459.

52. SGIA Robert Bruce to Visiting Superintendent George Ironside, June 25, 1851, NAC, DIA, RG 10, Superintendency Records, Northern (Manitowaning) Superintendency, Correspondence (Manitoulin Island), 1851–55, vol. 613, 172–73 (microfilm C-13386); Census of 1857 by Visiting Superintendent of Indian Affairs George Ironside, NAC, DIA, RG 10, Superintendency Records, Northern (Manitowaning) Superintendency, Statement of Indians Entitled to Annuities, 1846–57, vol. 621, 194–98 (microfilm C-13391, 13392).

53. Census of 1857 by Visiting Superintendent of Indian Affairs George Ironside, NAC, DIA, RG 10, Superintendency Records, Northern (Manitowaning) Superintendency, Statement of Indians Entitled to Annuities, 1846–57, vol. 621, 194–98 (microfilm C-13391, 13392); SGIA Robert Bruce to Visiting Superintendent George Ironside, June 25, 1851, NAC, DIA, RG 10, Superintendency Records, Northern (Manitowaning) Superintendency, Correspondence (Manitoulin Island), 1851–55, vol. 613, 172–73 (microfilm C-13386) AR, DIA, 1884, 183.

54. Indian Agent M. A. Leahy to CIA Thomas J. Morgan, September 10, 1891, AR, CIA, 1891, 469–70; Alice C. Fletcher, *Indian Education and Civilization: A Report Prepared in Answer to Senate Resolution of February 23, 1885,* Bureau of Education Special Report, 1888, 48th Cong., 2d sess., (1888), S. Exec. Doc. 95, serial 2264, 449–51.

55. Charles C. Royce, comp., "Indian Land Cessions in the United States," in *Eighteenth Annual Report of the Bureau of American Ethnology to the Secretary of the Smithsonian Institution, 1896–1897* (Washington, D.C.: Government Printing Office, 1899), 797, 841, 904; Leahy to Morgan, September 10, 1891, AR, CIA, 1891, 468–69; Federal Writers' Project, *Minnesota: A State Guide* (New York: Hastings House, 1938), 346; Fletcher, *Indian Education and Civilization,* 448–51.

56. Green Bay Agent M. M. Davis to CIA Dole, September 27, 1862, AR, CIA, 1862, 328–34.

57. Ibid.; Walter James Hoffman, "The Menomini Indians," in *Fourteenth Annual Report of the Bureau of American Ethnology for the Years 1892–93,* part 1 (Washington, D.C.: Bureau of American Ethnology, 1896), 31–32; Robert C. Nesbit, *The History of Wisconsin,* vol. 3, *Urbanization and Industrialization, 1873–1893* (Madison: State Historical Society of Wisconsin, 1985), 428–29.

58. Treaty with the Menominee, February 11, 1856, http://digital.library.okstate.edu/kappler/Vol2/treaties/men0755.htm (accessed April 10, 2007); Northern Superintendent Huebschmann to CIA George W. Manypenny, October 15, 1856, AR, CIA, 1856, 39–41; Davis to Dole, September 26, 1864, AR, CIA, 1864, 435–39; Davis to Cooley, September 25, 1865, AR, CIA, 1865, 435–39.

59. Special Agent for Wisconsin Stray Bands D. A. Griffith to CIA Ely S. Parker, September 20, 1870, AR, CIA, 1870, 323; La Pointe Agent to CIA, August 19, 1899, NARA, GLR (Chicago), OIA, RG 75, La Pointe Agency, LS to CIA; Nancy Oestreich Lurie, "Winnebago," in Trigger, *Handbook*, 702.

60. Treaty with the Chippewa, September 30, 1854, http://digital.library.ok state.edu/kappler/Vol2/treaties/chi0648.htm#mn2 (accessed April 7, 2007); L. H. Wheeler to Agent C. K. Drew, 1859, AR, CIA, 1859, 77; La Pointe Agent J. T. Gregory to CIA, August 29, 1888, NARA, GLR (Chicago), OIA, RG 75, La Pointe Agency, LS to CIA; Federal Writers' Project, *Wisconsin: A Guide to the Badger State* (New York: Duell, Sloan, and Pearce, 1941), 445. The 1854 treaty also assigned to the Bad River band two hundred acres on the northern tip of Madeline Island for a fishing ground.

61. Royce, "Indian Land Cessions," 797; Fletcher, *Indian Education and Civilization*, 668–69; Agent M. A. Leahy to CIA Thomas J. Morgan, September 10, 1891, AR, CIA, 1891, 468.

62. Leahy to Morgan, September 10, 1891, AR, CIA, 1891, 466–67; Fletcher, *Indian Education and Civilization*, 664–66; Bureau of Indian Affairs, *Indians of the Great Lakes Agency* (Washington, D.C.: Government Printing Office, 1968).

63. Michigan Agent Richard M. Smith to CIA N. G. Taylor, August 28, 1867, AR, CIA, 1867, 335–40; Smith to Taylor, September 17, 1868, AR, CIA, 1868, 298–300; Fletcher, *Indian Education and Civilization*, 419–20; Charles E. Cleland, *Rites of Conquest: The History and Culture of Michigan's Native Americans* (Ann Arbor: University of Michigan Press, 1992), 241–42.

64. Mackinac Agent D. C. Leach to CIA William P. Dole, October 17, 1863, AR, CIA, 1863, 374–80; Michigan Agent Captain James W. Long to CIA Ely S. Parker, October 20, 1870, AR, CIA, 1870, 313–17; Mackinac Agent George W. Lee to CIA, September 1, 1879, AR, CIA, 1879, 84–86.

65. Treaty with the Chippewa of Saginaw, Swan Creek, and Black River, October 18, 1864, http://digital.library.okstate.edu/kappler/Vol2/treaties/chi0868.htm#mn12 (accessed April 7, 2007); Michigan Agent George I. Betts to CIA Edward P. Smith, September 14, 1874, AR, CIA, 1874, 184–85; Cleland, *Rites of Conquest*, 238–39.

66. Smith to CIA D. N. Cooley, October 8, 1866, AR, CIA, 1866, 300–302; Betts to Smith, June 10, 1873, AR, CIA, 1873, 174–76; Lee to CIA, August 28, 1877, AR, CIA, 1877, 121–24; Tanner et al., *Atlas of Great Lakes Indian History*, 178.

67. "Indians in the United States in 1870," in U.S. Bureau of the Census, *Report on Indians Taxed and Indians Not Taxed in the United States (except for Alaska) in the Eleventh Census, 1890*, vol. 7 (Washington, D.C.: Government Printing Office, 1894), 22; Stewart Rafert, *The Miami Indians of Indiana: A Persistent People, 1654–1994* (Indianapolis: Indiana Historical Society, 1996), 115–24.

68. New York Agent D. Sherman to CIA Edward P. Smith, October 9, 1877, AR, CIA, 1877, 162–68; Fletcher, *Indian Education and Civilization*, 514–23; New York Agent A. W. Ferrin to CIA, August 30, 1900, AR, CIA, 1890, 297–306.

69. Ibid.

70. Cleland, *Rites of Conquest*, 234–35; Arrell M. Gibson, *The American Indian: Prehistory to the Present* (Lexington, Mass.: D. C. Heath and Company, 1980), 426–28; Prucha, *Great Father*, 1:580–81, 393; Philip Weeks, *Farewell, My Nation: The American Indian and the United States, 1820–1890* (Arlington Heights, Ill.: Harlan Davidson, 1990), 204–5, 217–18, 232–33.

71. AR, CIA Price, October 24, 1881, in Wilcomb E. Washburn, ed., *The American Indian and the United States: A Documentary History*, 4 vols. (New York: Random House, 1973), 1:300.

72. Robert W. Mardock, "Indian Rights Movement until 1887," and Hazel Whitman Hertzberg, "Indian Rights Movement, 1887–1973," in Wilcomb E. Washburn, ed., *Handbook of North American Indians*, vol. 4, *History of Indian-White Relations* (Washington, D.C.: Smithsonian Institution, 1988), 303–4, 305–6; Gibson, *American Indian*, 457–59, 494.

73. Murray quoted in Boyce Richardson, "Kind Hearts or Forked Tongues? The Indian Ordeal: A Century of Decline," *Beaver: Exploring Canada's History* 67 (February–March 1987), 18–23; E. Brian Titley, *A Narrow Vision: Duncan Campbell Scott and the Administration of Indian Affairs in Canada* (Vancouver: University of British Columbia Press, 1986), 201; Royal Commission on Aboriginal Peoples, *Report*, 1:188–91.

74. Prucha, *Great Father*, 1:582.

75. Roger Nichols, *Indians in the United States and Canada: A Comparative History* (Lincoln: University of Nebraska Press, 1998), 239–40.

76. Titley, *Narrow Vision*, 4–5, 13–14; Montgomerie, "Coming to Terms," 240–41n.

77. For comparative analyses of Canadian and U.S. Indian policies and administration, see Hana Samek, *The Blackfoot Confederacy, 1880–1920: A Comparative Study of Canadian and U.S. Indian Policy* (Albuquerque: University of New Mexico Press, 1987), and Nichols, *Indians in the United States and Canada*.

78. Lewis, "Reservation Leadership and the Progressive-Traditional Dichotomy: Willliam Wash and the Northern Utes, 1865–1928," in Albert L. Hurtado and Peter Iverson, eds., *Major Problems in American Indian History* (Lexington, Mass.: D. C. Heath and Company, 1994), 420–34.

79. Miller, *Skyscrapers Hide the Heavens: A History of Indian-White Relations in Canada*, rev. ed. (Toronto: University of Toronto Press, 1991), 190.

80. U.S. Bureau of the Census, *Report on Indians Taxed and Indians Not Taxed*, 624–25.

81. Cleland, *Rites of Conquest*, 243–44.

82. Royal Commission on Aboriginal Peoples, *Report*, 1:257.

83. Richardson, "Kind Hearts or Forked Tongues?" 24–27.

84. Red Jacket, "Address to White Missionaries and Iroquois Six Nations."

CHAPTER 1

1. Voget, "A Six Nations Diary, 1891–1894," *Ethnohistory* 16, no. 4 (Fall 1969): 345–60.

2. DIA, Report of DIA for the Year Ended 30th June, 1898, 62 Victoria, *Sessional Papers* (no. 14), 1899, xxi.

3. Bumsted, *The Peoples of Canada: A Post-Confederation History* (Toronto: Oxford University Press, 1992), 138–39.

4. Graham, *Medicine Man to Missionary*, 64–68; Elma E. Gray, *Wilderness Christians: The Moravian Mission to the Delaware Indians* (Ithaca, N.Y.: Cornell University Press, 1956), 314–15.

5. Report of the Deputy SGIA, December 31, 1878, 42 Victoria, *Sessional Papers* (no. 7), 1879, 216–17.

6. Ibid. Indians were the chief sources of information about nonfarm income as well as for the census and agricultural production. See Superintendent William Plummer to Rama Chief I. Benson, April 9, 1880, NAC, DIA, RG 10, Superintendency Records, Central (Toronto) Superintendency, Letterbook (William Plummer) Indexed, 1879–80, vol. 564, 671 (microfilm C-13370).

7. AR, DIA, 1896, 15.

8. Indian Agent John Thackeray to SGIA, August 21, 1885, AR, DIA, 1885, 13; Indian Agent John Beattie to SGIA, August 24, 1886, AR, DIA, 1886, 4.

9. Indian Superintendent Ebenezer Watson to SGIA, August 24, 1883, AR, DIA, 1883, 3; AR, DIA, 1885, 4; Wilson, *An Account of the Opening of a New Mission to the Indians of the Diocese of Huron, Canada* (Sarnia: "Observer" Steam Job Press, 1869), 10; Indian Agent A. English to SGIA, August 22, 1895, AR, DIA, 1895, 7–8.

10. Indian Agent John Thackeray to SGIA, August 23, 1884, AR, DIA, 1884, 14; Indian Agent George B. McDermot to SGIA, August 30, 1884, AR, DIA, 1884, 16; McDermot to SGIA, August 27, 1885, AR, DIA, 1885, 15.

11. See the reports of various agents in AR, DIA, 1892, 2–5, and 1896, 10, 15, 33, 35.

12. Sally M. Weaver, "The Iroquois: The Consolidation of the Grand River Reserve in the Mid-nineteenth Century, 1847–1875," in Rogers and Smith, *Aboriginal Ontario,* 186; Neal Ferris, "In *Their* Time: Archeological Histories of Native-Lived Contacts and Colonizations, Southwestern Ontario, A.D. 1400–1900" (Ph.D. diss., McMaster University, 2006), 258–61.

13. AR, DIA, 1890, xxxviii; Six Nations Indian Superintendent E. D. Cameron to SGIA, July 13, 1898, AR, DIA, 1898, 37; Weaver, "Six Nations," 529–30.

14. Quoted in Cameron to SGIA, July 13, 1898, AR, DIA, 1898, 37; Cameron to SGIA, September 6, 1894, AR, DIA, 1894, 1.

15. AR, DIA, 1890, xxxviii; visitor quoted in Horatio Hale, "Chief George H. M. Johnson, Onwanonsyshon: His Life and Work among the Six Nations," *Magazine of American History,* February 1885, 140.

16. AR, DIA, 1890, xxxviii.

17. Inspector of Indian Agencies A. Dingman to SGIA, October 26, 1889, AR, DIA, 1889, 157.

18. Weaver, "Iroquois," 186; Cameron to SGIA, August 24[?], 1896, AR, DIA, 1896, 35; Six Nations Visiting Superintendent J. T. Gilkison to SGIA, September 29, 1879, AR, DIA, 1879, 18; Weaver, "Six Nations," 529–30; Gilkison to SGIA, October 6, 1882, AR, DIA, 1882, 1; newspaper editor quoted in Gilkison SGIA, August 26, 1884, AR, DIA, 1884, 2; Howe to Gilkison, September 24, 1870, NAC, DIA, RG 10, Six Nations Superintendency, Correspondence, 1870, vol. 857, 391–93 (microfilm C-15117); Cameron to SGIA, August 30, 1893, AR, DIA, 1893, 1–2.

19. Weaver, "Six Nations," 530; Cameron to SGIA, September 6, 1894, AR, DIA, 1894, 1; Elizabeth Tooker, "Iroquois since 1820," in Trigger, *Handbook,* 464.

20. Sheila M. Van Wyck, "Harvests Yet to Reap: History, Identity, and Agriculture in a Canadian Indian Community" (Ph.D. diss., University of Toronto, 1992), 40; AR, DIA, 1875, 15; AR, DIA, 1898, 434.

21. Indian Agent Alexander McKelvey to SGIA, September 28, 1896, AR, DIA,

1896, 33; Register of Marriages, St. John the Baptist Church of England, 1896–1925, WIHC.

22. Legislative Assembly of the Province of Canada, Report of the Special Commissioners to Investigate Indian Affairs in Canada, Toronto, 1858, photocopy in WIHC; AR, DIA, 1898, 436; Van Wyck, "Harvests Yet to Reap," 44, 231–32, 242–43.

23. MacRae to Deputy SGIA Frank Pedley, July 6, 1904, NAC, DIA, RG 10, Red Series, vol. 3048, file 237 660-14 (microfilm C-11316).

24. Superintendent Thomas S. Walton to SGIA, August 26, 1884, AR, DIA, 1884, 8; Visiting Superintendent C. Skene to SGIA, August 19, 1882, AR, DIA, 1882, 8.

25. Special Commission quoted in Murray, *Muskoka and Haliburton,* 120; Visiting Superintendent of Indian Affairs W. R. Bartlett to SGIA R. T. Pennefather, July 12, 1860, NAC, DIA, RG 10, Superintendency Records, Central (Toronto) Superintendency, Letterbook (Bartlett) Indexed, 1860–61, NAC, RG 10, vol. 545, 90–91 (microfilm C-13358); Superintendent Thomas Walton to SGIA, September 8, 1894, AR, DIA, 1894, 8.

26. Nichols, *Indians in the United States and Canada,* 191–92.

27. Population data drawn from Wightman, *Forever on the Fringe,* 137, and from AR, DIA, 1894, 273.

28. Wightman, *Forever on the Fringe,* 137; Visiting Superintendent J. C. Phipps to SGIA, September 12, 1874, AR, DIA, 1874, 23; quoted in Phipps to SGIA, September 1880, NAC, RG 10, Manitowaning Agency Letterbook, vol. 10447, 562–66 (microfilm C-15235).

29. Wightman, *Forever on the Fringe,* 137.

30. Ibid., 135–37; Deputy Superintendent General William Spragge, NAC, DIA, RG 10, Ministerial Administration Records, Deputy Superintendent General's Office, Reports on Indian Affairs, [1868], vol. 722, 455 (microfilm C-13412); Phipps to SGIA, August 27, 1885, AR, DIA, 1885, 6–7.

31. William Van Abbott to SGIA, September 12, 1894, AR, DIA, 1894, 11; Agent J. P. Donnelly to SGIA, August 31, 1895, AR, DIA, 1895, 10.

32. Donnelly to SGIA, September 24, 1886, AR, DIA, 1886, 20; Donnelly to SGIA, August 25, 1892, 11; Donnelly to SGIA, August 31, 1894, 11–12.

33. Donnelly to SGIA, August 31, 1894, AR, DIA, 1894, 13–14; Donnelly to SGIA, August 31, 1895, AR, DIA, 1895, 9.

34. Donnelly to SGIA, August 31, 1894, AR, DIA, 1894, 11–12.

35. Donnelly to SGIA, August 25, 1892, AR, DIA, 1892, 11.

36. AR, DIA, 1898, 407, 434, 436, 440.

37. Donnelly to SGIA, August 31, 1893, AR, DIA, 1893, 13.

38. Morgan to Indian Agents and Superintendents of Indian Schools, January 30, 1890, NARA, GLR (Chicago), OIA, RG 75, La Pointe Agency, General Records, LR from CIA.

39. New York Agent Bela H. Colegrove to CIA Charles E. Mix, October 1, 1858, AR, CIA, 1858, 21–22; AR, CIA, 1865, appendix 7B, 497; U.S. Bureau of the Census, *Report on Indians Taxed and Indians Not Taxed,* 456ff.; U.S. Bureau of the Census, *The Six Nations of New York: The 1892 United States Extra Census Bulletin* (Washington, D.C.: Government Printing Office, 1892; reprint, Ithaca, N.Y.: Cornell University Press, 1995), 49–50.

40. Agent D. Sherman to CIA, October 9, 1877, AR, CIA, 1877, 162–68; Fletcher, *Indian Education and Civilization,* 578–79; quoted in U.S. Bureau of the Census, *Six Nations of New York,* 49–50.

41. U.S. Bureau of the Census, *Six Nations of New York,* 49–50; Sherman to CIA E. S. Parker, October 22, 1870, AR, CIA, 1870, 318–20; New York Agent Benjamin G. Casler to CIA, August 20, 1883, AR, CIA, 1883, 124–25; A. W. Ferrin to CIA, September 14, 1891, AR, CIA, 1891, 312–16; Ferrin to CIA, August 30, 1900, AR, CIA, 1900, 297–306; Fletcher, *Indian Education and Civilization,* 521–22.

42. Richard M. Smith to CIA N. G. Taylor, September 17, 1868, AR, CIA, 1868, 298–300.

43. Charles H. Titus, *Into the Old Northwest: Journeys with Charles H. Titus, 1841–1846,* ed. by George P. Clerk (East Lansing: Michigan State University Press, 1994), 99–100.

44. Special Agent H. J. Alvord to CIA L. V. Bogy, November 16, 1866, photocopy in WIHC; Fletcher, *Indian Education and Civilization,* 417; U.S. Bureau of the Census, *Report on Indians Taxed and Indians Not Taxed,* 332–34.

45. Article 2, Treaty with the Ottawa and Chippewa, July 31, 1855, http://digital.library.okstate.edu/kappler/treaties/ott0725.htm (accessed May 22, 2007); Agent A. M. Fitch to CIA A. B. Greenwood, June 18, 1859, NARA, OIA, RG 75, LR, Mackinac Agency; school officials quoted in Alice Littlefield, "Indian Education and the World of Work in Michigan, 1893–1933," in Littlefield and Martha C. Knack, eds., *Native Americans and Wage Labor: Ethnohistorical Perspectives* (Norman: University of Oklahoma Press, 1996), 103–4.

46. Robert Doherty, *Disputed Waters: Native Americans and the Great Lakes Fishery* (Lexington: University of Kentucky Press, 1990), 51–53; Littlefield, "Indian Education," 108, 115–16; Cleland, *Rites of Conquest,* 256–61.

47. Rafert, *Miami Indians of Indiana,* 161–63.

48. Memorial of November 18, 1868, enclosed in Green Bay Agent M. L. Martin to CIA, December 10, 1868, NARA, OIA, RG 75, LR, Green Bay Agency, 1868–69 (microfilm M-234, roll 326, frames 297–308); Lieutenant J. A. Manley to CIA Ely S. Parker, December 1, 1869, NARA, OIA, RG 75, LR, Green Bay Agency, 1868–69 (microfilm M-234, roll 326, frames 665–69); Fletcher, *Indian Education and Civilization,* 658; First Assistant Secretary, Department of the Interior, to CIA, January 26, 1895, NARA, OIA, RG 75, LR, 1895, no. 4175; School Supervisor William M. Moss to Superintendent of Indian Schools, December 12, 1895, NARA, OIA, RG 75, LR, 1895, no. 50542; quoted by Superintendent of Indian School Service W. N. Hailman to CIA, November 5, 1895, NARA, OIA, RG 75, LR, 1895, no. 45666.

49. U.S. Bureau of the Census, *Report on Indians Taxed and Indians Not Taxed,* 621.

50. Chiefs Memorial of November 18, 1868, enclosed in Green Bay Agent M. L. Martin to CIA, December 10, 1868, NARA, OIA, RG 75, LR, Green Bay Agency, 1868–69 (microfilm M-234, roll 326, frames 297–308); Green Bay Agent William T. Richardson to CIA F. A. Walker, October 18, 1872, AR, CIA, 1872, 203–8; Green Bay Agent Joseph C. Bridgman to CIA, August 20, 1878, AR, CIA, 1878, 142–44.

51. Fletcher, *Indian Education and Civilization,* 659; Charles S. Kelsey to CIA, August 28, 1891, AR, CIA, 1891, 463–65; A. D. Bonesteel to CIA, November 27, 1860, NARA, OIA, RG 75, LR, Green Bay Agency, 1856–60 (microfilm M-234, roll 323,

frames 1128–30); School Supervisor William M. Moss to Superintendent of Indian Schools, November 20, 1895, NARA, OIA, RG 75, LR, 1895, no. 47487.

52. Fletcher, *Indian Education and Civilization*, 653–54; Green Bay Agent A. D. Bonesteel to CIA Charles E. Mix, September 20, 1858, AR, CIA, 1858, 29–32; Government Farmer Friederich Haas to Bonesteel, September 8, 1859, AR, CIA, 1859, 46–49; M. M. Davis to Dole, September 27, 1862, AR, CIA, 1862, 328–34.

53. Bieder, *Native American Communities*, 157–60; Menominee leader quoted in David R. M. Beck, "Siege and Survival: Menominee Responses to an Encroaching World" (Ph.D. diss., University of Illinois at Chicago, 1994), 154–56; Remarks by Chiefs in Council, September 25, 1859, enclosed in Green Bay Agent A. D. Bonesteel to CIA, September 26, 1859, NARA, OIA, RG 75, LR, Green Bay Agency, 1856–60 (microfilm M-234, roll 323, frames 917–20); First Assistant Secretary, Department of the Interior, to CIA, January 26, 1895, NARA, OIA, RG 75, LR, 1895, no. 4175.

54. Beck, "Siege and Survival," 149–50; Bonesteel to CIA, June 15, 1859, NARA, OIA, RG 75, LR, Green Bay Agency, 1856–60 (microfilm M-234, roll 323, frames 897–98); Green Bay Agent D. P. Andrews to CIA, January 2, 1885, NARA, OIA, RG 75, LR, 1885, Green Bay Agency, no. 278; Felix M. Keesing, *The Menomini Indians of Wisconsin: A Study of Three Centuries of Cultural Contact and Change*, Memoirs of the American Philosophical Society 10 (Philadelphia: American Philosophical Society, 1939; repr. Madison: University of Wisconsin Press, 1987), 158–59, 172; citations are to the reprint edition; Bieder, *Native American Communities*, 157–60.

55. Keesing, *Menomini Indians*, 155–60; Green Bay Agent E. Stephens to CIA, March 4, 1882, NARA, OIA, RG 75, LR, Green Bay Agency, no. 4694.

56. Beck, *Siege and Survival: History of the Menominee Indians, 1634–1856* (Lincoln: University of Nebraska Press, 2002), 188ff.; Bieder, *Native American Communities*, 157–60.

57. Keesing, *Menomini Indians*, 155ff.; Green Bay Agent A. D. Bonesteel to CIA Charles E. Mix, September 20, 1858, AR, CIA, 1858, 29–32; Government Farmer Friederich Haas to Bonesteel, September 8, 1859, AR, CIA, 1859, 46–49; M. M. Davis to Dole, September 27, 1862, AR, CIA, 1862, 328–34; AR, CIA, 1870, Statement Showing Farming Operations of Different Indian Tribes, 342–43; Beck, "Siege and Survival," 154–56.

58. U.S. Bureau of the Census, *Report on Indians Taxed and Indians Not Taxed*, 622; Green Bay Agent Charles S. Kelsey to CIA, August 28, 1891, AR, CIA, 1891, 463–65; Keesing, *Menomini Indians*, 184–85.

59. W. H. Able to CIA, November 4, 1895, NARA, OIA, RG 75, LR, 1895, no. 44984.

60. Article 4, Treaty with the Chippewa, September 30, 1854, http://digital.library.okstate.edu/kappler/Vol2/treaties/chi0648.htm (accessed May 22, 2007).

61. La Pointe Agent W. A. Mercer to Government Farmer Roger Patterson, November 20, 1893, NARA, GLR (Chicago), OIA, RG 75, La Pointe Agency, LS; Mercer to Additional Farmer Peter Phalon, May 25, 1895, NARA, GLR (Chicago), OIA, RG 75, La Pointe Agency, LS; La Pointe Agent S. W. Campbell to Mr. Rodman, April 7, 1899, NARA, GLR (Chicago), OIA, RG 75, La Pointe Agency, LS; La Pointe Agent to Patterson, May 3, 1900, NARA, GLR (Chicago), OIA, RG 75, La Pointe Agency, LS; Campbell to Fred J. Vine, April 25, 1899, NARA, GLR (Chicago), OIA, RG 75, La Pointe Agency, LS.

62. La Pointe Agent to CIA, August 19, 1899, NARA, GLR (Chicago), OIA, RG

75, La Pointe Agency; Agent S. W. Campbell to CIA, April 8, 1899, NARA, GLR (Chicago), OIA, RG 75, La Pointe Agency, LS to CIA.

63. Agent S. E. Mahan to Acting CIA E. M. Marble, February 10, 1881, NARA, GLR (Chicago), OIA, RG 75, La Pointe Agency, LS to CIA; Farmer in Charge, La Pointe Agency, to Acting CIA H. Price, April 25, 1881, NARA, GLR (Chicago), OIA, RG 75, La Pointe Agency, LS to CIA; La Pointe Agent to CIA, June 24, 1881, NARA, GLR (Chicago), OIA, RG 75, La Pointe Agency, LS to CIA; Agent S. E. Mahan to Government Farmer J. D. Gurnoe, May 27, 1881, NARA, GLR (Chicago), OIA, RG 75, La Pointe Agency, LS to CIA; La Pointe Agent S. W. Campbell to CIA, April 8, 1899, NARA, GLR (Chicago), OIA, RG 75, La Pointe Agency, LS to CIA.

64. La Pointe Agent to CIA, March 20, [1879], and quote from April 1, 1879, NARA, GLR (Chicago), OIA, RG 75, La Pointe Agency, LS to CIA; La Pointe Agent to CIA H. Price, December 23, 1882, NARA, GLR (Chicago), OIA, RG 75, La Pointe Agency, LS to CIA.

65. La Pointe Agent C. K. Drew to Superintendent of Indian Affairs W. I. Cullen, July 22, 1860, enclosed in Cullen to CIA A. B. Greenwood, August 7, 1860, NARA, OIA, RG 75, LR, La Pointe Agency (microfilm M-234, roll 392); Leahy to CIA, September 19, 1890, NARA, OIA, RG 75, LR, La Pointe Agency; La Pointe Agent to CIA, August 19, 1899, NARA, OIA, RG 75, LR, La Pointe Agency.

66. La Pointe Agent to CIA, August 19, 1899, NARA, GLR (Chicago), OIA, RG 75, La Pointe Agency.

67. Superintendent W. I. Cullen to CIA A. B. Greenwood, August 7, 1860, NARA, OIA, RG 75, LR, La Pointe Agency (microfilm M-234, roll 392); Webb to Washburn, March 7, 1868, *Condition of the Lake Superior Chippewa*, 40th Cong., 2d sess., 1868, H. Exec. Doc. 246, serial 1341, 1–2; M. A. Leahy to CIA, September 19, 1890, NARA, OIA, RG 75, LR, La Pointe Agency. For a description of roaming Ojibwa from Red Cliff, Bad River, and Lac Court Oreilles reservations, see U.S. Bureau of the Census, *Report on Indians Taxed and Indians Not Taxed*, 314–17.

68. La Pointe Agent C. K. Drew to Superintendent of Indian Affairs W. J. Cullen, January 22, 1860, enclosed in Cullen to CIA A. B. Greenwood, February 1, 1860, NARA, OIA, RG 75, LR, La Pointe Agency (microfilm M-234, roll 392); La Pointe Agent to CIA, July 21, 1899, NARA, GLR (Chicago), OIA, RG 75, La Pointe Agency, LS to CIA; La Pointe Agent S. W. Campbell to Bois Fort Government Farmer Stephen Gheen, May 12, 1899, NARA, GLR (Chicago), OIA, RG 75, La Pointe Agency, LS; La Pointe Agent S. W. Campbell to Superintendent of Indian School at Tower, Minnesota, Oliver H. Gates, April 7, 1900, NARA, GLR (Chicago), OIA, RG 75, La Pointe Agency, LS; U.S. Bureau of the Census, *Report on Indians Taxed and Indians Not Taxed*, 449.

69. Durfee to CIA, May 14, 1885, NARA, OIA, RG 75, LR, La Pointe Agency, no. 11289.

70. Tanner et al., *Atlas of Great Lakes Indian History*, 20–21.

71. AR, DIA, 1898, 450.

CHAPTER 2

1. Danziger, *Chippewas of Lake Superior*, 94–95.
2. For a discussion of how the market system incorporated American Indian re-

sources, see Melissa L. Meyer, "'We can not get a living as we used to': Dispossession and the White Earth Anishinaabeg, 1889–1920," *American Historical Review* 96, no. 2 (April 1991): 368–94.

3. Van Wyck, "Harvests Yet to Reap," 183; quoted in Agent George B. McDermot to SGIA, August 27, 1885, AR, DIA, 1885, 15; McDermot to SGIA, September 1, 1892, AR, DIA, 1892, 18; Agent John Thackeray to SGIA, August 23, 1898, AR, DIA, 1898, 8.

4. Kane, *Wanderings of an Artist among the Indians of North America: From Canada to Vancouver's Island and Oregon through the Hudson's Bay Company's Territory and Back Again* (London: Longman et al., 1859; rev. ed., Toronto: Radisson Society of Canada, 1925; reprint, Rutland, Vt.: Charles E. Tuttle Company, 1968), 2; Agent John Crowe to SGIA, July 30, 1896, AR, DIA, 1896, 9; Agent James T. Conaway to SGIA, August 19, 1886, AR, DIA, 1886, 12; Economic Returns for Cape Croker Reserve, Spring 1876, NAC, DIA, RG 10, Ministerial Administration Records, Deeds, Reports, Census Returns, Accounts, Timber Bonds, 1885–97, vol. 466, 193 (microfilm C-13331); AR, DIA, 1889, 15.

5. Charles Hamori-Torok, "The Iroquois of Akwesasne (St. Regis), Mohawks of the Bay of Quinté (Tyendinaga), Onyota'a:ka (The Oneida of the Thames), and Waha Mohawk (Gibson)," in Rogers and Smith, *Aboriginal Ontario*, 270.

6. Visiting Superintendent J. C. Phipps to SGIA, November 24, 1885, Manitowaning Agency Letterbook, NAC, RG 10, vol. 10453, 660–66 (microfilm C-15237); AR, DIA, 1898, 442.

7. Agent William Van Abbott to SGIA, September 1, 1896, AR, DIA, 1896, 18; Agent J. P. Donnelly to SGIA, August 31, 1894, AR, DIA, 1894, 13; Agent John Thackeray to SGIA, August 31, 1895, AR, DIA, 1895, 9.

8. Richard M. Smith to CIA N. G. Taylor, September 17, 1868, AR, CIA, 1868, 298–300; U.S. Bureau of the Census, *Report on Indians Taxed and Indians Not Taxed*, 624; Fletcher, *Indian Education and Civilization*, 448; La Pointe Agent to Colonel Garrick Mallory (Special Agent in Charge of the 10th Census, Indian Division, Washington, D.C.), January 28, 1881, NARA, GLR (Chicago), OIA, RG 75, La Pointe Agency, LS to CIA.

9. Rae, *Newfoundland to Manitoba: A Guide through Canada's Maritime, Mining, and Prairie Provinces* (London: Sampson Low, Marston, Searle and Rivington, 1881), 148–50.

10. Robinson Treaty Made in the Year 1850 with the Ojibewa Indians of Lake Huron Conveying Certain Lands to the Crown and Robinson Treaty Made in the Year 1850 with the Ojibewa Indians of Lake Superior Conveying Certain Lands to the Crown, in Canada, *Indian Treaties and Surrenders*, 1:149–50, 147–50.

11. The three treaties are available online at http://digital.library.okstate.edu/kappler (accessed January 29, 2007).

12. Royal Commission on Aboriginal Peoples, *Report*, 2:498–99. For a summary of the legal controversy over Walpole Island fishing rights in the 1890s, see DIA Secretary J. D. M. Lean to Deputy Minister of Marine and Fisheries F. Gourdeau, June 8, 1898, transcription in WIHC. For a more detailed discussion, see J. Michael Thoms, "Ojibwa Fishing Grounds: A History of Ontario Fisheries Law, Science, and the Sportsmen's Challenge to Aboriginal Treaty Rights, 1650–1900" (Ph.D. diss., University of British Columbia, 2004).

13. Lytwyn, "Waterworld," 23–26. A thorough assessment of legal issues north of the international border may be found in Peggy Blair, "Taken for 'Granted': Aboriginal Title and Public Fishing Rights in Upper Canada," *Ontario History* 92, no. 2 (Spring 2000): 31–55.

14. Lytwyn, "Waterworld," 23–26. Wikwemikong oral tradition has him murdered by a white man because Gibbard could not pay a gambling debt after a night of whiskey and card playing on board a steamer between Penetanguishene and Sault Ste. Marie, according to historian David T. McNab (communiqué to author, September 27, 2001).

15. Kinoshaineg [sp?] to SGIA L. Vankoughnet, February 20, 1881, NAC, DIA, RG 10, Red Series, vol. 2111, file 20782 (microfilm C-11160).

16. Phipps to SGIA, November 24, 1885, Manitowaning Agency Letterbook, NAC, DIA, RG 10, vol. 10453, 660–61 (microfilm C-15237).

17. Acting Indian Agent to J. W. Stone of Barron, Wisconsin, December 21, 1897, enclosed in Charles [Lewiston, Deputy Commissioner,] State of Wisconsin Bureau of Labor, Census and Industrial Statistics, to Sam, May 12, 1899, NARA, GLR (Chicago), OIA, RG 75, La Pointe Agency, LR; Agent S. W. Campbell to Edward McIntosh, January 6, 1899, NARA, GLR (Chicago), OIA, RG 75, La Pointe Agency, LS; Assistant Commissioner of Indian Affairs to S. W. Campbell, June 22, 1899, NARA, GLR (Chicago), OIA, RG 75, La Pointe Agency, LR from CIA; Ronald N. Satz et al., *Chippewa Treaty Rights: The Reserve Rights of Wisconsin's Chippewa Indians in Historical Perspective* (Madison: Wisconsin Academy of Sciences, Arts and Letters, 1991), 79–83. Bogue's *Fishing the Great Lakes* reviews the rise of commercial fishing, changing fish habitats in the region, and the regulation of the industry by Canada and the United States during the 1800s. She writes: "It seems more than ironic that the first fishers [Indians] of the Great Lakes, the masters of technology that allowed them to secure a major part of their food needs from fishing, found themselves at the turn of the twentieth century being harassed by state and dominion authorities and denied their fishing rights to make way for sport and commercial fishermen. . . . The capital-intensive commercial fishery of the late nineteenth and early twentieth centuries required investments in boats and gear far beyond those that most Indian fishermen could muster, and they found themselves relegated to low-income jobs in the industry's hierarchy and, like other small fishermen, poor" (79–80).

18. AR, DIA, 1877, 161; Arthur Ray, *The Canadian Fur Trade in the Industrial Age* (Toronto: University of Toronto Press, 1990), 76–78, 85–88, figs. 21–22.

19. Visiting Superintendent J. C. Phipps to SGIA, September 12, 1874, AR, DIA, 1874, 31; Agent J. P. Donnelly to SGIA, August 31, 1893, AR, DIA, 1893, 12–13.

20. McKelvey to SGIA, December 1, 1885, NAC, DIA, RG 10, vol. 2118, file 22610.

21. James M. McClurken, "Wage Labor in Two Michigan Ottawa Communities," in Littlefield and Knack, *Native Americans and Wage Labor*, 78; Keesing, *Menomini Indians*, 159; U.S. Bureau of the Census, *Report on Indians Taxed and Indians Not Taxed*, 4; Indian Agent J. L. Mahan to CIA E. A. Hayt, April 21, 1879, NARA, GLR (Chicago), OIA, RG 75, La Pointe Agency, LS to CIA; William M. Moss to Superintendent of Indian Schools, November 4, 1895, NARA, OIA, RG 75, LR, 1895, no. 45347; Moss to Superintendent of Indian Schools, November 2, 1895, NARA, OIA, RG 75, LR, 1895, no. 45133. See, for example, David Calverly, "Who Controls the

Hunt? Ontario's Game Act, the Canadian Government, and the Ojibwa, 1800–1940" (Ph.D. diss., University of Ottawa, 1999).

22. Canada, *Indian Treaties and Surrenders*, 1:147–52.

23. Talfourd to Bury, April 14, 1855, NAC, DIA, RG 10, Field Office Records, Western (Sarnia) Superintendency, Deputy Superintendent General's Office Letterbook, February 20, 1856–59, vol. 584; Visiting Superintendent J. C. Phipps to Superintendent of Indian Affairs, July 5, 1880, NAC, DIA, RG 10, Manitowaning Agency Letterbook, vol. 10447, October 23, 1879–May 26, 1881, 426 (microfilm C-15235); Agent James Allen to SGIA, August 29, 1889, AR, DIA, 1889, 16; Agent J. R. Stevenson to SGIA, July 31, 1890, AR, DIA, 1890, 14; Agent William Van Abbott to SGIA, September 13, 1895, AR, DIA, 1895, 170.

24. U.S. Bureau of the Census, *Six Nations of New York*, 50; U.S. Bureau of the Census, *Report on Indians Taxed and Indians Not Taxed*, 330, 353; Sugar Island Indian Day School Teacher Mary E. Curry on School Report Form, April 30, 1882, and September 30, 1882, enclosed in Mackinac Agent Edward P. Allen to CIA, November 9, 1882, NARA, OIA, RG 75, LR, 1882, Mackinac Agency, no. 20382; Acting CIA to Leahy, June 2, 1890, NARA, GLR (Chicago), OIA, RG 75, La Pointe Agency, General Records, LR from CIA; Leahy to CIA, September 19, 1890, NARA, OIA, RG 75, LR, La Pointe Agency; La Pointe Agent W. A. Mercer to CIA, June 30, 1893, NARA, OIA, RG 75, La Pointe Agency, LR.

25. Visiting Superintendent William Plummer to SGIA, October 29, 1875, AR, DIA, 1875, 12; Plummer to SGIA, November 21, 1879, AR, DIA, 1879, 21–22; AR, DIA, 1898, 10, 450; David Landy, "Tuscarora among the Iroquois," in Trigger, *Handbook*, 522.

26. Minutes of Six Nations Council, March 27, 1885, NAC, DIA, RG 10, Six Nations Superintendency, Correspondence, January–April 1885, vol. 883, 136 (microfilm C-15123); Report of Inspector of Indian Agencies J. Ansdell Macrae to Deputy Superintendent General of Indian Affairs Frank Pedley, June 7, 1904, NAC, DIA, RG 10, Red Series, vol. 3048, file 237660-62 (microfilm C-11316); Memorandum of Deputy Superintendent General of Indian Affairs William Spragge, April 17, 1867, NAC, DIA, RG 10, Ministerial Administration Records, Deputy Superintendent General's Office, Reports on Indian Affairs, 1862–68, vol. 723, 79 (microfilm C-13412); AR, DIA, 1872, 5; Spragge, [September–October 1869], NAC, DIA, RG 10, Ministerial Administration Records, Deputy Superintendent General's Office, Reports on Indian Affairs, 1862–68, vol. 723, 180–81 (microfilm C-13412); Visiting Superintendent J. C. Phipps to Indian Office, January 19, 1875, AR, DIA, 1875, 17.

27. Jackson to CIA, February 13, 1888, NARA, OIA, RG 75, LR, 1888, New York Agency, no. 4375.

28. Superintendent William Plummer to John Sunday, February 3, 1875, NAC, DIA, RG 10, Superintendency Records, Central (Toronto) Superintendency, Letterbook (William Plummer) Indexed, 1874–75, vol. 557a, 228–29 (microfilm C-13364).

29. Agent George B. McDermot to SGIA, August 30, 1884, AR, DIA, 1884, 16; A. Dingman of Indian Affairs Department to Thomas Gordon, March 20, 1883, and Dingman to John M. Corneil, March 20, 1883, NAC, DIA, RG 10, Ministerial Administration Records, Superintendent General's Office, Correspondence, 1874–75, vol. 467, 183409–11 (microfilm C-13332); Agent Thomas Gordon to SGIA, August 26, 1887 AR, DIA, 1887, 6.

30. Superintendent T. G. Anderson to SGIA Lord Bury, August 13, 1855, NAC, DIA, RG 10, Superintendency Records, Central (Toronto) Superintendency, Letterbook (Anderson) Indexed, 1854–55, vol. 540, 400 (microfilm C-13356); Deputy SGIA William Spragge, April 5, 1871, NAC, DIA, RG 10, Ministerial Administration Records, Deputy Superintendent General's Office, Reports on Indian Affairs, 1862–68, vol. 723, 380–81 (microfilm C-13412); AR, DIA, 1872, 6–7; S. Y. Chesley to Special Indian Agent D. Thorburn, NAC, DIA, RG 10, Six Nations Superintendency, Correspondence, July–December 1856, vol. 833, 277–80 (microfilm C-15111); AR, DIA, 1877, 9.

31. Deputy SGIA William Spragge to Superintendent Charles J. Dupont, June 14, 1867, NAC, DIA, RG 10, Superintendency Records, Northern (Manitowaning) Superintendency, Correspondence (Manitoulin Island), 1866–68, vol. 6716, 471–72 (microfilm C-13388).

32. Brian Lee Dunnigan, foreword to Juliette Starr Dana, *A Fashionable Tour through the Great Lakes and Upper Mississippi: The 1852 Journal of Juliette Dana*, ed. David T. Dana III (Detroit: Wayne State University Press, 2004).

33. Patricia Jasen, "Native People and the Tourist Industry in Nineteenth-Century Ontario," *Journal of Canadian Studies* 28 (Winter 1993–94): 5ff.

34. Ibid.

35. Ibid.; Dana, *Fashionable Tour*, 37–39.

36. Agent J. P. Donnelly to SGIA, August 29, 1890, AR, DIA, 1890, 9, 11–13; Donnelly to SGIA, August 31, 1893, AR, DIA, 1893, 11; Donnelly to SGIA, August 31, 1894, AR, DIA, 1894, 12; Jasen, "Native People and the Tourist Industry," 5–6, 20–22; Mark Chochla, "Victorian Fly Fishers on the Nipigon," *Ontario History* 91, no. 2 (Autumn 1999): 151–63.

37. Cleland, *Rites of Conquest*, 256–61.

38. Special Indian Agent D. Thorburn to Superintendent General R. Pennefather, March 19, 1857, NAC, DIA, RG 10, Six Nations Superintendency, Correspondence, January–June 1857, vol. 834, 404–9 (microfilm C-15110); La Pointe Indian Agent to CIA, August 19, 1899, NARA, GLR (Chicago), OIA, RG 75, La Pointe Agency, LS; Deputy SGIA William Spragge, Memorandum of May 16, 1863, NAC, DIA, RG 10, Ministerial Administrative Records, Deputy Superintendent General's Office, Reports on Indian Affairs, 1862–68, vol. 722, 123–24 (microfilm C-13414); Robert F. Fries, *Empire in Pine: The Story of Lumbering in Wisconsin, 1830–1900* (Madison: State Historical Society of Wisconsin, 1951), 202; Satz et al., *Chippewa Treaty Rights*, 72–75.

39. Spragge, Memorandum of July 28, 1862, NAC, DIA, RG 10, Ministerial Administration Records, Deputy Superintendent General's Office, Reports on Indian Affairs, 1862–68, vol. 722, 65–66 (microfilm C-13412); AR, DIA, 1875, 18; Stockbridge and Munsee Delegate Jeremiah Slingerland to CIA, February 12, 1868, NARA, OIA, RG 75, LR, Green Bay Agency, 1868–69 (microfilm M-234, roll 326, frames 329–31); quoted in Superintendent Froome Talfourd to Deputy Superintendent General R. T. Pennefather, May 28, 1856, NAC, DIA, RG 10, Field Office Records, Western (Sarnia) Superintendency, Deputy Superintendent General's Office Letterbook, 20 February 1846–59, vol. 584; Council Minutes taken by Superintendent J. T. Gilkison and sent to William Spragge, March 19, 1873, NAC, DIA, RG 10, Ministerial Administration Records, Deputy Superintendent General's Office, Reports on Indian Affairs, 1872–74, vol. 724, 131–32 (microfilm C-13412).

40. Circular enclosed in DIA Accountant C. T. Walcot to Special Commissioner

D. Thorburn, November 15, 1861, NAC, DIA, RG 10, Six Nations Superintendency, Correspondence, September–December 1861, vol. 846, 45–47 (microfilm C-15114); Spragge to Solomon White, October 24, 1863, NAC, DIA, RG 10, Superintendency Records, Western (Sarnia) Superintendency, Correspondence, Spragge to F. Talfourd, 1862–64, vol. 452, 536–38 (microfilm C-9646); quoted in Spragge to Superintendent Charles J. Dupont, May 22, 1867, NAC, DIA, RG 10, Superintendency Records, Northern (Manitowaning) Superintendency, Correspondence (Manitoulin Island), 1866–68, vol. 616, 451–54 (microfilm C-13388).

41. Quoted in Secretary of the Interior O. H. Browning to CIA, June 1, 1868, NARA, OIA, RG 75, LR, Green Bay Agency, 1868–69 (microfilm M-234, roll 326, frames 123–25); Laurence M. Hauptman and L. Gordon McLester III, eds., *The Oneida Indians in the Age of Allotment, 1860–1920* (Norman: University of Oklahoma Press, 2006), 189.

42. Spragge to Visiting Superintendent of Indian Affairs William Plummer, October 9, 1871, NAC, DIA, RG 10, Superintendency Records, Northern (Manitowaning) Superintendency, Correspondence (Manitoulin Island), 1871–72, vol. 618, 363–65 (microfilm C-13389); Secretary of State Hector Lengevin to Plummer, February 4, 1869, NAC, DIA, RG 10, Superintendency Records, Northern (Manitowaning) Superintendency, Correspondence (Manitoulin Island) 1869–70, vol. 617, 61–62 (microfilm C-13388); Lengevin to Plummer, February 27, 1869, NAC, DIA, RG 10, Superintendency Records, Northern (Manitowaning) Superintendency, Correspondence (Manitoulin Island), 1869–70, vol. 617, 78–79 (microfilm C-13388); Visiting Superintendent of Indian Affairs W. R. Bartlett to Sampson Green and Joseph Cook, February 17, 1865, NAC, DIA, RG 10, Superintendency Records, Central (Toronto) Superintendency, Letterbook (Bartlett) Indexed, 1864–65, vol. 548, 406 (microfilm C-13359).

43. Weekly Scalers Report, Lac du Flambeau, June 1896, NARA, GLR (Chicago), OIA, RG 75, Lac du Flambeau Agency, LR by Superintendent, March 1896–December 1898, Agent W. A. Mercer to CIA, July 22, 1893, NARA, GLR (Chicago), OIA, RG 75, La Pointe Agency, LS.

44. Statement of General Council, October 9, 1869, WIHC; Memorandum to the Assistant Secretary, DIA, October 16, 1905, WIHC; Bird to Sir J. A. Macdonald, December 22, 1881, WIHC.

45. Agent C. L. D. Sims to Secretary, DIA, December 4, 1899, NAC, DIA, RG 10, Manitowaning Agency Letterbook, vol. 10523, April 1, 1899–August 25, 1899 (microfilm C-15253); Visiting Superintendent J. C. Phipps to SGIA L. Vankoughnet, February 18, 1890, NAC, DIA, RG 10, Manitowaning Agency Letterbook, vol. 10467, 59 (microfilm C-15240).

46. Visiting Superintendent J. C. Phipps to Nowagahbow, December 17, 1890, NAC, DIA, RG 10, Manitowaning Agency Letterbook, vol. 10470, October 8, 1890–May 16, 1891, 267 (microfilm C-15241).

47. For in-depth assessment of logging operations on a Great Lakes reservation within the United States, see the discussions in two books by David R. M. Beck: *Siege and Survival,* chaps. 5–6 and 8; and *The Struggle for Self-Determination: History of the Menominee since 1854* (Lincoln: University of Nebraska Press, 2005), chaps. 2, 4–6, and 10–11.

48. Miller to CIA, February 13 and December 10, 1868, and Martin to CIA, Feb-

ruary 3 and March 13, 1869, NARA, OIA, RG 75, LR, Green Bay Agency, 1868–69, (microfilm M-234, roll 326, frames 164–68, 288–90, 471–73, 495–501).

49. Quoted in Hazelton to CIA, May 18, 1881, and Hazelton to Secretary of the Interior, July 16, 1881, and Hazelton to CIA, January 7, 1882, NARA, OIA, RG 75, LR, 1881, nos. 8528, 12422, 418; Hauptman and McLester, *Oneida Indians,* 189.

50. CIA to Green Bay Agent, October 17, 1903, NARA, GLR (Chicago), OIA, RG 75, Green Bay Agency, LR; Green Bay Agent E. Stephens to CIA, May 16, 1882, NARA, OIA, RG 75, LR, 1882, Green Bay Agency, no. 9299; quoted in Green Bay Agent E. Stephens to CIA, January 19, 1882, NARA, OIA, RG 75, LR, 1882, Green Bay Agency, no. 1507; Secretary of the Interior to CIA, February 1, 1882, NARA, OIA, RG 75, LR, 1882, no. 2218.

51. Memorandum on the Application of Messer Muchmore to Purchase the Pine Timber on Lots Nos. 1, 2, 3 in the 5th Concession and Lot No. 8 on the 6th Concession of the Township of Tuscarora, Deputy Superintendent of Indian Affairs William Spragge, November 11, 1864, NAC, DIA, RG 10, Ministerial Administration Records, Deputy Superintendent General's Office, Reports on Indian Affairs, 1862–68, vol. 722, 207–10 (microfilm C-13412).

52. Weaver, "Iroquois," 188–89.

53. Minutes of Six Nations Council, February 10, 1885, NAC, DIA, RG 10, Six Nations Superintendency, Correspondence, January–April 1885, vol. 883, 83–85 (microfilm C-15123).

54. Minutes of Six Nations Council, February 15 and 17, 1885, NAC, DIA, RG 10, Six Nations Superintendency, Correspondence, January–April 1885, vol. 883, 86–91 (microfilm C-15123).

55. Minutes of Six Nations Council, February 20 and 27, 1885, NAC, DIA, RG 10, Six Nations Superintendency, Correspondence, January–April, vol. 883, 92–94, 97–100 (microfilm C-15123). The approved wood regulations included the following: only industrious farmers would be allowed to clear and farm land; each parcel of land must keep 30 to 100 acres as a woodlot; sugar maple groves must be protected and preserved; land proposed for clearing and farming must first be examined by a bailiff, who will report to the council; cut and piled timber may not be removed from a parcel unless approved by the council; a home market for Six Nations wood will be established in Oshweken; and wood products may not be exported from the reservation.

56. James T. Angus, "How the Dokis Indians Protected Their Timber," *Ontario History* 81, no. 3 (September 1989): 181–99. For a more detailed discussion of Ottawa's administration of Indian timber holdings, see Angus's *A Deo Victoria: The Story of the Georgian Bay Lumber Company, 1871–1942* (Thunder Bay: Severn Publications, 1990), chap. 14. That the Indian Department continued to harm Indian interests in the twentieth century is argued by Mark Kuhlberg in "'Nothing it seems can be done about it': Charlie Cox, Indian Affairs Timber Policy, and the Long Lac Reserve, 1924–40," *Canadian Historical Review* 84, no. 1 (March 2003): 33–63.

57. James A. Tuck, "Regional Cultural Development, 3000 to 300 B.C.," in Trigger, *Handbook,* 31; Rhonda Telford, "'Under the Earth': The Expropriation and Attempted Sale of the Oil and Gas Rights of the Walpole Island First Nation during World War I," in David T. McNab, ed., *Earth, Water, Air, and Fire: Studies in Cana-*

dian Ethnohistory (Waterloo, Ontario: Wilfrid Laurier University Press, 1998), 67–69; Danziger, *Chippewas of Lake Superior,* 5, 87–88; Nancy M. Wightman and W. Robert Wightman, "The Mica Bay Affair: Conflict on the Upper Lakes Mining Frontier, 1840–1850," *Ontario History* 83, no. 3 (September 1991): 202–5.

58. Vidal to D. B. Papineau, April 27, 1846, Ontario Archives, RG 1 A-1-6, vol. 25, 21675–77 (microfilm MS 563:22), transcription in WIHC.

59. Wightman and Wightman, "Mica Bay Affair," 193–208. For more about Ottawa's failure to safeguard Indian mineral resources, see two works by Rhonda Telford: "'The sound of the rustling of gold is under my feet where I stand. We have a rich country': A History of Aboriginal Mineral Resources in Ontario" (Ph.D. diss., University of Toronto, 1996) and "Aboriginal Resistance in the Mid-nineteenth Century: The Anishinabe, Their Allies, and the Closing of Mining Operations at Mica Bay and Michipicoten Island," in Bruce W. Hodgins, Ute Lischke, and David T. McNab, eds., *Blockades and Resistance: Studies in Actions of Peace and the Temagami Blockades of 1988–89* (Waterloo, Ontario: Wilfrid Laurier University Press, 2003), 71–84.

60. Crowley, "Rural Labour," in Paul Craven, ed., *Labouring Lives: Work and Workers in Nineteenth-Century Ontario* (Toronto: University of Toronto Press, 1995), 40, 67–69; AR, DIA, 1894, 1.

61. Crowley, "Rural Labour," 68; quoted in J. R. Stevenson to SGIA, August 1885, AR, DIA, 1885, 12.

62. Agent Thomas S. Walton to SGIA, August 23, 1890, AR, DIA, 1890, 9; Agent D. J. McPhee to SGIA, October 3, 1887, AR, DIA, 1887, 19–20; Agent William Van Abbott to SGIA, October 18, 1898, AR, DIA, 1898, 15.

63. La Pointe Agent Lieutenant W. A. Mercer to CIA, June 30, 1893, NARA, GLR (Chicago), OIA, RG 75, La Pointe Agency, LS.

64. Agent William Van Abbott to SGIA, August 23, 1884, AR, DIA, 1884, 9–10; McClurken, "Wage Labor in Two Michigan Ottawa Communities," 69, 94.

65. AR, DIA, 1898, 450; La Pointe Agent Lieutenant W. A. Mercer to CIA, June 30, 1893, NARA, GLR (Chicago), OIA, RG 75, La Pointe Agency, LS.

66. U.S. Bureau of the Census, *Report on Indians Taxed and Indians Not Taxed,* 334; First Assistant Secretary, Department of the Interior, to CIA, January 26, 1895, NARA, OIA, RG 75, LR, no. 4175; Bieder, *Native American Communities,* 160–64.

67. Kane, *Wanderings of an Artist,* 7–11.

68. Return of Indians for Presents, Distributed at Manitowaning, August 9, 1853, NAC, DIA, RG 10, Superintendency Records, Northern (Manitowaning) Superintendency, Correspondence (Manitoulin Island), 1851–55, vol. 613, 775–78 (microfilm C-13386). Great Britain ceased providing outright presents in the mid-1850s. See J. B. Clench to Honorable R. Bruce, December 29, 1853, NAC, DIA, RG 10, vol. 570 (microfilm C-13373), transcription in WIHC.

69. Kane, *Wanderings of an Artist,* 22.

70. Visiting Superintendent and Commissioner J. T. Gilkison to SGIA, November 15, 1875, AR, DIA, 1875, 9.

71. C. J. Walcot (in the Absence of Deputy Superintendent General of Indian Affairs) to C. J. Dupont, October 4, 1864, NAC, DIA, RG 10, Ministerial Administration Records, Deeds, Reports, Census Returns, Accounts, Timber Bonds, 1872–76, vol. 464, 541–47 (microfilm C-13331); Campbell to Walter B. Phillips of Grand Portage, June 8, 1900, NARA, GLR (Chicago), OIA, RG 75, La Pointe Agency, LS.

72. Voucher No. 4, Abstract D, 2nd Quarter 1879 to Property Return, Issues to Indians of Annuity Goods and Supplies by E. Stephens, Agent at Green Bay, June 30, 1879, NARA, GLR (Chicago), OIA, RG 75, Green Bay Agency, Records of Agent E. Stephens, 1879–85.

73. Mackinac Agent Edward P. Allen to CIA, May 28, 1885, NARA, OIA, RG 75, LR, 1885, Mackinac Agency, no. 12058.

74. Minutes of Six Nations Council, March 18 and April 14, 1880, NAC, DIA, RG 10, Six Nations Superintendency, Correspondence, January–April 1880, vol. 875, 8, 105–6 (microfilm C-15120).

75. Walpole Island Agency, Correspondence Relative to the Payment of the Accounts for the Repairs to the Council House, NAC, DIA, RG 10, Red Series, vol. 2606, file 122597 (microfilm C-11248); Pennefather to Froome Talfourd, January 13, 1857, NAC, DIA, RG 10, Field Office Records, Western (Sarnia) Superintendency, Deputy Superintendent General's Office Letterbook, 1846–59, vol. 584.

76. Secretary of State Hector Langevin to Superintendent of Indian Affairs William Plummer, October 14, 1868, NAC, DIA, RG 10, Superintendency Records, Northern (Manitowaning) Superintendency, Correspondence (Manitoulin Island), 1866–68, vol. 616, 775–77 (microfilm C-13388).

77. Acting CIA to Agent M. A. Leahy, May 28, 1890, NARA, GLR (Chicago), OIA, RG 75, La Pointe Agency, General Records, LR from CIA; Leahy to CIA T. J. Morgan, February 18, 1890 NARA, GLR (Chicago), OIA, RG 75, La Pointe Agency, Press Copies of LS to CIA.

78. Phipps to Deputy Superintendent General of Indian Affairs L. Vankoughnet, January 25, 1890, NAC, DIA, RG 10, Manitowaning Agency Letterbook, vol. 10467, 496–98 (microfilm C-15240); La Pointe Agent S. W. Campbell to Lac du Flambeau Government Farmer N. D. Rodman, January 19, 1899, NARA, GLR (Chicago), OIA, RG 75, La Pointe Agency, LS.

79. Royal Commission on Aboriginal Peoples, *Report*, 2:487.

80. Chute, *The Legacy of Shingwaukonse: A Century of Native Leadership* (Toronto: University of Toronto Press, 1998); Montgomerie, "Coming to Terms."

81. Quoted in Chute, *Shingwaukonse*, 123.

CHAPTER 3

1. Quoted in Robert W. Venables, introduction to U.S. Bureau of the Census, *Six Nations of New York*, xv–xvi.

2. Cleland, *Rites of Conquest*, 253–56.

3. Treaty with the Cherokee, July 8, 1817, http://digital.library.okstate.edu/kappler/Vol2/treaties/che0140.htm (accessed February 9, 2007); Gibson, *American Indian*, 489–90; Hayt quoted in Wilcomb E. Washburn, *The Assault on Indian Tribalism: the General Allotment Law (Dawes Act) of 1887* (Philadelphia: J. B. Lippincott, 1975), 6–7.

4. See http://digital.library.okstate.edu/kappler (accessed February 9, 2007) for the following: Treaty with the Chippewa, September 30, 1854, 648–52; Treaty with the Ottawa and Chippewa, July 31, 1855, 725–31; Treaty with the Stockbridge and Munsee, February 5, 1856, 742–55; Treaty with the Chippewa of Saginaw, Swan Creek, and Black River, October 18, 1864, 868–71. See also Tanner et al., *Atlas of Great Lakes Indian History*, 167–68.

5. Oberly 1888 AR quoted in Edmund Jefferson Danziger, Jr., "Native American Resistance and Accommodation during the Late Nineteenth Century," in Charles W. Calhoun, ed., *The Gilded Age: Essays on the Origins of Modern America*, 2d ed. (New York: Rowman and Littlefield Publishers, 2007), 177–78.

6. Ibid., 180; Dawes quoted in Alexandra Harmon, "American Indians and Land Monopolies in the Gilded Age," *Journal of American History* 90, no. 1 (June 2003): 106.

7. *U.S. Statutes at Large* 24 (1886): 388–91; Danziger, "Native American Resistance and Accommodation," 178.

8. 20 Victoria (1857), c. 26 (Province of Canada), in Derek G. Smith, ed., *Canadian Indians and the Law: Selected Documents, 1663–1972* (Toronto: McClelland and Stewart, 1975), 50–54; Miller, *Skyscrapers*, 110–13.

9. Deputy Superintendent Froome Talfourd to R. T. Pennefather, May 26, 1857, NAC, DIA, RG 10, Field Office Records, Western (Sarnia) Superintendency, Deputy Superintendent General's Office Letterbook, 1846–59, vol. 584; Deputy Superintendent General William Spragge to Agent for Indian Lands Joseph Wilson, November 28, 1863, NAC, DIA, RG 10, Superintendency Records, Northern (Manitowaning) Superintendency, Correspondence (Manitoulin Island), 1861–65, vol. 615, 303–4 (microfilm C-13387); Canada, *Indian Treaties and Surrenders*, 1:235–337.

10. 31 Victoria (1868), c. 42 (Canada); 32 and 33 Victoria (1869), c. 6 (Canada).

11. 39 Victoria (1876), c. 18 (Canada); Robert J. Surtees, "Canadian Indian Policies," in Washburn, *Handbook*, 91. Enfranchisement provisions applied only to eastern Indians of Canada, whom the federal government believed were prepared for assimilation.

12. Washburn, *Assault on Indian Tribalism*, 12; Gibson, *American Indian*, 496; Journeycake and Washakie quoted in Danziger, "Native American Resistance and Accommodation," 180.

13. Unidentified tribal leader quoted in Miller, *Skyscrapers*, 112, 114, 190.

14. Quoted in Gibson, *American Indian*, 496.

15. Bieder, *Native American Communities*, 161–62; Sarah R. Shillinger, "'They never told us they wanted to help us': An Oral History of Saint Joseph's Indian Industrial School" (Ph.D. diss., University of Pennsylvania, 1995), vi.

16. Van Wyck, "Harvests Yet to Reap," 249–50.

17. Agent S. E. Mahan to Acting CIA, February 17, 1881, NARA, OIA, RG 75, LR, 1881, La Pointe Agency; Petition of Lac Courte Oreilles to CIA, February 20, 1890, NARA, OIA, RG 75, LR, 1890, no. 5622; Matthew A. Leahy to CIA, July 30, 1890, NARA, GLR (Chicago), OIA, RG 75, La Pointe Agency, Press Copies of LS to CIA.

18. Jack Campisi and Laurence M. Hauptman, eds., *The Oneida Experience: Two Perspectives* (Syracuse, N.Y.: Syracuse University Press, 1988), 73–78, 85; Green Bay Agent A. D. Bonesteel to CIA, January 22, 1859, NARA, OIA, RG 75, LR, Green Bay Agency, 1856–60 (microfilm M-234, roll 323, frames 817–20); Petition of Oneida Opposed to Allotment, May 30, 1888, NARA, OIA, RG 75, LR, 1888, no. 14504; Proallotment Petition of May 7, 1888, NARA, OIA, RG 75, LR, 1888, no. 12560; Oneida Petition Favoring Allotment, enclosed in Agent Thomas Jennings to CIA, November 13, 1888, NARA, OIA, RG 75, LR, 1888, Green Bay Agency, no. 28447. The Wisconsin Oneida's involvement with allotment is detailed in Hauptman and McLester, *Oneida Indians*, 179ff.

19. Froome Talfourd to William Spragge, February 21, 1863, NAC, DIA, RG 10,

Field Office Records, Western (Sarnia) Superintendency, Deputy Superintendent General's Office Letterbook, 1846–59, vol. 585; Grand General Council of the Chippewas, Munsees, Six Nations, et al. *[Proceedings] Held on the Sarnia Reserve, June 25th to July 3, 1874* (Sarnia: Canadian Steam Publishing Establishment, 1874) enclosed in President of the Grand Council of the Indians H. P. Chase and First Vice President William Wawanosh to the Honorable Minister of the Interior, February 9, 1875, NAC, DIA, RG 10, Red Series, vol. 1942, file 4103 (microfilm C-1117).

20. Grand General Council of the Chippewas, Munsees, Six Nations, et al., *[Proceedings]*.

21. Ibid.

22. Ibid.

23. Campbell to Morrison, August 22, 1899, NARA, GLR (Chicago), OIA, RG 75, La Pointe Agency, LS; Campbell to Prophet, August 31, 1900, NARA, GLR (Chicago), OIA, RG 75, LA Pointe Agency, LS.

24. Indian Act, 1876, 39 Victoria (1876), c. 18 (Canada).

25. Spragge, February 3, 1873, NAC, DIA, RG 10, Ministerial Administration Records, Deputy Superintendent General's Office, Reports on Indian Affairs, 1872–74, vol. 724, 100 (microfilm C-13412); Secretary of State Joseph Howe to Chippewa Indians of Kettle Point, February 4, 1874, WIHC.

26. Macrae to Deputy SGIA Frank Pedley, May 9, 1905, NAC, DIA, RG 10, Red Series, vol. 3048, file 237660-16 (microfilm C-11316).

27. Acting CIA Thomas M. Nichol to Agent S. E. Mahan, February 28, 1881, enclosed in Acting CIA E. L. Stevens to Agent W. R. Durfee, August 24, 1882, NARA, GLR (Chicago), OIA, RG 75, La Pointe Agency, LR from CIA; CIA J. D. C. Atkins to La Pointe Agent James T. Gregory, September 16, 1885, NARA, GLR (Chicago), OIA, RG 75, La Pointe Agency, LR from CIA.

28. Acting CIA to Mercer, March 11, 1893, NARA, GLR (Chicago), OIA, RG 75, La Pointe Agency, LR from CIA.

29. Agency Clerk R. G. Redman, Jr., to Rice Harper, [1897], NARA, GLR (Chicago), OIA, RG 75, La Pointe Agency, LS to CIA.

30. Danziger, *Chippewas of Lake Superior*, 100–101.

31. Ibid., 101–2. See also Michelle M. Steen-Adams, Nancy Langston, and David J. Mladenoff, "White Pine in the Northern Forests: An Ecological and Management History of White Pine on the Bad River Reservation of Wisconsin," *Environmental History* 12 (July 2007): 614–48.

32. Oberly to James T. Gregory, December 8, 1888, NARA, GLR (Chicago), OIA, RG 75, La Pointe Agency, General Records, LR from CIA.

33. Danziger, *Chippewas of Lake Superior*, 101–2.

34. La Pointe Agent to CIA, September 11, 1895, NARA, GLR (Chicago), OIA, RG 75, La Pointe Agency, LS to CIA.

35. Danziger, *Chippewas of Lake Superior*, 101; Acting CIA A. G. Tourner to La Pointe Agent S. W. Campbell, February 11, 1899, NARA, GLR (Chicago), OIA, RG 75, La Pointe Agency, LR from CIA; Leahy to CIA T. J. Morgan, October 4, 1890, NARA, OIA, RG 75, LR, 1890, La Pointe Agency, no. 30981.

36. Mercer to Roger Patterson, October 22, 1895, NARA, GLR (Chicago), OIA, RG 75, La Pointe Agency, LS.

37. A. C. Tonner to La Pointe Agent S. W. Campbell, March 24, 1899, NARA,

GLR (Chicago), OIA, RG 75, La Pointe Agency, LS; Agent S. W. Campbell to Roger Patterson, June 9, 1899, NARA, GLR (Chicago), OIA, RG 75, La Pointe Agency, LS; Agent Campbell to William Denomie, May 15, 1900, NARA, GLR (Chicago), OIA, RG 75, La Pointe Agency, LS. The extent to which the Bad River Reservation economy was dominated and exploited by the Stearns Lumber Company and the local Indian agent is reviewed by Patty Loew in *Indian Nations of Wisconsin: Histories of Endurance and Renewal* (Madison: Wisconsin Historical Society Press, 2001), 73–75, and in "Newspapers and the Lake Superior Chippewa in the 'Unprogressive' Era" (Ph.D. diss., University of Wisconsin–Madison, 1998), chap. 2.

38. Whiteside to Agent S. W. Campbell, April 1, 1899, NARA, GLR (Chicago), OIA, RG 75, La Pointe Agency, LR.

39. Vilas quoted in Danziger, *Chippewas of Lake Superior,* 102.

40. Ibid.

41. Agent W. A. Mercer to CIA, June 7, 1893, and CIA D. M. Browning to Mercer, June 26, 1893, NARA, GLR (Chicago), OIA, RG 75, La Pointe Agency, LS to and LR from CIA. Recognizing that aged and disabled allottees might wish to lease their lands, Congress enacted legislation to regulate this process carefully, thereby creating even more paperwork for Indians and local federal agents. See section 3 of *U.S. Statutes at Large* 26 (1891): 795, approved February 28, 1891.

42. Schurz quoted in Danziger, "Native American Resistance and Accommodation," 179; Danziger, *Chippewas of Lake Superior,* 98; Arthur W. Thurner, *Strangers and Sojourners: A History of Michigan's Keweenaw Peninsula* (Detroit: Wayne State University Press, 1994), 107.

43. Port Arthur Agent J. P. Donnelly to SGIA, June 5, 1888 [1889?], enclosed with Circular, July 23, 1888, NAC, DIA, RG 10, Red Series, vol. 2425, file 87762 (microfilm C-11218).

44. McKelvey to SGIA, September 23, 1884, Walpole Island Agency, Correspondence regarding Farming Locations for Several Young Men on Walpole Island, NAC, DIA, RG 10, Red Series, vol. 2273, file 54616 (microfilm C-11192); McKelvey to SGIA, March 3, 1885, and Indian Office to McKelvey, March 27, 1885, NAC, DIA, RG 10, Red Series, vol. 2292, file 58185 (microfilm C-11196); quotations in McKelvey to SGIA, March 22, 1886, NAC, DIA, RG 10, Red Series, vol. 2326, file 66623 (microfilm C-11202); Walpole Island Allotment Records, 1913–44, NAC, DIA, RG 10, Red Series, vol. 2292, file 58185 (microfilm C-11196).

45. Garrett quoted in Laurence M. Hauptman, "Senecas and Subdividers: Resistance to Allotment of Indian Lands in New York, 1875–1906," *Prologue: Quarterly of the National Archives,* 25th anniversary issue (1994): 87–100.

46. Report of the Proceedings of the Chippewa Grand Council Approving the New Indian Act, 1876, NAC, DIA, RG 10, Red Series, vol. 1994, file 6829 (microfilm C-11115).

47. For a detailed discussion of the "Big Cut" and its impact on the region, see William Ashworth, *The Late, Great Lakes,* chap. 7.

48. Danziger, *Chippewas of Lake Superior,* 104.

49. Tanner et al., *Atlas of Great Lakes Indian History,* 168.

50. Wilkinson quoted in Satz et al., *Chippewa Treaty Rights,* 77–79; Bieder, *Native American Communities,* 164–65; Campisi and Hauptman, *Oneida Experience,* 73–78,

85. For a detailed discussion of Michigan Indian land loss because of allotment, see Cleland, *Rights of Conquest*, 236ff.

51. Rafert, *Miami Indians of Indiana*, 139ff.

52. Genetin-Pilawa, "'In the Interests of Harmony and Good Government': Allotment Era Politics in the Great Lakes Region" (M.A. thesis, Bowling Green State University, 2002), ii, 57–85. See also Leonard A. Carlson, *Indians, Bureaucrats, and Land: The Dawes Act and the Decline of Indian Farming* (Westport, Conn.: Greenwood Press, 1981).

CHAPTER 4

1. Twain quoted in James Axtell, *The Invasion Within: The Contest of Cultures in Colonial North America* (New York: Oxford University Press, 1985), 329; Gates quoted in James Wilson, *The Earth Shall Weep: A History of Native America* (New York: Grove Press, 1998), 310–11; Philip Cate Huckins, "Broken Vows, Broken Arrows: An Analysis of the U.S. Government's Off-Reservation Boarding School Program, 1879–1900" (Ph.D. diss., Boston College, 1995), 92. For a history of the responses of aboriginal people to Euro-American efforts to acculturate them coercively by means of formal schooling, see Jon Reyhner and Jeanne Eder, *American Indian Education: A History* (Norman: University of Oklahoma Press, 2004).

2. Wilson, *Earth Shall Weep*, 311–12; Huckins, "Broken Vows, Broken Arrows," 21–27; Morgan and Price quoted in Clyde Ellis, *To Change Them Forever: Indian Education at the Rainy Mountain Boarding School, 1893–1920* (Norman: University of Oklahoma Press, 1996), 3–6, 11, 16–17; Prucha, *Great Father*, 1:597; 2:700, 703, 814.

3. John S. Milloy, *"A National Crime": The Canadian Government and the Residential School System, 1879–1986* (Winnipeg: University of Manitoba Press, 1999), 11.

4. Miller, *Shingwauk's Vision: A History of Native Residential Schools* (Toronto: University of Toronto Press, 1996), 185ff.; Milloy, *"National Crime,"* 27.

5. Ellis, *To Change Them Forever*, 18–26; Margaret Connell Szasz and Carmelita Ryan, "American Indian Education," in Washburn, *Handbook*, 290–91.

6. Titley, *Narrow Vision*, 75; Miller, *Skyscrapers*, 105–8, 196–98; Miller, *Shingwauk's Vision*, 84, 135, 148; AR, DIA, 1869, 28–29; AR, DIA, 1893, 270–76.

7. Titley, *Narrow Vision*, 75; Paul W. Bennett, "'Little Worlds': The Forging of Social Identities in Ontario's Protestant School Communities and Institutions, 1850–1930" (Ph.D. diss., University of Toronto, 1990), 204–5; AR, DIA, 1869, 28; Weaver, "Iroquois," 197–99; U.S. Consul F. N. Blake to Secretary of State Hamilton Fish, January 6, 1870, in *Report on the Management of Indians in British America*, 2–3; Miller, *Shingwauk's Vision*, 122–23; Deputy SGIA William Spragge, August 4, 1866, NAC, DIA, RG 10, Ministerial Administrative Records, Deputy Superintendent General's Office, Reports on Indian Affairs, 1862–68, vol. 722, 307–8 (microfilm C-13412); Secretary of Indian Missions Committee of the Diocese of Huron Robert Ashton to SGIA, June 8, 1885, and SGIA to Ashton, June 25 and July 18, 1885, NAC, DIA, RG 10, Red Series, vol. 2301, file 60259 (microfilm C-11989).

8. Szasz and Ryan, "American Indian Education," 291; Prucha, *Great Father*, 2:693; Joshua Bolles Garritt, *Historical Sketch of the Missions among the North American Indians under the Care of the Board of Foreign Missions of the Presbyterian Church*

(Philadelphia: Women's Foreign Mission Society of the Presbyterian Church, 1881), 6–7; La Pointe Agent W. R. Durfee to CIA, August 16, 1881, NARA, OIA, RG 75, LR, La Pointe Agency, no. 14803; Shillinger, "'They never told us,'" 2–3.

9. Deputy SGIA Spragge, [November 1869], NAC, DIA, RG 10, Ministerial Administration Records, Deputy Superintendent General's Office, Reports on Indian Affairs, 1862–68, vol. 723, 187 (microfilm C-13412); Secretary of State Joseph Howe to Superintendent William Plummer, December 10, 1869, NAC, DIA, RG 10, Superintendency Records, Northern (Manitowaning) Superintendency, Correspondence, 1869–70, vol. 617, 252–54 (microfilm C-13389); Visiting Superintendent J. C. Phipps to the Reverend D. Dieronquet [sp?], S.J., July 31, 1879, NAC, DIA, RG 10, Manitowaning Agency Letterbook, vol. 10446, 584 (microfilm C-15234).

10. Green Bay Agent Lieutenant J. A. Manley to CIA Ely S. Parker, August 4, 1869, NARA, OIA, RG 75, LR, Green Bay Agency, 1868–69 (microfilm M-234, roll 326, frames 579–82); Agent S. W. Campbell to Sister Catherine Buckley at Odanah, Wisconsin, July 19, 1900, NARA, GLR (Chicago), OIA, RG 75, La Pointe Agency, LS; New York Agent D. Sherman to CIA, October 15, 1878, AR, CIA, 1878, 110–12; New York Agent Benjamin G. Caster to CIA, October 13, 1882, AR, CIA, 1882, 132–34; A. W. Ferrin to CIA, August 30, 1900, AR, CIA, 1900, 297–306; New York Agent Marcus H. Johnson to CIA George W. Manypenny, September 30, 1856, AR, CIA, 1856, 29–30.

11. Milloy, *"National Crime,"* 26–27; Eileen M. Antone, "The Educational History of the Onyota'a:ka Nation of the Thames," *Ontario History* 85, no. 4 (December 1993): 309–20; Correspondence regarding Grants to Schools, 1885–86, NAC, DIA, RG 10, Red Series, NAC, RG 10, vol. 2301, file 60259 (microfilm C-11198); the Reverend William Curry to CIA, July 18, 1882, LR, 1882, NARA, OIA, RG 75, no. 13226; SGIA R. Pennefather to Special Indian Commissioner D. Thorburn, February 5, 1861, NAC, DIA, RG 10, Six Nations Superintendency, Correspondence, January–April 1861, vol. 844, 218 (microfilm C-15113); Froome Talfourd to C. T. Walcot, January 20, 1862, NAC, DIA, RG 10, Field Office Records, Western (Sarnia) Superintendency, Deputy Superintendent General's Office Letterbook, vol. 585; Sarnia Council Proceedings, December 15, 1856, NAC, DIA, RG 10, Superintendency Records, Western (Sarnia) Superintendency, Miscellaneous Records, Collected by F. Talfourd, 1850–65, vol. 453, 19 (microfilm C-9646); Walpole Chief Peterwegeshick and Two Others to Superintendent F. Talfourd, August 4, 1862, NAC, DIA, RG 10, Superintendency Records, Western (Sarnia) Superintendency, Miscellaneous Records, vol. 453, 10 (microfilm C-9646).

12. Weaver, "Six Nations," 529–30; Minutes of Six Nations Council, June 4 and 5, 1880, NAC, DIA, RG 10, Six Nations Superintendency, Correspondence, vol. 876, 21, 29–32 (microfilm C-15120); Minutes of Six Nations Council, October 27, 1885, NAC, DIA, RG 10, Six Nations Superintendency, Correspondence, 1885, NAC, RG 10, vol. 885, 30 (microfilm C-15123).

13. See n. 41 for a representative list of these studies.

14. Data for this paragraph drawn from AR, DIA, 1870–1900.

15. John McFin [sp?] to Deputy Minister, October 13, 1890, Reports on the Wesleyan Methodist Schools in Ontario and Quebec, 1880–1917, NAC, DIA, RG 10, Red Series, vol. 2100, file 17960 (microfilm C-11157).

16. Inspector of Indian Agencies and Reserves and Acting Agent A. Dingman to SGIA, October 26, 1889, AR, DIA, 1889, 157–58.

17. Fletcher, *Indian Education and Civilization*, 417–18, 448–51, 515–24, 654, 658–60, 665–69.

18. Visiting Superintendent Phipps to Hebert, October 15, 1890; Phipps to Thessalon Chief Kewaidin, November 4, 1890; Phipps to Wakigigig, November 10, 1890; and Phipps to L. Vankoughnet, December 9, 1890—all in NAC, DIA, RG 10, Manitowaning Agency Letterbook, vol. 10470, 28, 107, 127, 243 (microfilm C-15241).

19. Peter E. Jones to Visiting Superintendent J. T. Gilkison, January 12, 1875, NAC, DIA, RG 10, Six Nations Superintendency, Correspondence, vol. 866, 49–50 (microfilm C-15119); AR, DIA, 1887, 15; AR, DIA, 1892, 14.

20. L. Vankoughnet to SGIA, November 19, 1890, Reports on the Wesleyan Methodist Schools in Ontario and Quebec, 1880–1917, NAC, DIA, RG 10, Red Series, vol. 2100, file 17960 (microfilm C-11157).

21. School reports in AR, DIA, 1860s–1890s.

22. Visiting Superintendent J. C. Phipps to Honorable Minister of the Interior, Indian Branch, October 28, 1878, Manitowaning Agency Letterbook, NAC, DIA, RG 10, vol. 10446, 119 (microfilm C-15234); AR, DIA, 1889, 7; AR, DIA, 1890, 5.

23. Visiting Superintendent W. R. Bartlett to the Reverend G. A. Anderson, February 6, 1860, NAC, DIA, RG 10, Superintendency Records, Central (Toronto) Superintendency, Letterbook (Bartlett) Indexed, 1858–60, vol. 544, 466 (microfilm C-13358); Bartlett to SGIA R. Pennefather, February 15, 1860, NAC, DIA, RG 10, Superintendency Records, Central (Toronto) Superintendency, Letterbook (Bartlett) Indexed, 1858–60, vol. 544, 471–72 (microfilm C-13358); Bartlett to Mohawk Councilors, March 30, 1860, NAC, DIA, RG 10, Superintendency Records, Central (Toronto) Superintendency, Letterbook (Bartlett) Indexed, 1860–61, vol. 545, 32 (microfilm C-13358); Bartlett to SGIA, July 9, 1860, NAC, DIA, RG 10, Superintendency Records, Central (Toronto) Superintendency, Letterbook (Bartlett) Indexed, 1860–61, vol. 545, 82–83 (microfilm C-13358).

24. Visiting Superintendent Bartlett to Mohawk Councilors of Tyendinaga, January 14, 1860, NAC, DIA, RG 10, Superintendency Records, Central (Toronto) Superintendency, Letterbook (Bartlett) Indexed, 1858–60, vol. 544, 443–44 (microfilm C-13358).

25. AR, CIA, 1888, 114; C. Skene to SGIA, August 30, 1883, AR, DIA, 1883, 7–8; Schmalz, *Ojibwa of Southern Ontario*, 189–90.

26. School reports in AR, DIA, 1860s–1890s; school inspectors quoted in Indian Agent Alex McKelvey to SGIA, September 28, 1896, AR, DIA, 1896, 32–34.

27. Agent P. E. Jones to SGIA, September 27, 1892, AR, DIA, 1892, 18–19; Act for the Gradual Enfranchisement of Indians, the Better Management of Indian Affairs, and to Extend the Provisions of the Act, 31 Victoria (1869) c. 42, s. 12 (Canada), in Smith, *Canadian Indians and the Law,* 76; Agent Alexander McKelvey to SGIA, August 30, 1889, AR, DIA, 1889, 1; Visiting Superintendent James C. Phipps to SGIA, August 27, 1885, AR, DIA, 1885, 7; Danziger, *Chippewas of Lake Superior,* 105.

28. Agent John Thackeray to SGIA, August 15[?], 1896, and Indian Agent J. P. Donnelly to SGIA, August 31, 1896, AR, DIA, 1896, 10, 21; Danziger, *Chippewas of Lake Superior,* 106.

29. Weaver, "Iroquois," 197–99; Bennett, "'Little Worlds,'" 204. Bennett's figures include a few schools outside the Great Lakes basin, which is the scope of this study.

30. Bennett, "'Little Worlds,'" 204.

31. Fletcher, *Indian Education and Civilization*, 417–18, 448–51, 515–24, 658, 619–20, 624–25, 667–69.

32. Superintendent Thomas S. Walton to SGIA, August 26, 1889, AR, DIA, 1889, 9; Nin-Da-Waab-Jig, *Walpole Island*, 61.

33. AR, DIA, 1880, 7; Superintendent William Plummer to SGIA, November 29, 1880, NAC, DIA, RG 10, Superintendency Records, Central (Toronto) Superintendency, Letterbook (William Plummer) Indexed, 1880–81, vol. 565, 207–16 (microfilm C-13370); Miller, *Shingwauk's Vision*, 129; Danziger, *Chippewas of Lake Superior*, 106; Agent W. A. Mercer to Mrs. Sullivan, December 2, 1893, NARA, GLR (Chicago), OIA, RG 75, La Pointe Agency, LS.

34. Agent A. English to SGIA, September 15, 1891, and Agent D. J. McPhee to SGIA, September 18, 1891, AR, DIA, 1891, 3, 17; Agent John Thackeray to SGIA, August 8, 1893, AR, DIA, 1893, 15–16; Report on the Indian School at Moraviantown Reserve under the Tuition of the Reverend L. Vogler, July 5, 1849, NAC, DIA, RG 10, Superintendency Records, Western (Sarnia) Superintendency, J. B. Clench Papers, School Reports, 1837–59, vol. 442; Agent John Thackeray to SGIA, August 3, 1891, and Agent Matthew Hill, October 12, 1891, AR, DIA, 1891, 14, 16.

35. Statement of the Condition of the Various Indian Schools in the Dominion, for the Year Ended 30th June, 1880, AR, DIA, 1880, 304–5.

36. Devens, *Countering Colonization: Native American Women and Great Lakes Missions, 1630–1900* (Berkeley: University of California Press, 1992), 108–11.

37. Report of Inspector R. Ashton for School Year Ended 30th June, 1884, to School Board of the Six Nations, AR, DIA, 1884, 18–19; Superintendent E. D. Cameron to SGIA, August 24, 1896, AR, DIA, 1896, 35–36; Moravian council quoted in Agent John Beattie to SGIA, August 14, 1885, AR, DIA, 1885, 5–6.

38. Weaver, "Iroquois," 197–99.

39. Walpole Island Agency, Correspondence Regarding the Proposed Erection of Another School House on Walpole Island, 1889–90, NAC, DIA, RG 10, Red Series, vol. 2469, file 97234 (microfilm C-11226).

40. Sutherland to SGIA, March 31, 1887, Reports on the Wesleyan Methodist Schools in Ontario and Quebec, 1880–1917, NAC, DIA, RG 10, Red Series, vol. 2100, file 17960 (microfilm C-11157); Schurz quoted in Cleland, *Rites of Conquest*, 244–45; AR, DIA, 1880, 7.

41. See, for example, the following general studies: Miller, *Shingwauk's Vision;* Milloy, *"National Crime";* Jeffrey Louis Hamley, "Cultural Genocide in the Classroom: A History of the Federal Boarding School Movement in American Indian Education, 1875–1920" (Ph.D. diss., Harvard University, 1994); Huckins, "Broken Vows, Broken Arrows." The Canadian government developed two types of residential schools in the 1880s: "boarding schools" that were located on or close to reservations and taught basic academic skills, such as arithmetic, reading, and writing, plus manual skills needed by farm families; and "industrial schools" that were larger, located closer to urban centers, and taught, in addition to a "plain English education," a variety of trades, including agricultural. In 1923, both types of schools were combined and henceforth referred to as "residential schools." See Milloy, *"National Crime,"* 7–8; Miller *Shingwauk's Vision*, 196–97. To minimize confusion, these institutions as well as similar ones in the United States will be referred to as boarding schools.

42. AR, CIA, 1897, xxvi; Miller, *Shingwauk's Vision*, 81–83, 105–8.

43. Leahy to CIA T. J. Morgan, July 30, 1890, NARA, GLR (Chicago), OIA, RG 75, La Pointe Agency, LS to CIA; Hayt and Teller quoted in Prucha, *Great Father*, 2:689; Colin G. Calloway, *First Peoples: A Documentary Survey of American Indian History*, 2d ed. (Boston: Bedford/St. Martin's, 2004), 384; Huckins, "Broken Vows, Broken Arrows," 70–71, 75; Shillinger, "'They never told us,'" 146.

44. Huckins, "Broken Vows, Broken Arrows," 20; Miller, *Skyscrapers*, 196–98; New York Agent A. W. Ferrin to CIA, August 30, 1900, AR, CIA, 1900, 297–306; New York Agent Marcus H. Johnson to CIA George W. Manypenny, September 30, 1856, AR, CIA, 1856, 29–30; Francis Paul Prucha, *Atlas of American Indian Affairs* (Lincoln: University of Nebraska Press, 1990), 62. For an overview of these institutions, see David Wallace Adams, *Education for Extinction: American Indians and the Boarding School Experience, 1875–1928* (Lawrence: University Press of Kansas, 1995), and Clifford E. Trafzer, Jean A. Keller, and Lorene Sisquoc, eds., *Boarding School Blues: Revisiting American Indian Educational Experiences* (Lincoln: University of Nebraska Press, 2006).

45. Quoted in Elizabeth Graham, "Uses and Abuses of Power in Two Ontario Residential Schools," in McNab, *Earth, Water, Air, and Fire*, 232.

46. Register of Pupils, 1893–1932, vol. A of 3:1893–1906, NARA, GLR (Chicago), OIA, RG 75, Records of Mount Pleasant Indian School; Statement of Arrival and Departure of Pupils, September 30, 1895, NARA, GLR (Chicago), OIA, RG 75, Tomah Indian Industrial School Reports of Employees, Students, Buildings, Positions; Shillinger, "'They never told us,'" 4, 164–67.

47. Miller, *Shingwauk's Vision*, 174–77; Elizabeth Graham, *The Mush Hole: Life at Two Indian Residential Schools* (Waterloo, Ontario: Heffle Publishing, 1997), 14–15, 58.

48. Report of Employees at the Tomah Indian Industrial School, September 30, 1896, NARA, GLR (Chicago), OIA, RG 75, Tomah Indian Industrial School Reports of Employees, Students, Buildings, Positions; Huckins, "Broken Vows, Broken Arrows," 74; quoted in Shillinger, "'They never told us,'" 58.

49. Statement Giving the Number and Description of Buildings Belonging to the United States, and Used for the Benefit of the Indian Service at Tomah, Wisconsin, Reservation, Belonging to the Tomah Indian Industrial School Agency, in the State or Territory of Wisconsin, March 31, 1897, NARA, GLR (Chicago), OIA, RG 75, Tomah Indian Industrial School Reports of Employees, Students, Buildings, Positions.

50. Wilson, *Earth Shall Weep*, 312; Szasz and Ryan, "American Indian Education," 291; Miller, *Shingwauk's Vision*, 153–60, 172, 178–81; Bennett, "'Little Worlds,'" 223–24; Milloy, *"National Crime,"* 34–38.

51. Atkins quoted in Prucha, *Great Father*, 2:690; Shillinger, "'They never told us,'" 100–102; Royal Commission on Aboriginal Peoples, *Report*, 1:341; Miller, *Shingwauk's Vision*, 173; Wilson quoted in Bennett, "'Little Worlds,'" 223.

52. Statement of Arrival and Departure of Pupils, September 30, 1895, NARA, GLR (Chicago), OIA, RG 75, Tomah Indian Industrial School Reports of Employees, Students, Buildings, Positions.

53. Miller, *Shingwauk's Vision*, 194–95, 197, 217–27; Shillinger, "'They never told us,'" 95; Milloy, *"National Crime,"* 40–41.

54. Miller, *Shingwauk's Vision*, 290–315; Wilson quoted in Bennett, "'Little Worlds,'" 224–25.

55. Miller, *Shingwauk's Vision*, 259–72; Bennett, "'Little Worlds,'" 229–32; Wilson

to E. A. Meredith, June 20, 1878, NAC, DIA, RG 10, Ministerial Administrative Records, Deeds, Reports, Census Returns, Accounts, Timber Bonds, 1877–84, vol. 465, 145–47 (microfilm C-13331); Visiting Superintendent J. C. Phipps to SGIA, April 15, 1885, NAC, DIA, RG 10, Manitowaning Agency Letterbook, vol. 10451, 965 (microfilm C-15237); E. A. Meredith to Robert McKenzie, October 8, 1875, NAC, DIA, RG 10, Superintendency Records, Western (Sarnia) Superintendency, Correspondence, Robert McKenzie, Land Records, Maps, Receipts, 1865–88, vol. 455, 401–3 (microfilm C-9647).

56. Antone, "Educational History," 312–13.

57. St. Martin to Superintendent, March 8, 1897, NARA, GLR (Chicago), OIA, RG 75, Records of Tomah Industrial School, LR; Acting Secretary of the Interior to CIA, February 8, 1895, NARA, OIA, RG 75, LR, 1895, no. 6515; La Pointe Agent S. W. Campbell to Tomah Superintendent, June 17, 1899, NARA, GLR (Chicago), OIA, RG 75, La Pointe Agency, LS.

58. Shillinger, "'They never told us,'" xi–xiii, 5, 82–86.

59. Deputy Superintendent Froome Talfourd to C. T. Wolcot, December 9, 1861, NAC, DIA, RG 10, Field Office Records, Western (Sarnia) Superintendency, Deputy Superintendent General's Office Letterbook, 1846–59, vol. 585; Deputy SGIA William Spragge, Memorandum, November 22, 1862, NAC, DIA, RG 10, Ministerial Administration Records, Deputy Superintendent General's Office, Reports on Indian Affairs, 1862–68, vol. 722, 85–88 (microfilm C-13412); Superintendent of Indian Schools to CIA, September 29, 1893, NARA, OIA, RG 75, LR, no. 3680; Bennett, "'Little Worlds,'" 232–33.

60. Tredo to Scott, August 30, 1897, NARA, GLR (Chicago), OIA, RG 75, La Pointe Agency, LR.

61. Morgan quoted in Shillinger, "'They never told us,'" 94–95.

62. Ellis, *To Change Them Forever*, 195–98; Shillinger, "'They never told us,'" 134, 146; Prucha, *Great Father*, 2:700.

63. Miller, introduction to Paul Robert Magocsi, ed., *Aboriginal Peoples of Canada: A Short Introduction* (Toronto: University of Toronto Press, 2002), 31.

64. Wilson, *Earth Shall Weep*, 320; Cleland, *Rites of Conquest*, 245–46; Hauptman and McLester, *Oneida Indians*, xiv, 8, 39–74.

65. Royal Commission on Aboriginal Peoples, *Report*, 1:601–2.

CHAPTER 5

1. Quoted in Anthony F. C. Wallace, *The Death and Rebirth of the Seneca* (New York: Vintage Books, 1972), 206.

2. Martin, *The Land Looks After Us: A History of Native American Religion* (New York: Oxford University Press, 1999), ix–13.

3. Cleland, *Rites of Conquest*, 66–67; Grant, *Profusion of Spires*, 6; Martin, *Land Looks After Us*, 33, 37; Brian S. Osborne and Michael Ripmeester, "The Mississaugas between Two Worlds: Strategic Adjustments to Changing Landscapes of Power," *Canadian Journal of Native Studies* 17, no. 2 (1997): 262–67.

4. Johnston, *The Manitous: the Spiritual World of the Ojibway* (Toronto: Key Porter Books, 1995), xxi–xxii, 1–2.

5. Grant, *Profusion of Spires*, 6–10; J. Garth Taylor, "Northern Algonquians on the Frontiers of 'New Ontario,' 1890–1945," in Rogers and Smith, *Aboriginal Ontario*, 330; Cleland, *Rites of Conquest*, 67.

6. Martin, *Land Looks After Us*, 34–37.

7. Grant, *Profusion of Spires*, 6–10; Taylor, "Northern Algonquians," 330–31; Cleland, *Rites of Conquest*, 65, 69.

8. Grant, *Profusion of Spires*, 6–7; Danziger, *Chippewas of Lake Superior*, 19–20. For further details on the Midéwiwin, see Helen Hornbeck Tanner, *The Ojibwa* (New York: Chelsea House Publishers, 1991), 27–31; Dewdney, *Sacred Scrolls*, 163–73; and Michael R. Angel, "Discordant Voices, Conflicting Visions: Ojibwa and Euro-American Perspectives on the Midéwiwin" (Ph.D. diss., University of Manitoba, 1997).

9. Grant, *Profusion of Spires*, 11–12.

10. Martin, *Land Looks after Us*, 39–41.

11. Eric Porter, "The Anglican Church and Native Education: Residential Schools and Assimilation" (Ph.D. diss., University of Toronto, 1981), 25–26, 101–4, 108–9; Robert Pierce Beaver, *Church, State, and the American Indians: Two and a Half Centuries of Partnership in Missions between Protestant Churches and the Government* (St. Louis: Concordia Publishing House, 1966), 71; Osborne and Ripmeester, "Mississaugas between Two Worlds," 270–72; C. L. Higham, *Noble, Wretched, and Redeemable: Protestant Missionaries to the Indians in Canada and the United States, 1820–1900* (Albuquerque: University of New Mexico Press, 2000), 20–21, 31–32, 36, 211–12.

12. Higham, *Noble, Wretched*, 15, 19–20, 29, 211–12.

13. Quoted in ibid., 20–23; Nichols, *Indians in the United States and Canada*, 170–71.

14. Higham, *Noble, Wretched*, 15–16.

15. Edward Francis Wilson, *Missionary Work among the Ojebway Indians* (New York: E and J. B. Young and Company, 1886), 49–50; Ruth Bleasdale, "Manitowaning: An Experiment in Indian Settlement," *Ontario History* 66, no. 3 (September 1974): 152–54; Virgil J. Vogel, "The Missionary as Acculturation Agent: Peter Dougherty and the Indians of Grand Traverse," *Michigan History* 51(1967): 200–201; Walter P. Schoenfuhs, "'O Tebeningeion'—O Dearest Jesus,'" *Concordia Historical Institute Quarterly* 37, no. 3 (1964): 110–13.

16. Wilson, *Missionary Work among the Ojebway Indians*, 5ff.; Johann Georg Kohl, *Kitch-Gami: Life among the Lake Superior Ojibway*, ed. Lascelles Wraxall et al. (London: Chapman and Hall, 1860; reprint, St. Paul: Minnesota Historical Society, 1985), 305.

17. John Webster Grant, *Moon of Wintertime: Missionaries and the Indians of Canada in Encounter since 1534* (Toronto: University of Toronto Press, 1984), 94–95, 173ff.; James M. McClurken, *Gah-Baeh-Jhagwah-Buk: The Way It Happened; A Visual Culture History of the Little Traverse Bay Bands of Odawa* (East Lansing: Michigan State University Museum, 1991), 19–27.

18. Miller, *Skyscrapers*, 100; Rogers, "The Algonquin Farmers of Southern Ontario, 1821–1890," in Rogers and Smith, *Aboriginal Ontario*, 125–26; W. H. Withrow, *Our Own Country: Canada, Scenic and Descriptive* (Toronto: William Briggs, 1889), 353–54; Ives Goddard, "Delaware," in Trigger, *Handbook*, 223; Rogers, "Northern Algonquians," 328–29. For one Methodist missionary's experiences in the mid-1800s, see

John H. Pitezel, *Lights and Shades of Missionary Life: Containing Travels, Sketches, Incidents, and Missionary Efforts, during Nine Years Spent in the Region of Lake Superior* (Cincinnati: Western Book Concern, 1860).

19. Miller, *Skyscrapers,* 100; Rogers, "Northern Algonquians," 328–29.

20. AR, DIA, 1895 and 1896. The only reserve with no Christians listed was Obidgewong on Manitoulin Island.

21. New York Agent D. Sherman to CIA Edward P. Smith, October 15, 1875, AR, CIA, 1875, 335–36; Garritt, *Historical Sketch of the Missions,* 7–9.

22. Jamieson quoted in James Miller, "The Reverend Simpson Brigham (1875–1926): The Worlds of Henry Ford and Simpson Brigham Collide," in McNab, *Earth, Water, Air, and Fire,* 81–89; James Miller, ed., "Three Letters Written by the Reverend Andrew Jamieson (1814–1885): June 1882, October 1882, February 1884" (unpublished photocopy, Port Lambton, Ontario), 1–3. For a discussion of Walpole Island's religious differences with Jesuit missionaries, see Denys Delâge and Helen Hornbeck Tanner, "The Ojibwa-Jesuit Debate at Walpole Island, 1844," *Ethnohistory* 41, no. 2 (Spring 1994), 295–321. Another evangelist who enjoyed some success because he and his family lived with Indians was Edward Baierlein, a German Lutheran. For his story, see E. R. Baierlein, *In the Wilderness with the Red Indians: German Missionary to the Michigan Indians, 1847–53,* ed. Howard W. Moll, trans. Anita Z. Boldt (Detroit: Wayne State University Press, 1996).

23. Ibid.

24. Ibid.; Jamieson to Mr. Viday [1885], quoted in Sheldon Krasowski, "'A Nuimay' (the Prayer People) and the Pagans of Walpole Island First Nation: Resistance to the Anglican Church, 1845–1885" (M.A. thesis, Trent University, 1998), 81–84. Krasowski's thesis presents an evaluation of Jamieson's Walpole ministry plus an appendix with transcriptions of many of the priest's letters.

25. Miller, "Reverend Simpson Brigham," 2–3.

26. Wilson, *Missionary Work among the Ojebway Indians,* 16ff.; quoted in David A. Nock, *A Victorian Missionary and Canadian Indian Policy: Cultural Synthesis vs. Cultural Replacement* (Waterloo, Ontario: Wilfrid Laurier University Press, 1988), 71–76.

27. Osborne, "Barter, Bible, Bush: Strategies of Survival and Resistance among the Kingston/Bay of Quinte Mississauga, 1783–1836," in Hodgins, Lischke, and McNab, *Blockades and Resistance,* 93–96.

28. Nock, *Victorian Missionary,* 75–76.

29. Higham, *Noble, Wretched,* 134; Beaver, *Church, State, and the American Indians,* 177–78.

30. Higham, *Noble, Wretched,* 144.

31. Graham, *Medicine Man to Missionary,* 62–64.

32. Weaver, *Medicine and Politics among the Grand River Iroquois: A Study of the Non-Conservatives,* Publications in Ethnology, no. 4 (Ottawa: National Museums of Canada, 1972), 15; U.S. Bureau of the Census, *Report on Indians Taxed and Indians Not Taxed,* 478.

33. Garritt, *Historical Sketch of the Missions,* 6–7. How white settlers obtained Indian land in northern Michigan is described in chapter 3 of the present study.

34. Martin, *Land Looks After Us,* 47, 81–82.

35. Ibid., 75, 81.

36. Bieder, *Native American Communities*, 157–60; Acting La Pointe Agent to Roger Patterson, February 14, 1898, NARA, GLR (Chicago), OIA, RG 75, La Pointe Agency, LS; Miller, *Thirty Years in the Itinerancy* (Milwaukee: I. L. Hauser and Company, 1875), 148–51.

37. Osborne, "Barter, Bible, Bush," 97–99.

38. Van Wyck, "Harvests Yet to Reap," 199–206; Peterwegeshick quoted in Krasowski, "'A Nuimay' (the Prayer People)," 55–58; Wilson, *Missionary Work among the Ojebway Indians*, 195.

39. Agent W. R. Durfee to CIA, August 16, 1881, NARA, OIA, RG 75, LR, La Pointe Agency, no. 14803; Jamieson quoted in Van Wyck, "Harvests Yet to Reap," 201–2. The role of Catholic missionaries is presented by Maureen Anna Harp in "Indian Missionaries, Immigrant Migrations, and Regional Catholic Culture: Slovene Missionaries in the Upper Great Lakes, 1830–1892" (Ph.D. diss., University of Chicago, 1996). For an in-depth discussion of how relations could be strained between a reservation community and a missionary, see Rebecca Kugel, "Of Missionaries and Their Cattle: Ojibwa Perceptions of a Missionary as Evil Shaman," *Ethnohistory* 41, no. 2 (Spring 1994): 227–44.

40. Krasowski, "'A Nuimay' (the Prayer People)," 92; Jamieson to the Reverend Thomas Bullock, January 9, 1877 and [no day or month] 1878, in ibid., appendix, 35–40; Indian Agent Alexander McKelvey to SGIA, August 25, 1884, AR, DIA, 1884, 3–4.

41. Keith and McMurray quoted in Chute, *Shingwaukonse*, 56–59.

42. In 1869, Walpole sent to Ottawa a three-man delegation, which included Jamieson, "to represent our interests in that city, and to make certain inquiries in the Indian office connected with the welfare of our tribe" (Walpole Councilors to William Spragge, September 27, 1869, WIHC).

43. Chute, *Shingwaukonse*, 54–55, 108.

44. Ferris, "Continuity within Change," 198–200.

45. Krasowski, "'A Nuimay' (the Prayer People)," 17; Wilson quoted in Graham, *Medicine Man to Missionary*, 61; Osborne, "Barter, Bible, Bush," 100; Ogista quoted in Chute, *Shingwaukonse*, 43.

46. Martin, *Land Looks After Us*, 78–80; Gibson, *American Indian*, 466; Nichols, *Indians in the United States and Canada*, 240.

47. Devens, *Countering Colonization*, 108–13, 120–28.

48. U.S. Bureau of the Census, *Report on Indians Taxed and Indians Not Taxed*, 447, 454–55, 476, 478–80; Harold Blau, Jack Campisi, and Elisabeth Tooker, "Onondaga," in Trigger, *Handbook*, 497.

49. U.S. Bureau of the Census, *Report on Indians Taxed and Indians Not Taxed*, 332–34.

50. Bieder, *Native American Communities*, 157–60, 170. For an analysis of the three-way religious struggle among the Menominee (Catholics versus Protestants versus non-Christians), see Beck, *Struggle for Self-Determination*, chap. 3.

51. Louise S. Spindler, "Menominee," in Trigger, *Handbook*, 716; Stephens quoted in Beck, "Siege and Survival," 181–86.

52. Bieder, *Native American Communities*, 171–72; Martin, *Land Looks After Us*, 102–6.

53. AR, DIA, 1890, 236–37; Weaver, *Medicine and Politics*, 15–16; Weaver, "Iroquois," 196–97; Dean R. Snow, *The Iroquois* (Oxford: Blackwell, 1994), 180–81.

54. Deputy Superintendent General Froome Talfourd, R. T. Pennefather, and Thomas Worthington to SGIA, [October 1858], NAC, DIA, RG 10, Field Office Records, Western (Sarnia) Superintendency, Deputy Superintendent General's Office Letterbook, 1846–59, vol. 584.

55. Wilson, *Missionary Work among the Ojebway Indians*, 55–56; Krasowski, "'A Nuimay' (the Prayer People)," 78–83, 92–93.

56. Joann Sebastian Morris, "Churches and Education," in Mary B. Davis et al., eds., *Native America in the Twentieth Century: An Encyclopedia* (New York: Garland Publishing, 1994), 114.

57. Graham, *Medicine Man to Missionary*, 87.

58. Martin, *Land Looks After Us*, 81–82.

CHAPTER 6

1. Jamieson Report of December 31, 1869, Andrew Jamieson Papers, Huron University College Library, University of Western Ontario, London, Ontario.

2. AR, DIA, 1872, 1–2.

3. Report of CIA T. J. Morgan, October 1, 1889, in Wilcomb E. Washburn, ed., *The American Indian and the United States: A Documentary History* (New York: Random House, 1973), 1:424–25.

4. Bieder, *Native American Communities*, 44–45; Sharon O'Brien, "Tribal Governments," in Davis et al., *Native America in the Twentieth Century*, 651.

5. Royal Commission on Aboriginal Peoples, *Report*, 2:119, 128.

6. John Kinzie letter to Lewis Cass quoted in Clifton, "Potawatomi," in Trigger, *Handbook*, 730–32; Spindler, "Menominee," 713–14.

7. Cleland, *Rites of Conquest*, 59–60; Chute, *Shingwaukonse*, 248–51; Bieder, *Native American Communities*, 26–27; Alexander von Gernet, "Iroquoians," in Magocsi, *Aboriginal Peoples of Canada*, 164.

8. Gernet, "Iroquoians."

9. Clifton, "Potawatomi," 730–32; Danziger, *Chippewas of Lake Superior*, 23; McClurken, *Gah-Baeh-Jhagwah-Buk*, 73; Royal Commission on Aboriginal Peoples, *Report*, 2:135–36.

10. Frederick E. Hoxie, *A Final Promise: The Campaign to Assimilate the Indians, 1880–1920* (Lincoln: University of Nebraska Press, 1984), 42–52; J. R. Miller, introduction to Magocsi, *Aboriginal Peoples of Canada*, 32; Weeks, *Farewell, My Nation*, 217–18, 228–30.

11. Jackson, *A Century of Dishonor: The Early Crusade for Indian Reform*, ed. Andrew F. Rolle (New York: Harper Torchbooks, 1965), 340–42.

12. Draft Statement of Deputy SGIA L. Vankoughnet, August 22, 1876, NAC, DIA, RG 10, Red Series, vol. 1995, file 6886 (microfilm C-11130); Montgomerie, "Coming to Terms," 260–61; Royal Commission on Aboriginal Peoples, *Report*, 1:261.

13. Royal Commission on Aboriginal Peoples, *Report*, 1:271–73; AR, DIA, 1897, xxv.

14. Royal Commission on Aboriginal Peoples, *Report*, 1:281; *Statutes of Canada* 1876, 39 Victoria (1876), c. 18 (Canada); Langevin quoted in Miller, *Skyscrapers*, 191;

Charlotte Coté, "Historical Foundations of Indian Sovereignty in Canada and the United States: A Brief Overview," *American Review of Canadian Studies* 31 (Spring–Summer 2001): 18.

15. 43 Victoria (1880), c. 28 (Canada); Miller, *Skyscrapers*, 189–90; Royal Commission on Aboriginal Peoples, *Report*, 1:280–89, 299–87.

16. Robert N. Clinton, "Sovereignty and Jurisdiction," in Davis et al., *Native America in the Twentieth Century*, 607–11; Sharon O'Brien, "Tribal Governments," 652; Coté, "Historical Foundations of Indian Sovereignty," 19–21.

17. *U.S. Statutes at Large* 16 (1871): 570; Gibson, *American Indian*, 437–38; Prucha, *Great Father*, 2:603, 646; William T. Hagan, "United States Indian Policies, 1860–1900," in Washburn, *Handbook*, 57–58; *U.S. Statutes at Large* 23 (1885): 385; *U.S. Statutes at Large* 24 (1886): 388–91.

18. Abbott to SGIA, September 12, 1894, AR, DIA, 1894, 9–11.

19. Hauptman, *The Iroquois in the Civil War: From Battlefield to Reservation* (Syracuse, N.Y.: Syracuse University Press, 1993), 13–16; Reginald Horsman, "The Wisconsin Oneidas in the Preallotment Years," in Campisi and Hauptman, *Oneida Experience*, 74; Beck, *Struggle for Self-Determination*, 17.

20. *Narrative: Visit of the Governor-General and the Countess of Dufferin to the Six Nation Indians, August 25, 1874*, comp. J. T. Gilkison, 2d ed. (n.p., 1875).

21. Weaver, *Medicine and Politics*, 17; U.S. Bureau of the Census, *Report on Indians Taxed and Indians Not Taxed*, 473–74; Tooker, "League of the Iroquois," 435–37; Visiting Superintendent of Indian Affairs J. C. Phipps to Minister of the Interior, Indian Branch, August 29, 1878, NAC, DIA, RG 10, Manitowaning Agency Letterbook, vol. 10446, 1878–79, 6 (microfilm C-15234).

22. Special Disbursing Agent J. O. Belleau to CIA W. A. Jones, May 24, 1899, NARA, OIA, RG 75, LR, Mackinac Agency, no. 25356.

23. Menominee political actions discussed in this and the following paragraphs are drawn from Beck, *Struggle for Self-Determination*, chaps. 1–2.

24. U.S. Consul F. N. Blake to Secretary of State Hamilton Fish, January 6, 1870, in *Report on the Management of Indians in British America*, 7.

25. Minutes of Six Nations Council, June 16, 1885, NAC, DIA, RG 10, Six Nations Superintendency, Correspondence, vol. 884, 137–39 (microfilm C-15123).

26. Talfourd to SGIA Viscount Bury, August 21, 1855, NAC, DIA, RG 10, Field Office Records, Western (Sarnia) Superintendency, Deputy Superintendent General's Office Letterbook, 1846–59, vol. 584; SGIA Lord Bury to F. Talfourd, September 28, 1855, Western (Sarnia) Superintendency, NAC, DIA, RG 10, Superintendency Records, vol. 451, 58 (microfilm C-9645).

27. Superintendent William Plummer to Chiefs and Principal Men of the Cape Croker Band, February 16, 1875, NAC, DIA, RG 10, Superintendency Records, Central (Toronto) Superintendency Letterbook (William Plummer) Indexed, 1874–75, vol. 557a, 301 (microfilm C-13364).

28. Rogers, "Algonquin Farmers of Southern Ontario," 147; C. T. Wolcot to Visiting Superintendent Charles J. Dupont, July 28, 1864, NAC, DIA, RG 10, Superintendency Records, Northern (Manitowaning) Superintendency, Correspondence (Manitoulin Island), 1861–65, vol. 615, 500–502 (microfilm C-13387); Pathmasters for 1885 Appointed in Council, May 15, 1885, NAC, DIA, RG 10, Six Nations Superintendency, Correspondence, 1885, vol. 884, 2ff. (microfilm C-15123).

29. Froome Talford to R. T. Pennefather, August 28, 1858, NAC, DIA, RG 10, Field Office Records, Western (Sarnia) Superintendency, Deputy Superintendent General's Office Letterbook, 1857–59, vol. 581; relief request quoted in Sarnia Agent E. Watson to DIA, January 20, 1883, NAC, DIA, RG 10, Red Series, vol. 2205, file 41089 (microfilm C-11179); Resolution of the Chippewa Council to Pay Certain Accounts and agent certification statement, 1898, NAC, DIA, RG 10, Red Series, vol. 2947, file 199675 (microfilm C-11302).

30. SGIA R. Pennefather to Special Commissioner D. Thorburn, August 29, 1859, NAC, DIA, RG 10, Six Nations Superintendency, Correspondence, 1859, vol. 838, 672–73 (microfilm C-15112); charges quoted in Pennefather to Thorburn, October 24, 1859, NAC, DIA, RG 10, Six Nations Superintendency, Correspondence, 1859, vol. 839, 58–61 (microfilm C-15112).

31. Beck, "Siege and Survival," 186–88.

32. New Credit Petition to Special Indian Agent D. Thorburn, April 6, 1859, NAC, DIA, RG 10, Six Nations Superintendency, Correspondence, 1859, vol. 838, 236–42 (microfilm C-15112).

33. Bieder, *Native American Communities*, 175–77; U.S. Bureau of the Census, *Report on Indians Taxed and Indians Not Taxed*, 473.

34. Miller, *Skyscrapers*, 190; Michael Ripmeester, "Intentional Resistance or Just 'Bad Behaviour': Reading for Everyday Resistance at the Alderville First Nation, 1837–76," in Hodgins, Lischke, and McNab, *Blockades and Resistance*, 119; Ferris, "Continuity within Change," 198–200.

35. Indian Speeches Made at a Council Held at Manitowaning on January 19, 1864, and Spragge to Dupont, July 25 and October 16, 1865, NAC, DIA, RG 10, Superintendency Records, Northern (Manitowaning) Superintendency, Correspondence (Manitoulin Island), 1861–65, vol. 615, 347–50, 910–11, 1010–12 (microfilm C-13387).

36. Sarnia Reserve Interpreter William Wawanosh to Indian Agent Adam English, August 25, 1886, NAC, DIA, RG 10, Red Series, vol. 2351, file 70569 (microfilm C-11206); quotation from President of the Grand Council Francis W. Jacobs to SGIA, April 4, 1898, NAC, DIA, RG 10, Red Series, vol. 2639, file 129690-91 (microfilm C-11255).

37. Bruce to Superintendent T. G. Anderson, May 16, 1851, NAC, DIA, RG 10, Superintendency Records, Central (Toronto) Superintendency, Correspondence, 1845–51, vol. 408 (microfilm C-9614).

38. Report of Macrae to Deputy SGIA General D. C. Scott, July 11, 1896, NAC, DIA, RG 10, Red Series, vol. 2639, file 129690-91 (microfilm C-11255). For a description of the grand council's 1879 meeting and its members views on the 1876 Indian Act, see Schmalz, *Ojibwa of Southern Ontario*, 194–204.

39. Indian Department to Secretary of the Grand Indian Council F. Lamorandiere, May 21, 1901, enclosed in Indian Department Secretary J. D. McLean to SGIA, June 4, 1901, NAC, DIA, RG 10, Red Series, vol. 2639, file 129690-91 (microfilm C-11255).

40. Weaver, *Medicine and Politics*, 16; Snow, *Iroquois*, 177–78.

41. La Pointe Agent W. A. Mercer to Peter Phelon, December 21, 1895, NARA, OIA, RG 75, LR, La Pointe Agency.

42. Chute, *Shingwaukonse*, 207–8; William Spragge's description of Ogista quoted

in Montgomerie, "Coming to Terms," 263; Montgomerie quoted in "Coming to Terms," 263.

43. Quotes regarding 1859 Menominee council from Kane, *Wanderings of an Artist*, 22–28; Statements of Chiefs, enclosed in Green Bay Agent E. Stephens to CIA, April 1, 1882, NARA, OIA, RG 75, LR, 1882, Green Bay Agency, no. 6463.

44. Sarnia Council Minutes, July 19, 1859, NAC, DIA, RG 10, vol. 453, 27–28 (microfilm C-9646); Bartlett to Chief John Sunday and Other Members of the Tribe, February 7, 1860, NAC, DIA, RG 10, Superintendency Records, Central (Toronto) Superintendency, Letterbook (Bartlett) Indexed, 1858–60, vol. 544, 468 (microfilm C-13358).

45. Wikwemikong Petitioners to Great Chief, June 18, 1866, NAC, DIA, RG 10, Superintendency Records, Northern (Manitowaning) Superintendency, Correspondence (Manitoulin Island), 1866–68, vol. 616, 70–72 (microfilm C-13388); Sarnia Chiefs, Headmen, and Warriors to F. Talfourd, January 31, 1860, Western (Sarnia) Superintendency, NAC, DIA, RG 10, Superintendency Records, vol. 450, 698–99 (microfilm C-9645); Ripmeester, "Intentional Resistance or Just 'Bad Behaviour,'" 114–15.

46. Circular enclosed in E. A. Meredith to Robert McKenzie, June 22, 1874, NAC, DIA, RG 10, Western (Sarnia) Superintendency Records, vol. 455, 156 (microfilm C-9647).

47. Minutes of Six Nations Council, February 14, 1870, NAC, DIA, RG 10, Six Nations Superintendency, Correspondence, 1870, vol. 857, 99–100 (microfilm C-15117).

48. Report of the Delegation to Ottawa, in Six Nations Council Minutes, April 26, 1870, NAC, DIA, RG 10, Six Nations Superintendency, Correspondence, 1870, vol. 857, 193–95 (microfilm C-15117).

49. Visiting Superintendent J. C. Phipps to L. Vankoughnet, August 28, 1879, NAC, DIA, RG 10, Manitowaning Agency Letterbook, vol. 10446, 657–58 (microfilm C-15234); Montgomerie, "Coming to Terms," 267–69; Chute, *Shingwaukonse*, 202–4.

50. Journal of William Elias, December 1885–March 1886, Shawanaga First Nation Administration Office, Nobel, Ontario; Visiting Superintendent J. C. Phipps to L. Vankoughnet, January 13, 1890, NAC, DIA, RG 10, Manitowaning Agency Letterbook, vol. 10467, 452 (microfilm C-15240).

51. Petition of Menominee Chiefs, Headmen, and Warriors to Congressman P. Sawyer, July 6, 1868, NARA, OIA, RG 75, LR, Green Bay Agency, 1868–69 (microfilm M-234, roll 326, frames 358–62); La Pointe Agent to Alexander Stewart, April 12, 1900, and to John C. Spooner, May 10, 1900, NARA, OIA, RG 75, LR, La Pointe Agency, LS.

52. Beck, "Siege and Survival," 165–66. Chapter 1 of Beck's *Struggle for Self-Determination* is a devastating indictment of incompetent and corrupt Menominee Indian agents during the early reservation years.

53. Menominee Chiefs and Headmen to Allen, January 4, 1869, enclosed in Allen to Honorable Philetus Sawyer, January 20, 1869, NARA, OIA, RG 75, LR, Green Bay Agency, 1868–69 (microfilm M-234, roll 326, frames 699–703); Green Bay Agent B. L. Martin to CIA, December 15, 1868, NARA, OIA, RG 75, LR, Green Bay Agency, 1868–69 (M-234, roll 326, frames 309–15); Green Bay Agent Thomas Jennings to CIA, February 21, 1890, NARA, OIA, RG 75, LR, Green Bay Agency, no. 5844.

54. Jennings to CIA, February 21, 1890, NARA, OIA, RG 75, LR, Green Bay Agency, no. 5844. For a discussion of skillful politicking and research by Michigan Ot-

tawa leaders while in Washington, D.C., see McClurken, *Gah-Baeh-Jhagwah-Buk,* 81–82.

55. Pennefather to Superintendent George Ironside, July 6, 1860, NAC, DIA, RG 10, Superintendency Records, Northern (Manitowaning) Superintendency, Correspondence (Manitoulin Island), 1856–60, vol. 614, 407–9 (microfilm C-13387); Pennefather to D. Thorburn, July 6, 1860, NAC, DIA, RG 10, Six Nations Superintendency, Correspondence, 1860, vol. 841, 450–52 (microfilm C-15113). Also see Ian Radforth's "Performance, Politics, and Representation: Aboriginal People and the 1860 Royal Tour of Canada," *Canadian Historical Review* 84, no. 1 (March 2003): 1–32. He notes that Canadian Indians "benefited little from their 1860 appeal to the monarch and their professions of loyalty," yet "in future years First Nations in Canada would sometimes pursue a similar strategy . . . [including] pilgrimages to London." Other strategies included "appeals to opposition politicians, to the media, and to international organizations, so as to embarrass British and Canadian governments into taking corrective action." But Radforth writes, "In 1860, however, the Native people had little leverage, and they operated in a context where the colonialism and race politics were daunting indeed" (22).

56. Montgomerie, "Coming to Terms," 269–70.

57. Ripmeester, "Intentional Resistance or just 'Bad Behaviour,'" 114; Froome Talfourd to SGIA R. T. Pennefather, July 18, 1856, NAC, DIA, RG 10, Field Office Records, Western (Sarnia) Superintendency, Deputy Superintendent General's Office Letterbook, vol. 580; Talfourd to William Spragge, February 11, 1863, NAC, DIA, RG 10, Field Office Records, Western (Sarnia) Superintendency, Deputy Superintendent General's Office Letterbook, vol. 585.

58. Campbell to Deputy SGIA Hayter Reed, January 12, 1895, NAC, DIA, RG 10, vol. 2119, file 22610, part 2.

59. Phipps to Indians of the Unceded Part of Manitoulin Island, June 21, 1877; Phipps to Honorable Minister of the Indian, June 30, 1877; and Phipps to Lewis W. Word, June 2, 1877—all in NAC, DIA, RG 10, Manitoulin Agency Letterbook, vol. 10445, 1878, 149, 159, 196.

60. Gregory to CIA J. D. G. Atkins, August 12, 1888, NARA, OIA, RG 75, LR, La Pointe Agency.

61. Campbell to Morrison, August 22, 1899, NARA, GLR (Chicago), OIA, RG 75, La Pointe Agency, LS; W. A. Mercer to M. R. Baldwin, November 12, 1895, NARA, GLR (Chicago), OIA, RG 75, La Pointe Agency, LS; Minutes of Six Nations Council, January 28 and 31, 1870, NAC, DIA, RG 10, Six Nations Superintendency, Correspondence, 1870, vol. 857 (microfilm C-15117).

62. Sarnia Council Minutes, July 19, 1859, NAC, DIA, RG 10, vol. 453, 27–28 (microfilm C-9646).

63. Keesing, *Menomini Indians,* 168–69.

64. Green Bay Agent Thomas Jennings to CIA, December 30, 1889, NARA, OIA, RG 75, LR, 1890, Green Bay Agency, no. 285; Agent Charles S. Kelsey to CIA, October 10, 1890, NARA, OIA, RG 75, LR, Green Bay Agency, no. 31966.

65. Petition of Red Cliff Chiefs, enclosed in La Pointe Agent to CIA Ezra A. Hayt, December 7, 1878, NARA, GLR (Chicago), OIA, RG 75, LR, La Pointe Agency; CIA to Acting Agent Lieutenant W. A. Mercer, July 22, 1895, NARA, GLR (Chicago), OIA, RG 75, La Pointe Agency, LR from CIA.

66. Abler and Tooker, "Seneca," in Trigger, *Handbook,* 511; George H. J. Abrams, "Seneca," in Davis et al., *Native America in the Twentieth Century,* 581; Campisi, "Oneida," in Trigger, *Handbook,* 486–87; Hauptman and McLester, *Oneida Indians,* 89–90.

67. Bieder, *Native American Communities,* 163.

68. Policy quotation from Deputy SGIA James A. Smart to SGIA, December 31, 1897, AR, DIA, 1897, xxv–xxvi; Plummer to Indian Department, January 17, 1881, NAC, DIA, RG 10, Red Series, vol. 2116, file 22155 (microfilm C-11161).

69. Deputy SGIA William Spragge to Talfourd, October 9, 1863, Letterbook copy, WIHC; "J.S.T" for Talfourd [who was ill] to Spragge, November 28, 1863, NAC, DIA, RG 10, Field Office Records, Western (Sarnia) Superintendency, Deputy Superintendent General's Office Letterbook, vol. 585.

70. Van Wyck, "Harvests Yet to Reap," 219–28.

71. Weaver, *Medicine and Politics,* 17, 25–28; Weaver, "Iroquois," 201–9.

72. In Davis et al., *Native America in the Twentieth Century,* see Patricia A. Dyer, "Ottawa/Odawa," 414; James M. McClurken, "Potawatomi in Northern Michigan," 466; Thomas W. Topash and James M. McClurken, "Potawatomi in Southern Michigan," 467–68; Nicholas L. Clark, Sr., "Miami," 337–38.

73. Superintendent E. D. Cameron to SGIA, August 30, 1893, and Western Superintendent—3d Division to SGIA, August 29, 1893, AR, DIA, 1893, 2, 4.

74. Chute, *Shingwaukonse,* 220–21.

CONCLUSION

1. Pokagon, "The Red Man's Greeting," in *Talking Back to Civilization: Indian Voices from the Progressive Era,* ed. Frederick E. Hoxie (Boston: Bedford/St. Martin's, 2001), 31–35.

2. Tanner et al., *Atlas of Great Lakes Indian History,* 182.

3. "Statement of Reconciliation," in Canada, *Gathering Strength—Canada's Aboriginal Action Plan* (Ottawa: Minister of Indian Affairs and Northern Development, 1997), http://dsp-psd.pwgsc.gc.ca/Collection/R32-192-2000E.pdf (accessed July 14, 2008); "Remarks of Kevin Gover, Assistant Secretary of the Interior—Indian Affairs, Department of the Interior, at the Ceremony Acknowledging the 175th Anniversary of the Establishment of the Bureau of Indian Affairs, September 8, 2000," http://www.tahtonka.com/apology.html (accessed May 1, 2007).

4. Royal Commission on Aboriginal Peoples, *Report,* 1:249–50.

5. There were of course some differences in Canadian and American legislation pertaining to Indians, their legal status in each country, and each country's federal Indian services. For brief discussions of these differences, see Genetin-Pilawa, "In the Interests of Harmony and Good Government," 85–87, and Nichols, *Indians in the United States and Canada,* conclusion.

6. Pratt, "The Advantages of Mingling Indians with Whites," extract of *Official Report of the Nineteenth Annual Conference of Charities and Correction* (1892), reprinted in Francis Paul Prucha, ed., *Americanizing the American Indians: Writings by the "Friends of the Indian," 1880–1900* (Cambridge, Mass.: Harvard University Press, 1973), 262.

7. See, for example, Ripmeester, "Intentional Resistance or Just 'Bad Behaviour,'" 125–26, and Bieder, *Native American Communities,* 175–76.

8. Donald B. Smith, *Sacred Feathers: The Reverend Peter Jones (Kahkewaquonaby) and the Mississauga Indians* (Lincoln: University of Nebraska Press, 1987), 238–39; Cleland, *Rites of Conquest,* 239.

9. U.S. Consul F. N. Blake to Secretary of State Hamilton Fish, January 6, 1870, in *Report on the Management of Indians in British North America.*

10. Bellfy, "Division and Unity," 150; Frederick A. Norwood, "Conflict of Cultures: Methodist Efforts with the Ojibway, 1830–1880," *Religion in Life* 48, no. 3 (1979): 360–76; David T. McNab, "'Those freebooters would shoot me like a dog': The Borders of Knowledge and Homeland Security in the Journals of William A. Elias" (unpublished photocopy, Canadian Studies Department, York University), 5–13.

11. U.S. Bureau of the Census, *Census Reports,* cxxiv, 488, 563.

12. U.S. Bureau of the Census, *Report on Indians Taxed and Indians Not Taxed,* 448; Carrington quoted in Landy, "Tuscarora among the Iroquois," in 522.

13. U.S. Bureau of the Census, *Report on Indians Taxed and Indians Not Taxed,* 330–32, 335.

14. Indian office records quoted in Danziger, *Chippewas of Lake Superior,* 107.

15. Quoted material from ibid., 107–8.

16. Campisi and Hauptman, *Oneida Experience,* 77–78.

17. Danziger, *Chippewas of Lake Superior,* 107; U.S. Bureau of the Census, *Report on Indians Taxed and Indians Not Taxed,* 354.

18. Reporter quoted in Danziger, *Chippewas of Lake Superior,* 109.

19. Macrae to Deputy SGIA Frank Pedley, May 9, 1905, NAC, DIA, RG 10, Red Series, vol. 3048, file 237660-16 (microfilm C-11316).

20. Agricultural and Industrial Statistics appended to AR, DIA, 1898, 434–50.

21. Ibid.; Indian Agent John McIver to SGIA, June 30, 1898, AR, DIA, 1898, 2–3.

22. Indian Agent William Van Abbott to SGIA, October 18, 1898, AR, DIA, 1898, 14–15.

23. Indian Agent J. F. Hodder to SGIA, August 31, 1898, AR, DIA, 1898, 17–18.

24. Surtees, "Canadian Indian Policies," 88–91; Miller, *Skyscrapers,* 115–16.

25. AR, CIA Morgan, 1891, in Washburn, *American Indian and the United States,* 1:529, 532–33.

26. AR, DIA, 1898, xxi; AR, CIA, 1886, in Washburn, *American Indian and the United States,* 1:393.

27. AR, CIA, 1882, in Washburn, *American Indian and the United States,* 1:331, 336; Danziger, "Native American Resistance and Accommodation," 173, 178–79.

28. AR, DIA, 1891, x; 1894, xxi; 1897, xxvi; 1889, x–xii.

29. AR, DIA, 1897, xxv; AR, CIA, 1888, 422; Danziger, "Native American Resistance and Accommodation," 173.

30. AR, CIA, 1888, in Washburn, *American Indian and the United States,* 1:421.

31. Little Raven quoted in Danziger, "Native American Resistance and Accommodation," 167, 182.

32. Sitting Bull quoted in Danziger, "Native American Resistance and Accommodation," 177.

33. Danziger, "Native American Resistance and Accommodation," 176–77; Calloway, *First Peoples,* 346–47, 351–52.

34. R. David Edmunds et al., *The People: A History of Native America* (Boston: Houghton Mifflin Company, 2007), 325–27, 337–38; Calloway, *First Peoples,* 338–39.

35. Chief Joseph quoted in Calloway, *First Peoples*, 325.
36. Paul S. Boyer et al., *The Enduring Vision: A History of the American People*, 6th ed. (Boston: Houghton Mifflin Company, 2008), 533.
37. Porter, "Industrialization and the Rise of Big Business," in Calhoun, *Gilded Age*, 12–13.
38. Mary Beth Norton et al., *A People and A Nation: A History of the United States*. 7th ed. (Boston: Houghton Mifflin Company, 2007), 357.
39. Arnesen, "American Workers and the Labor Movement in the Late Nineteenth Century, " in Calhoun, *Gilded Age*, 56–60; Norton et al., *A People and A Nation*, 329; J. L. Granastein et al., *Nation: Canada since Confederation*, 3d ed. (Toronto: McGraw-Hill Ryerson, 1990), 91–95.
40. Granastein et al., *Nation: Canada since Confederation*, 84–86; Bumsted, *Peoples of Canada*, 117–18, 162–63; Stacy A. Cordery, "Women in Industrializing America," in Calhoun, *Gilded Age*, 128–32.
41. Roger Daniels, "The Immigrant Experience in the Gilded Age," in Calhoun, *Gilded Age*, 76–89; Norton et al., *A People and A Nation*, 343.
42. Daniels, "Immigrant Experience in the Gilded Age," 91–92; Arnesen, "American Workers and the Labor Movement," 59; Norton et al., *A People and A Nation*, 344. For a more detailed discussion of how the American dominant culture viewed immigrants and Indians, see Alan Trachtenberg, *Shades of Hiawatha: Staging Indians, Making Americans, 1880–1930* (New York: Hill and Wang, 2004).
43. Bumsted, *Peoples of Canada*, 397; Macdonald quoted in Alvin Finkel et al., *History of the Canadian Peoples: 1867 to the Present*, 2 vols. (Toronto: Copp Clark Pitman, 1993), 1:116–19.
44. Finkel et al., *History of Canadian Peoples*, 1:119–20; Arnesen, "American Workers and the Labor Movement," 59; Leslie H. Fishel, Jr., "The African-American Experience," in Calhoun, *Gilded Age*, 144–45, 157.
45. For an interesting cross-cultural study, see Michael C. Coleman, "The Responses of American Indian Children and Irish Children to the School, 1850s–1920s: A Comparative Study in Cross-Cultural Education," *American Indian Quarterly* 23 (Summer and Fall 1999): 83–112.
46. Nichols, *Indians in the United States and Canada*, 243–45. Great Lakes Indians within the United States totaled 23,581 in 1900 (U.S. Bureau of the Census, *Census Reports*, cxxiv). Canadian natives numbered 17,283 (AR, DIA, 1896, 426–27).
47. Nichols, *Indians in the United States and Canada*, 243–45.
48. Keesing, *Menomini Indians*, 225.
49. Ibid., 222–28.
50. Hoxie, *Talking Back to Civilization*, 3–5.
51. Hoxie, *Final Promise*, x–xii; Prucha, *Great Father*, 2:864–65, 896; Lawrence C. Kelly, "United States Indian Policies, 1900–1980," in Washburn, *Handbook*, 66.
52. Quoted in Miller, *Skyscrapers*, 207.
53. Quoted in Miller, *Skyscrapers*, 206; Miller, introduction to Magocsi, *Aboriginal Peoples of Canada*, 32.
54. Miller, *Skyscrapers*, 211–14; Surtees, "Canadian Indian Policies," 93.
55. Duane Champagne, "Bureau of Indian Affairs (BIA)," in Davis et al., *Native America in the Twentieth Century*, 81; Gibson, *American Indian*, 517.
56. Calloway, *First Peoples*, 354–60.

57. Campisi, "Oneida," 487.

58. "Laura Kellogg Attacks the Government's System of Indian Education, 1913," in Hoxie, *Talking Back to Civilization*, 54. The continued impact of boarding schools on native families and their children is discussed by Brenda J. Child, *Boarding School Seasons: American Indian Families, 1900–1940* (Lincoln: University of Nebraska Press, 1998).

59. Danziger, *Chippewas of Lake Superior*, 110–12, 114.

60. Oshkosh quoted in the introduction to Hoxie, *Talking Back to Civilization*, 22.

61. Patrick K. Ourada, *The Menominee Indians: A History* (Norman: University of Oklahoma Press, 1979), 170–73.

62. Ojibwa leader quoted in Miller, *Skyscrapers*, 217–18.

Bibliography of Works Cited

PRIMARY SOURCES

Archival Collections

Huron University College Library, University of Western Ontario (London, Ontario)
    Andrew Jamieson Papers

National Archives and Records Administration (Washington, D.C.)
    Office of Indian Affairs, Record Group 75
        Letters Received
            Department of the Interior
            Green Bay Agency
            La Pointe Agency
            Mackinac Agency
            New York Agency
            Superintendent of Indian School Service

National Archives and Records Administration, Great Lakes Region (Chicago)
    Office of Indian Affairs, Record Group 75
        Green Bay Agency
            Letters Received
            Records of Agent E. Stephens, 1879–85
        Lac du Flambeau Agency
        La Pointe Agency
            Letters Received
            Letters Sent
        Records of Mount Pleasant Indian School
        Records of Tomah Indian Industrial School

National Archives of Canada (Ottawa), Department of Indian Affairs (microfilmed documents from RG 10)
    Correspondence regarding Grants to Schools

Deputy Superintendent General's Office
    Letterbooks
    Reports of Inspectors of Indian Agencies
Field Office Records
    Manitowaning Agency
    Walpole Island Agency
    Western (Sarnia) Superintendency
Ministerial Administration Records
    Deeds, Reports, Census Returns, Accounts, Timber Bonds
    Deputy Superintendent General's Office
    Superintendent General's Office
Superintendency Records
    Central (Toronto) Superintendency
    Northern (Manitowaning) Superintendency
    Six Nations Superintendency
    Western (Sarnia) Superintendency

Shawanaga First Nation Administrative Office (Nobel, Ontario)
    Journal of William Elias

Walpole Island Heritage Centre, Walpole Island First Nation (Wallaceburg, Ontario)
    Fishing Rights Document File (photocopies and transcriptions)
    Land Claims Document File (photocopies and transcriptions)
    Register of Marriages, St. John the Baptist Church of England, 1896–1925

PUBLISHED FEDERAL DOCUMENTS

Bureau of Indian Affairs. *Indians of the Great Lakes Agency.* Washington, D.C.: Government Printing Office, 1968.

Canada. *Gathering Strength—Canada's Aboriginal Action Plan.* Ottawa: Minister of Indian Affairs and Northern Development, 1997. http://dsp-psd.pwgsc.gc.ca/Collection/R32-192-2000E.pdf (accessed July 14, 2008).

Canada. *Indian Treaties and Surrenders, from 1680 to 1890.* 2 vols. Ottawa: Brown Chamberlin, 1891.

Canada. *Sessional Papers.* Department of Indian Affairs. Annual Reports, 1869–1900.

Canada. *Statutes of Canada.* Various Indian acts between 1850 and 1900.

Condition of the Lake Superior Chippewa. 40th Cong., 2d sess., 1868. H. Exec. Doc. 246, serial 1341.

Environment Canada et al. *The Great Lakes: An Environmental Atlas and Resource Book.* Chicago: Great Lakes National Program Office of the U.S. Environmental Protection Agency, 1987.

Federal Writers' Project. *Minnesota: A State Guide.* New York: Hastings House, 1938.

Federal Writers' Project. *Wisconsin: A Guide to the Badger State.* New York: Duell, Sloan, and Pearce, 1941.

Fletcher, Alice C. *Indian Education and Civilization: A Report Prepared in Answer to Senate Resolution of February 23, 1885.* Bureau of Education Special Report, 1888. 48th Cong., 2d sess., 1888. S. Exec. Doc. 95, serial 2264.

Gover, Kevin. "Remarks of Kevin Gover, Assistant Secretary of the Interior—Indian Affairs, Department of the Interior, at the Ceremony Acknowledging the 175th

Anniversary of the Establishment of the Bureau of Indian Affairs, September 8, 2000." http://www.tahtonka.com/apology.html (accessed May 1, 2007).
Hoffman, Walter James. "The Menomini Indians." In *Fourteenth Annual Report of the Bureau of American Ethnology for the Years 1892–93*, part 1, 1–328. Washington, D.C.: Bureau of American Ethnology, 1896.
Kappler, Charles J., ed. *Indian Affairs: Laws and Treaties*. 7 vols. http://digital.library.okstate.edu/kappler (accessed April 10, 2007).
Nixon, Richard M. Special Message to the Congress on Indian Affairs. July 8, 1970. In *Public Papers of the Presidents of the United States: Richard Nixon, Containing the Public Messages, Speeches, and Statements of the President, 1970*, 564–76. Washington, D.C.: Government Printing Office, 1971.
Report on the Management of Indians in British America by the British Government. 41st Cong., 2d sess., 1870. H. Misc. Doc. 35, serial 1433.
Royal Commission on Aboriginal Peoples. *Report of the Royal Commission on Aboriginal Peoples*. Vol. 1, *Looking Forward, Looking Back*. Ottawa: Minister of Supply and Services Canada, 1996.
Royal Commission on Aboriginal Peoples. *Report of the Royal Commission on Aboriginal Peoples*. Vol. 2, *Restructuring the Relationship*. Ottawa: Minister of Supply and Services Canada, 1996.
Royal Commission on Aboriginal Peoples. *Report of the Royal Commission on Aboriginal Peoples*. Vol. 3, *Gathering Strength*. Ottawa: Minister of Supply and Services Canada, 1996.
Royce, Charles C., comp. "Indian Land Cessions in the United States." In *Eighteenth Annual Report of the Bureau of American Ethnology to the Secretary of the Smithsonian Institution, 1896–1897*. Washington, D.C.: Government Printing Office, 1899.
U.S. Bureau of the Census. *Census Reports. Volume I, Twelfth Census of the United States, Taken in the Year 1900, Population Part I*. Washington, D.C.: United States Census Office, 1901.
U.S. Bureau of the Census. *Report on Indians Taxed and Indians Not Taxed in the United States (except for Alaska) in the Eleventh Census, 1890*. Vol. 7. Washington, D.C.: Government Printing Office, 1894.
U.S. Bureau of the Census. *The Seventh Census of the United States, 1850*. Washington, D.C.: Robert Armstrong, 1853.
U.S. Bureau of the Census. *The Six Nations of New York: The 1892 United States Extra Census Bulletin*. Washington, D.C.: Government Printing Office, 1892. Reprint, Ithaca, N.Y.: Cornell University Press, 1995.
U.S. Office of Indian Affairs. *Annual Reports, 1850–1900*. National Cash Register Microfiche Edition. Dayton, Ohio: National Cash Register, 1969.
U.S. Statutes at Large, 16, 23, 24, 26.

FIRSTHAND BOOK ACCOUNTS

Baierlein, E. R. *In the Wilderness with the Red Indians: German Missionary to the Michigan Indians, 1847–53*. Ed. Howard W. Moll. Trans. Anita Z. Boldt. Detroit: Wayne State University Press, 1996.
Bartram, John, et al. *A Journey from Pennsylvania to Onondaga in 1743*. Barre, Mass.: Imprint Society, 1973.

Dana, Juliette Starr. *A Fashionable Tour through the Great Lakes and Upper Mississippi: The 1852 Journal of Juliette Dana.* Ed. David T. Dana III. Detroit: Wayne State University Press, 2004.

Garritt, Joshua Bolles. *Historical Sketch of the Missions among the North American Indians under the Care of the Board of Foreign Missions of the Presbyterian Church.* Philadelphia: Women's Foreign Mission Society of the Presbyterian Church, 1881.

Grand General Council of the Chippewas, Munsees, Six Nations, et al. *[Proceedings] Held on the Sarnia Reserve, June 25th to July 3, 1874.* Sarnia: Canadian Steam Publishing Establishment, 1874.

Hauptman, Lawrence M., and L. Gordon McLester III, eds. *The Oneida Indians in the Age of Allotment, 1860–1920.* Norman: University of Oklahoma Press, 2006.

Jackson, Helen Hunt. *A Century of Dishonor: The Early Crusade for Indian Reform.* Ed. Andrew F. Rolle. New York: Harper Torchbooks, 1965.

Kane, Paul. *Wanderings of an Artist among the Indians of North America: From Canada to Vancouver's Island and Oregon through the Hudson's Bay Company's Territory and Back Again.* London: Longman et al., 1859. Rev. ed., Toronto: Radisson Society of Canada, 1925. Reprint, Rutland, Vt.: Charles E. Tuttle Company, 1968.

Kohl, Johann Georg. *Kitchi-Gami: Life among the Lake Superior Ojibway.* Ed. Lascelles Wraxall et al. London: Chapman and Hall, 1860. Reprint, St. Paul: Minnesota Historical Society, 1985.

Kingston, William H. G. *Western Wanderings, or A Pleasure Tour in the Canadas.* 2 vols. London: Chapman and Hall, 1856.

Lafitau, Father Joseph François. *Customs of the American Indians Compared with the Customs of Primitive Times.* Ed. and trans. William N. Fenton and Elizabeth Moore. 2 vols. Toronto: Champlain Society, 1974.

Lewis, Herbert S., and L. Gordon McLester III, eds. *Oneida Lives: Long-Lost Voices of the Wisconsin Oneidas.* Lincoln: University of Nebraska Press, 2005.

Miller, W. G. *Thirty Years in the Itinerancy.* Milwaukee: I. L. Hauser and Company, 1875.

Murray, Florence, ed. *Muskoka and Haliburton, 1615–1875: A Collection of Documents.* Toronto: Champlain Society, 1963.

Narrative: Visit of the Governor-General and the Countess of Dufferin to the Six Nation Indians, August 25, 1874. Comp. J. T. Gilkison. 2d ed. N.p., 1875.

Pitezel, John H. *Lights and Shades of Missionary Life: Containing Travels, Sketches, Incidents, and Missionary Efforts, during Nine Years Spent in the Region of Lake Superior.* Cincinnati: Western Book Concern, 1860.

Rae, William Fraser. *Newfoundland to Manitoba: A Guide through Canada's Maritime, Mining, and Prairie Provinces.* London: Sampson Low, Marston, Searle and Rivington, 1881.

Smith, Derek G., ed. *Canadian Indians and the Law: Selected Documents, 1663–1972.* Toronto: McClelland and Stewart, 1975.

Thwaites, Reuben Gold, ed. *The Jesuit Relations and Allied Documents: Travels and Explorations of the Jesuit Missionaries in New France, 1610–1791.* 73 vols. New York: Pageant Books, 1959.

Titus, Charles H. *Into the Old Northwest: Journeys with Charles H. Titus, 1841–1846.* Ed. George P. Clark. East Lansing: Michigan State University Press, 1994.

Washburn, Wilcomb E., ed. *The American Indian and the United States: A Documentary History.* 4 vols. New York: Random House, 1973.
Wilson, Edward Francis. *An Account of the Opening of a New Mission to the Indians of the Diocese of Huron, Canada.* Sarnia: "Observer" Steam Job Press, 1869.
Wilson, Edward Francis. *Missionary Work among the Ojebway Indians.* New York: E. and J. B. Young and Company, 1886.
Withrow, W. H. *Our Own Country: Canada, Scenic and Descriptive.* Toronto: William Briggs, 1889.

FIRSTHAND ESSAY ACCOUNTS

Hale, Horatio. "Chief George H. M. Johnson, Onwanonsyshon: His Life and Work among the Six Nations." *Magazine of American History,* February 1885, 130–42.
Kellogg, Laura. "Laura Kellogg Attacks the Government's System of Indian Education, 1913." In Frederick E. Hoxie, ed., *Talking Back to Civilization: Indian Voices from the Progressive Era,* 51–56. Boston: Bedford/St. Martin's, 2001.
Megapolensis, Johannes. "A Short Account of the Mohawk Indians, 1644." In J. Franklin Jameson, ed., *Narratives of New Netherland, 1609–1664,* 38–47. New York: Charles Scribner's Sons, 1909. Reprint, New York: Barnes and Noble, 1959.
Pokagon, Simon. "The Red Man's Greeting." In Frederick E. Hoxie, ed., *Talking Back to Civilization: Indian Voices from the Progressive Era,* 31–35. Boston: Bedford/St. Martin's, 2001.
Pratt, Richard H. "The Advantages of Mingling Indians with Whites." Extract of *Official Report of the Nineteenth Annual Conference of Charities and Correction* (1892), 46–59. Reprinted in Francis Paul Prucha, ed., *Americanizing the American Indians: Writings by the "Friends of the Indian," 1880–1900,* 260–71. Cambridge, Mass.: Harvard University Press, 1973.
Red Jacket. "Address to White Missionaries and Iroquois Six Nations." http://www.americanrhetoric.com/speeches/nativeamericans/chiefredjacket.htm (accessed March 23, 2007).
Van den Bogaert, Harmen. "Narrative of a Journey into the Mohawk and Oneida Country, 1634–35." In J. Franklin Jameson, ed. *Narratives of New Netherland, 1609–1664,* 135–62. New York: Charles Scribner's Sons, 1909. Reprint, New York: Barnes and Noble, 1959.

SECONDARY SOURCES

Books

Adams, David Wallace. *Education for Extinction: American Indians and the Boarding School Experience, 1875–1928.* Lawrence: University Press of Kansas, 1995.
Angus, James T. *A Deo Victoria: The Story of the Georgian Bay Lumber Company, 1871–1942.* Thunder Bay: Severn Publications, 1990.
Aquila, Richard. *The Iroquois Restoration: Iroquois Diplomacy on the Colonial Frontier, 1701–1754.* Detroit: Wayne State University Press, 1983.
Ashworth, William. *The Late, Great Lakes: An Environmental History.* Detroit: Wayne State University Press, 1987.

Axtell, James. *The Invasion Within: The Contest of Cultures in Colonial North America.* New York: Oxford University Press, 1985.

Barry, James P. *Georgian Bay: The Sixth Great Lake.* Toronto: Clarke, Irwin and Company, 1968.

Beaver, Robert Pierce. *Church, State, and the American Indians: Two and a Half Centuries of Partnership in Missions between Protestant Churches and the Government.* St. Louis: Concordia Publishing House, 1966.

Beck, David R. M. *Siege and Survival: History of the Menominee Indians, 1634–1856.* Lincoln: University of Nebraska Press, 2002.

Beck, David R. M. *The Struggle for Self-Determination: History of the Menominee since 1854.* Lincoln: University of Nebraska Press, 2005.

Berton, Pierre. *The Great Lakes.* Toronto: Stoddart Publishing Company, 1996.

Bieder, Robert E. *Native American Communities in Wisconsin, 1600–1960: A Study of Tradition and Change.* Madison: University of Wisconsin Press, 1995.

Bogue, Margaret Beattie. *Fishing the Great Lakes: An Environmental History, 1783–1933.* Madison: University of Wisconsin Press, 2000.

Bothwell, Robert. *A Short History of Ontario.* Edmonton: Huntig Publishers, 1986.

Boyer, Paul S., et al. *The Enduring Vision: A History of the American People.* 6th ed. Boston: Houghton Mifflin Company, 2008.

Bumsted, J. M. *The Peoples of Canada: A Post-Confederation History.* Toronto: Oxford University Press, 1992.

Calloway, Colin G. *First Peoples: A Documentary Survey of American Indian History.* 2d ed. Boston: Bedford/St. Martin's, 2004.

Campisi, Jack, and Laurence M Hauptman, eds. *The Oneida Experience: Two Perspectives.* Syracuse, N.Y.: Syracuse University Press, 1988.

Carlson, Leonard A. *Indians, Bureaucrats, and Land: The Dawes Act and the Decline of Indian Farming.* Westport, Conn.: Greenwood Press, 1981.

Child, Brenda J. *Boarding School Seasons: American Indian Families, 1900–1940.* Lincoln: University of Nebraska Press, 1998.

Chute, Janet. *The Legacy of Shingwaukonse: A Century of Native Leadership.* Toronto: University of Toronto Press, 1998.

Cleland, Charles E. *Rites of Conquest: The History and Culture of Michigan's Native Americans.* Ann Arbor: University of Michigan Press, 1992.

Coatsworth, Emerson S. *The Indians of Quetico.* Toronto: University of Toronto Press, 1957.

Danziger, Edmund Jefferson, Jr. *The Chippewas of Lake Superior.* Norman: University of Oklahoma Press, 1978.

Devens, Carol. *Countering Colonization: Native American Women and Great Lakes Missions, 1630–1900.* Berkeley: University of California Press, 1992.

Dewdney, Selwyn. *The Sacred Scrolls of the Southern Ojibway.* Toronto: University of Toronto Press, 1975.

Doherty, Robert. *Disputed Waters: Native Americans and the Great Lakes Fishery.* Lexington: University of Kentucky Press, 1990.

Edmunds, R. David, et al. *The People: A History of Native America.* Boston: Houghton Mifflin Company, 2007.

Ellis, Clyde. *To Change Them Forever: Indian Education at the Rainy Mountain Boarding School, 1893–1920.* Norman: University of Oklahoma Press, 1996.

Finkel, Alvin, et al. *History of the Canadian Peoples: 1867 to the Present.* 2 vols. Toronto: Copp Clark Pitman, 1993.

Fries, Robert F. *Empire in Pine: The Story of Lumbering in Wisconsin, 1830–1900.* Madison: State Historical Society of Wisconsin, 1951.

Gibson, Arrell M. *The American Indian: Prehistory to the Present.* Lexington, Mass.: D. C. Heath and Company, 1980.

Graham, Elizabeth. *Medicine Man to Missionary: Missionaries as Agents of Change among the Indians of Southern Ontario, 1784–1867.* Toronto: Peter Martin Associates, 1975.

Graham, Elizabeth. *The Mush Hole: Life at Two Indian Residential Schools.* Waterloo, Ontario: Heffle Publishing, 1997.

Granastein, J. L., et al. *Nation: Canada since Confederation.* 3d ed. Toronto: McGraw-Hill Ryerson, 1990.

Grant, John Webster. *Moon of Wintertime: Missionaries and the Indians of Canada in Encounter since 1534.* Toronto: University of Toronto Press, 1984.

Grant, John Webster. *A Profusion of Spires: Religion in Nineteenth-Century Ontario.* Toronto: University of Toronto Press, 1988.

Gray, Elma E. *Wilderness Christians: The Moravian Mission to the Delaware Indians.* Ithaca, N.Y.: Cornell University Press, 1956.

Graymont, Barbara. *The Iroquois in the American Revolution.* Syracuse, N.Y.: Syracuse University Press, 1972.

Hauptman, Laurence M. *The Iroquois in the Civil War: From Battlefield to Reservation.* Syracuse, N.Y.: Syracuse University Press, 1993.

Higham, C. L. *Noble, Wretched, and Redeemable: Protestant Missionaries to the Indians in Canada and the United States, 1820–1900.* Albuquerque: University of New Mexico Press, 2000.

Hodgins, Bruce W., and Jamie Benickson. *The Temagami Experience: Recreation, Resources, and Aboriginal Rights in the Northern Ontario Wilderness.* Toronto: University of Toronto Press, 1989.

Hoxie, Frederick E. *A Final Promise: The Campaign to Assimilate the Indians, 1880–1920.* Lincoln: University of Nebraska Press, 1984.

Hoxie, Frederick E., ed. *Talking Back to Civilization: Indian Voices from the Progressive Era.* Boston: Bedford/St. Martin's, 2001.

Jenness, Diamond. *The Ojibwa Indians of Parry Island: Their Social and Religious Life.* Ottawa: J. O. Patenaude, 1935.

Johnston, Basil H. *The Manitous: The Spiritual World of the Ojibway.* Toronto: Key Porter Books, 1995.

Keesing, Felix M. *The Menomini Indians of Wisconsin: A Study of Three Centuries of Cultural Contact and Change.* Memoirs of the American Philosophical Society 10. Philadelphia: American Philosophical Society, 1939. Reprint, Madison: University of Wisconsin Press, 1987.

Loew, Patty. *Indian Nations of Wisconsin: Histories of Endurance and Renewal.* Madison: Wisconsin Historical Society Press, 2001.

Martin, Joel W. *The Land Looks After Us: A History of Native American Religion.* New York: Oxford University Press, 1999.

McClurken, James M. *Gah-Baeh-Jhagwah-Buk: The Way It Happened; A Visual*

Culture History of the Little Traverse Bay Bands of Odawa. East Lansing: Michigan State University Museum, 1991.

McCrady, David G. *Living with Strangers: The Nineteenth-Century Sioux and the Canadian-American Borderlands.* Lincoln: University of Nebraska Press, 2006.

Miller, J. R. *Shingwauk's Vision: A History of Native Residential Schools.* Toronto: University of Toronto Press, 1996.

Miller, J. R. *Skyscrapers Hide the Heavens: A History of Indian-White Relations in Canada.* Rev. ed. Toronto: University of Toronto Press, 1991.

Milloy, John S. *"A National Crime": The Canadian Government and the Residential School System, 1879–1986.* Winnipeg: University of Manitoba Press, 1999.

Morrison, James. *Aboriginal Peoples in the Archives: A Guide to Sources in the Archives of Ontario.* Toronto: Archives of Ontario, 1992.

Nesbit, Robert C. *The History of Wisconsin.* Vol. 3, *Urbanization and Industrialization, 1873–1893.* Madison: State Historical Society of Wisconsin, 1985.

Nichols, Roger. *Indians in the United States and Canada: A Comparative History.* Lincoln: University of Nebraska Press, 1998.

Nin-Da-Waab-Jig. *Walpole Island: The Soul of Indian Territory.* Walpole Island: Nin-Da-Waab-Jig, 1987.

Nock, David A. *A Victorian Missionary and Canadian Indian Policy: Cultural Synthesis vs. Cultural Replacement.* Waterloo, Ontario: Wilfrid Laurier University Press, 1988.

Norrie, Kenneth, and Douglas Owram. *A History of the Canadian Economy.* Toronto: Harcourt Brace Jovanovich, 1991.

Norton, Mary Beth, et al. *A People and a Nation: A History of the United States.* 7th ed. Boston: Houghton Mifflin Company, 2007.

Ourada, Patrick K. *The Menominee Indians: A History.* Norman: University of Oklahoma Press, 1979.

Penny, David W. *Great Lakes Indian Art.* Detroit: Wayne State University Press and Detroit Institute of Arts, 1989.

Prucha, Francis Paul. *Atlas of American Indian Affairs.* Lincoln: University of Nebraska Press, 1900.

Prucha, Francis Paul. *The Great Father: The United States Government and the American Indians.* 2 vols. Lincoln: University of Nebraska Press, 1984.

Rafert, Stewart. *The Miami Indians of Indiana: A Persistent People, 1654–1994.* Indianapolis: Indiana Historical Society, 1996.

Ray, Arthur. *The Canadian Fur Trade in the Industrial Age.* Toronto: University of Toronto Press, 1990.

Reyhner, Jon, and Jeanne Eder. *American Indian Education: A History.* Norman: University of Oklahoma Press, 2004.

Richter, Daniel K. *The Ordeal of the Longhouse: The Peoples of the Iroquois League in the Era of Colonization.* Chapel Hill: University of North Carolina Press, 1992.

Samek, Hana. *The Blackfoot Confederacy, 1880–1920: A Comparative Study of Canadian and U.S. Indian Policy.* Albuquerque: University of New Mexico Press, 1987.

Satz, Ronald N., et al. *Chippewa Treaty Rights: The Reserve Rights of Wisconsin's Chippewa Indians in Historical Perspective.* Madison: Wisconsin Academy of Sciences, Arts and Letters, 1991.

Schmalz, Peter S. *The Ojibwa of Southern Ontario.* Toronto: University of Toronto Press, 1991.
Smith, Donald B. *Sacred Feathers: The Reverend Peter Jones (Kahkewaquonaby) and the Mississauga Indians.* Lincoln: University of Nebraska Press, 1987.
Snow, Dean R. *The Iroquois.* Oxford: Blackwell, 1994.
Strickland, W. P. *Old Mackinaw, or the Fortress of the Lakes and Its Surroundings.* Philadelphia: James Challen and Son, 1860.
Tanner, Helen Hornbeck. *The Ojibwa.* New York: Chelsea House Publishers, 1991.
Tanner, Helen Hornbeck, et al., eds. *Atlas of Great Lakes Indian History.* Norman: University of Oklahoma Press, 1987.
Thurner, Arthur W. *Strangers and Sojourners: A History of Michigan's Keweenaw Peninsula.* Detroit: Wayne State University Press, 1994.
Titley, E. Brian. *A Narrow Vision: Duncan Campbell Scott and the Administration of Indian Affairs in Canada.* Vancouver: University of British Columbia Press, 1986.
Tooker, Elisabeth. *Ethnography of the Huron Indians, 1615–1649.* Bureau of American Ethnology Bulletin 190. Washington, D.C.: Bureau of American Ethnology, 1964.
Trachtenberg, Alan. *Shades of Hiawatha: Staging Indians, Making Americans, 1880–1930.* New York: Hill and Wang, 2004.
Trafzer, Clifford E., Jean A. Keller, and Lorene Sisquoc, eds. *Boarding School Blues: Revisiting American Indian Educational Experiences.* Lincoln: University of Nebraska Press, 2006.
Trigger, Bruce C. *The Children of Aataentsic: A History of the Huron People to 1660.* 2 vols. Montreal: McGill-Queen's University Press, 1976.
Trigger, Bruce C., ed. *Handbook of North American Indians.* Vol. 15, *Northeast.* Washington, D.C.: Smithsonian Institution, 1978.
Wallace, Anthony F. C. *The Death and Rebirth of the Seneca.* New York: Vintage Books, 1972.
Washburn, Wilcomb E. *The Assault on Indian Tribalism: The General Allotment Law (Dawes Act) of 1887.* Philadelphia: J. B. Lippincott, 1975.
Weaver, Sally M. *Medicine and Politics among the Grand River Iroquois: A Study of the Non-Conservatives.* Publications in Ethnology, no. 4. Ottawa: National Museums of Canada, 1972.
Weeks, Philip. *Farewell, My Nation: The American Indian and the United States, 1820–1890.* Arlington Heights, Ill.: Harlan Davidson, 1990.
White, Randall. *Ontario, 1610–1985: A Political and Economic History.* Toronto: Dundurn Press, 1985.
Wightman, W. R. *Forever on the Fringe: Six Studies in the Development of Manitoulin Island.* Toronto: University of Toronto Press, 1982.
Wilson, James. *The Earth Shall Weep: A History of Native America.* New York: Grove Press, 1998.

Articles and Book Chapters

Abler, Thomas S., and Elisabeth Tooker. "Seneca." In Bruce G. Trigger, ed., *Handbook of North American Indians,* vol. 15, *Northeast,* 505–17. Washington, D.C.: Smithsonian Institution, 1978.

Abrams, George H. J. "Seneca." In Mary B. Davis et al., eds., *Native America in the Twentieth Century: An Encyclopedia,* 580–82. New York: Garland Publishing, 1994, 580–82.

Angus, James T. "How the Dokis Indians Protected Their Timber." *Ontario History* 81, no. 3 (September 1989): 181–99.

Antone, Eileen M. "The Educational History of the Onyota'a:ka Nation of the Thames." *Ontario History* 85, no. 4 (December 1993): 309–20.

Arnesen, Eric. "American Workers and the Labor Movement in the Late Nineteenth Century." In Charles W. Calhoun, ed., *The Gilded Age: Perspectives on the Origins of Modern America,* 53–73. 2d ed. Lanham, Md.: Rowman and Littlefield Publishers, 2007.

Blair, Peggy. "Taken for 'Granted': Aboriginal Title and Public Fishing Rights in Upper Canada." *Ontario History* 92, no. 2 (Spring 2000): 31–55.

Blau, Harold, Jack Campisi, and Elisabeth Tooker. "Onondaga." In Bruce G. Trigger, ed., *Handbook of North American Indians,* vol. 15, *Northeast,* 491–99. Washington, D.C.: Smithsonian Institution, 1978.

Bleasdale, Ruth. "Manitowaning: An Experiment in Indian Settlement." *Ontario History* 66, no. 3 (September 1974): 147–57.

Buffalohead, Priscilla K. "Farmers, Warriors, Traders: A Fresh Look at Ojibway Women." *Minnesota History* 48 (Summer 1983): 236–44.

Campisi, Jack. "Oneida." In Bruce G. Trigger, ed., *Handbook of North American Indians,* vol. 15, *Northeast,* 481–90. Washington, D.C.: Smithsonian Institution, 1978.

Champagne, Duane. "Bureau of Indian Affairs (BIA)." In Mary B. Davis et al., eds., *Native America in the Twentieth Century: An Encyclopedia,* 80–84. New York: Garland Publishing, 1994.

Chochla, Mark. "Victorian Fly Fishers on the Nipigon." *Ontario History* 91, no. 2 (Autumn 1999): 151–63.

Clark, Nicholas L., Sr. "Miami." In Mary B. Davis et al., eds., *Native America in the Twentieth Century: An Encyclopedia,* 337–38. New York: Garland Publishing, 1994.

Cleland, Charles E. "An Overview of Chippewa Use of Natural Resources." In James M. McClurken, comp., *Fish in the Lakes, Wild Rice, and Game in Abundance: Testimony on Behalf of Mille Lacs Ojibwe Hunting and Fishing Rights,* 8–16. East Lansing: Michigan State University Press, 2000.

Clifton, James A. "Potawatomi." In Bruce G. Trigger, ed., *Handbook of North American Indians,* vol. 15, *Northeast,* 725–42. Washington, D.C.: Smithsonian Institution, 1978.

Clinton, Robert N. "Sovereignty and Jurisdiction." In Mary B. Davis et al., eds., *Native America in the Twentieth Century: An Encyclopedia,* 605–11. New York: Garland Publishing, 1994.

Coleman, Michael C. "The Responses of American Indian Children and Irish Children to the School, 1850s–1920s: A Comparative Study in Cross-Cultural Education." *American Indian Quarterly* 23 (Summer and Fall 1999): 83–112.

Cordery, Stacy A. "Women in Industrializing America." In Charles W. Calhoun, ed., *The Gilded Age: Perspectives on the Origins of Modern America,* 119–41. 2d ed. Lanham, Md.: Rowman and Littlefield Publishers, 2007.

Coté, Charlotte. "Historical Foundations of Indian Sovereignty in Canada and the United States: A Brief Overview." *American Review of Canadian Studies* 31 (Spring–Summer 2001): 15–23.

Crowley, Terry. "Rural Labour." In Paul Craven, ed., *Labouring Lives: Work and Workers in Nineteenth-Century Ontario*, 13–104. Toronto: University of Toronto Press, 1995.

Daniels, Roger. "The Immigrant Experience in the Gilded Age." In Charles W. Calhoun, ed., *The Gilded Age: Perspectives on the Origins of Modern America*, 75–99. 2d ed. Lanham, Md.: Rowman and Littlefield Publishers, 2007.

Danziger, Edmund Jefferson, Jr. "Historical Importance of Great Lakes Aboriginal Borders." In Jill Oakes et al., eds., *Aboriginal Cultural Landscapes*, 1–9. Winnipeg: Aboriginal Issues Press, 2004.

Danziger, Edmund Jefferson, Jr. "Native American Resistance and Accommodation during the Late Nineteenth Century." In Charles W. Calhoun, ed., *The Gilded Age: Essays on the Origins of Modern America*, 167–86. 2d ed. New York: Rowman and Littlefield Publishers, 2007.

Delâge, Denys, and Helen Hornbeck Tanner. "The Ojibwa-Jesuit Debate at Walpole Island, 1844." *Ethnohistory* 41, no. 2 (Spring 1994): 295–31.

Dunnigan, Brian Lee. Foreword to Juliette Starr Dana, *A Fashionable Tour through the Great Lakes and Upper Mississippi: The 1852 Journal of Juliette Dana*, ed. David T. Dana III. Detroit: Wayne State University Press, 2004.

Dyer, Patricia. "Ottawa/Odawa." In Mary B. Davis et al., eds., *Native America in the Twentieth Century: An Encyclopedia*, 413–15. New York: Garland Publishing, 1994.

Fenton, William N. "The Iroquois in History." In Eleanor Burke Leacock and Nancy Oestreich Lurie, eds., *North American Indians in Historical Perspective*, 129–68. New York: Random House, 1971.

Fenton, William N. "Northern Iroquoian Culture Patterns." In Bruce G. Trigger, ed., *Handbook of North American Indians*, vol. 15, *Northeast*, 296–321. Washington, D.C.: Smithsonian Institution, 1978.

Fenton, William N. "Structure, Continuity, and Change in the Process of Iroquois Treaty Making." In Francis Jennings, ed., *The History and Culture of Iroquois Diplomacy: An Interdisciplinary Guide to the Treaties of the Six Nations and the League*, 3–36. Syracuse, N.Y.: Syracuse University Press, 1985.

Fishel, Leslie H., Jr. "The African-American Experience." In Charles W. Calhoun, ed., *The Gilded Age: Perspectives on the Origins of Modern America*, 143–65. 2d ed. Lanham, Md.: Rowman and Littlefield Publishers, 2007.

Gernet, Alexander von. "Iroquoians." In Paul Robert Magocsi, ed., *Aboriginal Peoples of Canada: A Short Introduction*, 153–73. Toronto: University of Toronto Press, 2002.

Goddard, Ives. "Delaware." In Bruce G. Trigger, ed., *Handbook of North American Indians*, vol. 15, *Northeast*, 213–39. Washington, D.C.: Smithsonian Institution.

Graham, Elizabeth. "Uses and Abuses of Power in Two Ontario Residential Schools." In David T. McNab, ed., *Earth, Water, Air, and Fire: Studies in Canadian Ethnohistory*, 231–44. Waterloo, Ontario: Wilfrid Laurier University Press, 1998.

Hagan, William T. "United States Indian Policies, 1860–1900." In Wilcomb E. Washburn, ed., *Handbook of North American Indians*, vol. 4, *History of Indian-White Relations*, 51–65. Washington, D.C.: Smithsonian Institution, 1988.

Hamori-Torok, Charles. "The Iroquois of Akwesasne (St. Regis), Mohawks of the Bay of Quinté (Tyendinaga), Onyota'a:ka (Oneida of the Thames), and Waha Mohawk (Gibson)." In Edward S. Rogers and Donald B. Smith, eds., *Aboriginal Ontario: Historical Perspectives on the First Nations,* 258–72. Toronto: Dundurn Press, 1994.

Harmon, Alexandra. "American Indians and Land Monopolies in the Gilded Age." *Journal of American History* 90, no. 1 (June 2003): 106–33.

Hauptman, Laurence M. "Senecas and Subdividers: Resistance to Allotment of Indian Lands in New York, 1875–1906. *Prologue: Quarterly of the National Archives,* 25th anniversary issue (1994): 87–100.

Hertzberg, Hazel Whitman. "Indian Rights Movement, 1887–1973." In Wilcomb E. Washburn, ed., *Handbook of North American Indians,* vol. 4, *History of Indian-White Relations,* 305–23. Washington, D.C.: Smithsonian Institution, 1988.

Horsman, Reginald. "The Wisconsin Oneidas in the Preallotment Years." In Jack Campisi and Laurence M. Hauptman, eds., *The Oneida Experience: Two Perspectives,* 65–82. Syracuse, N.Y.: Syracuse University Press, 1988.

Jacobs, Dean M. "'We have but our hearts and the traditions of our old men': Understanding the Traditions and History of Bkejwanong." In Dale Standon and David McNab, eds., *Gin Das Winan: Documenting Aboriginal History in Ontario; A Symposium at Bkejwanon, Walpole Island First Nation, September 23, 1994,* 1–13. Occasional Papers, no. 2. Toronto: Champlain Society, 1996.

Jasen, Patricia. "Native People and the Tourist Industry in Nineteenth-Century Ontario." *Journal of Canadian Studies* 28 (Winter 1993–94): 5–27.

Kelly, Lawrence C. "United States Indian Policies, 1900–1980." In Wilcomb E. Washburn, ed., *Handbook of North American Indians,* vol. 4, *History of Indian-White Relations,* 66–80. Washington, D.C.: Smithsonian Institution, 1988.

Kugel, Rebecca. "Of Missionaries and Their Cattle: Ojibwa Perceptions of a Missionary as Evil Shaman." *Ethnohistory* 41, no. 2 (Spring 1994): 227–44.

Kuhlberg, Mark. "'Nothing it seems can be done about it': Charlie Cox, Indian Affairs Timber Policy, and the Long Lac Reserve, 1924–40." *Canadian Historical Review* 84, no. 1 (March 2003): 33–63.

Landy, David. "Tuscarora among the Iroquois." In Bruce G. Trigger, ed., *Handbook of North American Indians,* vol. 15, *Northeast,* 518–24. Washington, D.C.: Smithsonian Institution, 1978.

Lewis, David Rich. "Reservation Leadership and the Progressive-Traditional Dichotomy: William Wash and the Northern Utes, 1865–1928." In Albert L. Hurtado and Peter Iverson, eds., *Major Problems in American Indian History,* 420–34. Lexington, Mass.: D. C. Heath and Company, 1994.

Littlefield, Alice. "Indian Education and the World of Work in Michigan, 1893–1933." In Alice Littlefield and Martha C. Knack, eds., *Native Americans and Wage Labor: Ethnohistorical Perspectives,* 100–21. Norman: University of Oklahoma Press, 1996.

Lurie, Nancy Oestreich."Winnebago." In Bruce G. Trigger, ed., *Handbook of North American Indians,* vol. 15, *Northeast,* 690–707. Washington, D.C.: Smithsonian Institution, 1978.

Lytwyn, Victor P. "Waterworld: The Aquatic Territory of the Great Lakes Nations." In Dale Standon and David McNab, eds., *Gin Das Winan: Documenting Aboriginal History in Ontario; A Symposium at Bkejwanon, Walpole Island First*

Nation, September 23, 1994, 14–28. Occasional Papers, no. 2. Toronto: Champlain Society, 1996.

Mardock, Robert W. "Indian Rights Movement until 1887." In Wilcomb E. Washburn, ed., *Handbook of North American Indians,* vol. 4, *History of Indian-White Relations,* 301–5. Washington, D.C.: Smithsonian Institution, 1988.

McClurken, James M. "Potawatomi in Northern Michigan." In Mary B. Davis et al., eds., *Native America in the Twentieth Century: An Encyclopedia,* 466–67. New York: Garland Publishing, 1994.

McClurken, James M. "Wage Labor in Two Michigan Ottawa Communities." In Alice Littlefield and Martha C. Knack, eds., *Native Americans and Wage Labor: Ethnohistorical Perspectives,* 66–99. Norman: University of Oklahoma Press, 1996.

Meyer, Melissa L. "'We can not get a living as we used to': Dispossession and the White Earth Anishinaabeg, 1889–1920." *American Historical Review* 96, no. 2 (April 1991): 368–94.

Miller, James. "The Reverend Simpson Brigham (1875–1926): The Worlds of Henry Ford and Simpson Brigham Collide." In David T. McNab, ed., *Earth, Water, Air, and Fire: Studies in Canadian Ethnohistory,* 81–94. Waterloo, Ontario: Wilfrid Laurier University Press, 1998.

Miller, J. R. Introduction to Paul Robert Magocsi, ed., *Aboriginal Peoples of Canada: A Short Introduction.* Toronto: University of Toronto Press, 2002.

Morris, Joann Sebastian. "Churches and Education." In Mary B. Davis et al., eds., *Native America in the Twentieth Century: An Encyclopedia,* 113–16. New York: Garland Publishing, 1994.

Norwood, Frederick A. "Conflict of Cultures: Methodist Efforts with the Ojibway, 1830–1880." *Religion in Life* 48, no. 3 (1979): 360–76.

O'Brien, Sharon. "Tribal Governments." In Mary B. Davis et al., eds., *Native America in the Twentieth Century: An Encyclopedia,* 651–55. New York: Garland Publishing, 1994.

Osborne, Brian S. "Barter, Bible, Bush: Strategies of Survival and Resistance among the Kingston/Bay of Quinte Mississauga, 1783–1836." In Bruce W. Hodgins, Ute Lischke, and David McNab, eds., *Blockades and Resistance: Studies in Actions of Peace and the Temagami Blockades of 1988–89,* 85–104. Waterloo, Ontario: Wilfrid Laurier University Press, 2003.

Osborne, Brian S., and Michael Ripmeester. "The Mississaugas between Two Worlds: Strategic Adjustments to Changing Landscapes of Power." *Canadian Journal of Native Studies* 17, no. 2 (1997): 259–91.

Porter, Glenn. "Industrialization and the Rise of Big Business." In Charles W. Calhoun, ed., *The Gilded Age: Perspectives on the Origins of Modern America,* 11–27. 2d ed. Lanham, Md.: Rowman and Littlefield Publishers, 2007.

Radforth, Ian. "Performance, Politics, and Representation: Aboriginal People and the 1860 Royal Tour of Canada." *Canadian Historical Review* 84, no. 1 (March 2003): 1–32.

Richardson, Boyce. "Kind Hearts or Forked Tongues? The Indian Ordeal: A Century of Decline." *Beaver: Exploring Canada's History* 67 (February–March 1987): 16–41.

Ripmeester, Michael. "Intentional Resistance or Just 'Bad Behaviour': Reading for Everyday Resistance at the Alderville First Nation, 1837–76." In Bruce W. Hodgins, Ute Lischke, and David McNab, eds., *Blockades and Resistance: Studies* in *Actions of Peace and the Temagami Blockades of 1988–89*, 105–26. Waterloo, Ontario: Wilfrid Laurier University Press, 2003.

Rogers, Edward S. "The Algonquian Farmers of Southern Ontario, 1830–1945." In Edward S. Rogers and Donald B. Smith, eds., *Aboriginal Ontario: Historical Perspectives on the First Nations*, 122–66. Toronto: Dundurn Press, 1994.

Rogers, Edward S. "Northern Algonquians and the Hudson's Bay Company, 1821–1890." In Edward S. Rogers and Donald B. Smith, eds., *Aboriginal Ontario: Historical Perspectives on the First Nations*, 307–43. Toronto: Dundurn Press, 1994.

Schoenfuhs, Walter P. "'O Tebeningeion'—'O Dearest Jesus.'" *Concordia Historical Institute Quarterly* 37, no. 3 (1964): 95–114.

Spindler, Louise S. "Menominee." In Bruce G. Trigger, ed., *Handbook of North American Indians*, vol. 15: *Northeast*, 708–24. Washington, D.C.: Smithsonian Institution, 1978.

Steen-Adams, Michelle M., Nancy Langston, and David J. Mladenoff. "White Pine in the Northern Forests: An Ecological and Management History of White Pine on the Bad River Reservation of Wisconsin." *Environmental History* 12 (July 2007): 614–48.

Surtees, Robert J. "Canadian Indian Policies." In Wilcomb E. Washburn, ed., *Handbook of North American Indians*, vol. 4, *History of Indian-White Relations*, 81–95. Washington, D.C.: Smithsonian Institution, 1988.

Szasz, Margaret Connell, and Carmelita Ryan. "American Indian Education." In Wilcomb E. Washburn, ed., *Handbook of North American Indians*, vol. 4, *History of Indian-White Relations*, 284–300. Washington, D.C.: Smithsonian Institution, 1988.

Taylor, J. Garth. "Northern Algonquians on the Frontiers of 'New Ontario,' 1890–1945." In Edward S. Rogers and Donald B. Smith, eds., *Aboriginal Ontario: Historical Perspectives on the First Nations*, 344–72. Toronto: Dundurn Press, 1994.

Telford, Rhonda. "Aboriginal Resistance in the Mid-nineteenth Century: The Anishinabe, Their Allies, and the Closing of Mining Operations at Mica Bay and Michipicoten Island." In Bruce W. Hodgins, Ute Lischke, and David McNab, eds., *Blockades and Resistance: Studies in Actions of Peace and the Temagami Blockades of 1988–89*, 71–84. Waterloo, Ontario: Wilfrid Laurier University Press, 2003.

Telford, Rhonda. "'Under the Earth': The Expropriation and Attempted Sale of Oil and Gas Rights of the Walpole Island First Nation during World War I." In David T. McNab, ed., *Earth, Water, Air, and Fire: Studies in Canadian Ethnohistory*, 65–79. Waterloo, Ontario: Wilfrid Laurier University Press, 1998.

Tooker, Elisabeth. "Iroquois since 1820." In Bruce G. Trigger, ed., *Handbook of North American Indians*, vol. 15, *Northeast*, 449–65. Washington, D.C.: Smithsonian Institution, 1978.

Tooker, Elisabeth. "The League of the Iroquois: Its History, Politics, and Ritual." In Bruce G. Trigger, ed., *Handbook of North American Indians*, vol. 15, *Northeast*, 418–41. Washington, D.C.: Smithsonian Institution, 1978.

Topash, Thomas W., and James M. McClurken. "Potawatomi in Southern Michigan." In Mary B. Davis et al., eds., *Native America in the Twentieth Century: An Encyclopedia*, 467–68. New York: Garland Publishing, 1994.

Tuck, James A. "Regional Cultural Development, 3000 to 300 B.C." In Bruce G.

Trigger, ed., *Handbook of North American Indians,* vol. 15, *Northeast,* 28–43. Washington, D.C.: Smithsonian Institution, 1978.
Venables, Robert W. Introduction to U.S. Bureau of the Census, *The Six Nations of New York: The 1892 United States Extra Census Bulletin.* Washington, D.C.: Government Printing Office, 1892. Reprint, Ithaca, N.Y.: Cornell University Press, 1995.
Vogel, Virgil J. "The Missionary as Acculturation Agent: Peter Dougherty and the Indians of Grand Traverse." *Michigan History* 51 (1967): 185–201.
Voget, Fred. "A Six Nations Diary, 1891–1894," *Ethnohistory* 16, no. 4 (Fall 1969): 345–60.
Weaver, Sally M. "The Iroquois: The Consolidation of the Grand River Reserve in the Mid-nineteenth Century, 1847–75." In Edward S. Rogers and Donald B. Smith, eds., *Aboriginal Ontario: Historical Perspectives on First Nations,* 182–212. Toronto: Dundurn Press, 1994.
Weaver, Sally M. "Six Nations of the Grand River, Ontario." In Bruce G. Trigger, ed., *Handbook of North American Indians,* vol. 15, *Northeast,* 525–36. Washington, D.C.: Smithsonian Institution, 1978.
Wightman, Nancy M., and W. Robert Wightman. "The Mica Bay Affair: Conflict on the Upper Lakes Mining Frontier, 1840–1850." *Ontario History* 83, no. 3 (September 1991): 193–208.

Unpublished Studies

Angel, Michael R. "Discordant Voices, Conflicting Visions: Ojibwa and Euro-American Perspectives on the Midéwiwin." Ph.D. diss., University of Manitoba, 1997.
Beck, David R. M. "Siege and Survival: Menominee Responses to an Encroaching World." Ph.D. diss., University of Illinois at Chicago, 1994.
Bellfy, Phillip. "Division and Unity, Dispersal and Permanence: The Anishnabeg of the Lake Huron Borderlands." Ph.D. diss., Michigan State University, 1995.
Bennett, Paul W. "'Little Worlds': The Forging of Social Identities in Ontario's Protestant School Communities and Institutions, 1850–1930." Ph.D. diss., University of Toronto, 1990.
Calverly, David. "Who Controls the Hunt? Ontario's Game Act, the Canadian Government, and the Ojibwa, 1800–1940." Ph.D. diss., University of Ottawa, 1999.
Ferris, Neal. "Continuity within Change: Settlement-Subsistence Strategies and Artifact Patterns in Southwestern Ontario Ojibwa, A.D. 1780–1861." M.A. thesis, York University, 1989.
Ferris, Neal. "In *Their* Time: Archeological Histories of Native-Lived Contacts and Colonizations, Southwestern Ontario, A.D. 1400–1900." Ph.D. diss., McMaster University, 2006.
Genetin-Pilawa, C. Joseph. "'In the Interests of Harmony and Good Government': Allotment Era Politics in the Great Lakes Region." M.A. thesis, Bowling Green State University, 2002.
Hamley, Jeffrey Louis. "Cultural Genocide in the Classroom: A History of the Federal

Boarding School Movement in American Indian Education, 1875–1920." Ph.D. diss., Harvard University, 1994.

Harp, Maureen Anna. "Indian Missionaries, Immigrant Migrations, and Regional Catholic Culture: Slovene Missionaries in the Upper Great Lakes, 1830–1892." Ph.D. diss., University of Chicago, 1996.

Huckins, Philip Cate. "Broken Vows, Broken Arrows: An Analysis of the U.S. Government's Off-Reservation Boarding School Program, 1879–1900." Ph.D. diss., Boston College, 1995.

Krasowski, Sheldon. "'A Nuimay' (the Prayer People) and the Pagans of Walpole Island First Nation: Resistance to the Anglican Church, 1845–1885." M.A. thesis, Trent University, 1998.

Loew, Patty. "Newspapers and the Lake Superior Chippewa in the 'Unprogressive' Era." Ph.D. diss., University of Wisconsin–Madison, 1998.

McMullen, Stephanie Louise. "Disunity and Dispossession: Nawash Ojibwa and Potawatomi in the Saugeen Territory, 1836–1865." M.A. thesis, University of Calgary, 1997.

Montgomerie, Deborah Anne. "Coming to Terms: Ngai Tahu, Roberson County Indians, and the Garden River Band of Ojibwa, 1840–1890; Three Studies of Colonialism in Action." Ph.D. diss., Duke University, 1993.

Porter, Eric. "The Anglican Church and Native Education: Residential Schools and Assimilation." Ph.D. diss., University of Toronto, 1981.

Shillinger, Sarah R. "'They never told us they wanted to help us': An Oral History of Saint Joseph's Indian Industrial School." Ph.D. diss., University of Pennsylvania, 1995.

Telford, Rhonda. "'The sound of the rustling of gold is under my feet where I stand. We have a rich country': A History of Aboriginal Mineral Resources in Ontario." Ph.D. diss., University of Toronto, 1996.

Thoms, J. Michael. "Ojibwa Fishing Grounds: A History of Ontario Fisheries Law, Science, and the Sportsmen's Challenge to Aboriginal Treaty Rights, 1650–1900." Ph.D. diss., University of British Columbia, 2004.

Van Wyck, Sheila M. "Harvests Yet to Reap: History, Identity, and Agriculture in a Canadian Indian Community." Ph.D. diss., University of Toronto, 1992.

Personal Files of the Author

McNab, David T. Communiqué to author. September 27, 2001.

McNab, David T. "'Those freebooters would shoot me like a dog': The Borders of Knowledge and Homeland Security in the Journals of William A. Elias." Unpublished photocopy, Canadian Studies Department, York University, Toronto, Ontario.

Miller, James, ed. "Three Letters Written by the Reverend Andrew Jamieson (1814–1885): June 1882, October 1882, February 1884." Unpublished photocopy, Port Lambton, Ontario.

Index

Abbott, William Van, 195
Agriculture: Canadian government encouragement of, 32–36, 41, 56–59, 237; Indian response to, 31–32, 34–57, 225–26; Peter Hill experience with, 31–32, 57; U.S. government encouragement of, 44–45, 56–59, 237. *Also see individual reservations*
Alderville First Nation, Ontario, 206, 211, 224
Alderville School on Alnwick Reservation, 136
Algonquian people, xiii, 3–9, 16, 18
Allegany Reservation, New York, 21, 45–46, 70, 115–16, 140, 164, 179, 197, 204, 215
Allen, Thomas J., 210
Allotment, 48; Canadian policy, 99–100, 226–27; government management of lumbering allotments, 110–12; Henry Dawes support for, 95; impact of, 47–48, 116–17, 119–20; implementation challenges, 106–11; Indian response to, 100–106; Lucy Penaseway experiences, 96, 117, 118; U.S. policy, 96–99, 250. *See also* Enfranchisement; Location tickets
Alnwick Reservation, Ontario, 35–36, 60, 69, 104, 115, 136, 140
American Board of Commissioners for Foreign Missions, 160, 170
Amherstburg, 15, 163
Anglican Church missions, 163, 168, 170, 176, 178
Angus, James T., 82
Anishinaabeg. *See* Algonquian people
Annuities and presents, 86–92
Arapaho, Southern, 240
Arnesen, Eric, 243
Ashland, Wisconsin, 19, 60, 62, 63, 231
Ashland Daily News, 234
Ashworth, William, 14
Atkins, J. D. C., 145
Au Sable River Reservation, Ontario, 17

Bad River Reservation, Wisconsin, 19, 54–55, 60, 106, 108–14, 119, 134, 140, 164, 173, 180, 204, 209, 213, 215, 231, 250
Baraga, Michigan, 140, 231
Barry, James P., 12
Bartlett, W. R., 132, 206
Batchewana Reservation, Ontario, 18, 40, 63, 99, 205, 208–9
Bay Mills, 128
Bay of Quinté. *See* Mohawk Bay of Quinté Reservation (Tyendinaga)
Bayfield, Wisconsin, 60
Beausoleil Reservation, Ontario, 17, 40, 203

Beck, David R. M., 51, 197, 201
Bellfy, Phillip, 228
Benedict, R. P., 51
Berton, Pierre, x
Bieder, Robert E., 202, 224
Big Heads Reservation, Ontario, 18, 195
Big Jake, Chief, 173
Black River Ojibwa, Michigan, 20
Blake, F. N., 227–28
Board of Indian Commissioners, 97
Bois Forte Reservation, Minnesota, 55, 130, 213. *See also* Grand Fork Reservation, Minnesota; Nett Lake Reservation, Minnesota; Vermilion Lake Reservation (Bois Forte band), Minnesota
Brantford, Ontario, 211
Brigham, Reverend Simpson, 167
Brisette, Michael, 108
Brotherton of Wisconsin, 97, 146
Brown, George, 12, 25
Browning Ruling, 150
Bruce, Robert, 203
Bruce Peninsula, 15, 17, 71
Buffalo Creek Reservation, New York, 156
Buhkwujjenene, 205
Bumsted, J. M., 33
Burning, Chief N. H., 105, 207
Bury, Viscount, 67

Campbell, James J., 212
Campbell, S. W., 53, 54, 89, 106, 107, 112, 213
Campisi, Jack, 231
Canada, 23, 214; Department of Indian Affairs, xii, 15, 23, 41, 69, 70, 71, 74, 76, 77, 78, 82, 84, 85, 90, 107, 115, 127, 130, 131, 132, 137, 138, 139, 182, 187, 192–93, 198–201, 203–8, 211–12, 214, 216, 222–23, 235, 237–38, 247–48; Gradual Civilization Act of 1857, 99, 100, 103, 192; Gradual Enfranchisement of Indians Act of 1869, 99, 133, 152, 192, 216; Indian Act of 1868, 99; Indian Act of 1869, 207; Indian Act of 1876, 70, 136, 192, 223; Indian Act of 1880, 193; Indian policy of, xi, xiii, 12, 14, 15–18, 64, 86–92, 106, 125, 129, 227–29; permeability of national borders for native peoples, 228–29; political reforms proposed, 191, 222–23, 236–38; Proclamation of 1763, 192; Robinson-Huron Treaty of 1850, 16, 18, 41, 64, 67, 81, 83; Robinson-Superior Treaty of 1850, 16, 64, 67, 83; Royal Commission on Aboriginal People, 2, 26, 92, 145, 153, 223
Canadian Pacific Railway, 41, 244
Cape Croker Reservation (Nawash), Ontario, 17, 40, 62, 104, 115, 131, 199, 203–4, 235
Carlisle Indian School, Pennsylvania, 140, 143, 224, 250
Carrington, Henry, 230
Catholic Missions, Bureau of, 142
Cattaraugus Reservation, New York, 21, 45–46, 57, 115–16, 128, 140, 164, 167, 179, 197, 204, 215
Cayuga Indians, 8, 21
Chicago World's Columbian Exposition, 220, 242
Chippewa. *See* Ojibwa
Chippewa and Munsee of the Thames, 16, 70, 104, 115, 117, 128, 140–42, 147–49
Christian churches: Anglican, 160, 163, 168, 170, 175–76, 178; Baptist, 160; Church of England, 128, 163, 175, 182, 202; Congregationalist, 160; encouragement of Indian agriculture, 33, 50; Episcopal, 170; Jesuit order, 175, 183; Methodist, 160, 162; missionaries, 160–70, 172, 175–76, 183; Moravian, 163; Presbyterian, 160; Protestant, 164; Roman Catholic, 163, 173, 175. *See also* Methodist Church of Canada
Christian Islands Reservation, Ontario, 17, 209
Chute, Janet, 93, 178, 205, 209, 218
Citizenship. *See* Dawes Severalty Act; Enfranchisement
Civilization Fund of 1819, 124
Clay, Henry, 14

Cleland, Charles E., 25, 73, 119, 157, 225, 249
Cleland, Robert, 152
Clifton, James A., 190
Cockburn Island Reservation, Ontario, 17, 18, 40
Colborne, Sir John, 175
Collier, John, 247
Condecon, Maggie, 111
Condecon, Tom, 111
"Conservative" ("non-progressive" or "vagabond") Indian factions, 224, 229, 231
Copway, George, 163
Cornplanter Tract Reservation, Pennsylvania, 21, 164
Countess of Dufferin, 196
Crowley, Terry, 84
Cushway, Joseph H. *See* Joseph H. Cushway and Company

Dana, Juliette Starr, 72
Dawes, Henry L., 98
Dawes Severalty Act, xv, 98, 100, 101, 102, 103, 104, 105, 106, 107, 108, 116, 117, 118, 133, 152
Delaware Indians, 4, 163
Denomie, Sam, 113
Deven, Carol, 137, 179
Dokis, Chief Michel, 81–82
Dokis Reservation, Ontario, 17, 40, 81–82
Dream Dance (Drum Dance), 181
Duke of Newcastle, 211
Duluth and Winnipeg Railroad, 60
Dupont, Charles J., 203
Durfee, W. R., 55, 175

Education: boarding schools, 139–55, 238; Canada and U.S. policy toward, 123–28, 136–39; Carlisle Indian School, Pennsylvania, 140, 143; day schools, 129–39; funding by local Indian communities, 129; importance of, summarized, 153–55; Indian response to, 153–55; Indian schools established, 125–28, 238; role of Christian churches, 129, 153–55; role of Indian parents, 137, 249
Elias, William A., 115, 209, 229
Enfranchisement, 99, 100, 103–6, 107. *See also* Allotment; Location tickets
Episcopal Church, 170
Erie Confederacy, 8

Farming. *See* Agriculture
Fish, Hamilton, 227–28
Fishing, 60–66, 74, 92, 226, 249
Five Civilized Tribes, 241
Fletcher, Alice, 135
Fond du Lac Reservation, Minnesota, 18, 55–56, 67–68, 130, 134, 164
Fort Buford, Dakota Territory, 240
Fort Erie, 227
Fort Snelling, Minnesota, 181
Fort William, 16, 66, 72, 163
Fort William Reservation, 18, 42–44, 58, 85, 132, 137, 140, 236
Fox Indians. *See* Mesquakie (Fox)
French Canadians, 244
French River, 81
French River Reservation, Ontario, 17, 81–82
Friends of the Indian, 22, 95, 98, 100, 160

Garden River Reservation, Ontario, 16, 18, 42, 62, 68, 85, 93, 102, 135, 140, 146–48, 161–63, 167–68, 170, 174–75, 177–78, 205, 208–9, 217–18, 236
Garrett, Philip C., 116
Garritt, Joshua Bolles, 164
Gates, Merrill, 123
Gathering of wild foods, 61, 67–69, 82, 226, 249
General, Chief Jacob, 196
General Allotment Act. *See* Dawes Severalty Act
Genetin-Pilawa, C. Joseph, 119
Georgian Bay, 17, 18, 163
Geronimo, 241, 253
Ghost Dance, 241
Gibbard, William, 65
Gibson, Arrell M., 22, 100, 248

INDEX

Gilkison, J. T., 80–81, 208
Globe, 12
Gogebic Iron Range, 60
Golden Lake Reservation, Ontario, 115
Goulais Bay Reservation, Ontario, 62, 99
Graham, Elizabeth, 183
Grand Fork Reservation, Minnesota, 19
Grand General Council of Ontario, 103, 104, 105, 203
Grand Haven, Michigan, 20
Grand Island, Michigan, 20
Grand Medicine Society (Midéwiwin), 7, 159, 180, 181
Grand Portage, Minnesota, 19, 58
Grand Portage Reservation, Minnesota, 18, 55, 58, 61, 67, 89, 114, 130, 132, 134, 164, 213, 228, 234
Grand Rapids, Michigan, 20
Grand River Reservation. *See* Six Nations of the Grand River Reservation, Ontario
Grand Traverse Bay Reservation, Michigan, 20, 172
Grant, John Webster, 158, 159
Grant, Ulysses S., 170, 190
Grape Island, 169
Great Lakes, x, 1–2, 12, 25
Great Lakes Indians, x–xii, 2–3, 12, 119. *See also* Algonquian people; Iroquois Indians; Iroquois of New York; *individual reservations*
Great Western Railway, 212
Green, Chief Sampson, 215
Greenbird, Chief J. G., 78
Gregory, James T., 112, 113, 213
Gull Bay Reservation (Nipigon), Ontario, 236

Handsome Lake, 179, 197
Haudenosaunee. *See* Six Nations Confederacy; Six Nations of the Grand River Reservation, Ontario
Hauptman, Laurence M., 116, 195, 231
Hayt, Ezra A., 97, 140
Hazelton, G. W., 79
Hebert, Father, 130

Henry, George, 163
Henry, Chief John, 104, 105
Henvey's Inlet Reservation, Ontario, 17, 39–44, 57
Higham, C. L., 160, 170
Hill, David, 208
Hill, John, 208
Hill, Josiah, 208
Hill, Peter, 31–32
Hopi Indians, 157, 240
Howe, John, 207
Hoxie, Frederick E., 246
Huckins, Philip, 143
Hudson's Bay Company, 16, 41, 66, 67, 161, 177, 237
Hunting and trapping, 7, 66, 226, 249
Huron Confederacy, 2, 8

Illinois tribes, 15
Indian Rights Association, 22, 98
Indian Territory, 241
Industrial revolution in North America, impact on Chinese, immigrants, Indians, women, 242–45
Iroquois Indians, xiii, 3, 8–11, 15, 16, 21, 22, 72–73, 116, 127, 128, 140, 154, 157, 159, 178, 190–91, 220
Iroquois of New York, 57, 154, 164, 171, 179, 181, 189, 195, 204, 228, 230
Isabella Reservation, Michigan, 20, 47–48, 164, 180

Jackfish Island Reservation (Nipigon), Ontario, 236
Jackson, Helen Hunt, 190
Jackson, T. W., 70
Jacobs, John, 167
Jacobs, Peter, 163
Jamieson, Andrew, 165, 166, 167, 171, 175, 176, 177, 178, 182, 183, 184, 187, 198, 216
Jefferson, Thomas, 97
Johnston, Basil, 158
Jones, Chief Peter, 148, 162, 169, 171, 225, 229, 253
Joseph, Chief, 241

Joseph H. Cushway and Company, 85, 110
Journeycake, Chief Charles, 100
J. S. Stearns Lumber Company, 109, 110

Kane, Paul, 62, 87
Keith, George, 177
Kellogg, Laura, 249
Keshena Indian Agency (Menominee), Wisconsin, 246
Kettle Point Reservation, Ontario, 17, 104, 107, 182
Keweenaw Bay, Michigan, 20, 98, 114
Kickapoo Indians, 4, 15
Kingston, Ontario, 15
Kingston, William H. G., ix, x
Kinoshaineg, William, 65
Kirkwood, Samuel J., 201
Knox, Henry, 97
Kohl, Johann Georg, 162
Krasowski, Sheldon, 178, 182–83

La Follette, Robert M., 251
La Pointe Agency, Wisconsin, 63, 108
Lac Court Oreilles Reservation, Wisconsin, 20, 24, 53–54, 102, 107, 111, 114, 134, 139, 164, 180, 233, 253
Lac du Flambeau Reservation, Wisconsin, 20, 25, 53, 85, 110, 114, 119, 140, 149, 164, 180–81
Lac Vieux Desert Reservation, Michigan, 20, 90, 197
Laird, D., 116
Lake Huron, 72
Lake Mohonk Conferences, New York, 98, 123
Lake Nipigon Reservation, Ontario, 18, 58, 163
Lake Nipissing Reservation, Ontario, 17, 40
Lake Simcoe, 68
Lake Superior, 72
Lake Winnebago, 19
Langevin, Hector, 193
L'Anse, Michigan, 140, 231
L'Anse Reservation, Michigan, 20, 90, 114, 140, 164, 197, 229

League of the Iroquois, 2. *See also* Six Nations Confederacy; Six Nations of the Grand River Reservation, Ontario
Leahy, Matthew A., 68, 111, 139
Leasing, 68–71, 74, 92, 226
Leupp, Francis, 248
Lewis, David Rich, 24
Little Raven, Chief, 240
Little Traverse Bay Reservation, Michigan, 20, 172
Location tickets, 99, 100, 114–15. *See also* Allotment; Enfranchisement
Loft, Catherine, 131
Long Lake Reservation, Ontario, 18, 42–44, 66
Longfellow, Henry Wadsworth, 73
Lorne, Lord, 208–9
Lytwyn, Victor, 65

Macdonald, John A., 244
Macgregor, Chief William, 199
MacKay, James, 67
Mackinac Agency, 20
MacRae, J. Andsell, 39, 107, 204, 235
Magnetawan Reservation, Ontario, 17, 18
Manitou, 158
Manitoulin Island, 4, 8, 12, 15, 17, 18, 40, 65, 71, 87, 99
Manitoulin Island Reservations, Ontario, 40–44, 57–59, 62, 66, 78, 91, 131, 163, 197, 202–3, 209, 211, 213, 228–29
Manitowaning Superintendency, 18, 40–44, 86, 91
Manitowaning Village, 15, 40, 87, 203
Maracle, Phoebe, 214
Marshall, Chief Justice John, 193
Martin, Joel W., 157, 159, 172, 181, 184
Mason County, Michigan, 180
McClurken, James M., 85
McCrady, David G., xi
McDougall, William, 15
McKelvey, Alexander, 67, 90, 114, 115, 137, 138, 212
McLean, James, 201
McMurray, William, 177

Menominee of Wisconsin, 4, 5, 19, 67, 146, 172
Menominee Reservation, Wisconsin, 48, 50–52, 57–59, 67, 86–87, 89–90, 101, 114, 127, 130, 140, 142, 148, 150, 154, 164, 180, 190, 196–98, 200, 205, 209–11, 214–15, 232, 246–52
Mercer, William A., 108, 111
Meshingomesia Reservation (Miami), Indiana, 119
Mesquakie (Fox), 4, 15
Methodist Church of Canada, 129, 138, 162–63, 174
Miami Indians, Indiana, 4, 5, 15, 21, 46–48, 119, 217
Mica Bay, 83
Michipicotin Reservation, Ontario, 18, 41, 63, 163, 177, 195
Middle Village, Michigan, 172
Midéwiwin Society, 7, 159, 180, 181
Miller, J. R., 24, 99, 127, 142, 145, 152, 237, 248
Miller, M. L., 79
Miller, Reverend W. G., 173
Milloy, John, 128
Mining, 74, 82–84
Missionary Herald, 160
Mississauga people, 4, 17, 206, 212, 225
Mississauga River Reservation, Ontario, 169, 174–75, 202, 206–7
Mohawk Bay of Quinté Reservation (Tyendinaga), 16, 69, 76, 130–32, 136, 162–63, 169, 174, 215
Mohawk Institute, Brantford, Ontario, 129, 140, 142
Mohawk of Gibson Reservation, 17, 62, 85, 115, 135
Mohawk people, 8, 9, 132
Mohawk Valley, New York, 163
Montgomerie, Deborah Anne, 93, 205
Moravian Church, 163
Moravians of the Thames Reservation, 5, 16, 75, 99, 104, 115, 117, 137, 217–18
Morgan, Thomas Jefferson, 44, 124, 133, 150, 188, 237
Morrison, George A., 106, 213
Mount Elgin Industrial School, Muncytown, Ontario, 140, 141, 142, 147, 148, 149
Mount Pleasant Boarding School, Michigan, 47–48, 140, 152
Mud Lake Reservation, Ontario, 16, 104
Munsee people. *See* Chippewa and Munsee of the Thames
Murray, Sir George, 22, 125

Nab-na-ga-ghing, Chief, 83
National Indian Defense Association, 98, 100
Native American Church, 181
Nawash Reservation. *See* Cape Croker Reservation (Nawash), Ontario
Neopit, 101, 246, 251
Nett Lake Reservation, Minnesota, 19
Neutral Indians, 8
New Credit Reservation, Ontario, 16, 104, 105, 115, 128, 130, 133, 157, 171, 201
New England Company, 129
Nichols, Roger, xi
Nipigon of Gull Bay Reservation, Ontario, 236
Nipigon of Jackfish Island Reservation, Ontario, 236
Nipigon River, 73
Nixon, President Richard M., xv
Nock, David, 169, 170
Northern Pacific Railroad, 60

Oberly, John H., 98, 109
Oconto, 251
Odanah, Wisconsin, 110, 140, 231
Off-reservation employment, 48, 84, 92, 226, 249
Ogista, Chief, 177, 205, 209
Oil Spring Reservation, New York, 21
Ojibwa, xiv, 3, 4, 5, 7, 14, 16, 17, 19–20, 63, 64, 66, 73, 78, 91, 98, 109–12, 116, 146, 157–58, 173, 178, 180–81, 197, 203, 214–15, 228, 231, 236, 251–52
Ojibwa of Georgina Island Reservation, Ontario, 115
Ojibwa of Keweenaw Bay, 231
Ojibwa of Lake Huron, 17–18
Ojibwa of Lake Superior, 4, 5, 57, 97,

108–10, 113–14, 117–18, 130, 133, 189, 197, 204, 231, 235, 250
Ojibwa of L'Anse, Michigan, 113
Ojibwa of Nawash. *See* Cape Croker Reservation (Nawash), Ontario
Old Village, Lac du Flambeau Reservation, Wisconsin, 181
Oneida, New York, 21
Oneida people, 8, 233, 250
Oneida Reservation, Ontario, 16, 78–79, 128, 182, 197
Oneida Reservation, Wisconsin, 19, 48–50, 78–79, 102–3, 114, 119, 130, 140, 146, 164, 173, 196, 215, 231, 249
Onondaga people, 8
Onondaga Reservation, New York, 21, 45–46, 164, 179
Osborne, Brian S., 169, 174
Oshkosh, 251
Oshkosh, Chief, 205
Oshkosh, Reginald, 250
Ottawa people, 4, 5, 14–17, 67, 78, 85, 98, 180
Ottawa Reservations, Michigan, 20, 217
Otter, Joseph, 90

Parry Island Reservation, Ontario, 17
Parry Sound Superintendency, 39–44
Pays Plat River Reservation, Ontario, 18, 41, 63
Penaseway, Lucy, 96, 117, 118
Penetanguishene, 16, 209
Pennefather, Richard T., 91, 211
Peterborough, Canada, 16
Peterwegeshick, Chief, 175, 216
Phipps, J. C., 65, 91, 130, 213
Pic River Reservation, Ontario, 18, 177
Plummer, William, 215–16
Point Grondine Reservation, Ontario, 17
Pokagon, Chief Simon, 220, 241–42, 253
Politics: Canadian and U.S. governments involvement in, 187–88, 191–94, 199, 203–5, 217, 222–23, 246–53; Indian responses to federal government reforms, 188, 194–96, 201–2, 224–29, 239–42, 246, 249; intertribal cooperation, 202, 211; land use issues, 211–13; money matters, 213; relations with Indian agents, 196, 215; resource protection, 214; traditional Indian governance, 189–94; tribal membership, 213. *See also individual reservations*
Port Arthur, Ontario, 13, 72, 86, 114
Porter, Glenn, 242
Porter, Nicodemus, 208
Potawatomi people, 4, 5, 14, 15, 16, 19–20, 78, 90, 177, 180, 190, 217, 220
Powwows, 73
Pratt, Richard, 140, 143, 152, 224
Price, Hiram, 22, 124
Prince of Wales, 211
Progress Party, 212
Progressive Era, 246
"Progressive" Indian factions, 224, 229, 231
Prophet, J. L., 107
Protestant reservation missions. *See* Christian churches
Prucha, Francis Paul, 23, 152

Quay, Matthew, 116
Quebec-Superior Mining Association, 83

Rae, William Fraser, 63
Rafert, Stewart, 21, 119
Rama Reservation, Ontario, 17, 40, 85, 104, 115, 136, 167
Red Cliff Reservation, Wisconsin, 19, 54–55, 60–61, 108, 114, 134, 214, 250
Red Cloud, Chief, 241
Red Jacket, Chief, xvi, 1, 11, 26, 27, 156, 240, 253
Red Lake, Minnesota, 107
Red Power movement, 253
Red Rock/Helen Island Reservation, Ontario, 18, 42–44, 135
Reed, Hayter, 33
Religion: Indian response to Christianity, 171–83; mixing of Christian and traditional beliefs, 178–79; traditional Indian spirituality, 156–59, 178–83. *See also* Christian churches; *individual reservations*

Requa, Reverend Henry, 173
Reservations. *See individual entries and the map, which lists all reservations and their locations*
Reserves. *See individual entries for reservations and the map, which lists all reservations and their locations*
Residential (boarding) schools. *See under* Education
Rice, John, 206
Rice Lake Reservation, Ontario, 16, 19, 69, 107–8, 136, 235
Ripmeester, Michael, 206–7, 212, 224
Ritchie, George, 209
Robinson, William B., 83
Roman Catholic Church, 163–64, 175
Royal Commission on Aboriginal People, 2, 26, 92, 145, 153

Sac people, 146
Saginaw Ojibwa, 20
Salt, Allen, 163
Samek, Hana, xi
Sandy Island Reservation. *See* Shawanaga Reservation, Ontario
Sarnia, Ontario, 75, 107
Sarnia Reservation, Ontario, 15, 17, 36, 104, 128, 136, 148, 150, 178, 182, 199, 202–3, 206, 211–12, 214
Saugeen Reservation, Ontario, 17, 62, 65–66, 104, 116–17
Saugeen River, 62
Sauk people, 4, 15
Sault Ste. Marie, 63, 72, 83, 161, 162, 218
Sawyer, Chief Joseph, 201
Sawyer, Philetus, 198, 209
Schmalz, Peter, 132
Schurz, Carl, 97, 113, 138, 139
Scott, D. C., 247
Scugog Lake Reservation, Ontario, 16, 36, 62, 69, 75, 104
Seneca Indians of New York, 8, 9, 21, 70, 101, 115–16, 197, 215. *See also* Allegany Reservation, New York; Cattaraugus Reservation, New York; Tonawanda Reservation, New York; Tuscarora Reservation, New York

Serpent River Reservation, Ontario, 18
Shawanaga Reservation (Sandy Island), Ontario, 17, 40
Shawano Businessmen's Association, 210
Shawnee people, 5, 15
Shawnee Prophet, 179
Sheguiandah Reservation, Ontario, 18, 40
Sheshegwaning Reservation, Ontario, 18, 40, 131
Shingwauk, Chief, 83, 168, 175, 177, 178, 229, 253
Shingwaukonse, Chief, 93
Sickles, Reverend Abram, 105
Sickles, Chief, 103, 182
Sigennok, Chief, 87
Simpson, Chief John, 206
Sitting Bull, 240–41, 253
Six Nations Confederacy, 8–9, 10, 136
Six Nations of the Grand River Reservation, Ontario, 16, 89–90, 163, 171, 181, 230, 235; agriculture on, 31, 34, 37–44, 57, 58; allotment of, 119; alternatives to agriculture, 69, 78, 80–81, 85; education on, 127–29, 131, 135, 137; enfranchisement, 104–5; politics on, 196–200, 202, 204, 206, 208, 211, 213–14, 216–18, 228
Skinaway, Andrew, 111
Skolaskin, 241
Skyler, Chief Moses, 182
Smart, James A., 32
Smith, Peter, 200
Smoholla, 241
Snake, Chief, 17
Snake Island Reservation, Ontario, 17, 104
Society for the Propagation of the Gospel in Foreign Parts, 163
Society of Friends, 170
South Bay Reservation, Ontario, 18, 40
Spanish River Reservation, Ontario, 18
Spragge, General William, 15, 75, 76, 77, 80, 107, 203
St. Ignace, 20
St. Martin, Mary S., 148
St. Mary's River, 20, 63, 73, 177, 236

Stearns, J. S. *See* J. S. Stearns Lumber Company
Steinhauer, Henry, 163
Stephens, Ebenezer, 89, 180, 181
Stockbridge and Munsee Reservation, Wisconsin, 19, 48–50, 75, 98, 114, 130, 146
Stoney Point Reservation, 203
Sucker Creek Reservation, Ontario, 18, 40, 115
Sucker Lake Reservation, Ontario, 18
Sugar Island, 20
Sugar making, 67–68
Sun Dance, 240–41
Sunday, John, 163, 229
Susquehannock people, 8
Sutherland, A., 138, 139
Sutton, Catherine Sunegoo, 163
Swan Creek Ojibwa, 20

Tahgaiewenene Reservation, Ontario, 17
Talfourd, Froome, 67, 199, 216
Tanner, Helen Hornbeck, xiv, 56, 118
Taylor, Hattie, 136
Tecumseh, x, 253
Thessalon Reservation, Ontario, 18, 78, 130
Thomas, David, 208
Thompson, William, 96, 118
Thoreau, Henry David, 100
Thunder Bay, 228
Timber industry, 60–61, 74, 78, 92, 108, 111, 226, 249–50, 252. *See also individual reservations*
Tomah Indian Industrial School, 140, 142–44, 146, 148
Tonawanda Reservation, New York, 21, 45–46, 164, 179
Toronto, Canada, 13
Tourism, 71–76, 92, 226, 249
Transportation revolution, 14
Trapping. *See* Hunting and trapping
Treaties. *See* Canada, Indian policy of; United States, Indian policy of
Tredo, Alice, 149–50
Trigger, Bruce C., xiv
Tuscarora people, 9

Tuscarora Reservation, New York, 21, 45–46, 164, 179, 230–31
Twain, Mark, 123, 155
Tyendinaga. *See* Mohawk Bay of Quinté Reservation (Tyendinaga)

United States, 86, 91, 97, 251; agriculture, encouragement of, 44–45, 56–59; allotment of reservations, 96–99; Browning Ruling, 150; Chinese Exclusion Act, 244; Civilization Fund of 1819, 124; Dawes Severalty Act, xv, 98, 100, 101, 102, 103, 104, 105, 106, 107, 108, 116, 117, 118, 133, 152, 194, 223, 247–49; educational reforms proposed, 152–53; Federal Relief Fund, 90–92; Indian policy of, xi, xiii, 12, 14–15, 86–92, 112, 227–29; Major Crimes Act of 1885, 194; Office of Indian Affairs, xii, 21–24, 91, 97, 98, 101, 107, 108, 109, 110, 112, 113, 118, 125, 127, 128, 140, 173, 183, 197, 209, 215, 217, 222, 238, 240–41, 247, 250; political reforms proposed, 191, 222–23, 236–38; treaties, 60, 67, 83, 107, 211

Van Voorhis, John, 116
Vankoughnet, L., 209
Vermilion Lake Reservation (Boise Forte band), Minnesota, 18, 19, 67, 130, 134, 140, 213
Vidal, Alexander, 83
Vilas, William F., 113

Wah-ka-ke-zhik, Chief, 202
Wai-she-guon-gai, Chief, 203
Waiskee Bay, 20
Wakigigig, Victoria, 130
Walker, W. G., 215
Walker, Bishop William D., 116
Walpole Island Reservation, Ontario, 16, 62, 67, 74–75, 78, 90, 104, 147, 167, 235; agriculture on, 34, 38–44, 57; Christianity on, 163, 165–67, 170–71, 174–78, 182–83; education on, 128, 131–33, 135–38, 148, 150; location tickets on, 101, 114–16, 119; politics on, 187–88, 198, 200, 211–13, 216, 218

Walton, Thomas, 82
War of 1812, x, 11, 220
Wash, William, 23
Washakie, Chief, 100
Wawanosh, Chief David, 199, 202, 206
Wawanosh, Chief William, 104, 105
Waywaynosh, Chief, 202
Wea Indians, 4
Weaver, Sally M., 80, 171
Wedge, William, 208
Wenro people, 8
West and Davis Company, 90
West Bay Reservation, Ontario, 18, 40, 131, 135
White Fish Lake Reservation, Ontario, 18, 66–68
White Fish River Reservation, Ontario, 18, 40, 78, 135
Whiteside, Daisy M., 112
Wikwemikong, 17, 206, 213

Wikwemikong Reservation, Ontario, 17–18, 40–41, 65, 130, 137, 140, 204
Wikwemikongsing Reservation, Ontario, 18, 40
Wilkinson, Charles F., 119
Wilson, Reverend Edward F., 36, 146–48, 161–62, 167–68, 170, 171, 175, 178
Wilson, James, 152
Wilson, Joseph, 90
Winnebago people of Wisconsin, 4, 19, 52, 146, 180–81
Women's National Indian Association of Philadelphia, 98
Wright, Asher, 164
Wyandot people, 4, 15, 16, 90

Younghusband, E., 212

Zoar Menominee, 181